DISCARD

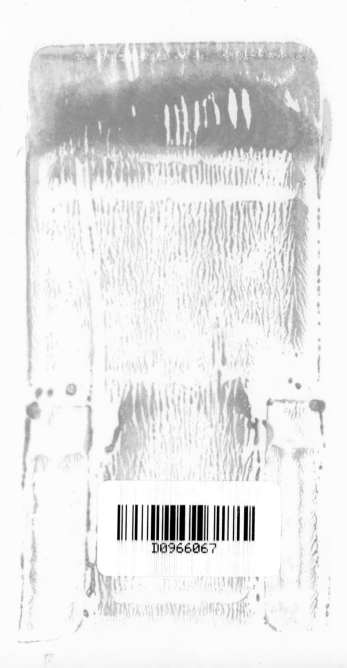

STUDIES IN FRENCH-CLASSICAL TRAGEDY

STUDIES IN
FRENCH-CLASSICAL
TRAGEDY

BY
LACY LOCKERT

Nashville
THE VANDERBILT UNIVERSITY PRESS
1958

To

MARY BELLE HOPKINS

*who, when someone asked her in speaking of me,
"Does he know he is not your brother?"
replied, "I hope nobody tells him."*

CONTENTS

INTRODUCTION

E ACH of the studies contained in this book is practically a separate article, more or less independent of the others.[1] I have brought together here all that I have written about French-classical tragedy, whether previously published or not, that each part of it may be read in connection with the rest, and that some treatment of the whole subject—of the major and also the chief minor dramatists—may be found in a single volume. None of the chapters on these lesser playwrights has appeared earlier,[2] and those chapters constitute more than half of the book.

Though seventeenth-century France, like the England of Elizabeth and the first two Stuarts, was notable for one

---

[1] They were not written in the order in which they stand. The chapters on *Andromaque, Britannicus, Phèdre,* and *Athalie* were the earliest in date; they are reprinted, with slight alterations, from my book, *The Best Plays of Racine* (Princeton University Press, Princeton, 1936), where they serve as introductions to the translations of these dramas. "Racine's *Bérénice,*" published in *The Romanic Review* in February, 1939, was written next, and then the chapters dealing with Tristan l'Hermite, Rotrou, and *Iphigénie* —all before 1940. The first, long chapter, on Corneille, which I have used in a shortened form for my introduction in *The Chief Plays of Corneille* (Princeton, 1952), was among those done later; the very last of all were the chapters on *Bajazet* and *Mithridate.* These two chapters and those on *Bérénice* and *Iphigénie* serve, little modified, as the introductions in my *Racine's Mid-Career Tragedies* (Princeton, 1958).

[2] Passages in them have been condensed or quoted in the brief introductions to the translated plays in my book, *The Chief Rivals of Corneille and Racine* (Vanderbilt University Press, Nashville, 1956), from which most of the verse translations in the present volume are taken.

of the four or five really great flourishings of dramatic literature that have ever occurred, critical and historical investigation of this French "classical" drama—more properly called "neo-classical"—was long confined to its major figures. To speak of tragedy alone, to a consideration of which this book is limited, not until the latter part of the nineteenth century were any serious efforts made to rescue from oblivion the almost forgotten contemporaries of Corneille and Racine—efforts comparable to those of Lamb, Hazlitt, Gifford, and others in renewing interest in the contemporaries of Shakespeare, more than two generations earlier. And whereas the study of Elizabethan drama begun by these pioneers has progressed steadily ever since their day, the monographs of Gustave Reynier on Thomas Corneille and N. M. Bernardin on Tristan l'Hermite,[3] inadequate though they were, have been followed and superseded by no others on either of these dramatists or any of their fellow-writers of tragedy, with the sole exception of the huge, exhaustive volume on Quinault by Etienne Gros[4]—not, that is, in France itself. There, except for that single book and for a few pages in histories of literature and in books about the major dramatists, there seems to have been no critical discussion of the minor ones for many decades—until the tercentenary of Rotrou's death evoked some small interest in him, which subsided immediately afterwards. Only in the monumental work of the eminent American scholar Henry Carrington Lancaster have we been given a detailed history of the entire period, in which the development of its several

---

[3] *Thomas Corneille,* Paris, 1892, and, much better done, *Un Précurseur de Racine, Tristan l'Hermite, sieur du Solier,* Paris, 1895.

[4] *Philippe Quinault, sa vie et son œuvre,* Paris and Aix-en-Provence, 1926.

dramatic types has been traced and every author and extant play received attention.[5]

[5] *A History of French Dramatic Literature in the Seventeenth Century,* The Johns Hopkins Press, Baltimore: Part I, 1929; Part II, 1932; Part III, 1936; Part IV, 1940; Part V, 1942.

While French critics have for so many years been almost completely ignoring their minor "classical" dramatists, the *Cumulative Book Index* of books in English has listed (exclusive of editions of any Elizabethan plays) in a mere six-year period, shortly after World War II, six new books about Marlowe, six about Jonson, three about Beaumont and Fletcher, two about Chapman, one about Middleton, one about Webster, and one about Ford. In approximately the same six years the *International Index to Periodicals* listed eighty-eight articles concerning Elizabethan dramatists: thirteen dealing with Marlowe, seventeen with Jonson, ten with Beaumont and Fletcher, ten with Middleton, seven with Massinger, seven with Greene, four with Chapman, four with Heywood, three with Tourneur, two with Lyly, two with Kyd, two with Marston, two with Webster, one with Peele, one with Rowley, and one with Ford. Such industry in a field that had been similarly tilled for perhaps three-quarters of a century!—during which time had appeared the lengthy books on Elizabethan drama as a whole by Ward and by Schelling and the later, really admirable one by Parrott and Ball, besides books on some single playwright, and yet other books dealing each with a number of playwrights (e.g., Swinburne's *The Age of Shakespeare* and Una Ellis-Fermor's *The Jacobean Drama*), nor should we overlook the some 430 pages devoted to Elizabethan dramatists in *The Cambridge History of English Literature* as against the 120 pages devoted to their French analogues in the similar *Histoire* of French literature edited by Petit de Julleville. And throughout all this time there has been a continual reprinting of Elizabethan plays, often with notably excellent factual and critical introductions: in volumes of selected plays (volumes each containing plays of a single dramatist as in the old Mermaid and Belles-Lettres series, or large anthologies of plays of the entire period like Oliphant's) or in definitive editions of all the plays of a dramatist like the Parrott *Chapman,* the Allardyce Nicoll *Tourneur,* the Lucas *Webster,* and the Herford and Simpson *Jonson*—whereas very few plays indeed out of all the

Yet some acquaintance with the lesser dramatists of a great period of drama is necessary if anyone is to see its great men with proper perspective and appreciation. This has long been recognized by British and American students of Shakespeare. Since the appearance of Lancaster's volumes, there has been a greater realization of it by French critics—notably Mornet and J. Scherer. But some of the lesser French dramatists are worth knowing for their own sake also, just as the Elizabethans are. Critics generally have held them in slight esteem, and—perhaps on that account—have too often been strangely careless even as to facts.

Let us take, for instance, the treatment accorded to Thomas Corneille, one of the most prolific and important of them.

Jules Lemaître begins a discussion of *Andromaque*—his brilliant though idolatrous *Jean Racine*[6] is the publication of a course of lectures—by stating that to realize the originality of this play one must know what sort of tragedies had been written in the years immediately preceding its appearance.

"Between 1660 and 1667 were produced Pierre Corneille's *Othon, Sophonisbe, Agésilas,* and *Attila;* Quinault's *Astrate. Bellérophon,* and *Pausanias;* and Thomas Corneille's *Camma, Pyrrhus, Maximian, Persée et Démétrius,* and *Antiochus.*" [7]

Lemaître says that he has read, "of course," the ones by Pierre Corneille, and has either read or "glanced through"

---

work of all the lesser French-classical dramatists are in print today, or have been recently.

[6] Paris, 1908.

[7] Translated from *op. cit.,* p. 129. Actually, neither *Pausanias* nor *Bellérophon* was written until after this period; but several other tragedies by these authors—Pierre Corneille's *Sertorius,* Quinault's *Stratonice* and *Agrippa,* and Thomas Corneille's *Stilicon*—fall within it. See Lancaster, *op. cit.,* Part III, pp. 865-868.

(*parcouru*) those by Thomas Corneille and Quinault. He then says, however, that he will speak of none of these, but of Thomas Corneille's *Timocrate,* dated 1656.

It might be supposed that he would at least have read *Timocrate,* and not merely have glanced through it. He makes merry over the absurdities of this fantastic "romanesque" drama, in which the hero fights alternately on his own side and on the enemy's, now as Timocrates and now under the name of "Cleomenes." "He has won, as the perfect lover," says Lemaître, "the heart of the princess Eriphyle; she is his for the taking. But he wants also to deserve her as a hero and a great commander; and that is why, as soon as his father's death sets him on the throne, he comes, without a word to her, and besieges the city of the woman whom he adores. And in truth, 'such gallantry is unusual.' " [8]

It is much more than unusual; it simply does not exist in the play *Timocrate.* There, a far greater barrier of hate stood between the hero and his beloved than that which separated Romeo and Juliet. Eriphyle's father, the king of Argos, had been captured in war by Demochares, king of Crete, and had died a prisoner; his queen believed his death foully encompassed and, though she had to make peace at that time, was determined to avenge him. Soon afterwards, the Messenians attacked Argos, and the unknown soldier of fortune, "Cleomenes," came to its defense, defeated them, and then disappeared. Now the Queen launched her blow against Crete, sweeping all before her; Demochares was besieged in his last city, and triumph seemed within her grasp, when the prince Timocrates, long absent and supposed to be dead, arrived in the nick of time and routed her forces. Demochares died; Timocrates became king of Crete. He could not reasonably aspire to her daughter's hand as the

---

[8] Translated from *ibid.,* p. 132.

adventurer "Cleomenes." As Timocrates, the son of her hated foe and the thwarter of her vengeance, he was doubly hated. The story of his twin roles, in which he drew his sword now on one side and now on the other[9] that he might win his heart's love, is of course sheer stuff of romance. Yet how else could he have won her? [10]

It may be objected that this is only an instance of the carelessness in details that is individually characteristic of the brilliant Lemaître. But the mistakes are not his alone— nor even primarily his. He must have prepared himself for his lecture, not by "glancing through" *Timocrate,* but by reading about it in Gustave Reynier's *Thomas Corneille,* a book which he recommends[11] and from which he quotes the phrase *"la galanterie est rare."* A perusal of Reynier's discussion of *Timocrate* (too long to reproduce here) discloses the fact that Lemaître has only followed him in the misstatements which I have cited above, though adding later at least one of his own.[12]

---

[9] There is no statement, however, that he actually killed any of his own soldiers.

[10] It might even be asked, further: How else could he so well and promptly have brought about a lasting peace between Argos and Crete? As matters stood, the implacable Queen of Argos was sure to re-open the war once more as soon as she believed that she had a chance of success. Disregard the impracticality of Timocrates' course, suppose he could go through with it successfully as he is represented as doing, and he is justified in it from the point of view of State policy as well as from that of love. It is not as regards political morality that the play is absurd.

[11] *Jean Racine,* p. 130.

[12] Lemaître says that one of Timocrates' reasons for "declaring war" on Argos was that he wished "after the life of a languishing lover, to acquaint himself with a life of action" (*"après la vie langoureuse, connaître la vie énergique"*—*Jean Racine,* p. 134). *Timocrate* furnishes no basis for this assertion—nor does Reynier. Timocrates had not been languishing; he had already had full ex-

Lemaitre, as we have seen, had selected this drama for contrast with the one which was the subject of his lecture. But Reynier's mistakes were made in a monograph on the author of *Timocrate* itself, an entire book on Thomas Corneille, the only book ever devoted to him. And the errors in it regarding *Timocrate* are by no means its only flagrant ones. If that was Thomas Corneille's most influential play and the one which had the greatest immediate success, his *Ariane* has been the most habitually praised. Let us turn to Reynier's treatment of this tragedy, which deals with the desertion of Ariadne by Theseus.

According to *Ariane,* the heroine's younger sister, Phaedra, has fled with them from Crete after the killing of the Minotaur; and Theseus and Phaedra fall in love and abandon Ariadne in Naxos. The king of that island loves Ariadne; but Reynier has no warrant whatever to call his pity for her, when she is forsaken, "hypocritical" (p. 180)— nor to say of Pirithoüs that by his "base inaction" he "made himself an accomplice in the treachery of his friend" (p. 181), for Pirithoüs is unmistakably represented as convinced that nothing could be done to rectify the situation. Reynier proceeds:

"And Phaedra? Can this vicious little person inspire the slightest interest? She was not impelled by affection to follow her sister, but rather by a craving for adventure; she has stolen her sister's lover in the most nonchalant manner. She at first resists Theseus, but only from coquetry, in order to inflame his passion the more; she presently goes off with him, well satisfied and light-hearted, as if she recked nothing of her crime—but she is practical, too, taking care to exact solemn promises from him before yielding:

---

perience of a life of action; he had fought and conquered in two campaigns.

And who will assure me that thou wilt be faithful?

THESEUS.

My troth, which neither time nor angry heaven . . .

PHAEDRA.

My sister had that, when she fled with thee. . . .
Thou leavest her in Naxos, bowed with grief;
Thy fickleness might leave me somewhere else. . . .

Who would recognize in her the Phaedra of Euripides
and Racine—the destined victim of Venus? It seems that
she has no heart, nor even any sense. She does not love
Theseus, no matter what she may say about it. But she
enjoys having made a 'conquest' of an already famous hero,
a king's son who will soon be king himself, and a man whom
her sister adores." [13]

There is nothing in the play which supports any of the
statements derogatory to Phaedra in that paragraph. Some
of them—those in the last two sentences, for instance—
are indeed not positively contradicted by the text; others,
however, are demonstrably untrue. Ariadne says it was only
with great difficulty that she persuaded her sister, reluctant
and in tears, to flee with her:

Je vous fis malgré vous accompagner ma fuite.[14]

[13] Translated from Reynier's *Thomas Corneille,* p. 181. The
verse lines translated are as follows in the original:

Et qui me répondra que vous serez fidèle?
THÉSÉE.
Ma foi, que ni le temps ni le ciel en courroux . . .
PHÈDRE.
Ma sœur l'avait reçue en fuyant avec vous. . . .
Vous la laissez dans Naxe en proie à ses douleurs,
Votre légèreté peut me laisser ailleurs. . . .

[14] Despite thyself, I made thee share my flight.

> . . . Phèdre, elle de qui les pleurs
> Semblaient en s'embarquant présager nos malheurs!
> Avant que la résoudre à seconder ma fuite,
> A quoi, pour la gagner, ne fus-je pas réduite!
> Combien de résistance et d'obstinés refus!

On Phaedra's first appearance in the play, she tells Theseus that they must renounce each other and part, for though she loves him she cannot forget Ariadne's tremendous claims on him. Later, she proves too weak for her suggested self-sacrifice and accepts his plan of trying to persuade her sister to be reconciled to his inconstancy and marry King Oenarus; but when the forsaken woman begs her to plead with Theseus for her, she does this, against her own interests, so eloquently that Pirithoüs is convinced that her lack of success makes plain the uselessness of any further efforts to persuade the recreant lover to fulfil his obligations—yet still she wishes to try once more. Only when she learns of Ariadne's determination to discover the object of Theseus' affections and kill her, does she consent, in terrified dismay, to fly with him; and even then she remains keenly conscious of the piteousness of her sister's position.

> Dieux! qu'elle en souffrira! que d'ennuis! que de
>   larmes! [15]
> Je sens naître en mon coeur les plus rudes alarmes:
> Il voit avec horreur ce qui doit arriver.

> . . . Phaedra, her whose tears
> Seemed, when we sailed, a presage of misfortune!
> Before I could persuade her to accompany
> My flight, what was I not obliged to do!
> How loath she was! how stubbornly she refused!

[15] How she will suffer! Gods! What woe! what tears!
I feel born in my heart the ghastliest fears.
I see with horror what must come to pass.

There is here, surely, no nonchalance observable in her attitude, no complacency or light-heartedness or callousness,
no ground for charging her with coquetry or with not loving
Theseus or with finding a piquancy in taking her sister's
lover from her.

Nor have French critics become very much more careful,
in their statements about these lesser dramas and diamatists
of the seventeenth century, since the days of Reynier and
Lemaître. The late Daniel Mornet is scarcely more successful than they were in his attempt to sketch the plot of
Timocrate,[16] and he, like them, appears to be more interested
in being facetious than in being accurate about it. According
to him, the hero was already king of Crete when he went to
Argos as "Cleomenes"; and Mornet says that it would seem
as though kingdoms in those days could somehow dispense
with a ruler, and represents Crete as being without one in its
final expedition against Argos while Timocrates-Cleomenes
is still in that city. But according to the play itself, Timocrates' lengthy absence from Crete occurred during his
father's lifetime and reign; he returned to Crete to repel
the Argive invasion of the island, and was there at the
time of—and after—his father's *subsequent* death; and he
led the final Cretan expedition against Argos, absenting
himself from his newly acquired royal duties for only a
few hours to reappear briefly in Argos as "Cleomenes" when
the play opens. Robert Brasillach in his interesting *Pierre
Corneille*[17] repeats (on page 347) some of Lemaître's and
Reynier's misrepresentations of *Timocrate*.

Criticism of Thomas Corneille—to continue to use him
as our example—has been no less inadequate than inaccurate.
Neither in Reynier's monograph nor in the brief treatment
accorded him by others has anyone before me, I believe,

[16] In his excellent book, *Jean Racine,* Paris, 1944, p. 42.
[17] Paris, 1938.

stressed his "ability to invent striking if melodramatic situations, of immense effectiveness on the stage, which was his
greatest gift as a dramatist." Nor has anyone pointed
out that the principal defect of his dramaturgy is a tendency
to relegate crucial plot-details to the intervals between the
acts instead of having them occur before the eyes of the
audience, or off-stage while the act is playing. In other
words, there has been no study of him at all as a manipulator
of dramatic effects, which is what he largely was.

The work of the minor playwrights of this great period of
drama should be more carefully examined and appraised,
as that of the Elizabethans has been, not by one critic or by
a few critics but by many with diverse views. The endeavor
of this book is to make some contribution to that end and
also to a better understanding of the careers of Corneille
and Racine themselves and to a more discriminating judgment of their tragedies.

To this task I believe I can justly claim to bring certain
qualifications of value in dealing with it. My lifelong interest in drama has been concentrated on that of no type or
country or period to the neglect of others. It began not unnaturally with Shakespeare and his fellow playwrights, but
was soon extended to the drama of Greece and Rome, to
that of the Spain of Lope de Vega and Calderon, to that of
these neo-classicists with whom I have largely been occupied
for more than twenty-five years, and to that of the age of
romanticism and that developed thereafter and still regnant.
I bring to my discussion of French-classical tragedy no
prejudice either for or against any particular school of
drama, but a desirable perspective.

Every important type of drama has its distinctive merits, and to demand that it should have those of some other
dramatic type results in such unintelligent and unappreciative criticism as Rymer's and Voltaire's of Shakespeare by
neo-classical canons, Saintsbury's of Corneille and Racine

by those of Shakespearean tragedy, and William Archer's of the Elizabethans by those of the school of Ibsen.[18] But on the other hand there are certain features of good drama which will be found in the best plays of every period, and certain things which are to be condemned wherever they occur. The perception of these latter—or at least the full force of them—may sometimes escape the specialist who is familiar only or chiefly with his own field; the widest possible acquaintance with drama is desirable for the best dramatic criticism. Jules Jusserand's pages treating of Elizabethan drama in his history of English literature showed how its faults in their worst extremes, often little censured by English enthusiasts, appeared to a French critic who had not grown callous to them through long specialization in it.

---

[18] Real comprehension in England and America of the greatness of Racine may perhaps be said to date from Giles Lytton Strachey, though of course Racine was praised earlier in the introductions and notes in editions of plays of his for use in schools. But obtuseness about alien genius is not peculiar to ourselves; I quote a passage by Emile Faguet, one of the most celebrated French critics of drama whose life extended into the twentieth century, on *King Lear:*

"In most of Shakespeare's tragedies gross, atrocious melodrama is mingled with the work of art . . . In *King Lear* we have scarcely anything but the gross, atrocious melodrama; it is almost unmixed. Except, that is, for some beauties of lyric eloquence in the famous 'scene on the heath' and some philosophical reflections—quite profound, if one takes the trouble to fathom them—in the rightly called mad scenes, and in truth these things are quickly summed up; all the rest is only an accumulation of stupid crimes, senseless horrors, and absurd flaws of character. . . . Save for the very brief parts that I have excepted, nothing would be easier to concoct. No one in Europe at that particular time, or indeed for a good century afterwards, could have written *Hamlet,* or *Othello,* or even *The Tempest.* Almost anyone, save for a few touches which, all combined, would not fill more than a single page, could have written *King Lear.*" (Translated from his *Propos de Théâtre,* vol. iii, Paris, 1906, pp. 58-59.)

There is one point which seems to me of primary importance in appraising drama of any sort or period whatsoever,
but which traditional French dramatic criticism has not
sufficiently taken into account. I therefore have been obliged
to stress it in my own criticism of French-classical tragedies.

For a play to be effective, some, at least, of its characters
must be able to elicit sympathy. Almost every critic of these
plays, in considering the characters for whom one's sympathy is necessary if the proper dramatic effect is to be
secured, thinks any conduct or feelings of theirs acceptable
which would have been approved by that public for which
the plays were first produced. But their conduct or mental
attitude is usually what was prescribed or sanctioned by the
frequenters of the salons of that period, whose highly artificial code of behavior is generally observed in the tragedies
written then. Students of those dramas become so habituated
to such behavior of the dramatis personae as to lose all natural reactions to it, both of the intellect and of the moral sense,
and cease to realize how abhorrent it often is to those who
encounter it without the familiarity that breeds acceptance.[19]
Yet unless the intendedly "sympathetic" characters in a

---

[19] I do not say this merely because of my own feelings. Again
and again I have seen people richly endowed with imagination and
good taste, widely read in drama and in literature in general, and
not at all unappreciative of the French-classical type of tragedy,
*but not habituated to its sanctions to the point of insensitivity in
such matters,* who find some of its supposedly "sympathetic" characters—e.g., the insanely jealous Atalide of Racine's *Bajazet*—nothing short of revolting. It seems to me that critics are gravely in
error when they fail to take account of such reactions of intelligent
people, about which they seem totally unaware. Mornet actually
says (in his *Andromaque,* Paris, 1947, p. 207) that Racine's Titus,
Berenice, and Atalide are "entirely good" (*tout bons*); and many
other critics have regarded them with similar approval, especially
in modern times. It was not always so, even in France, as I show
in my chapter on *Bajazet.*

play can win the sympathy of people in subsequent times as well as in its own, that play will fail to produce a satisfactory dramatic effect in subsequent times and therefore—to the extent that such sympathy is important—should be recognized as of somewhat ephemeral value.

We do not, of course, have to see absolutely eye to eye, on moral issues, with a dramatist and his intendedly sympathetic characters; but the behavior of these characters must be such that we can, while the play in which they appear is before us, at least view them with imaginative sympathy. This we can do, for example, in plays dealing sympathetically with revenge, whatever our own ethical ideas, professed or sincere, about that—as the success of such plays, from the *Coëphoroe* down through *Hamlet* and the *Cid* to *Monte Cristo* and still later, abundantly testifies. Calderon's *The Devotion of the Cross,* on the other hand, depicts a bandit who has many crimes on his head but who is miraculously saved from hell and admitted to heaven because in all his nefarious career he has never said or done anything disrespectful to the Cross! That drama may have been acceptable to a Spanish audience of the seventeenth century, but it certainly has no abiding appeal. As a matter of fact, in regard to all plays —be they Elizabethan, Greek, or whatever else—except those of the French-classical period, critics have not failed to judge the attractiveness or unattractiveness, the acceptableness or unacceptableness, of the characters by permanent standards of behavior rather than by eccentric notions prevalent when the plays were written, and have appraised accordingly the effect and merit of each play for all time, and not for its own brief age.[20]

[20] Within the last generation we have finally had an important exception to this rule in *Shakespeare's Problem Comedies,* by W. W. Lawrence, New York, 1931. This author seems to think he vindicates Shakespeare's achievement in *All's Well that Ends Well* and *Measure for Measure* by showing that the low moral code im-

The need for people of the present day to be able to sympathize with the characters in a play for whom our sympathy is required is implicitly assumed by me hereafter as axiomatic, without further argument except in my chapter on Racine's *Bérénice*—where I recur to it explicitly, with some unavoidable repetition. It could be assumed without being mentioned, in criticizing the drama of any other land or time.[21]

Most of my departures from the traditional appraisals of the plays which I discuss result from the importance that I attach to this matter. If I deny the word "great" to some plays which are generally accorded it, this is because I think the word is much over-used, and thereby cheapened, in literary studies; I would likewise deny it to nearly three-fourths of Shakespeare's work and to all of that of the other Elizabethans. It should be reserved for plays in which really notable subject matter receives really adequate treatment, unmarred by serious faults or else possessed of such extraordinary merits that the defects are redeemed and overshadowed by them and the total-effect is admirable.

French criticism of drama has tended, more than English criticism, to generalize about an author, or consider succes-

---

plied in them was taken for granted by an Elizabethan audience. Shakespeare's better work needs no such defense. However excellent in other respects, Lawrence's book should not be imitated in this one.

21 On the other hand, I have not inveighed, as critics even in France often have, against the artificial "language of gallantry" employed more or less in all amatory passages or references in the tragedies of the period. This is indeed a serious obstacle to our enjoyment of these plays today; but where it occurs to only a moderate degree, we can scarcely more legitimately consider it a fault than that the *Aeneid* is not written in English! An author of distinction may be expected to have moral insight superior to the average of his contemporaries; but any author must needs use the language, the idiom, and the connotations that are furnished him.

sively different aspects of his work, rather than deal with his plays one after another.[22] More than English criticism it has tended to limit its discussion of individual plays to a study of their characters, though such study is of course a prominent, if not the main, topic in dramatic criticism everywhere.[23] Naturally, it is prominent in my own criticism,

[22] This sort of criticism is seen at its best in the brilliant pages of Gustave Lanson (in his edition of *Mithridate,* Hachette *Classiques française,* Paris, n.d., pp. 22 ff.) on the difference between Corneille's and Racine's treatment of history.

[23] A challenging article by Jean Boorsch, "Remarques sur la Technique Dramatique de Corneille," in *Yale Romanic Studies,* vol. xviii, 1941, New Haven, pp. 101-162, goes to the opposite extreme in regard to Corneille, urging that his tragedies should be considered merely as mechanisms (*machines*) to produce emotion in his audiences, and maintaining that such was his real concern. Professor Boorsch even argues that Corneille does not attempt to draw consistent, lifelike characters; and, apparently not perceiving that he would thus make of him only a minor dramatist, asks in connection with *Rodogune,* whose theatrical devices he admires but which has generally been pronounced a melodrama: "Why this scholarly disdain for melodrama unless one is blinded by the idea that drama is a study of souls?" (I translate his French words.) According to the logic implied in that question, *East Lynne* might be as great as *Macbeth* or *Ghosts.*

I speak at such length of Professor Boorsch's article because it seems to have won some following. The truth is that almost all dramatists, being playwrights dependent on public favor, have written with their audiences directly in mind, with the intention of interesting them and moving them. But obviously, as all dramatists of any considerable magnitude must have recognized, an audience can be most deeply interested and moved by characters who seem real people, not arbitrarily manipulated puppets. In making them seem real, the genuinely creative writer will himself be gripped by them, and they will become even more real to him than to his audiences.

There is much of value, however, in Professor Boorsch's article. Its opening pages are wholly admirable; what it primarily pleads for, a thorough study of Corneille's dramatic technique, is indeed

but I have tried in the case of each play to deal with whatever seemed most worthy of treatment in that particular instance. I frequently point out analogies between Elizabethan and French-classical playwrights or plays; for I believe that anyone who is familiar with either of these two schools of drama, which flourished so near each other in both time and place and which exhibit so many contrasts and parallels, will find such analogies enlightening. As the minor French dramatists are little known and even their best plays are rarely accessible, I quote extensive passages from these, in order that one may thus have some idea of their work.[24]

These quotations are in every case translated into English verse in footnotes, which are so arranged, for the convenience of the reader, that as nearly as possible each English line is on the same page as the corresponding French line. Translations from Racine, from whom also I quote at some length, are in rhyming couplets because that is the medium I used in translating his plays; but blank verse is employed in my renderings of all the passages quoted from the other dramatists—save once (p. 117, note 7) where a few lines of Tristan l'Hermite fell naturally into an English version of the French alexandrines. My quotations from French critics have been made in English, except for a few phrases where the French words are so nearly the same as English ones that their sense cannot be mistaken. In short, I have wished the book to be intelligible throughout to all who are in-

---

very desirable, and its discussion of the later plays of this dramatist is, to say the least, suggestive.

[24] Texts of plays by the lesser French-classical dramatists are often difficult to obtain; and I consequently have had to take my quotations from whatever editions were available. I have modernized their spelling, but have not tried to harmonize their differing usage in regard to capitalization in the case of certain words (*Madame, Etat*, etc.) or in some other particulars.

terested in drama, whether they have any knowledge of French or not.

Concerning one problem, I cannot do better than to repeat a few sentences from my Translator's Foreword in *The Chief Plays of Corneille.* "No English translator or critic of French classical tragedies has been consistent in altering or preserving the French names of the dramatis personae. All keep at least some of them, and all alter at least some to the forms familiar in English. I have, therefore, attempted no consistency in this respect—even within the limits of a single play. As a rule I have changed proper names to the form, classical or otherwise, that we customarily use in English." Where I do not, there is some reason or other for my keeping the French form, though that reason may not always be apparent.

Largely the same people who were of service to me in my earlier volumes of translation and criticism aided me in this one. Dr. C. Maxwell Lancaster and the late Mrs. W. F. Peirce were again helpful in regard to passages which I have translated; Miss Louise Allen has again been the principal critic of my verse renderings; and the late Philip W. Timberlake again gave me the benefit of his criticism of these and of my discussion of the dramatists. I have been fortunate indeed to have such willing and capable helpers.

CHAPTER I

THE AMAZING CAREER OF
PIERRE CORNEILLE

THE career of Pierre Corneille, called "the Great" by his admirers and thus conveniently distinguished from his younger brother Thomas, is perhaps without parallel in the history of literature. At the age of thirty he dazzled France with a masterpiece of tragic drama; he wrote three other very famous plays within the next half-decade; then in thirty years more he never again even approached the standard which he himself had set, and much of his work in that long period is simply execrable. Yet there was at no time any marked diminution in his poetic powers, as with Wordsworth in later life, nor in his capacity for characterization, nor in his technical skill as a dramaturgist.

How, then, are we to account for the frustration of this author's undeniable genius? What was there in the man, in his life, in his environment, or in all three together, which can explain such a descent from the heights he had formerly reached? In seeking an answer, let us review one by one the successive steps of that lamentable progress, his tragedies themselves, appraising each anew, to observe just what was the nature of his own tragedy as an artist and the course it took. We may disregard his comedies, which are important because of their place in the development of the comic genre in France rather than for intrinsic merit; we may also pass over his productions for music and spectacle (*Andromède, la Toison d'Or,* and the collaborated *Psyché*) ; only his serious dramas are of real significance.

27

I

Born at Rouen in Normandy in 1606, Corneille was educated for the profession of law. Between 1629 and 1636
he wrote eight plays—six of them called comedies, and two
called tragedies though the earlier of this pair, *Clitandre,*
is really an extravagant tragi-comedy and should not be
(and never is) taken into account in any consideration of the
tragedies of Corneille. The other, *Médée* (1635), his first
genuine tragedy, is not altogether lacking in merit—though
indeed, with Euripides and Seneca as guides, it would have
been hard to spoil completely the subject of Medea's vengeance. Corneille handled with praiseworthy adroitness the
complication furnished by Aegeus (which is a stone of stumbling in all dramatic versions of this story), binding it closely
to the plot and giving it new and useful turns; *Médée* contains
a number of striking passages. On the whole, it is a better
piece of work than Racine's analogous maiden effort, by
odd coincidence similarly based on Euripides and Seneca,
la Thébaïde. But it is somewhat stiff, somewhat mechanical
throughout. Nerina's attitude towards the crimes of her
mistress is ambiguous and inconsistent. Medea's magic powers are represented as being so great that her difficulties
should always have been easily disposed of and everyone
should have feared her more. Her past love for Jason and
her love for her children are emphasized much less than
her thirst for revenge; on that account, and in comparison
with the deaths of Creon and Creusa (which only Corneille
has presented on the stage), the killing of the children,
properly the climax in any drama on this subject, loses effectiveness; and practically all sense of the sorrow which
the death of his offspring should cause in Jason is destroyed
by the atrocious invention of his own impulse to kill them
in order to bring pain to Medea. There is, indeed, nothing
in the play as good as the later acts of Mairet's *Sophonisbe,*

which inaugurated French "classical" tragedy a few months before—nor anything to suggest that real genius was at work in that field and was on the point of bursting into full flower. Yet the very next year, Corneille wrote the *Cid,* his masterpiece.

The literary Brahmins of the seventeenth century preferred *Cinna,* the literary Brahmins of today prefer *Polyeucte,* but the great mass of theater-goers and play-readers have never wavered in their allegiance to the *Cid.* It took Paris by storm and made its author the popular idol; "as beautiful as the *Cid"* became a proverbial phrase. It is the work which one instinctively associates in one's mind with Corneille, even more than one thinks first of *Phèdre* in connection with Racine or of *Hamlet* in connection with Shakespeare.

Nor is this to be wondered at. When the youthful playwright, by happy chance, went rummaging about in the vast store-house of material furnished by the national drama of Spain, then at its apogee, and lighted upon the *Mocedades del Cid* of Guillén de Castro, he found in that inchoate chronicle-play a subject which is perhaps more universal and irresistible in its appeal than any other in the dramatic literature of mankind. All the world loves a lover; and all the world can sympathize with a man's or a woman's devotion to the imperative claims of honor, whether or not the particular code that institutes those claims is still in vogue; and hence all the world must thrill to the story of Rodrigue, bound by honor to avenge the intolerable insult to his aged father by the father of the woman he loves, and of Chimene, obligated no less to seek his death in turn, despite her love for him.[1] The nobility of the young lovers, their steadfast

---

[1] The compulsion under which Chimene acted may, indeed, have to be explained today to be rightly understood. In an age when it devolved on a slain man's family rather than on a public

adherence to what they conceive to be their duty, and the greatness of their love for each other in spite of everything, have always captured and will always capture the hearts of people everywhere.

The *Cid* is an astonishing work. It is essentially the work of a young man.; it has all the freshness and exuberance of youth. In this respect it is somewhat like Racine's *Andromaque* and still more like *Romeo and Juliet*. But there is also a note of Marlowe here: it makes the blood tingle, like a flourish of trumpets in the morning. A minor French critic has not only compared the *Cid* with *Romeo and Juliet* but has pronounced the two dramas approximately equal in greatness.[2] True, like a good patriot, he has been careful to point out to his readers only those details in which he thinks the play written by his fellow-countryman is superior to Shakespeare's, never those in which the case is the reverse; but his appraisal is correct: these two tragedies, so similar in nature and in their date in the careers of their respective authors, are indeed of a surprisingly exact parity of merit. The *Cid* does, however, in its best scenes rise to greater heights than its English rival ever attains.

Its chief defect is, obviously, the role of the Infanta. The struggle between her love for Rodrigue and her pride which forbids her to marry a man not of royal blood, a theme which often recurs in dramas of the period, does not vitally affect the action and is tiresome in itself, though the disingenuousness of her advice to Chimene at times and the

---

prosecutor to bring a slayer to justice, she was obligated to take every step against Rodrigue that her father would have wished to be taken. He being helpless in death, common loyalty made her his deputy, no matter if she herself thought his foe blameless. The situation is unfamiliar to us, but needs no further statement to be sufficiently comprehended.

[2] F. Hémon in *Cours de Littérature, le Cid, Paris*, ed. of 1930, pp. 44-46.

uncertainty of how she may intervene in the course of events do increase in some small degree the tension of the tragic predicament. Almost every other alleged blemish proves, upon closer inspection, to be a positive excellence. Is Chimene's plea when she first comes before the King, demanding her lover's death, flamboyantly rhetorical? She speaks from a sense of duty, asking for what she does not really desire; the note of insincerity here, sounded by her exaggerated rhetoric, is precisely right. Are the arguments with which she and Rodrigue justify the positions they take oversubtle and wire-drawn, as Corneille himself felt to be the case? Yes, they are increasingly so as the play proceeds; and that is natural with certain people of an intellectual type who are enmeshed in an agonizing situation with which they try to deal rationally, reasoning their way through it, while the strain to which it subjects them increases steadily and makes their suppression of hysteria more and more difficult. Do they go to extremes in stickling for the "point of honor"? Jules Lemaître has cleverly observed [3] that they often express not the sentiments which they have, but those which they think they ought to have; that they are conscious of the noble figure they cut, each in the other's eyes, and that they want to compel each other's admiration and prove themselves worthy of being loved; that constantly in all their anguish they thus are, after a fashion, making love to each other: it is a very delicate and beautiful touch. Is Rodrigue's boast of invincibility, when Chimene tells him to fight his best for her hand, outrageous rhodomontade? Nothing could be truer to life: he has been stumbling blindly through a dark maze from which he saw no prospect of escape; he has perceived at last a little glimmer of light and groped his way towards it; and then suddenly it is brighter than he

[3] In L. Petit de Julleville's *Histoire de la Langue et de la Littérature française,* Paris [1897], vol. iv., p. 279.

could possibly have expected, and the path lies plain and straight before him with nothing required to gain his heart's desire but simple hard-hitting, in which he knows his adequacy. A man's instinctive reaction in such a case would be to throw up his head, square his shoulders, and shout aloud what he feels in his sheer relief: "I can thrash all creation!" And that, in the language of poetry, is just what Rodrigue says.

The twin peaks of the *Cid* are the two interviews between the lovers. Here are the essence and the greatness of the play. Each of these scenes is pivotal. The first of them clears up every possible misunderstanding that either Rodrigue or Chimene might have had of the other's attitude. "Rodrigue offers his life, and Chimene demands it; but in spite of the feud which a rigorous obligation imposes on them, they adore each other; they will adore each other even unto death, which (it is their sole hope) will reunite them soon." [4] The second interview breaks the deadlock established in the first; it shows to Rodrigue (and to us) that Chimene may yet be his, for a situation has developed in which she will accept this outcome rather than the only other alternative; it ends with her promise to wed him if he will save her from that, and he undoubtedly can. But far more wonderful than the dramatic effectiveness of these scenes, or even than their psychological insight, is their emotional power—the beauty and vital force of the eloquent depiction here of the heart's true feelings bursting into irrepressible utterance despite every code and convention that would throttle them. This breath-taking triumph of sincerity is an almost incredible thing.

For, if we are to judge by its literature, there was never, perhaps, in all human annals an age more convention-ridden,

[4] Translated from L. Petit de Julleville: *Théâtre choisi de Corneille,* Paris, n.d., pp. 21-22.

a society more artificial, than that in which the *Cid* was written and first produced. The characters in the plays of that century were governed by catchwords rather than by realities; Racine's Andromache offers merely the most consistent and thorough-going example of the common vice. Legal relationships were of paramount importance; the Tomyris of Quinault's *la Mort de Cyrus,* who is desperately in love with Cyrus and is forced into a detested marriage to save his life, thereupon finds her sense of duty to her "husband" so strong that she cannot kill, as she has planned to do as soon as she attains her object, the villain who has thus compelled her to wed him—and afterwards, when Cyrus himself kills him, she feels that she is obligated to put her lover to death! Appearances were at any cost to be preserved. Everyone was forever posturing. "By this action I shall become an illustrious example"—of this or that—is an idea frequently expressed. Yet it was then, and at no other time, that a great dramatist represented a daughter letting herself be plighted to her father's slayer, within twenty-four hours of his deed—because he did only what he ought to have done, and he still really deserved her love, and she could not but love him still.

The audiences of the day were enraptured. Moralists were scandalized. Propriety joined hands with envy and enmity in an attack on the author. We need not review the famous "Quarrel of the *Cid,*" which followed and which threw the subject finally into the hands of the French Academy. Suffice it to say that the judgment of that august tribunal, declaring the marriage of Chimene to Rodrigue so flagrant an affront to decency that it would have been better not to write a play at all than to set girls such an example, and condemning many other details of the plot as unethical, unseemly, or improbable, wrought a vital change in the nature of Corneille's work and affected all his subsequent career. We must not for a moment suppose that the verdict of the

Academicians either crushed or curbed him; he could have defied it and triumphantly walked his own path, assured of the support of an idolatrous public. It did worse: it convinced him. Not immediately, for he resented it at first; but soon in large degree, and still more as time went on, though not so much in regard to its specific criticisms as in regard to the principles and viewpoint underlying it. In consequence, the great romantic dramatist that, as the *Cid* shows us, might have been (a figure such as Victor Hugo would have liked to be and doubtless did fondly imagine himself) never was. The extent of Corneille's metamorphosis may be measured by the fact that in his *Examen* of the *Cid* in the edition of 1660 he points out that his heroine never consents to wed Rodrigue; that she is silent when the King decrees that their marriage shall take place at the end of a year, and silence when royalty has spoken does not imply consent but the reverse; therefore we may well believe that she will persist in her refusal!

This argument is of course absurd—though it has been approved by certain modern critics who are the spiritual descendants of those who were shocked by the play when it first appeared.[5] In reality, Chimene's final speech and the King's speech that follows, taken together, permit no reasonable doubt that the lovers will "marry and live happily ever afterwards." [6] This, having been the outcome in the source

[5] They surprisingly include Petit de Julleville (*Théâtre choisi de Corneille,* p. 222, note 3), whose discussion of the *Cid* is for the most part brilliant and penetrating.

[6] Chimene says that she has already revealed her love of Rodrigue, that she cannot deny it now, and that she is obligated to do whatever her sovereign bids her do—only she asks the King if he himself can sanction this marriage which he has commanded, and can justly use her to pay his own debt to Rodrigue in a manner that will dishonor her.

No, she does not ask even this; it is what the Corneille of 1660

of Corneille's drama, is to be assumed, unless he specifically indicated the contrary. The audiences that first acclaimed the *Cid* understood it thus—or they perhaps would not have

---

substituted for the lines he had originally written and had let stand till then. The point about Rodrigue's value to the State had been raised by the Academy as the only possible justification for Chimene's union with him; that, beyond doubt, is what made Corneille introduce it at long last. Originally Chimene had said only that it would be a monstrous thing if *in one same day* she buried her father and wedded Rodrigue; this would be to compound her father's death, to be untrue to his memory, and to bring everlasting reproach upon herself.

> Mais à quoi que déjà vous m'ayez condamnée,
> Sire, quelle apparence, à ce triste hyménée,
> Qu'un même jour commence et finisse mon deuil,
> Mette en mon lit Rodrigue et mon père au cercueil?
> C'est trop d'intelligence avec son homicide,
> Vers ses mânes sacrés c'est me rendre perfide,
> Et souiller mon honneur d'un reproche éternel
> D'avoir trempé mes mains dans le sang paternel.

"But to whatever you have already condemned me, sire, how would it appear, with this sad marriage, for the selfsame day to begin and end my mourning, place Rodrigue in my bed and my father in the tomb? This is too nearly a connivance at his death; makes me unfaithful to his sacred ashes; besmirches my honor with the eternal shame of having dyed my hands with a father's blood."

It is this original speech, rather than its emended version, that the King's reply directly answers: he says that it would be indeed unseemly for Chimene to wed Rodrigue on that very day, but that he has not prescribed the date; in a year it will be quite legitimate and she shall wed him then. Yet in either version the gist of the matter is the same: Chimene protests, but says she will obey the King's decision—"Vous êtes mon roi, je vous dois obéir" ("You are my King; I ought to obey you") in 1637; "Quand un roi commande, on lui doit obéir" ("When a king commands, he ought to be obeyed") in 1660—and the King answers her objection and decides that she still must marry Rodrigue.

been so delighted. The people who censured it, including the
Academy, understood it thus. The people who defended it
understood it thus. If Corneille himself had meant it to be

The only evidence in support of the idea that Chimene will never
relent is that cited by the aging Corneille from the scene earlier in
Act V between her and Elvira. Here she declares that even if
Rodrigue should prevail in his duel with Don Sancho, she will
defy the royal mandate and refuse marriage with him. Corneille
argues in 1660 that what she says in this scene has especial validity
because she is speaking to her confidante, to whom she would not
lie. But neither would she lie to the man whom she loves and honors—
not at least in a matter of supreme importance when his action is
based on his confidence in her good faith. The fact is that she no
longer knows her own mind; she is the prey of veering impulses.
A few moments after her statement adduced by Corneille, she tells
Elvira that her love for Rodrigue is less potent than her aversion
to Don Sancho in moulding her desires concerning the outcome
of the duel. Let him believe it who can!
    Dramatically, this declaration of Chimene's, that under no cir-
cumstances will she wed Rodrigue, is needed to maintain the suspense; for otherwise the denouement of the play would have been
too obvious after their interview in V, i; that scene and her subsequent scene with Elvira, the mistake about the result of the duel,
Chimene's public avowal of her love, Rodrigue's generous renunciation of his rights, her final forgiveness of him but objection to their
nuptials, alternately presage and seem to thwart the ultimate solution that is reached only with the King's pronouncement, at the
very end of the drama. But Corneille, with the subtlety characteristic of his best work, has made a virtue of necessity. The un-
compromising attitude taken by his heroine in talking with Elvira
is psychologically explainable as her instinctive revulsion from
having permitted herself, just previously, to assure Rodrigue that
he can win her by winning the duel and that she wishes him to.
When she thereupon goes to the opposite extreme and hysterically
insists she will never wed him, she says also that she will raise up
a thousand of other champions to espouse her cause if Don Sancho
fails; but in the end she accepts the outcome of a single duel as
terminating her efforts to avenge her father, just as the arrangement had been that she would accept it; and similarly she may be

understood otherwise, he would most surely have said so during the controversy. The interpretation which he offered in the *Examen* of 1660 is hence merely a perverse and graceless attempt—like that of Tennyson in *Locksley Hall Sixty Years After*—to unsay in old age what he had said magnificently in youth. In the same *Examen*, Corneille admits that he would not write the two colloquies between the lovers, if it were to do over again!

What he did write, when three years after the *Cid* he first offered another play to the public, was a tragedy of early Rome, *Horace,* or, as it is often called, *les Horaces.* The latter would seem, to modern English ears, the more suitable title; for the theme here treated was the legendary combat of the Horatii and the Curiatii, and when the name "Horatius" is used, we think today rather of the Roman hero who held the bridge against the army of Lars Porsena as told by Macaulay—whereas "Horace" suggests the great poet of the Age of Augustus. But Corneille entitled his drama *Horace,* and that fact should refute those critics who have maintained that the play has two chief characters of equal importance, or that its hero is not the young warrior but his father. Corneille calls the father "le vieil Horace" ("Old Horatius"), the son "Horace" alone.

Yet this play is a study of the reactions not only of one

---

expected to abide also by her promise to Rodrigue that she will marry him if he is victorious. Nor could she honorably do anything else, for it was on that condition alone that he would not let Don Sancho kill him. True, he releases her from her pledge—he knows best how to capture her heart utterly!—but he waives his claim to her hand only that he may first do whatever deeds are necessary to satisfy her. There has never been any suggestion that he would consent to live, if forgiven but deprived of her forever. They both know that. When Chimene surrenders her vengeance, she in effect surrenders herself also.

If she did not, the problem of the Infanta would be reopened and left unsolved; the play would not really end, but only terminate.

man but of a number of people to a tragic situation in which conflicting claims are made on their loyalty. A similar situation had been the essence of the *Cid;* there the conflict between love and filial duty was long undecided, but love had the final word. In *Horace* the conflict is between love in its various phases on the one hand and patriotism on the other, and no two of the characters concerned react in the same way. To young Horatius, beside the claims of his country everything else is as nothing. In old Horatius the counterclaims of affection are no less inexorably rejected, but they make themselves felt more strongly—though the difference perhaps results only from the mellowing effect of age on a nature fundamentally much the same as his son's. The Alban champion, Curiatius, exemplifies normal humanity in contrast to these austere extremists. He feels the full force of both claims; like the brave man he is, he does his duty unhesitatingly, but with torn heart. Naturally it is he who falls in his combat with the single-minded zealot, Horatius.

The remaining major characters in the play are the two women, Sabina and Camilla. Alban by birth and Roman by marriage, at once the affectionate sister of the three Curiatii and the devoted wife of Horatius, Sabina finds no alternatives in prospect but the subjection of her adopted or of her native city, the death of her husband or of all her brothers; and her dominant wish, to which she recurs again and again in this intolerable position, is to escape from it by her own death. Horatius' sister, Camilla, is at the opposite extreme from him. With her, feeling is everything, principle nothing. When she sees Curiatius in Rome, she at first supposes him a deserter for her sake, and she is proud and happy to think that he loves her so much. Whichever side may win the triple duel, she will hate the victor who bereaves her of brother or lover; and when Horatius returns exultant with the blood of her betrothed on his hands, the only possible outcome of the meeting between this fanatical patriot and the frantic, resentful girl—who curses not only him but Rome also—is the sword-stroke with which he punishes such blasphemy.[7]

This turn of the plot was believed by Corneille, no doubt correctly, to account for the original imperfect success of *Horace;* and it has been a target of adverse criticism ever since. It violates the only one of the famous three Unities that is of real importance, unity of action, by violating what has been called "the unity of peril": hitherto the subject of this drama had been the combat between the Horatii and the Curiatii, by which the life of the hero was endangered; but now, with that danger past, he is again in peril—in peril of being put to death for killing his sister—and the fifth act is concerned with the entirely new subject of his arraignment for this deed. Attempts to defend the play as written, or to suggest an improvement, have been unsatisfactory.

The murder of the Horatii's sister by her surviving brother and his escape from punishment for it when brought to trial are, however, a part of the legend itself which Corneille dramatized; and indeed something more than a duel successfully fought, even under the harrowing circumstances of such close ties between the combatants and when so much depends on its result, is necessary for an adequate tragic action. The native genius of the author, which was really remarkable, seems to have groped instinctively towards a right solution of his difficulty, and might have found it if he had not been governed at this time by unfortunate prepossessions.

---

[7] It should be noted, in illustration of Corneille's delicate sense of character, that he does not represent Camilla here as one whom grief and anger have made reckless of all consequences, even loss of life. His "Camille" is of too frail fiber for anything approaching heroism. Clearly she never conceives that her death may be the cost of her imprecations; she flees in panic when her brother attacks her.

That a character should undergo some change in the course of a play is universally regarded as one of the finest achievements of dramatic art. We are told it can rarely occur in classical drama, where the action takes place within the limits of a single day. Yet it occurs in *Horace*. When the young hero of this tragedy first appears—it is at the beginning of Act II—he knows that he and his brothers have been selected to represent Rome in the impending combat, but not that the Curiatii are to represent Alba. He is proud of the distinction accorded him, but modest withal. He feels that many others might better have been chosen than he— though he believes that the fervor and determination which he will bring to the task assigned can make him invincible. Then he discovers who will be his adversaries. He must kill the betrothed of his own sister, the brothers of his own wife, men whom he himself loves devotedly; or Rome will henceforth forever wear the yoke of Alba. The conflict which is waged in his soul is not portrayed in words, as that in Rodrigue's is portrayed in the *Cid* before he goes to meet the father of Chimene. An actor perhaps could partially reveal it. In the text it may only be inferred from his immediate change in tone and temper. When Curiatus is overwhelmed on learning that he and his brothers are to fight against the Horatii, Horatius tries to help him by arguing that the very poignancy of the situation, which is a challenge to their manhood, will augment their glory. Here something of strain and excess is already evident. And when Curiatus protests against the inhumanity of his attitude, he becomes arrogant and contemptuous. To attain to the unwavering, obsessive resolution which he considers needful in this crisis, he has had to do violence to his gentler feelings, and in the degree that this was difficult his self-esteem for having so done is magnified, and he cannot permit any question that he is right. It is true that he can still be moved by the distress of his wife and his sister—while the combat is still to be fought. But when it is over, and what he ruthlessly purposed he has actually performed no less ruthlessly, he comes home triumphant—great in his own eyes as he deems the importance great of Rome's victory, which was due to him alone—flaunting the spoils of his once-beloved antagonists, without comprehension or toleration of Camilla's anguish. And when finally he is tried for killing her, he is quite devoid of any sense of having disgraced himself by this brutal crime; standing on the scene of it, when his victim's body has scarce yet grown cold, he complacently asks for death because, he says, he has now reached the very pinnacle of heroic renown, and any further life that he might live must needs be less glorious!

It should be clear, then, what kind of ending this play ought to have. Hémon, to whom I am largely indebted for the substance of the preceding paragraph,[8] points out that even though our sympathies are with the temperate, warm-hearted Curiatius, we must realize that the man who can best serve his country in her hour of need is he who, when a great cause is at stake, abandons himself to it utterly; and therefore the blind devotion of Horatius to the task entrusted to him was the right reaction at such a time, being the reaction most likely to bring success and hence most conducive to the public weal. But however right, it was ruinous to him as a man. It was right because in comparison with the fortunes of an entire people his individual fate was of slight importance, but its inevitable consequence was a perversion of his character. The violence done to his natural feelings, the identification of himself with his country's cause, could only result in callousness and egotism. Purely specious was his father's argument: that it was on impulse that Horatius slew his sister, and the impulse sprang from his patriotic ardor, a virtue in him, because of which he

---

[8] Cf. his *Cours de Littérature, Horace,* Paris, ed. of 1930, pp. 18 ff.

legitimately was enraged by Camilla's treasonous words. Even if he killed her in hot blood, he was cool and calm when later, at the bar of justice, he exhibited no vestige of remorse but only proud self-satisfaction. Regardless of the King's verdict, this drama is indeed the "tragedy" of Horatius; for to have become the man he is in the last two acts, is assuredly tragic—and that he became such a man as a result of having answered his country's call in the best of all possible ways, may well excite in us both "pity and terror." And the fact, which we may also realize, that this perfect response of his, which enabled him to do his duty better than it could otherwise have been done, would have been impossible for anyone who did not have originally in his nature a certain imperfection—his "tragic flaw," which could develop as it did—is a part of the complexity and the wonder and the mystery and the truth of life.

But something more overtly and actively tragic than the mere demonstration of the impairment of Horatius' character is needed. Indubitable disaster should befall him, of a sort to make his error obvious—to the audience, at least, if not to him. One is perhaps safe in saying that it is of chief importance that his wife should kill herself. Many critics have found Sabina's role, with her often reiterated eagerness to die, monotonous and ineffectual. As the consummation of her recurrent desire and a pivotal feature of the denouement, her suicide would greatly lessen the force of that reproach. It would be a very hard blow to Horatius, who has shown a tendency to display human weakness only where she is concerned. And it would be a very natural step for her to take, and natural that she should take it directly in consequence of his murder of Camilla. Sabina might have reconciled herself to resume her wifely place at his side in spite of the death of her three brothers by his hand, for that was in fair fight and "in line of duty" by the necessity of war; and yet, even though she loved him still, she might have felt it impossible for her to live with a husband who had butchered his own sister merely because of the girl's frenzied grief and the vain words, however culpable, which it prompted—his sister, who was Sabina's sister-in-law and house-mate, of whom she had grown fond. These things she could have told Horatius with great dramatic effectiveness before taking her own life—and told him, too, that though Rome was so much in his debt that he could not be punished, everyone would recoil from association with him. After this it would make little difference what "curtain" might be devised for Horatius himself—whether suicide in his turn, or a stubborn refusal to believe that he was wrong, or a bewildered sense of isolation somewhat like Anthony's final "I no longer understand the world" in the *Maria Magdalena* of Hebbel.

But Corneille, who had been blamed for depicting in the *Cid* the triumph of love over duty as commonly conceived, was bent on showing in this next tragedy the triumph of the manly passion of patriotism, regarded as a supreme duty, over all gentler passions, with death the penalty incurred by one who put love highest and the infliction of that penalty excused if not vindicated. Hence he would not follow the logic of what his genius divined and perhaps despite him portrayed; he followed the old story, and even modified it in favor of Horatius, who in the legend was first sentenced to die but then was pardoned because of his great service to the State. The fifth act of the play, in large part devoted to formal speeches at the trial of the hero, is in consequence stiffly rhetorical; but indeed there is a certain rigidity about this drama as a whole, with its symmetrical differentiation of the several characters to illustrate the different possible attitudes towards the problem posed, and with its severe economy of dialogue. Another fault, which seems oddly to have escaped comment though much of the general dissatisfaction with the last part of *Horace* may be caused by it, is the failure to provide at the end of Act IV anything to make one look forward to what will follow. At this point one sees that Horatius' relations with his wife offer a problem, and of course one does feel that his killing of his sister must have serious consequences; but there is no definite indication that he will be prosecuted for murder, and there ought to be. Indeed, there is nothing said that would suggest any consequences whatever of his crime; as it stands, the drama might almost conclude with the end of the fourth act. Because of these defects, *Horace,* in spite of all its excellent features noted above and the martial vigor and magnificent swell and crash and resonance of its verse, is not to be reckoned like the *Cid* a truly great play, if one sets the standard of greatness as high as one should; but a very fine play it unquestionably is.

II

From rigidity, Corneille passes in *Cinna* to frigidity. This we encounter at its very outset, with a heroine who in monologue apostrophizes her *"impatients désirs d'une illustre vengeance,"* weighs her love for Cinna against her hatred for Augustus, and, in connection with the latter passion, speaks also of her rage (*fureur, ardents transports, bouillant mouvement*) though hate cherished for many years because of an old wrong must surely be an emotion of cold malevolence rather than of flaming anger. A large part of the first act is consumed with an account, part summary and part verbatim quotation, of a previous impassioned harangue; and most of the second act is a formal debate in which one of the two participants does not argue sincerely. In Corneille's own day, however, *Cinna* was regarded as his masterpiece. Its somewhat too "stately" rhetoric was in keeping with the literary taste of the times; its discussion of whether a republic or a monarchy is the best form of

government, whether justice or mercy is more to be commended in a ruler, and whether tyrannicide is justifiable
were of absorbing interest in a period when these questions
could not be argued save on the stage without risk of going
to the Bastille; and in Emilia all recognized a portrait of
one of the high-born ladies of that generation, such as
Madame de Chevreuse, Madame de Longueville, or the
Princesse de Condé, who combined love and intrigue, who
conspired ceaselessly against Richelieu and a few years later
would create the Fronde. Yet modern critics tell us that
in the age in which this play was most admired, it was not
admired understandingly. Then, Cinna and "Emilie" were
the center of sympathetic interest, Augustus was the adversary whose eventual change of heart fortunately spared
them; and this view of the play, modern critics tell us, is
wrong. Pointing to the complete title, *Cinna, or the Clemency
of Augustus,* they explain how cleverly Corneille has wrought
—how in the first act he lets Augustus be seen through the
eyes of the conspirators as a ruthless tyrant and themselves
as heroic champions of liberty, and how in the subsequent
acts we bit by bit discover his noble qualities and the ingratitude, self-seeking, and perfidy of those who plot against
him, until at last we behold him in all his greatness and
them in all their baseness and pettiness. Such criticism
forgets that to write a play thus is to ignore one of the
cardinal facts of drama: that when the sympathies of an
audience are once enlisted, they cannot afterwards be transferred effectively. In evidence of this fact is the stage-history
of *Cinna:* whatever the pronouncements of literary authorities, theater-goers in general have always regarded Cinna
himself and Emilia as the hero and heroine of the play.

I shall have the temerity to defend Corneille on this point,
in part at least, against his scholarly admirers. He has not
been as ill-advised as they represent him. If his intention
had been to shift all sympathy from the conspirators to

Augustus, he would never have made Cinna display such courage when confronted with the prospect of death— and still less, when Augustus reproaches Emilia for the way in which she has repaid his unnumbered acts of loving kindness, would she have been given the most impressive line in the entire play:

Ceux de mon père en vous firent mêmes effets.[9]

Professor Paul Landis comes much nearer the truth when he praises "the dexterity with which Corneille in *Cinna* first throws the sympathy to Cinna, then to Augustus, and finally extracts and unites the virtues of both." [10] While older than Rodrigue and Chimene, both Cinna and Emilia are still quite young; they are thrilled by the excitement of conspiring and by the picture they paint of themselves as the deliverers of Rome; they are easily thrown into a panic by the sobering threat of discovery. But there is true pathos in Emilia's cry, when faced with failure, that she has done all she could. Her incomprehension of Cinna's scruples and her readiness to assume the worst hypothesis to account for his hesitancy are a blemish only too characteristic of "lovers" in French-classical tragedy, but she has the excuse that she has just been under great tension. As for Augustus, his eventual pardon of the conspirators is attributed by different critics to sagacity, humanity, or ambition to behave nobly. Lancaster suggests that he may well have been actuated by all three at once.[11] But I think that his successive reactions to the successive disclosures warrant little doubt as to which

[9] Those of my father
Produced the same results in thee.

[10] *Six Plays by Corneille and Racine*, New York, 1931, p. xi.
[11] *A History of French Dramatic Literature in the Seventeenth Century*, Part II, p. 315.

was the dominant factor in determining his course. When he first learns of the conspiracy, his reflections leave him undecided, but at least he rejects the advice of Livia, which is to do precisely what he finally does. In the fifth act, at the end of his scene with Cinna there is no hint of leniency: he says he will see whether Cinna's fortitude will persist unshaken to the end; and he tells the culprit to choose his own punishment according to what is just. Then the horrified Emperor discovers that Emilia, too, has conspired against his life, yet he still has no thought of mercy; she begs to be united with Cinna in a common doom, and he declares that he will indeed unite this treacherous and ungrateful pair and make the whole world blench at their punishment as at their crime. Then Maximus appears, his savior Maximus—and confesses to being the worst, the most perfidious, of all his foes. "Have I any subject still faithful!" cries Augustus, and forthwith pardons them all. Dramatically, the scene is defective, in that his change is too sudden to be easily understood; but that change, coming as it does, can only be a result of his realization that all his previous severity has left him no one whom he can trust, that this policy has ended in complete bankruptcy, and that there is nothing left for him to do but to try its opposite.

Even with such an interpretation of Augustus' conduct, and with the necessary modification of that extreme reversal of sympathies which modern criticism has seen in this play, we still must recognize that Corneille has over-reached himself in his design. The difference between the Augustus described in the first act and the Augustus shown to us in the second act remains bewilderingly, unacceptably great. The temperate, kindly, conscientious ruler, whom we find anxiously debating the proper course to pursue, can never have been, by any stretch of the imagination, the blood-stained proscriber of whom we have heard; he seems to us more like George Washington deciding not to accept a third term as President and about to write his famous Farewell Address. And Emilia, too, is inconceivable, on any thoughtful envisagement of her conduct. Even waiving all question of the ethical status of revenge in general (since it is true that no other theme has a more potent dramatic appeal at all times), many critics have declared that she could not be justified in taking vengeance, though for a father's death, upon one on whose bounty she had lived so long with pretended reciprocation of his love; but this is not really the main point of the difficulty about her. Life in a royal household would not involve nearly so close a relationship between its members as in a private family; yet with all necessary allowance made for that fact, the truth is that she could not have concealed so completely and so long the intense hatred which she felt for Augustus—not unless deceitfulness to a repulsive degree was a strong, fundamental trait in her nature, which Corneille certainly did not mean to be the case. Nor is it humanly possible that, having hated Augustus so bitterly for so many years, she could in a twinkling reverse her feelings towards him as one takes off or puts on a garment. She might indeed be convinced, when he pardoned all, that thanks and admiration and loyal service were now his due from her, instead of death. But she could have said only something like this: "Sire, I am overwhelmed by your magnanimity. I owe everything to you. After what you have just done, I could not conspire against you; I would henceforth give my life to serve you and defend you. But I cannot live in constant loving association with you, whose face, whose voice, whose person have been linked in my mind, since childhood, with all the hatred of which I was capable. Permit me, sire, to go to the farthest bounds of your empire, where I shall never see you again." The whole effect of the conclusion is that of the forced "happy ending" so frequently encountered in comedy and tragicomedy. The facile supposition that people can let any and all bygones be bygones may be very convenient in bringing a drama to a pleasant close, but it is very untrue to life.

There is a similar want of imaginative grasp elsewhere in this play. Cinna claims that he could not avenge Emilia on Augustus if the Emperor were to abdicate; but though the conspiracy would of course collapse when it no longer had the object of regaining the liberties of Rome, as a private citizen Augustus could be killed all the more easily by one determined man.[12] It is unbelievable that any human being would have been fatuous enough to declare his love in the circumstances and in the manner in which Maximus declares his to Emilia; and, indeed, that he secretly loves her, and betrays the conspiracy in the hope of destroying his "rival" and winning her hand, is the most hackneyed of possible turns that the play could take. Augustus concludes his great soliloquy by expressing a sentiment, "Either let me die or let me reign," which it was conventional to ascribe to all sovereigns, but which is at complete variance with the feelings of this particular sovereign as previously and subsequently portrayed. *Cinna* contains much eloquence and some really striking thoughts and workmanship; but only the tenacious traditionalism which at all times has characterized the appraisals of French "classical" drama could have preserved for this tragedy a place beside or near its two immediate predecessors and *Polyeucte,* which followed it.

In Corneille's own century *Polyeucte,* though a favorite of the general public, was not held by "the judicious" to be one of his best plays. There were two reasons for its failure to win their plaudits. In the first place, they preferred the

---

[12] True, the plea of personal revenge for a past crime of Augustus might not, in that case, save the murderer if he were discovered—but this would be an inglorious consideration for the professed lover to be governed by! Neither Cinna nor Emilia ever conceives the situation clearly.

more elevated style of *Cinna,* whereas we consider the greater naturalness of expression in *Polyeucte* a point of excellence, and its verse is commonly thought today to be the finest its author ever wrote. In the second place, its religious subject was long deemed unsuitable for treatment on the stage.

This tragedy of an early Christian martyr seeks to depict the workings of Divine Grace in the human soul. With his fondness for symmetrical structure, Corneille offers three examples of this, in which the miraculous element is increasingly evident. The first instance, Polyeucte's resolve to interrupt a pagan sacrifice, break the images of the gods, and thus win martyrdom, does not seem miraculous at all, but merely the fervor of a newly baptized convert. The third and last instance, the sudden conversion of the ignoble, cowardly Felix, cannot possibly be anything but a miracle— and as such it is usually considered the chief defect of the play. The best that can be said for it is, that it is of a piece with the world of saints'-legends from which *Polyeucte* derives and something of whose atmosphere is preserved throughout this drama, nor could one easily imagine any other, more satisfactory ending that would conclude the action with sufficient finality to have been acceptable to its original public. Between these two manifestations of Grace there is yet another, the conversion of Pauline; this one is surprising in its suddenness and can be regarded as supernatural, but it also admits of rationalistic explanation as a consequence of the transfer of her love from Severus to Polyeucte. Her position between these two men—her lost lover and her husband—is the heart and core of the play.

Herein has lain always the principal interest in *Polyeucte;* and herein does modern criticism find grounds for maintaining that it is Corneille's masterpiece. In certain of its scenes—most of all in the great scene between Severus and Pauline in the second act—we encounter a strength, a subtlety, a maturity of genius which cannot be matched by anything in the *Cid* or elsewhere in his work. But by strange coincidence it was now, and only now, immediately on the heels of *Cinna,* that he repeated the fundamental mistake of that play and again asked of his audience an impossible shift of their sympathies. True, the shift would be less violent here; both Severus and Polyeucte were meant by him to be admired, but first the one and then the other in the higher degree. Yet even more surely here than in *Cinna,* what Corneille attempted was doomed to failure. There is nowhere—there never has been—an audience that would not give its heart, at once and beyond recall, to a worthy young man who is denied the hand of his sweetheart because of his poverty.

So it was from the first with this play. "Is there anyone," asked the Prince de Conti, the brother of the great Condé, "who would not be a thousand times more touched by the anguish of Severus when he finds Pauline married than by the martyrdom of Polyeucte?" In the next century Voltaire observed a secret joy in the audiences when they saw that Polyeucte was going to break the statues of the gods, because they anticipated that he would be put to death for it and Severus would then wed Pauline. One is safe in saying that this would still be, and will always be, the reaction of the average undirected spectator. But Corneille unquestionably intended to represent the change in his heroine's feelings as a growth from a youthful, romantic love for Severus —admirable enough in its way, but essentially earthly—to a nobler, higher, more spiritual love for her husband. Regardless of whether we like this change, we must recognize that he has motivated it with great subtlety and complexity. Many things have been pointed out as involved in causing it: her fear of her love for Severus, her wish to love Polyeucte, her instinctive cherishing of one for whom she has given up so much, the fact that it is now he (as it formerly was Severus) who is in a distressing situation and her heart goes out by nature and habit to the unfortunate, the necessity of declaring and emphasizing her love for him in order to put the strongest pressure that she can both on Felix to grant him mercy and on Polyeucte himself not to persist in his fatal resolution, her pique in being then rejected by him, and, most of all, the attraction of the mysterious and the unknown—the seemingly heroic and the professedly supernal—which she feels when he talks of religious values beyond her ken and renounces her and goes to his death for them, so that in comparison with him Severus, ready to accept her from his hand and uttering the conventional phrases of courtship, appears to her small and commonplace.[13] But all these factors combined could not have produced the result they did, if it had not been for

[13] Cf. the briefer and neater but similar analysis of her feelings by Lemaître in Petit de Julleville's *Histoire de la Langue et de la Littérature française,* vol. iv, p. 290. Translated, it is: "She resolves to love her husband, not only because he is in danger and is going to die, but also because he is mad and because in the depths of her heart the wisdom of Severus seems a little insipid beside this madness. She loves her husband from a sense of duty, it is true, but also from a sense of pity, and at the same time from a sense of admiration, and still more because she does not understand him and feels the attraction of the unexplained and the unknown."

This generally accepted interpretation of Pauline's character and conduct was first set forth by Sarcey. Faguet was one of its most convincing expositors (see his *En lisant Corneille*), but he at one time entertained, and presented in his *Propos de Théâtre* (vol. i, Paris, 1903, pp. 121 ff.), very different views regarding her feelings. Substantially these views have been reiterated by Octave Nadal in his *le Sentiment de l'amour dans l'œuvre de Pierre Corneille,* Paris, 1948. According to them, Pauline is very much in love with Polyeucte at the beginning of the play; her youthful fancy for Severus is by that time merely a tender memory! Such a thesis can be maintained only by selecting the passages

one circumstance which Corneille supplied with the un-
erring instinct of genius working at its best: she had been
married to Polyeucte only fourteen days. Her feelings towards him were still easily subject to change; he had won
her esteem and affection by his kindly, considerate treatment
of her as well as by displaying his own great love for her;
she may even be said to have begun to love him at the opening of the play, though too little not to be torn by the
more powerful tug of her old love when this was given fresh
strength—but he must have been in large measure a stranger
to her still. She could not yet have explored the major portion of his mind or soul. She had not yet had a long-
continued daily life with him, which would have made him
familiar to her beyond possibility of glamor. Hence, when

---

which can seem to accord with it and conveniently disregarding those
which demolish it.

In his article, "Doutes à l'égard de *Polyeucte*," in *French Studies,*
vol. ii (1948), pp. 1-34, R. Chauviré challenged the credibility of
the chief figures in *Polyeucte,* especially of Pauline. He was answered in later issues of the same periodical by R. Lebègue ("Remarques sur *Polyeucte*," vol. iii, pp. 212-218) and by P. J. Yarrow
("A Further Comment on *Polyeucte*," vol. iv., pp. 151-155). Professor Chauviré belongs to the school of Professor Boorsch in
viewing Corneille as a dramatist whose chief aim is theatrical effects,
without concern for any psychological consistency in the characters. He suggests that the same fault could be found in *Horace*
and *Cinna,* and also in later plays; it is noteworthy that he does not
mention the *Cid* in his indictment. Everything that he finds inconsistent in Pauline can easily be accounted for by Sarcey's interpretation of her, as here reproduced and augmented. Professor
Chauviré says it is unnatural that so base a man as Felix should
have such a daughter. To interject considerations of this sort about
characters in a play is not proper dramatic criticism at all, but an
instance of what A. J. A. Waldock called "the documentary fal-
lacy" in his stimulating *Sophocles the Dramatist* (Cambridge, 1951).
No responsible critic has ever pronounced it a flaw in *King Lear*
that Cordelia was born of the same parents as Goneril and Regan.

she discovered him dedicated to an otherworldliness whose claims he asserted in lofty-sounding words, her imagination could invest him with the grandest qualities, and he speedily became almost a god to her, and the luckless Severus as nothing in comparison.

Now this representation of the change in Pauline is wonderfully well conceived in the only way in which it could have taken place. Most people in Corneille's lifetime, and long afterwards, doubtless were glad for the heroine to become a Christian in any way and so escape damnation. Modern scholarly critics, on their part, are so engrossed in admiring the masterly genius of the portraiture that they have not regarded with their natural human reactions the thing that is portrayed. But rightly considered, for people too far removed from the Middle Ages to believe in the excellence of martyrdom or in the supreme importance of correct theological dogma, the spectacle of a woman so dazzled by the aura of false saintliness which surrounds a religious enthusiast that she loses all love for her noble, greatly-tried lover, and will not marry him when fate at last removes every legitimate obstacle to their union, is decidedly unpleasant.

We must recognize today that Severus is altogether the more admirable man. Where religion is not concerned, Polyeucte exhibits many attractive qualities—a grave courtesy, an understanding and magnanimous nature, a zest for life, and a lack of jealousy which, one regrets to say, can hardly be paralleled elsewhere in French-classical drama. He has served in war, we gather, with exceptional distinction. But there is no reason to suppose that he could even have approached the achievements which made Severus the hero of the empire; and in the realm of the spirit, Polyeucte's inferiority is greater still. His chief concern in seeking martyrdom is to enjoy the delights of heaven sooner and to avoid the danger he would run of losing them by backsliding if he continued to live. These are the considerations that he talks of most. Severus, on the other hand, is actuated wholly by principle—by a love of rectitude and nobility for their own sake—when he tries to save his rival and declares that he will intercede with the Emperor for the Christians though at the risk of his life. Both in abilities and in moral grandeur, the man who loses Pauline's heart is far above the man who wins it.[14]

The fact is that with enlightened people of today whose imagination is keen enough to make real to them what is depicted in literature, Polyeucte's behavior in the temple may well put him entirely beyond the pale of sympathy. Religious intolerance, carried to the point of using force, is particularly abhorrent to us. Granted that it appears in its least objectionable form in Polyeucte, who would have killed or harmed no one in the name of religion. He had a moral right to express his convictions publicly, denouncing the pagan faith and proclaiming the virtues and truth of his own. But his violation of the sanctities of others by doing this in the midst of their ceremonies of worship, which he broke up, and then destroying their sacred vessels and the statues of their gods, was an outrage for which he deserved to be very severely punished.

Pauline herself, even apart from her misguided change of affections, seems to me by no means so admirable as traditional criticism has pronounced her. No other heroine of Corneille, says Lancaster, "unites such intensity of feel-

[14] Lemaître's idea, given unfortunate prominence by being stated in so notable a place as the pages of Petit de Julleville's great *Histoire,* that when Severus calls Pauline *"trop vertueux objet"* he reveals that he has hoped to seduce her (vol. iv, p. 291), is exploded by reference to the text of the play. He calls her "too virtuous" when she reminds him that it was never in her power to marry him, for filial duty subjected her to her father's will.

ing with such understanding of others and such strength." [15]
It is true that, like Severus, she acts from principle, according to what she conceives to be right, however intense her
emotions; and she shrewdly realizes that no fear of punishment will make her husband abjure his faith, and is under
no illusions about her father. But she continually, and always wrongly, expects the unworthiest conduct of Polyeucte
and Severus in their relations with each other, though recog-
nizing that her fears insult them both. A climax is reached
in Act IV when she imagines that Severus' object in coming
to see Polyeucte is to taunt him in his misfortunes! [16] It
may be the same persistent distrust of a man of admitted
nobility which partly inspires her vehement assertion that
nothing could make her wed one who was, however innocently, the cause of her husband's death; she probably believes that Severus will not do his best to save him if the
least prospect remains of marrying her in case of Polyeucte's
execution. At any rate, she here brings to mind by contrast
Chimene, who can in the end marry one who deliberately,
with his own hand, killed her father, since she knows that
he was blameless in doing so; and we may be sure that the
people who were horrified by Chimene applauded Pauline.
But Chimene had never ceased to love Rodrigue, and Pauline
by this time has almost completed the transference of her
love to Polyeucte. Her last vestige of affection for Severus
appears in her final words of this scene, when she tells him

---

[15] *Op. cit.,* Part II, p. 325. Lancaster's more sympathetic analysis
of Pauline's character is the best succinct statement of the traditional
view of her that I know of.

[16] This immediate, wholly gratuitous conjecture is, perhaps, in
some degree a result of blind anger; her husband has just rejected
her in favor of his religion, and it actually would seem from her
words that she is on the point of leaving him to his fate; but
Severus unluckily arrives at that very moment, and she vents her
ill temper on *him*.

that if he is not generous enough to intercede for her husband's life, she does not wish to know it. Thereafter, as Lancaster observes,[17] he drops so utterly out of her thoughts and heart that when Polyeucte has suffered martyrdom and she has become a Christian, she exclaims on learning that her father, too, is converted,

Cet heureux changement rend mon bonheur parfait.[18]

She says this in the presence of Severus himself, to whom, moreover, she speaks no word and pays no attention at any time in the entire scene. With her, out-of-love is indeed out-of-mind—and out of any sort of fondness whatever. Though she must believe that salvation depends on conversion, she feels not the slightest concern for the noble, heroic man whom she formerly has loved, who loves her still, and who has tried to save his rival for her sake.

I have stated the matter thus sharply because there is no other possible interpretation of her behavior in this concluding scene of the play, and it seems to me that here we have a sufficient answer, even without the other points discussed above, to those who see a spiritual development in her merely because her love for a gallant pagan soldier is supplanted by an infatuation for a Christian martyr. It is a blemish in any literary work if the characters whom the author meant to be esteemed cannot hold the sympathies of people in all subsequent times, as I believe Polyeucte and Pauline cannot. But this blemish, though serious, does not necessarily prevent a play which is marred by it from being a great play.[19] The very fact that different periods and dif-

17 *Op. cit.*, Part II, p. 325.

18 This glad change makes my happiness complete.

19 Molière's *Tartuffe* does not provide an exact parallel, for no one has ever sympathized with Orgon's conduct in casting his son out with almost murderous mood and trying to force his daughter to marry Tartuffe. But parental tyranny was formerly

ferent critics can interpret Polyeucte and Pauline differently and cannot agree in liking or disliking them, just as we differ about people in real life, is a proof of the complexity and lifelikeness of their portraiture. All, in fact, of the major characters in *Polyeucte* are masterfully drawn. No further comment on Severus is needed, and, except for his miraculous conversion, we have in Felix a wonderful study of base fatuity, where a large and delicious element of comedy, which is usually excluded from the French tragic stage, testifies to Corneille's powers in that vein. Though a religious drama, *Polyeucte* is its author's most broadly human play.

III

Since neither its subject matter nor its verse, however, had pleased those whose approval he most desired, he went back to Roman themes and resounding rhetoric in his next tragedy. Instead of simply *Pompée,* it was at first entitled *la Mort de Pompée*—and rightly so, for Pompey himself is not one of the dramatis personae, whereas the play deals with matters leading up to and following his death. Evidently, Corneille's intention was to repeat the great success of *Cinna,* and in the opinion of his contemporaries he accomplished his aim. Till the end of his life, at least, the *Cid, Horace, Cinna,* and *Pompée* were considered his supreme achievements; *Polyeucte* was never put beside them, then. The original estimate of *Pompée* has preserved for it even yet, in traditional repute, a place among the best seven or eight tragedies of its author. But most modern critics, be-

---

condoned enough, especially as a stage convention, for people to be satisfied with a denouement in which Orgon recognizes his error, whereas he now arouses emotions not so easily purged. Yet no one would deny the greatness of *Tartuffe.*

ginning with Lemaître and Faguet, would rank it among his worst.

Imitating *Cinna,* it has the characteristic faults of imitation; it exaggerates the defects of the earlier play. Its verse is the most grandiose that Corneille ever wrote. Attempting to rival the debate between Cinna and Maximus over the proposed abdication of Augustus, it opens with a formal discussion by the young king Ptolemy and his counselors as to whether to welcome the vanquished Pompey, refuse asylum to him, or kill him. At every opportunity all through the play, there are long narrative speeches; the one describing the death of Pompey tells, with a grotesque assumption of omniscience, what his thoughts were when the murderers struck him down!

This tragedy does not really have a plot; "a mere sequence of events logically connected" does not constitute one. There is no conflict of opposites that are matched evenly enough to create suspense. Julius Caesar does not appear until the second scene of Act III, and Cornelia, Pompey's widow, not until the last scene of that act. The brief clash between these two—between, on the one hand, her resolve to make him pay for her husband's death and, on the other, Caesar's magnanimity, which arouses her unwilling admiration but cannot turn her from her purpose—has been much praised because it is the single truly dramatic thing in the play; many critics regard the role of Cornelia as its only excellence. But on adequate inspection she will be found to be a far from attractive figure. The "duty" to which the heroines of Corneille consecrate themselves has become more and more questionable. Chimene, in the world in which she lived, was genuinely obligated to take action against Rodrigue. If vengeance is justifiable at all, even Emilia's pursuit of it may be defended; everything that Augustus had done for her was not enough to atone for her father's blood, which he had foully spilled. But no credible logic could show it to be Cornelia's duty to seek Caesar's death in retaliation for Pompey's. The quarrel between these great men was political, not personal. Caesar in victory was eager to treat his vanquished foe with kindness and honor; he was horrified by the murder of Pompey and pledged himself to avenge it. After his generous conduct towards Cornelia, it was most ungenerous of her to doubt his sincerity, as she tried hard to do; her implacable hatred of him is in the blind and senseless spirit of a vendetta.[20] Yet Corneille certainly intended her to be admired.

The chief offense to most people, however, in *la Mort de Pompée* is its depiction of the love of Caesar for Cleopatra. According to this play, he fell in love with her when she came to Rome, while a young girl, with her father; he has written her almost daily letters throughout all his campaigns; he conquers the world only to lay it at her feet! A new influence has now become of major importance in the work of Corneille. Early in the seventeenth century the enormous vogue of D'Urfé's interminable pastoral romance, the *Astrée,* introduced into French drama its preoccupation with love, its strained conventions of gallantry and decorum, and its stereotyped love-jargon of "sighs" and "flames" and "conquests." This element, called "romanesque" because of its derivation from the *Astrée* and subsequent romances, was perpetuated and increased by the influence of the fashionable drawing-room society, which had its heyday from 1630 to 1650, upon French life and letters—particularly the influence of the coterie that frequented the famous *chambre bleue* of the Marquise de Rambouillet. These took as their models the heroes and heroines of D'Urfé. "In entering a seven-

---

[20] To justify her, some critics have asserted that she hates Caesar mainly for having destroyed the liberties of Rome, but the text of the play makes it clear that this is only a secondary consideration with her. Quite in character is her sharp rebuff of Cleopatra's well-meant condolences.

teenth-century drawing-room," says Irving Babbitt,[21] "one entered an intensely artificial Arcadia . . . from which the cares and concerns of ordinary life were banished and where one was free to discourse of love. This discourse of love, it is true, often ran into mere *préciosité,* into what has been termed wire-drawn and supersubtilized gallantry, but at the same time a great deal of real insight into the passions resulted from all this anatomizing of the heart."

Unfortunately, insight into the passions, which has ever since been a boasted virtue in the literature of France, was not the sole result, as we shall note only too often in French-classical drama. Love being apotheosized, whatever feelings were observed frequently to attend it were accepted complacently as "natural" and therefore excusable or even right and proper. Thus, for example, the indulgence shown to jealousy, however base or contemptible, in French literature, in striking contrast to its treatment in English literature, which has no such convention;[22] and thus the sympathetic attitude, by people steeped in French literature, towards this and other ignoble human weaknesses which would not be condoned in the characters delineated in the literature of any other country. The ignoble is not less bad in being natural, and to rise above the worst side of human nature is the very essence of goodness and nobility.

Prominent authors had free access to the Hôtel de Rambouillet, and Corneille was among those who went to it. He contributed some of the verses written for the *Guirlande de Julie,* which was presented to the daughter of the Mar-

---

[21] In his *Racine's Phèdre,* Boston, New York, and Chicago, 1910, p. xiv.

[22] Cf., at the opposite extreme, Arethusa in Beaumont and Fletcher's *Philaster:*

> She that loves my lord,
> Curst be the wife that hates her.

quise. It is said that he read all his plays to the gatherings there, from the *Cid* to *Rodogune*—and that *Polyeucte* met with great disfavor. All these tragedies, like all others of their period, have romanesque touches, be it only some use of the conventional love-language; but in *Pompée* the romanesque element runs riot. There is but one thing that can account for its sudden extreme prominence in this drama: the advent just then of a new literary type, degenerative in its effect on the taste of cultured high society, at the very time when Corneille must have been anxious not to displease again. In place of the previous pastoral romances, the pseudo-historical or "heroic" romance was coming into vogue; and it is even possible that by 1642, the year in which *Pompée* was written, he had heard in the *chambre bleue* the opening chapters of Madeleine de Scudéry's *le Grand Cyrus,* with its wonderfully valiant and absurdly gallant heroes, in all whose doings of war or statecraft, as in those of Corneille's Julius Caesar, love such as the frequenters of the drawing-rooms would have love be was an important consideration. The first volume of this colossal work was not published until 1648; but its author's earlier romance, *Ibrahim* or *l'Illustre Bassa,* had appeared in 1641 and the first volume of La Calprenède's *Cassandre* in 1642. The latter, especially, anticipated the characteristics of *Cyrus,* and its setting in the Near East during the break-up of the empire of Alexander the Great pointed the way for dramatists to exploit the Hellenistic world, whose petty kingdoms, with obscure annals, allowed free scope to romanesque invention.

It was to this very world that Corneille, after writing two comedies, *le Menteur* and *la Suite du Menteur,* next turned. *Rodogune,* produced in 1644-1645, was his own favorite of all his plays, and therefore is significant as revealing what he came to value most in drama. An involved plot, largely of his own invention, with extraordinary situations which culminate in a sensational climax—it was on this that he especially prided himself; and here in a single drama, he asserted, are combined a beauty of subject-matter, power and fluency of verse, soundness of reasoning, violence of passions, and tenderness of love and affection, so that his other plays have few merits which *Rodogune* does not possess. But the fact is that its love is the gallant love of the romances, its passions are strained, its logic is often fantastic, its verse less grandiloquent than that of *Pompée* but still too rhetorical,[23] and its subject-matter and conduct are such that it is a melodrama rather than a tragedy.

Melodrama bears the same relation to tragedy that farce does to comedy; in both melodrama and farce the interest excited is found in the plot rather than in the characters. Hence in melodrama the characters are likely to be simplified—to be altogether good or altogether bad—and the plot is likely to be devised to secure the maximum possible tension and shock, frequently of a naive or crude sort, and sheer chance may be a factor in what occurs. And when, for the sake of the plot, something is made to happen as it would not happen in real life, or the consistency of a character is violated, the melodrama becomes bad melodrama. *Rodogune* is a bad melodrama.

The exposition of what has previously taken place and of the situation at the opening of this play is clumsier, perhaps, than any elsewhere in Corneille, and is so long that to make it endurable he had to interrupt it with scenes of a more dramatic nature and resume it after them. Demetrius Nicanor, king of Syria, was taken prisoner, it explains, by the Parthians and was reported dead. His wife, "Cleopatre" —to use the French form of her name and avoid confusion

[23] Its over-use of apostrophe in soliloquies is especially flagrant. Sometimes a speaker apostrophizes first one abstraction or inanimate object and then immediately afterwards another. E.g., the first speech in Act II and the first speech in Act V.

with the famous Cleopatra of Egypt—then married his brother, who at length died; and later she learned that Nicanor was still alive, an honored captive in his adversaries' hands. He would accept no excuses for her second marriage, and himself planned to wed Rodogune, the young sister of the Parthian king; but when he brought this princess home to marry her, the outraged Cleopatre killed him and subjected her to the cruelest imprisonment until her brother came with an avenging Parthian army and forced the Queen to agree to a treaty arranging for Rodogune to wed the elder of Cleopatre's twin sons, who would then mount the throne of Syria. At the opening of the play, these two young men have recently arrived from Egypt, where they were sent when little children for safe rearing in the troubled times through which their country has passed. Only the Queen knows which of them was born first—here at the outset we encounter one of the improbabilities frequent in melodrama—and she, unaware that both have fallen in love with Rodogune, tells them that she will name as the true heir to the crown the one that will kill the Princess for her. When they both refuse to do this, she tries to turn them against each other; but their mutual devotion is unshaken by her wiles, so she secretly stabs to death one of the twins, Seleucus, and feigning to be reconciled with his brother Antiochus and with Rodogune, intends to poison them at their wedding.

The supreme situation planned by Corneille for the climax of this drama was that now, in the fifth act, Antiochus should be faced with the certainty that either his mother or his bride seeks his life, but should not know which. For this, it was necessary that what he learns of Seleucus' death should clearly indicate that the murderer must be one of the two women and might be either of them. It was also necessary that there should have been something earlier in the play that would make Rodogune as natural an object of suspicion as the perfidious, sanguinary Queen herself. To supply this indispensable preparation for the culminating scene, Corneille gave the plot a startling turn indeed.

After Cleopatre has promised, in Act II, to yield the throne to whichever of the twins will kill Rodogune, they decide to ask the Princess herself to choose the one who shall wed her and reign. She has secretly been informed of the Queen's offer to them, and when they come to her to learn her preference, she tells them that she will wed whichever will avenge his father by killing his mother for her!

This instigation to matricide is introduced into the play purely by arbitrary will of the author, to enable him to have his climacteric scene and in violence to every other consideration. From Rodogune, who both earlier and later is a typical romanesque heroine, so atrocious a proposal is entirely out of character. Of course it produces a sensational surprise, but it lessens the effectiveness of her role by showing her to be no less savage and dangerous than her enemy, just when most sympathy for her should be evoked. In her predicament it was the worst possible maneuver. Corneille said that she made it only to avoid choosing either of the princes and to enlist them both in her defense by giving them equal hopes; but the result really to be anticipated from it was that she would alienate them both—perhaps make them think their mother was quite right in wanting to kill such a person. She did alienate one of them.[24]

[24] Rodogune does not even excuse herself to them by explaining that she knows of the Queen's fell designs against her. To do so, might risk the life of her informant.

Several critics have attempted to interpret Rodogune as a consistent character—each, usually, by neglecting the passages that conflict with his explanation of her. The most recent effort, which at least is not guilty of this fault, is that of René Jasinski in the *Revue d'Histoire littéraire de la France,* vol. xlix, pp. 209-219, 322-338. His thesis is that what seems strange to us in her conduct is quite in accordance with the conventions of the heroic romances, but he merely asserts this to be a fact without citing any specific

Corneille further said that she did not expect or even wish her demands to be granted; but these explanations were made more than fifteen years after he wrote the play, and at the time when he misrepresented the conclusion of the *Cid*. Though Rodogune herself says much the same thing to Antiochus in the scene in Act IV in which she admits that she loves him, her statements then are sharply at variance with her soliloquy in Act III. There, after having been advised to find shelter from the Queen's hate in the love of the two princes, she deliberately works herself up, with frigid rhetoric and strained reasoning, to a determination to avenge her late betrothed. From this speech, one might well think that she loves Nicanor, who cannot have been dead very long, and his son also! [25] She declares that it would be ignoble to ask the protection of men in love with her, that she becomes a free agent once more when Cleopatre breaks the treaty and when Antiochus and Seleucus let her choose be-

---

parallels in them to support his statement. He thinks, as I do, that her concern for Nicanor is deliberately worked up by her in Act III; but he does not succeed in making either her monologue then or her demand on the princes at all credible. She could not have expected to form, as he says, "a party of the princes against that of the Queen," or have "rallied them to her," by a demand which she herself later admitted was monstrous—rather should she have expected to accomplish the exact reverse. Her invocation to her "long stifled sentiments of grief and rage" is too abrupt to suggest the complex mental processes which Professor Jasinski imagines in her (with nothing in the text to support his hypothesis) as having prompted it. . . . He also insists that she is concerned lest any indication of her heart's preference would bring down the Queen's wrath on Antiochus; but she never utters a word, either in soliloquy or in dialogue, which would indicate such an anxiety.

[25] Some recent critics have assumed that Rodogune must have been much older than the twins, merely because she had been engaged to their father. There is nothing improbable about a royal marriage being arranged for a monarch of forty or more with a princess of twenty or less.

tween them, and that as a free agent it is her "duty" to seek vengeance for the man who was slain when about to wed her. But when the Queen pretends a reconcilement, Rodogune is all deference and amity again. It would seem that she is able not merely to hide her feelings; she can turn them on and off like water at a faucet.[26]

The circumstances of Seleucus' death which cast equal suspicion on both women are no less unnatural. Found dying, he gasps:

> Une main qui nous fut bien chère,[27]
> Venge ainsi le refus d'un coup trop inhumain.
> Régnez; et surtout, mon cher frère,
> Gardez-vous de la même main.
> C'est . . .

and then expires. No man at death's door with such information to impart would speak thus, withholding the all-important fact of his murderer's name so long—with the result that he dies before uttering it. This is but a familiar expedient of melodrama.

At least, the scene achieved at such cost is a tremendous one. *Rodogune* is mainly famous for it and for the stark figure of Cleopatre. She too, however, belongs essentially to melodrama; she is simply a human tigress, consumed by

---

[26] Corneille's characters, especially his women, again and again assert a complete mastery over their emotions. Pauline's claim of it is so extreme as to evoke a cry of anguished protest from Severus. Fortunately for truth-to-life, their strength of will generally proves to be much less potent than they suppose it to be. But in Rodogune it goes beyond the bounds of nature.

> [27] A hand that was beloved by us
> Avenges a cruel deed's refusal thus.
> Reign; and above all, brother dear,
> Of that same hand beware, beware.
> It is . . .

ambition and hatred, yet, with melodramatic naïveté, calling her own deeds "crimes" and making conventional references to the motherly instincts to which she did violence—as though she, portrayed as she is, would have any thought of such instincts! Her sons, on the other hand, have generally been considered the play's worst blemish. Both of these youths appear at first as sighing lovers out of the *Astrée* or *le Grand Cyrus,* but Seleucus later exhibits shrewdness and a sense of values which make him the one really likable character in this drama. He wants no bride who bids him kill his mother, and he is aware of his mother's villainy and minces few words with her. Therefore it was inevitable that he should be less admired than his brother in an age when fashions in men were set by the Hôtel de Rambouillet, from whose ideas and gestures Antiochus never departs—and no less inevitable that it should be Antiochus who survives to wed and reign. The weight of tradition in the field of French "classical" tragedy is such that, amazingly, most critics ever since have also preferred this priggish young chevalier *à la mode,* who is always tenderly respectful to his mother and unshaken in his love for his heart's mistress, no matter what they do. When his brother cries out in horror at the Queen's malignant offer, this perfect son chides him:

Gardons plus de respect aux droits de la nature.[28]

When Rodogune makes an even worse demand and Seleucus exclaims that one so barbarous ought to be the daughter of Cleopatre, this perfect lover says:

Plaignons-nous sans blasphème.[29]

Unlike Seleucus, he does not cease to love either of them; and therefore critics speak approvingly of his "moderation"

[28] Let us have more respect for natural ties.

[29] Let us lament without blaspheming.

or "magnanimity"—even of his being the "maturer" of the twins. A lack of revulsion from people of abominable wickedness is not regarded elsewhere as moderation or magnanimity or maturity. Perhaps his magnanimity is to be seen in his professed willingness for Seleucus to have Rodogune, though he knows that it is himself whom she loves; without the slightest regard for *her* happiness, he must be the perfect brother also. In the final scene he wishes to die rather than find out which woman is the criminal, despite the fact that his death would leave the other one to her tender mercies; and, to crown all, when his mother, trapped at last, herself drinks the poisoned draft which she had prepared for him, and refuses all aid, he bleats:

> Ah! vivez pour changer cette haine en amour.[30]

Yet he has just learned that she had murdered his beloved twin-brother!

Fortified by the success of *Pompée* and *Rodogune,* Corneille again undertook a tragedy about an early Christian martyr. Despite the criticisms which *Polyeucte* had incurred, he was still attracted to such a theme, for it embodied more than any other his favorite topics of inexorable duty and unfaltering will. Duty to one's God is the highest of all duties; and, as everything else must be renounced if need be in its performance, it can furnish the most extreme test of one's constancy. Polyeucte gave up love and life; but Corneille conceived of a yet greater sacrifice. "Theodore," the heroine of his play by that name, is faced with the choice of renouncing Christianity or being thrown into a house of ill fame.

Of course a drama involving that situation was foredoomed to failure in an age when tragedy had to be decorous beyond the utmost decorum of Victorian England. Only an

---

[30] Ah, live to change this hate to love!

almost incredible ingenuousness could have enabled its author to hope that it would be acceptable. He could not depict his virgin martyr in the place to which she is consigned. But the method of presentation which he employed instead—successive incomplete reports of her plight, and of her rescue from it by a Christian youth who loves her, heard by another man who also loves her and who is frantic with anxiety and jealousy—is not undramatic. *Théodore* can be judged on its merits as it stands, regardless of how it was received in the seventeenth century or whether its subject could be handled better now.

Corneille selected characters and circumstances well calculated to produce a tragic result. Valens, the Roman governor of Antioch, is a puppet in the hands of his wife, Marcella, who had saved him when the Emperor had condemned him to death. Placidius, his son by a former wife, was betrothed in childhood to Flavia, Marcella's idolized daughter by a former husband. The young man cannot endure Flavia, who is wasting away for love of him; he takes a perverse delight in angering his step-mother, whom he hates; and he vainly pays court to Theodora, who Marcella discovers is secretly a Christian. It is thought that he will be cured of his love for her better by her defilement than by her death. She has taken a vow of perpetual virginity; and though threatened with the loss of this anyhow and in the worst of ways, she refuses his offer to save her if she will marry him, but begs him to kill her or enable her to kill herself—a deed which she says God plainly sanctions because He makes the idea of it occur to her! Placidius' passion is thoroughly selfish; he has persisted in his unwelcome attentions though reminded that they are dangerous to her; now, he surely could procure her instant release if he would promise never to see her again, but he hopes for advantage to himself from her predicament. At the prospect of her being ravished, he is largely concerned with the dishonor that this would bring upon *him*; when she escapes from the house of prostitution, he is slow to believe in the innocence of her relations with Didymas, her rescuer.

Here the fourth act ends—and with only minor changes in what has gone before, the play could be made to end here, too. Up to this point it has been moderately good, though no more than that. It contains better, soberer, less romanesque work than *Rodogune,* its verse in the main is of high quality, and Placidius, Marcella, and Valens are well drawn. But there is practically no struggle in the breast of any of the characters; they contend only against each other. None of them excites any sympathy. There are no really impressive scenes or great moments.

The chief source of potential effectiveness in this tragedy lay in Corneille's initial conception: the monstrousness of the sacrifice demanded of the heroine; but obviously her sacrifice cannot seem great when she exhibits little distress at the prospect of it. She remains cold and self-possessed throughout. Had she been overwhelmed with fear and horror of the fate decreed her, not only would her efforts to escape it have supplied the emotional element which is lacking, but when they proved of no avail her unhesitating refusal to forsake her faith would be the more impressive as the alternative had been shown to be terrible to her. And this would have been the climax of the play, which, as it stands, has none.

The fifth act only worsens the whole. Didymas is held a prisoner in place of Theodora; and now she comes to surrender herself to his jailors. She would let him die to save her from shame but not to save her from death, she says; and it is her death instead of her dishonor that Marcella now desires; God, Theodora says, has revealed this to her—thus casually and conveniently is the miraculous again introduced! One who can have information direct from heaven ought surely to know, as anyone else would know, that since Didymas is a Christian she could not save his life by returning, but would only lose hers as well. That is what does take place: Marcella kills them both. She then commits suicide, an act which is doubtfully motivated and without adequate dramatic preparation. The play ends with Placidius stabbing himself, cursing his craven father, and swooning from loss of blood.

How needlessly Corneille had botched his subject! A Christian maiden, confronting the alternatives of apostasy and shame, did not have to be represented as one who was vowed to virginity; she could have loved Placidius without her dilemma being any less dreadful, and thus she would have preserved the needed human warmth. And Placidius could have loved her more nobly. If Flavia had been dead already at the opening of the play, no offer of his could possibly have saved Theodora from his vengeful step-mother. The role of Didymas would not have been required at all. Thus simplified, thus conventionalized if one please, this drama would be far more effective. But Corneille was infatuated with extremes: he wished his virgin martyr to have no concern except for God and her purity; he wished her serene otherworldliness to be so dominant that nothing could make her quail; he wished to set her in isolation amidst baleful people. And his stubborn instinct for reality irresistibly led him to portray in Placidius not the conventional, devoted hero but the complex, all-too-human sort of "lover" who he felt would most surely be the architect of her disaster. In every way he over-reached himself, as he was presently to no small extent aware.

He went back to melodrama, to melodrama so highly involved that *Rodogune* seems simple in comparison. For extreme complication, his *Héraclius* (1646-1647) has become a legend—quite as Browning's *Sordello* has for obscurity. Corneille himself said that no one could understand it completely on seeing it only once. The difficulty, which for the most part lies in the identity of the characters, is not actually as great as that. Even in reading the play for the first time, one does not find it hard to keep track of the dramatis personae; and in a stage performance, where they are before one's eyes, this would be still easier. To describe the windings of the plot, however, is too long a task. Suffice it to say that the author has taken some names from the history of the Byzantine Empire and put them into a story that is entirely of his own devising. Opposed to Phocas, who has usurped the throne of the Emperor Maurice and murdered him, are two young men; one of them is supposed to be Martian, the son of Phocas, but is really Heraclius, the son of Maurice, and the other is supposed to be Leontius, a young nobleman, but really is Martian. The real Martian has never doubted that he is Leontius till after the opening of the play, and then he is led to believe that he is Heraclius; the real Heraclius, supposed to be Martian, knows that he is Heraclius. Consequently, both of them hate Phocas and desire his death. A daughter of Maurice has survived, and Phocas tries to compel a marriage between her and his supposed son, who knows himself to be really her brother; she and the real Martian are in love and of course Martian, upon coming presently to believe himself Heraclius, believes himself her brother! All these complications lead up to a stirring climax when Phocas learns that whereas one youth is certainly his son, the other is no less certainly his mortal foe; and he does not know which is which; and the woman who originally was responsible for the confusion, and who knows the truth, will not reveal it to him but challenges him to divine it if he can and choose between them if he dares.

In the end, Phocas is killed by neither of them, but by a band of conspirators. The denouement is thus no logical consequence of the action which precedes it; yet this action, throughout the drama, is full of excitement, suspense, sharp turns, and striking situations, so that though *Héraclius* never equaled *Rodogune* in renown, a good argument could be made that it is the better play. It has no scene as theatrically

effective as the last scene in *Rodogune* and no figure to match
"Cleopatre," but it is almost as well written, is little marred
with gallantry, and is peopled by characters who are in the
main likable and who generally behave as they naturally
would under the given circumstances. Even the villain Phocas, in his craving for a son's love and his tortured patience
when both the young men defy him, at times arouses sympathy.

In the later acts an old and wide-spread superstition is
curiously introduced: the idea that one feels instinctively an
impulse of affection for one's unrecognized kindred when
one encounters them. The French have a name for this alleged
impulse: *"la voix du sang"*—"the voice of the blood," heard
when the presence of a kindred strain is mysteriously sensed.
It has often found a place in cheap, conventionalized literature, but never (at least since ancient times) in the dramas
of a master-genius, unless he was working at a further
remove from reality than usual, like Shakespeare in *Cym-
beline*. Even in the melodrama of *Héraclius,* Corneille did not
create a world in which it is operative—save fleetingly, perhaps, in Martian at the news of Phocas' death—but he
created a world in which people believe in it and, ludicrously,
listen for it in vain. Phocas wonders distractedly why the
voix du sang does not reveal his son to him; Martian argues
that he must be the true Heraclius because otherwise he
would shrink from killing Phocas; and Heraclius doubts his
own identity because Phocas shows a love for him which he
thinks may be possible only in one's real father. These be-
lievers in the *voix du sang* are invariably mistaken whenever
it would have guided them if there were any such thing. Phocas finally imagines that Heraclius, being the youth whom
he instinctively prefers, must be his son; and he is wrong.
Heraclius hopes that his sister will by her sisterly feelings
prove to him that he is her brother; and she is more inclined
to believe that Martian is. She explains the love between her

and Martian as a misunderstood emotion prompted by the *voix du sang;* and they really are not related. Never has any superstition been so derided elsewhere, save in comedy.

Don Sanche d'Aragon (1649), the very next play that Corneille wrote (not counting *Andromède*) again makes the *voix du sang* ridiculous, but this time by representing it as a genuine phenomenon with fantastic consequences. A usurper rules Aragon. Its king is dead, and his daughter Elvira and her mother are living in exile at the Court of Castile. Here Carlos, a youthful soldier of unknown origin, has won great distinction by his prowess in war. Isabella, the young queen of Castile, secretly loves him; and he loves her —but is equally devoted to the princess Elvira! And Elvira appears to be in love with Carlos and with Don Alvar, a Castilian nobleman, both at the same time. These strange acrobatics of the heart are finally accounted for by the discovery that Carlos, who has believed himself a poor fisherman's son, is Sancho, the rightful king of Aragon; the *voix du sang* had aroused mutual love in him and Elvira, and as they never dreamed they were brother and sister, they mistook their affection for being in love with each other, although each was conscious of being in love with someone else!

It seems impossible that Corneille did not realize that such nonsense was nonsense. He had put nothing like it into any of his tragedies. True, he called *Don Sanche* a *comédie héroïque* because, he explained, of the high rank of its characters on the one hand and the absence from it of all tragic perils on the other, and *he saw nothing in it which could move one to laughter*. This play must indeed be grouped with his tragedies, not his comedies—or else it would not be discussed here. But we have already found comic elements in some of his tragedies and shall find them later in others; and it is true that his *reductio ad absurdum* of the *voix du sang* does not create laughable scenes but simply helps to give the play an atmosphere of make-believe not unlike, in some degree, that of a modern musical comedy. We can accept in a slightly unreal, slightly conventionalized stage-world Isabella's outburst of jealousy about Carlos and Elvira, surely excessive in its virulence even by romanesque standards; we can smile at it as a part of the convention, whereas if regarded soberly it would render despicable an otherwise attractive heroine.

Thus taken not too seriously, *Don Sanche* is one of the very best of Corneille's lesser plays. Its opening act has great verve and brilliancy,—is cloak-and-sword drama of the finest sort, quite in the vein of Hugo and the other French romanticists of the nineteenth century and superior to anything they wrote. There is perhaps no other single act of Corneille's after *Polyeucte* that is as good. He was unable to continue the play on the same high level of excellence; thenceforth it lacks the stirring scenes and swift succession of incidents that a drama of this sort should have; it is too largely devoted to dialogues about the situation created by the first act. The claims of personal merit and achievement, asserted by Carlos, cease to be an issue when it is learned that he himself is a king's son. No other denouement would have been tolerated in seventeenth-century France; yet only by facing that issue, and arriving at some impressive worthy conclusion about it, could this drama have risen above mere good entertainment—or so at least we feel, with our own convictions. It would be a mistake, however, to think that Corneille at all conceived of any such handling of his subject matter and then shirked it. The task which he proposed to himself from the first was instead to demonstrate that "blood will tell." He sought to show how one who was a king's son would always, though believing himself of the humblest origin, behave in the noblest manner; the plot is shaped to exhibit him doing this in various trying situations. Thus viewed, the play will be seen to have been devised with undeniable cleverness. The characterization, moreover, is excellent throughout—especially that of Isabella, Carlos, and the haughty grandees who resent the honors accorded a hero of dubious antecedents.

Don Sanche was a failure, we are told, because it displeased a certain exalted personage whose identity Corneille does not disclose. The difference that its success might have made in its author's career is an interesting subject for speculation. It was decidedly the best play he had written since *Polyeucte,* and in it he again exploited the chivalric Spain of the *Cid,* his natural field and one in which he seemed to recover immediately, at least for a moment, something of the freshness, zestful vigor, and boldly provocative ideas that distinguished the masterpiece of his youth. He was still near the peak of his ability, ready to do notable work when he had a theme affording sufficient opportunities for it; that fact his next drama was to prove. But just as he had turned from the Spain of the *Cid* to the Rome of *Horace,* so now from the Spain of *Don Sanche* he turned to the Rome of *Nicomède.*

This time the Rome that he depicts is not the Rome of the kings, taking her first steps towards greatness, nor Rome at the height of her power, the assured mistress of the world, under her kingly emperors, but republican Rome (dominant already throughout the whole Mediterranean area) in her dealings—now wily, now tyrannical—with the petty kings of Asia Minor; and he treats his subject from the viewpoint of those unfortunate monarchs. Among his contemporaries, Corneille enjoyed an especial reputation as a historical dramatist; but he allowed himself much license with prominent figures of history, altering at will their motives, their characters, and the events in their lives. What he was at pains to reproduce, as well as he could with the limited knowledge that people in his day had of the past, was the political background, the forces at work and in conflict, and

the general nature of the periods in which he laid his tragedies. Nowhere else has he done this so notably as in *Nicomède*.

He chose for his hero, whose name the play bears, the
son of King Prusias of Bithynia. According to history, Prusias tried to kill Nicomedes but was killed by him. Corneille
rejected so terrible a denouement and made the really undistinguished prince an impressive figure by representing him
as having learned the art of war from Hannibal during the
great Carthaginian's last days in exile at the Bithynian court,
as having already caused Rome anxiety by his conquests,
and as embodying Asiatic nationalist resistance to Roman
aggression, before which the cowardly Prusias cringes.

In Corneille's play, Nicomedes is the son of Prusias' first
marriage; and the King's second wife, Arsinoë, hates her
step-son and wants her own son to succeed to the throne in
his stead. To her influence and her machinations, to the no
less dangerous hostility of her ally, the Roman envoy Flaminius, and to the base jealousy and suspicions which Nicomedes' victories and the love felt for him by the populace
excite in Prusias himself, he opposes a bold demeanor, a cool
courage, and a barbed, eloquent tongue. Irony is the keynote
of this drama, and admiration—not "pity or terror"—the
feeling which it arouses. There results a somewhat too great
monotony of effect: Nicomedes' successive clashes with his
several adversaries, in which everybody is equally ironical,
are too much alike; and his betrothed, Laodice, the Queen
of Cappadocia, who also engages in duels of wits and words
with them, is nearly—not quite—his "double." These constantly repeated encounters are purely thrust and parry and
counter-thrust; one may be hurt or angered or baffled in
them, but no one (with a single exception) is influenced by
what another says, as the characters in the *Cid* or *Polyeucte*
are influenced, and hence the dialogue, though always spirited
and often quite stirring, is not so dramatic as in those plays.

Lemaître sees in Nicomedes an earlier D'Artagnan, ever intrepid and ever capable—to the confusion of all miscreants. In reality, Corneille has not created so conventional a hero. This valiant, straight-forward soldier, marvelously competent in war, is without experience in Court intrigues and falls at once into the trap which Arsinoë sets for him; it is Laodice, not he, who divines that there must be something in the situation besides what meets the eye. But the trouble is that this play needs the conventional hero imagined by Lemaître. One who speaks always with the proud assurance characteristic of Corneille's Nicomedes must live up to his words, or he to some extent forfeits sympathy. This self-confident prince cuts an inglorious figure when, after all his "tall talk," the first and only real act against him finds him devoid of resources to thwart it, and he can do nothing but exclaim in helpless surprise, "Thou sendest me to Rome?" and owes his deliverance to no effort of his but to his despised brother, Attalus. Here we have one of the two or three serious defects in this excellent play.

Yet in some sense Nicomedes was, truly, himself the cause of his eventual triumph. It was his example—his bravery in the face of odds, his gallant bearing, his frank speech, his loftiness of soul—that first kindled the dormant spark of manhood in the breast of Attalus. The transformation of this youth from the complacent protégé of Rome and spoiled darling of his mother to the noble lad who comes to his elder brother's rescue is perhaps the finest single thing in *Nicomède*. Here we again have that great achievement of genius, so rare in plays of the "classical" type: a change or development of character, convincingly depicted, in the course of a drama.

The revelation that it was Attalus who saved Nicomedes is a very effective *coup de théâtre*. In other respects, the denouement of this tragedy is its weakest point. Even more than in *Cinna*, matters have gone too far, feelings have been too intense and purposes too grim, for any finale of forgiveness and reconciliation to be appropriate. Such an ending is palpably forced. It has been argued that Corneille made Prusias so ignoble a figure that, like Felix in *Polyeucte,* he arouses amusement rather than abhorrence; and beyond doubt the dramatist did intend to justify thus the way in which he concludes the play. There is, indeed, a large comic element in Prusias.[31] But though Felix was fatuous, craven, and selfish, he was not by nature unkindly, whereas Prusias was malignant as well as base. Nicomedes did not know of his father's intention to kill him and throw down his head to the rioters; but he might some day learn of it, perhaps from Attalus—and then what tolerable relations could exist between him and Prusias? The feelings which this vile king evokes in us, like those evoked by the Orgon of *Tartuffe,* cannot be placated by anything short of veritable disaster for him. And what faith can Nicomedes—or we—have in Arsinoë's professions of regret and amity?

Appreciation of *Nicomède* has grown steadily greater. Voltaire and La Harpe coupled it with *Sertorius* as merely one of the best tragedies of Corneille's long decline, inferior to his *Rodogune* and, of course, to his then-admired *Pompée.* In the nineteenth century it was generally thought to be next in merit to "the four masterpieces"—the *Cid, Horace, Cinna,* and *Polyeucte.* That is still the opinion of some critics —notably of Lancaster, who is inclined to conservatism (quite properly in such work as his) in regard to the acceptance or rejection of traditional appraisals.[32] But, beginning

---

[31] This is particularly true in his scenes with Arsinoë, which may have suggested Molière's Argan and Béline in *le Malade imaginaire.*

[32] Perhaps he would rate *Nicomède* higher, but for a strange error in his recollection of it. In his *History of French Dramatic Literature in the Seventeenth Century,* Part II, p. 692, he says: "Corneille apologizes for the fact that he makes Flaminius, the

with Lemaître, modern criticism has tended to rank this play above *Cinna* and consequently fourth among the dramas of its author, a place it surely deserves.

There is a scene in *Nicomède* in which Prusias commands his hero-son to choose between the throne and Laodice, and Nicomedes chooses Laodice. Corneille beyond doubt was attracted by the dramatic possibilities in this situation, for a similar one determined, so he himself tells us, the subject of his next play, *Pertharite roi des Lombards* (1651). Its opening scene reveals that Pertharite has been defeated in war and driven from his kingdom by Grimoald, the Count of Beneventum. He is believed to be dead, and Grimoald wooes his wife, Rodelinde, breaking troth with the princess Eduige in doing so; but the dispossessed monarch comes to place himself in the power of his conqueror, and offers to give up all claims to his realm and all efforts to regain it, if Grimoald will restore Rodelinde to him. Such behavior was unacceptable to Corneille's public; they thought it unworthy of a king, and the drama depicting it was a complete failure. Drastic changes were made in the second edition of the text; the offending passages were removed and a different reason for Pertharite's return was supplied. These alterations only left a bad play worse; they eliminated the most original and interesting thing in it and, in the taste of the times of its revision, increased its romanesque gallantry. It had, even in its original form, many objectionable features. The prompt

---

king, and the queen return at the end of the play after having set out to sail for Rome. . . . It is, indeed, difficult to believe that Prusias and Arsinoé would have returned merely to avoid an accusation of cowardice. . . . Apart from this slip the play is well constructed." Really, according neither to the play itself nor to Corneille's statement to which Lancaster refers was Arsinoë one of the party who set out for Rome—nor was the King, strictly speaking—and Prusias declares that he and Flaminius returned to protect her from the mob or die in her defense.

reversion of Grimoald's love to Eduige after the appearance of Pertharite in the third act, as it seems to be quite genuine, is unconvincing; the plot of this tragedy, the action initiated at its beginning, is here given a new turn and its proper unity is thus destroyed. Up to this point, moreover, Rodelinde has been the center of interest, and thenceforth she is not.

A good deal of vigor and effectiveness are to be found in some of the scenes of the first two acts, where the situation is almost a duplicate—and evidently the model—of that with which Racine was to achieve the tremendous success of *Andromaque*. In both plays a princess forsaken by her royal fiancé offers her hand to another man if he will avenge her, and the faithless monarch tries to force a captive woman to wed him by threatening to kill her little son. Corneille's heroine, indeed, has better grounds than Racine's for an unconquerable aversion to marriage with her captor; he had been the cause of her husband's overthrow and (as she thinks) death, whereas it was only the father of Pyrrhus, not Pyrrhus himself, who had slain Andromache's husband. But Rodelinde, when told by Grimoald that he will kill her child if she does not marry him, replies that she will marry him, then, but solely on the condition that he does kill her child—and proceeds to justify herself by the most fantastic casuistry! The fact is that Corneille was now completing anew, but in briefer time and on a lower plane, the same perverse sequence as earlier. Beginning with the *Cid,* he had proceeded through *Horace, Cinna, Polyeucte,* and *Pompée* to *Rodogune* and *Héraclius;* now likewise, from *Don Sanche* through *Nicomède* to *Pertharite* he passed from Spain to Rome to melodrama. Characters in *Pertharite* are repeatedly discovered to have feigned the thoughts, feelings, or intentions which they have professed, the audience as well as their fellow characters being kept ignorant of the sham in order that melodramatic effects may be achieved—a meretricious device used without stint in late-Elizabethan drama of the school of Fletcher, but happily infrequent in French "classical" drama. *Pertharite* has always been adjudged one of the very worst plays of Corneille. In his discouragement over its reception, however, he felt that he had lost touch with his public; and he probably realized that the France of that immediate day, at the end of the civil strife of the Fronde, had little relish for tragedies. He resolved to write no more for the stage, and in this resolve he persisted for seven years.

IV

When at length in 1659 he again addressed himself to dramatic composition, the great minister Fouquet suggested to him three subjects from which to choose. Preciosity and gallantry now reigned supreme. Madeleine de Scudéry's *Cyrus* had been followed by her still more extravagant *Clélie,* with its map of the Land of Tender Love; and, beginning with the *Timocrate* (1656) of Corneille's younger brother Thomas, romanesque plays dominated the stage, to which they brought all the absurdities, the complications, and the complete disregard of historical verisimilitude that were characteristic of the romances themselves. Amid such a world, Pierre Corneille's choice, in preference to the other two themes offered him, was the grim story of King Oedipus of Thebes!

It would be entirely wrong, however, to view his *Œdipe* as an attempt to rival Sophocles' immortal masterpiece. He well knew that any such play would be intolerable to his audiences. He undertook, instead, to write an involved melodrama, somewhat like *Héraclius;* and in the fabrication of his plot—fitting its various details, both legendary and invented, into their place—he showed remarkable skill. But in order to provide "heart-interest," he created a daughter of Laius and Jocasta, Dirce by name, and made her the beloved of no less a personage than Theseus, who as here portrayed might have stepped from the pages of *Clélie* itself. During a large portion of the play their love is given much greater prominence than the affairs of Oedipus. People who see in Corneille a resolute foe of the romanesque vogue do not take sufficient note of his *Œdipe,* in which he surrenders abjectly to prevailing tastes. Its Theseus is the very opposite of the typical Corneillian hero who sets duty above everything else; if Dirce dies, he will die, regardless of all obligations to his country or mankind; nothing matters to him but love. In three scenes (IV, ii-iv), as it gradually comes to light that Oedipus had killed Laius, the dramatic power of the situation cannot fail to manifest itself; but throughout the ensuing dialogue of Oedipus with Jocasta, whose real relationship to him is still unrevealed, they consider only her plight in being bound to love him because he is her husband, yet also bound to hate him because she had been the wife of the man he slew—the question of the rightness or wrongness of his deed is not weighed by them. Such a question had finally been of primary importance to Chimene; but Corneille was now repentant for having depicted her so, and would not offend again. After the culminating discovery of Oedipus' unwitting parricide and incest, instead of the play ending as quickly as possible or attention at least being focused thenceforth on his fearful past and on his present predicament, he and Dirce and Theseus engage in conversations, in which the *voix du sang* is freely alleged by them to explain feelings which had hitherto puzzled them. Thus the tension is relaxed and the tragic horror largely dissipated; the eventual reports of the suicide of Jocasta and the self-blinding of Oedipus are quite devoid of impressiveness. Yet this sorry play was greeted with an enthusiasm which must have restored its author's faith in his power to please.

What his true preference was, however, when he felt he could safely follow it, can be learned from his next tragedies. The success of his brother's *Stilicon* and *Camma* in the interim had shown that the public would now again accept dramas of a less tinsel kind, grounded to some extent in actual history; and he accordingly produced *Sertorius* in 1662, *Sophonisbe* in 1663, and *Othon* in 1664. These are the most characteristic plays of the latter part of his career, and they embody the principles set forth in his critical writings which appeared in 1660, and which were the ablest dramatic criticism in France up to that time. Love is a passion of too little impressiveness, he maintained, to serve as the chief subject of a tragedy, where it should not be absent but should be relegated to a secondary part. For this opinion, subsequent critics have never ceased to berate him; and they have pointed to his dramas of this period as lamentable proof of its erroneousness. Let love be the main theme or exclude it altogether, these critics say; reduced to a subordinate role, it is inevitably frigid, a mere perfunctory embellishment that does not embellish. But the fact is that the entire history of drama supports Corneille against them. Although love has very little place in Greek tragedy, its small but definite presence in the *Antigone* and the *Iphigenia in Aulis* does not injure either of these great plays, and obviously they would not be injured if their love-element were a good deal enlarged—as it certainly would be if a modern author were to rewrite them. Nor does Ophelia injure *Hamlet*. On the other hand, no extant drama of the highest degree of greatness has been written about honorable love.[33] Desertion and marital jealousy have been the subjects, respectively, of such supreme masterpieces as the *Medea* of Euripides and *Othello;* a wife's illicit passion is the basis of the *Hippolytus* and of *Phèdre;* but we have no greater play than *Romeo and Juliet* or the *Cid* which treats, on the first plane, the guiltless love between man and maid.

[33] The lost *Andromeda* of Euripides, apparently "an unclouded love-romance," may have been greater than any that we possess. It had enormous fame in antiquity.

The trouble with these later tragedies of Corneille is not that love is stressed too little in them. The trouble is that it is stressed too much. Nearly every character is represented as in love with somebody. In every decision on matters of great historical note, some love or other, generally invented outright by the author, is involved. The eternal recurrence of such factors, in the most important questions of war or policy, is annoying. It quite transforms history and the figures of history. Yet it does not make them more dramatic by introducing any violent passions which result in stirring words or deeds. It merely keeps the characters in a state of indecision till the five acts required by invariable custom in French "classical" tragedy have run their course. Each of these plays consists of a dreary series of dialogues between two of the dramatis personae in continually new pairings, each new dialogue modifying an infirm purpose which has just been formed in a previous dialogue. The characters profess intense love; even when great things are at stake they frequently listen to love's promptings to an extent that would have horrified Chimene; but in the end they do not obey its promptings. Moreover, they talk about their love frigidly, and often in the conventional phrases of gallantry, so that though it intrudes into all their affairs, it seems almost an impersonal consideration.

In *Sertorius,* the great Roman general of that name, who, after the triumph of Sulla, maintained the cause of the Marian party in Spain, is represented as in love, though an aging man, with a fictitious Lusitanian queen, Viriate. She is anxious to marry him, because she admires his genius and it can serve her ambition; and he dares not offend her, for her subjects are his chief allies; but his lieutenant, Perpenna, to whom he owes much, also loves her, and if Sertorius were to marry Aristia instead, whom Pompey, the Roman commander opposing him, has divorced at the bidding of Sulla, he would gain the support of all her friends at Rome. He cannot make up his mind; and Aristia, who still loves Pompey but feels that in her humiliating position as a cast-off wife she must have an illustrious husband immediately, cannot make up hers, either. And Perpenna, envious but not quite devoid of conscience, cannot make up his about assassinating Sertorius !

A certain degree of ineptness and irresolution is of course not unnatural in a veteran soldier who loves a beautiful young woman and is constantly aware of his own physical unattractiveness; such a man might indeed suppose that he could disregard his feelings and resign her to a friend for the sake of policy, and then might find his act of renunciation far more difficult than he had anticipated. But a Sertorius would never talk of dying if he should lose her to a rival, as Corneille makes him talk in a scene with Viriate, one moment unable to control himself and the very next moment thinking of expediency again, continually failing to keep his true goal in mind, proposing to behave in bad faith towards Perpenna and the friends of Aristia, and not meeting the issue when Viriate would have him leave his own Roman followers in the lurch. He should evoke no healthy sympathies after this scene.

Aristia also forfeits all sympathy. Though she discovers that Pompey still adores her, she refuses to wait for him even for the brief interval till the end of Sulla's regime will permit him to return to her; unless he will break with the Dictator forthwith, she will marry Sertorius—so much greater is her pride in the figure that she cuts than is her love, or her concern for her country's best interests! And Pompey, who has made such sacrifices for what he believes to be the good of Rome, thereupon declares that he will abandon all attempts to conciliate the insurgent faction, and will break the truce between the two armies and wage war to the death for his own personal ends! But these scenes at least interject some stir of life into this cold, dull play, which elsewhere has none till Perpenna's murder of the "hero" in the fifth act produces a crisis that is followed by a really dramatic conclusion depicting Viriate's dignity in her despair, the exultant traitor's discomfiture and death, and Pompey's magnanimity in victory.

Sertorius made a very successful debut, however, and has traditionally been regarded as the best of all the dramas written by Corneille after his seven years' retirement. Its poetry, with numerous quotable lines, is superior to that of any of the others of this period, and style has always been accorded undue weight in the critical judgments of his countrymen. A long scene of political discussion, when Sertorius and Pompey meet, has been much praised, like similar scenes in *Cinna* and *la Mort de Pompée,* and indeed it is beside the latter of these two tragedies that *Sertorius,* for better or for worse, has usually been ranked and should rightly stand. Significantly, Faguet and Lemaître, the most eminent French critics since Brunetière in the field of drama, have liked it least. Faguet's verdict is devastating: "The play is extremely poor because, however hard one tries, one cannot, I think, be interested in anybody in it." [34]

Sophonisbe, on the other hand, met with little success from the first. Taking the same subject as that of Mairet's *Sophonisbe,* which after some thirty years was still played and admired, Corneille felt obliged to impose on himself the handicap of dispensing with everything invented by his predecessor in dramatising Livy's narrative. This restriction kept him from using the best scenes afforded by his theme—such as Sophonisba's first meeting with the victorious Masinissa, her suicide, and her lover's grief at her death—and led him to substitute the little-known figure of Scipio's lieutenant Laelius for the great general himself as the embodiment of Roman policy; like Livy and unlike Mairet, Corneille repre-

[34] Translated from his *En lisant Corneille,* p. 196.

sents Sophonisba's husband as surviving her defeat, and hence her marriage with his conqueror as bigamous. Love, however, is not the ruling passion of Corneille's heroine. As a young girl she had indeed loved Masinissa when for reasons of State she wedded the much older Syphax instead; she loved him still when the fortunes of war placed her in his power. In fact, her love seems more real than that alleged by any of the characters in *Sertorius*. But it is rigorously controlled by an inflexible will. Patriotism and pride dominate her in the main; she married Syphax to gain an ally for Carthage; she keeps him at war with Rome, despite all reverses, until complete disaster overtakes him, and then she callously discards him and, while he yet lives, weds Masinissa in the hope of winning him, too, over to the side of her native city, or at least of saving herself from the shame of gracing a Roman triumph—to avoid which she is ready to take her own life if necessary, as she eventually does. Thus portrayed, she could be—and at times appears—an imposing if stark and unlovely figure, a female counterpart of the younger "Horace." But Corneille had long forsaken such simplicity for the complex and the romanesque. He must needs invent another North-African queen, Eryxa, whom Masinissa had intended to marry after losing Sophonisba to Syphax. He must needs portray his heroine as so jealously possessive that though she had broken troth with the man she loved, she still wished to have sway over his life and therefore was unwilling for him to wed anyone else unless she herself might choose his bride! On this account she had made her husband take up arms against Eryxa, who is her prisoner at the opening of the play; and her determination to prevent Masinissa from marrying her "rival" is no less potent a factor in causing her to oppose a negotiated peace, and later in persuading her to contract her hasty, bigamous union with him, than is her solicitude for the interests of Carthage in the one case and her wish to escape the hu-

miliation of being led in chains in the other. Such despicable-
ness destroys any vestige of sympathy that we might otherwise feel for her, but doubtless seemed only "human" to
seventeenth-century anatomizers of the heart; and it gave
Corneille an opportunity to introduce not one but several of
those verbal tilts, chiefly ironical in tone, in which the women
in his plays, beginning with *Pompée,* engage with weari-
some monotony. *Sophonisbe* is considered by every critic
one of his poorest tragedies. It contains, more than any of
the others, nearly all the characteristic questionable features
of its author's work subsequent to the *Cid,* and exhibits them
in their worst form, much as a cartoon exaggerates the distinctive, salient details of someone's face. But at least its
dramatis personae, quite refreshingly unlike those of *Sertorius,* know their own minds and go straight towards the
goal of their desires; and in this respect it is less typical than
Sertorius of Corneille's later manner.

In *Othon,* veering decisions again fill an entire play, but
here Corneille for once found a theme in which they are not
inappropriate or objectionable: the struggle for power—even
for survival—at the Court of the well-meaning but aged and
pliable Roman emperor Galba, who is dominated by three
rapacious scoundrels, the consul Vinius, the freedman Martianus, and the pretorian prefect Laco. Otho, who of old
had been a companion of Nero in his pleasures but subsequently had shown to better advantage as a provincial governor, has tried to avoid the fate of Nero's other associates
by seeking marriage with Vinius' daughter, Plautina; he
has won her heart but lost his own to her when better acquaintance showed him the fineness of her character. But
Laco and Martianus combine against Vinius. All hangs on
who shall wed Galba's niece, Camilla, and be named heir to
the imperial throne. Laco urges the Emperor to select Piso,
an upright but stupid man whom the prefect and Martianus
can easily control. Vinius foresees his own destruction and

Otho's unless Otho gives up Plautina and himself wins Camilla's hand; and to this course the lovers are constrained to agree. Martianus has the effrontery to tell Plautina that if she will marry him he will exert his decisive influence in Otho's behalf, but naturally she scorns this vile ex-slave. Galba names Piso his successor; Camilla, who has listened only too eagerly to Otho's wooing, has no mind to marry a Piso. Very well, says Galba, Nero's minion shall have her but not the principate; Piso shall have that—and Plautina for his bride. With things come to such a pass, Otho, greatly embarrassed, tries to explain to Camilla that he cannot accept her sacrifice of empire for his sake. She sees through his pretenses, dismisses him, and in her anger promises Plautina, willing or unwilling, to Martianus. But the army mutinies on learning of Galba's choice of Piso; he, Galba, Vinius, and Laco alike perish in the ensuing disorders, Martianus is held for execution, and Otho becomes emperor. We have had, throughout, nothing but "closet intrigues, which defeat one another," as Corneille himself put it.

All this, however, is excellent material for a play—except the final outcome, which is dramatically defective as being wholly the work of the rebellious soldiery and no whit attributable to any initiative on the part of Otho himself. The opening scene is perhaps the most skilfully managed piece of exposition that Corneille ever achieved. Some of his friends pronounced *Othon* equal or superior to any previous work of his pen, and in recent years it has again had a few fervent admirers, among whom Brasillach is the most eloquent. The cold objectivity with which it depicts a corrupt Court no doubt endears it to modern lovers of disillusion; but a writer's coldness of detached observation should not be communicated to his dramatis personae and their passions —and here these, too, as in most of Corneille's later plays, are mortally cold. Really notable tragedy cannot exist at this temperature, continuously maintained. There is genuine feel-

ing in some of Plautina's words when she sends Otho to woo
Camilla—and the author has drawn no other woman who
is always so commendable—but nothing that Otho has said
about his love for her suggests an intensity of it which could
adequately prepare us for his sudden proposal to commit
suicide at this juncture; and when he is sent back to her by
Camilla, her analysis of his desperate plight is all intellect,
without a trace of emotion, and it is the same with all the
other characters at all times. Yet at least their motivation
and conduct are not unnatural,[35] however frigid their speech,
so that *Othon,* unlike anything else that Corneille had written
since *Nicomède,* may be called "a good play."

Only his incredible mislabeling of *Agésilas* (1666) as
a tragedy could have secured it a place among his serious
dramas and brought down upon it the scorn of critics, from
Boileau with his *"Hélas"* to the present day, as the most
insipid and worthless of them all. It is no more a tragedy
than *A Midsummer Night's Dream* is, but only an inept experiment in a new kind of light comedy, with a nominally
classical setting and colorless characters who in all but their
classical names are French gallants. The conflicting loves of
these constitute the sole subject matter, with the exception
of a single scene between Agesilaus and Lysander in which
the author's fondness for presenting a political situation
momentarily mastered him. Written in lines of irregular
length and varying rhyme patterns, this play suggests the
scenario of an opera; it was doubtless meant to compete with
the purely romanesque dramas of Quinault, which had cul-

---

[35] Plautina's behavior in the final scene appears to be the single
exception to this fact. The tie between her and her father, whose
unscrupulous opportunism is at the farthest extreme from her high
principles, and who has just exhibited his readiness to trample on
her feelings and sacrifice her for his advantage, cannot have been
close enough for her to be so completely paralyzed with grief at
his death.

minated in *Astrate* a year earlier and were all the vogue while *Sophonisbe* and *Othon* were finding few admirers. "If the public wants nothing but love, gallant love," Corneille must have said to himself, "it should be given to them in a vehicle like *Agésilas,* not with the trappings of tragedy." But his venture was ill received, and he returned to weightier themes in *Attila* (1667).

Here, at last, genuine emotion reappears and with it a protagonist of tremendous impressiveness. Attila the Hun is the one gigantic figure that Corneille ever drew, of far larger mould than any character in his best plays. He depicts him not so much as a resistless conqueror, beating down all opposition by sheer brute force, but rather as a wily despot, a Louis XI, a monstrous, gloating King Spider who likes to gain his ends by craft more than by risking the hazards of the battlefield and who winds his toils around all within the range of his power. Two princesses are in his camp, each of whom has come there expecting to wed him as arranged by treaty with the royal brother of each, and at his good pleasure he will choose one of them to be his bride and will give the other in marriage to some subject king. One is the haughty, ambitious Honoria, the sister of the Roman emperor; she wishes to put love aside and marry even this savage monarch to share his greatness. The other is the pure and beautiful Ildione, the sister of the king of the Franks; she is ready to sacrifice her own love and wed Attila, despite her loathing of him, that she may kill him and rid the world of his presence. The two young kings their lovers, Valamir and Ardaric, are his vassals and attend him, virtually prisoners; and he enjoys humiliating them and playing them against each other. The beauty of Ildione has infatuated him, and for this very reason he would rather marry Honoria, because he does not want a wife who might have some power over him; yet that either king should dare to love either of them, or (still worse) should be loved by one of them, he regards as intolerable presumption, worthy of death. There is interest from the first, and steadily mounting tension; Ildione gives more evidence of real love for Ardaric than a Corneillian heroine is accustomed to show towards her "beloved"; the scene in which these two bare their hearts to each other is genuinely moving; angry passions flame in stormy colloquies between Attila and Honoria, who becomes infuriated at the prospect of wedding him when she learns that he preferred Ildione. The terror and the menace of him hang constantly over all, and the action works up to a fine climax when, dilating to demoniac proportions, he glories in being "the scourge of God" and declares that he will give the princesses to whatever two base-born fellows will kill Ardaric and Valamir. But the grotesque fate which overtakes him, though in accord with history and not without dramatic foreshadowing in the play itself, is quite out of keeping with tragic dignity; it simply will not do for the hero of a tragedy to die of a "nosebleed." A variant tradition offered Corneille the obviously right alternative, that Ildione should wed Attila and then seize the first chance to kill him as she had intended to do; but by thus playing Judith to his Holophernes she would no doubt have forfeited the sympathy of seventeenth-century audiences, in whose opinion her marital vows, once taken, should have protected her husband against her, regardless of the circumstances.[36]

---

[36] The scruples which beset her, when the time for the deed she had planned drew near, seem absurd to us today in view of the situation; but the fact is that the dramatist displayed no small daring in representing her as continuing to cherish her purpose despite these scruples, as she evidently does when she persuades Attila to postpone his vengeance till the morrow. To let her carry out that purpose was more than could be expected of Corneille in the case of one of his most attractive heroines, which Ildione is. Her flash of spiteful pride in making it clear to her

Besides the denouement, the chief defect in this tragedy is found in its portrayal of Attila's infatuation for Ildione, which is represented as too nearly the same sort of courtly love that Corneille's lovers feel in all his plays, and is expressed in too nearly the same gallant language. Here, however, the fault is as much in us as in Corneille. His Attila is in every other respect so vigorously drawn that he seems to us indeed the savage Mongolian conqueror, who would be ignorant of any love but sheer animalism—and therefore his passion for the Frankish princess appears wholly out of character, alike in its nature and in its expression. Yet even the grimmest lines of his portrait could equally well belong to a very different kind of man, not incapable of some refinements of speech and feeling: one of the ruffianly, scheming despots or condottieri of the Renaissance, conscienceless and grandiosely ambitious, a Sforza or a Borgia, or even

---

"rival" that she herself could wed Attila if she chose, would have been condoned more in the author's time than now. Her reproof of Ardaric for asking her to use a word so *"rude"*—"bold" would be the best translation here, I think—as "love" in regard to her feelings towards him, has often been considered a ridiculous manifestation of fantastic delicacy, but only because it has not been understood. In the first place, she considered herself plighted to Attila, and betrothal was a far more solemn and binding thing in the seventeenth century than now. More important still, in that century an avowal of love evidently carried with it a conscious envisagement of—and was thought of as expressing a desire for— the physical consummation of love, as it does not carry now in even a remotely comparable degree. In no other way can the reluctance which the heroines of the dramas of those days exhibit about admitting their love be explained—or the "hate" which they feel for the suitor whose love they do not reciprocate. It is a point which should be kept in mind by students of French-classical tragedy.

Ildione does confess her love for Ardaric when she sees that complete frankness between them is needed. That she does not do so as unhesitatingly as Honoria avows hers to Valamir shows a difference between them which Corneille wished to emphasize.

some wolfish, sardonic great French lord of the author's own lifetime. In view of the meager historical imagination then possessed by anyone, it is entirely probable that this was as near as Corneille came to divining what the real Attila, so remote from him in time and of so unfamiliar a race, was like. He is at fault in having drawn, consequently, a figure whom people living in any period with more accurate historical conceptions cannot identify in their minds with the famous king of the Huns; but we too are at fault if we think that this figure which he drew is not self-consistent or is like no men that ever lived or is without dramatic value.[37] This tragedy—instead of *Sertorius* as critics formerly held, or *Othon* or *Suréna* as some now hold—is the best of the later plays of Corneille, and ought to be more widely known.

It enjoyed a fair amount of popularity, in spite of the fact that subjects taken from the early Dark Ages met with scant favor in literary circles (idolatrous as these were of things-classical) in seventeenth-century France—a fact which no doubt had contributed to the humiliating failure of *Pertharite*. Might even such moderate success have been enough to confirm the author in his return to dramatic vitality and warmth of human emotions? We cannot know. Hardly more than eight months later, Paris was in ecstasies over Racine's *Andromaque,* and Corneille saw his laurels fade in the blaze of glory which attended the advent at last of a rival who could have challenged his supremacy in his palmiest days—a rival, moreover, whose themes and ideas were in extreme contrast to his own. Racine's depiction of men and women as the helpless prey of their passions must have seemed to him—who had always insisted on the sovereignty

[37] In actual presentation on the stage a good deal of the difficulty could be overcome by making him quite different in garb and appearance from any mental picture that we may have of the real Attila.

of the human will—profoundly immoral, insidious, even in-
decent. He was openly contemptuous of Racine's plays.
Jealousy of each other's greatness increased the bad feeling
between these two sensitive, acrimonious men, whose antipa-
thetic conceptions would have bred hostility in any case.
For three years Corneille wrote nothing. Then in 1670 he
wrote *Tite et Bérénice*.

The old story that this drama and Racine's *Bérénice,*
which was produced just one week earlier, were written in
competition with each other at the behest of Henrietta of
England has been shown to be without foundation. The
truth seems to be that Racine discovered the subject of the
new play on which Corneille was at work and hastened to
write a play of his own on it, rightly confident that his would
be the better and that thus he would humiliate his enemy.
Yet it is not improbable that Corneille did undertake his
Tite et Bérénice in deliberate rivalry with Racine—not in
emulation of *Bérénice* but in emulation of *Andromaque.* Its
dramatis personae, like those of *Andromaque,* are eight in
number and similarly consist of four major characters and
their four respective confidants—a confidant for every major
character. There is no other play of Corneille's in which
this is the case; and it would be a surprising coincidence, if
it were only a coincidence, that the sole occasion of this
exact correspondence with *Andromaque* should be in his
first play after *Andromaque.* In both dramas, with their
thus precisely parallel casts of characters, the essential problem is: who will marry whom? In *Tite et Bérénice* a situation roughly corresponding to that of *Andromaque*—love
at odds with love or with other considerations in two men
and two women—is merely given a Corneillian instead of a
Racinian handling.

In *Andromaque* Orestes loves Hermione, who loves Pyrrhus, who loves Andromache, who loves her dead husband.
In *Tite et Bérénice* Titus and Berenice love each other, and

Domitian and Domitia love each other, but Domitia's ambition to be empress makes her bent on marrying Titus, who is deterred from marrying Berenice by his knowledge of the Roman people's abhorrence of queens. Domitia and he are to celebrate their nuptials in four days, when the woman he has never ceased to love appears upon the scene; he realizes that if he breaks off his engagement and flouts public opinion by marrying Berenice, his life will be threatened endlessly by plots and Domitia herself will implacably seek vengeance upon him—he must either wed her or put her to death. In consequence, we have another late-Corneillian drama of irresolution, in which Corneille's reaction against the frenetic emotionalism of *Andromaque* not unnaturally leads him to revert to something of the frigidity from which he had escaped in *Attila*. Titus never does decide what he will do, and with his weakness can arouse no sympathy nor interest. Berenice in some ways is more attractive than Racine's Berenice, but any interest or sympathy which she may arouse is dissipated before the end of the fifth act. She wishes Titus, if he cannot marry her, to marry someone whom he will never love—not her "rival," whose beauty, constantly implied to be very great, might make him forget her—and when the Senate eventually confers Roman citizenship on her and sanctions her union with him, she declares that now, with her "honor" satisfied, she will renounce him in order to avoid the risk he might yet run from the murderous hand of some unreconciled individual; and Titus, who could now have his heart's wish, does not even protest against her decision!

As for the steel-hard, feline Domitia, in her utter selfishness, in the unblushing effrontery of her claims on others, and in the transparent dishonesty of her occasional attempts to persuade when effrontery fails, she is the most despicable woman Corneille ever drew—yet, though not really essential to the story of Titus and Berenice, she has the longest role in the play. To be empress, she says, she would have married Nero himself, with all his crimes. She tells Domitian to follow her example and seek marriage with another, but when he seems to take her advice and pay court to Berenice, she is furious. He, too, forfeits interest and sympathy—by loving such a woman as Domitia. Yet everyone is continually referring to her fine qualities, and Domitian's confidant defends her selfishness as common to all mankind, and her dog-in-the-manger attitude towards her lover as characteristic of her sex in general! What are we to make of this? Did Corneille deliberately portray in her an odious woman, to match Racine's Hermione, and ironically pretend to justify her (with a professed cynical view of human nature derived from La Rochefoucauld) for those who had delighted in the characters of *Andromaque?* Or had he really come to have no better knowledge of what is good and what is bad—of what can be admired or at least be sympathized with and what must be detested—than his presentation of Domitia would indicate? The whole matter of the effect of Racine's success upon the last plays of Corneille needs fuller study than it has yet received.

It is more probably *Pulchérie* (1672), his next drama, that was written in emulation of Racine's *Bérénice*. Its subject, also, is a royal marriage, in which considerations of State oppose the dictates of the heart. Pulcheria, who has ruled the Byzantine Empire in her brother's name, must, now that he is dead, marry whatever man the Senate may elect as his successor. She hopes it will be Leo, a young soldier in whom she thinks she discerns a budding greatness; she loves him and he loves her; but when the Senate instead elects her empress and leaves to her the choice of her consort, she realizes that if she were to choose Leo, other aspirants for her hand and crown—older men of higher birth than he and already famous for their achievements in war (the ambitious, unscrupulous Aspar exemplifies them in the play)—might raise the standard of revolt. Consequently, for Leo's own sake and the realm's, she chooses to wed in a nominal, celibate marriage an elderly general and statesman revered by all, Martian, who she learns has long cherished a love for her which he has considered hopeless because of their difference in age; but she arranges that Leo shall marry Martian's daughter, who secretly loves him, and shall be the heir to the throne. It is thus—Corneille seems to say— thus with dignity and intelligence that such unhappy situations should be dealt with, not by tearing a passion to tatters.

Pulchérie, doubtless because of its unromantic conclusion and this very sobriety which its author sought after, was little appreciated. In modern times Lancaster seems to be almost alone in giving it some measure of the praise it deserves. Yet though it is another play that consists of a series of conversations without excitement or tension, it is surpassed among Corneille's later dramas only by *Attila*— and perhaps by *Suréna,* which followed it. Despite its quiet tone, one senses the presence of true emotion in its characters; with them, strong feeling seems restrained, not absent. They are all subtly and consistently portrayed; their conduct is natural; and the action progresses to the final denouement without being open to severe criticism at any point. Indeed, so great is Corneille's technical mastery in this play that, as Lancaster observes,[38] he has managed to dispense entirely with the conventional figure of the confidant; none of the members of its dramatis personae could be considered one, nor in lack of a confidant are there any soliloquies; everything is brought out naturally in dialogue between characters of importance. In this respect, *Pulchérie* perhaps stands unique among serious dramas in seventeenth-century France.

Throughout his duel with Racine, Corneille persisted in

---

[38] *Op. cit.,* Part III, p. 582.

the tactical blunder of trying to surpass his rival in Racine's special field, instead of attempting to show his superiority in tragedies in which he could follow his own bent. After *Andromaque* he would write of nothing but love. *Suréna* (1674) appears to be in emulation of *Bajazet*—and possibly, to some extent, of *Mithridate* also.[39] No other work of Corneille's, except *Pompée,* has been so diversely appraised. When produced, it encountered such a dismal reception that he once more abandoned play-writing, this time permanently. It was long looked upon as one of the feeblest of his tragedies, a view held by as late and able a critic as Petit de Julleville. Lemaître, however, has words of commendation for it; Faguet pronounces it, if not one of its author's plays of the first rank, at least very near them in merit; Brasillach declares that it is surpassed only by the *Cid* and *Polyeucte;* and Schlumberger thinks the role of its heroine comparable to none but that of Racine's Phaedra.[40] The truth lies, surely, between these extremes of praise and blame. *Suréna* is not a bad play, but neither is it a very good play. It contains passages of no small eloquence, which reveal Corneille as a great poet to the last. Especially famous are the lines spoken by its hero when he is urged to marry and perpetuate, in his children, himself and his noble forefathers:

Que tout meure avec moi, madame: que m'importe[41]

[39] Eurydice's indignation at Pacorus' effort to discover whom she really loves, and her consequent indefinite postponement of their nuptials, is strikingly like Monime's indignant refusal to marry Mithridates after he had tricked her into revealing her love for Xiphares.

[40] Petit de Julleville: *Théâtre choisi de Corneille,* p. xviii. Lemaître in Petit de Julleville's *Histoire de la Langue et de la Littérature française,* vol. iv, pp. 339-340; *Jean Racine,* pp. 230-231. Faguet: *En lisant Corneille,* p. 238. Brasillach: *Pierre Corneille,* p. 462. Schlumberger: *Plaisir à Corneille,* Paris, 1936, p. 258.

[41] Let all die with me, madam. What care I

Qui foule après ma mort la terre qui me porte?
Sentiront-ils percer par un éclat nouveau
Ces illustres aïeux, la nuit de leur tombeau?
Respireront-ils l'air où les feront revivre
Ces neveux qui peut-être auront peine à les suivre,
Peut-être ne feront que les déshonorer,
Et n'en auront le sang que pour dégénérer?
Quand nous avons perdu le jour qui nous éclaire,
Cette sorte de vie est bien imaginaire,
Et le moindre moment d'un bonheur souhaité
Vaut mieux qu'une si froide et vaine éternité.

The plot of this drama is fashioned with no little artfulness, and in its characters we again encounter—and to a greater degree than in *Pulchérie*—intense but restrained emotions. The action depicts the stages by which two lovers, both of whom are required to marry someone else, gradually betray to others the secret of their love, which they try to conceal. We are shown how, in the misery in which their plight has plunged them, they are unable to avert the destruction that consequently threatens the hero.

He is that Parthian general who annihilated the Roman army of Crassus; Corneille mistook his title, Surenas, which

---

After my death who treads the earth above me?
Will my illustrious ancestors perceive
The darkness of their tomb pierced by new rays
Of glory? Will they breathe again the air
In which they shall be made to live once more
By these descendants who may find it hard
To follow in their steps and who perchance
Will but dishonor them and will have the same
Blood as theirs only to become degenerate?
When we have lost the light of day, such life
Is but a fancied blessing, and the briefest
Moment of longed-for happiness is better
Than such a cold and vain eternity.

means "lord," for his name. The play represents that he
and the Armenian princess Eurydice have secretly fallen in
love when he was an envoy at her father's Court; now, after
the war, a treaty consigns her to wed the son and heir of
King Orodes of Parthia, Pacorus, who has loved Surenas'
sister, Palmis, but is now captivated by the beauty of Eurydice. Orodes wishes to give his daughter, Mandane, in marriage to Surenas and thus assure himself of the loyalty of
his too-powerful subject. Yet with so many political considerations involved, Surenas, Eurydice, Pacorus, and Palmis
are all, like the characters whom Racine depicts, actuated
primarily by the passion of love; "interests of State" count
for little with them. *Suréna* is a tragedy of love and jealousy,
like the tragedies of Racine.

Eurydice's coldness makes Pacorus suspect that she does
not love him or even loves another. When he insists on her
being frank with him about her feelings, she tells him she
indeed does love someone else, but will not say whom. She
says that she will wed none but Pacorus, yet because he has
pried into her heart's secret, she will not wed him on the
morrow as she had been ready to do, but only when at some
future time she has come to love him instead of the man
she now loves. Though her anger at being forced to confess
her feelings is not unnatural, it naturally angers Pacorus in
turn; for his desire to know the truth was reasonable, and
had she apprised him of it in a different spirit, he might (we
are made to realize) have released her from their engagement—but treated as he is, he will not. From this situation
the tragedy develops as it becomes more and more apparent
that Surenas is Eurydice's unknown lover. Had she declared roundly that now she would never marry Pacorus,
she might evoke more sympathy; but the stand she does take
has an element of mere punctiliousness, and is really an expedient which she instinctively seizes upon to put off the
marriage; and being persisted in till Surenas' death, it makes

one have little patience with her. Even by letting him wed
Mandane she could save his life; but she wishes, like Corneille's Sophonisba, herself to choose the wife of the lover
whom she has to renounce, yet when asked to suggest one
for him, she cannot bring herself to do that, either; she
wilfully shuts her eyes to his approaching doom, despite
the entreaties of Palmis, till too late. Moreover, there was
the alternative that Orodes might only banish Surenas, but
to this proposal she replies that during his banishment she
will not wed Pacorus. The fate of such a "heroine" (who
possibly derives from the Atalide of *Bajazet*) can arouse
no concern. Surenas, on his part, assures Eurydice that his
greatness would bring about his destruction in any case; if
this were true—and in other scenes Orodes shows clearly
it is not—the whole dilemma with which the play deals
would be unimportant. And the mighty general, its hero, a
mature and war-hardened man, declares in all seriousness
that he will shortly die of grief at losing his beloved! Romanesque dramatists continually put such statements in the
mouths of their characters—yet they must have known that
lovers do not die of grief, for they never represent any of
them as doing so. Not die of grief over disappointment in
love, that is; but Eurydice does die of grief when Surenas
is killed.[42] With this climax of romanesque unreality, Corneille ends his career as a playwright.

V

In our survey of his work we may observe four sharply
differentiated periods. During the first of these, he wrote

[42] At least she says she is dying, and loses consciousness. The
only rational alternatives are that she is mistaken and only swoons
or that the shock she suffers can result in her death because she
has some organic weakness with which she could not have lived
long in any event. On either hypothesis the denouement would be
lame indeed.

according to his own taste and judgment, following the impulses of his own native genius. Unhappily, after his apprenticeship, only the *Cid* was written under these conditions.

In the second period he wrote according to his taste and judgment as these had been modified by the storm of criticism which the *Cid* evoked. The fruit of the change thus wrought in him is to be found in *Horace, Cinna,* and *Polyeucte.*

In the third and by far the longest period, beginning with *Pompée* and extending (across his seven years' retirement in middle life) down to and including *Attila,* his work was further modified by the influence of the gallant pseudo-historical romances, which embodied and exaggerated the artificial ideals of the Hôtel de Rambouillet.

The fourth period, which produced *Tite et Bérénice, Pulchérie,* and *Suréna,* is that in which his work underwent a final modification in consequence of his rivalry with Racine.

The sensitiveness—the responsiveness—to external influences which these successive radical changes in the matter and manner of his plays reveal does not accord with the usual conception of this "dramatist of the Will" as himself a heroic figure. The truth is that there is no evidence to support such a conception of him. The facts, as we have seen, all indicate him to have been just the reverse of this; and, indeed, that was the more natural presumption. It is the man who is himself weak, and who suffers from his weakness, that is most likely to be fond of drawing inflexible supermen; thus vicariously he enjoys the strength and heroism which he does not possess. A dramatist who shared the resolute self-confidence of Nicomedes would not have grown to regret his depiction of Rodrigue and Chimene, or, having written the *Cid,* have gone on to write *Cinna* and *Pompée* and *Rodogune* and *Sertorius* and *Suréna*—still less *Œdipe* and *Sophonisbe* and *Tite et Bérénice.*

As though by a strange fatality, each time when it seemed that he might adjust himself to the compromise which then governed him and do better work than he had yet done under its terms, some new thing persuaded him to write in a different and less effective vein. *Polyeucte* was his best play subsequent to the *Cid,* and after its ill success with the coterie of the Hôtel de Rambouillet he surrendered to the conventions of the romances which were their favorite reading. *Don Sanche d'Aragon,* with its momentary promise, was a failure. In *Attila,* Corneille at long last again depicted intense emotions—and the vogue of Racine's emotional dramas of love drove him to what was at once an imitation of them and a reaction against them.

One cannot turn from one's natural bent, discard one's own ideas of what is attractive and noble in deference to the ideas of others, transform one's writing in compliance with prevailing literary fashion, save at a heavy cost. The verve and passion and warmth of human sympathies which characterized the *Cid* were never quite captured by Corneille again; and, anxious to please though he was, he was often unable to gauge the effect of what he would offer to an audience when no longer following his own instincts; hence the last act of *Horace,* the change of sympathies that he vainly sought in *Cinna* and *Polyeucte,* the abject failure of *Théodore* and *Pertharite,* the lack of appeal in most of his later dramas. As the years passed, his plays grew colder and colder. And especially, and most naturally, did he who had distrusted and renounced his own sense of right-and-wrong become increasingly confused as to ethical values. In *Horace* he does with remarkable acuteness perceive them all in a highly complex situation and errs solely in his relative emphasis among them and in considering as palliable and pardonable an atrocity which is neither. But in both the hero and heroine of *Polyeucte* he evidently approves of that which ought to be censured; and he proceeds in subsequent plays to expect sympathy and even admiration for characters whose conduct is vicious, absurd, or contemptible. Perhaps this descent to moral sanctions approximating those of the romances and of the minor romanesque dramatists is the most important single factor in Corneille's decline.

The pity of it all was that though inferior to Racine as a poet, he seems to have been in some respects more richly endowed with the specific gifts of a dramatist. We have observed three instances—Horatius, Pauline, and Attalus—in which, despite the very limited time of the action in classical tragedies, he succeeded in depicting the change or development of a character in the course of a play; there is no example of this in any drama of Racine's.[43] Great characters, characters of an impressiveness such as Racine's Phaedra, Hermione, Athaliah, Roxana, Achmet, or Jehoiada, he has not drawn—except his Attila in a minor play. Yet these personages of Racine are delineated with the economy of means characteristic of classical art in general—with few, simple strokes that sketch a vividly conceived, obviously consistent and easily understood figure—in striking contrast to the detailed portrait-painting of Shakespeare, which has the complexities, the surprises, and the apparent irrelevances and contradictions of life itself. Aeschylus, Sophocles, and Euripides, though constrained to even greater brevity than the French "classical" dramatists, manage to achieve touches of subtlety and surprise and a complexity of characterization that can hardly be matched outside of Shakespeare. But Corneille, in depicting character and motivation, approaches the complexity of Shakespeare and of

---

[43] That alleged of Nero in Racine's *Britannicus* is not a change of character but merely a breaking away from restraint. It can be canceled together with that alleged of Augustus in Corneille's *Cinna,* each being a spurious instance of this difficult achievement of dramatic genius.

life more nearly than any other neo-classical dramatist certainly, if not more nearly than any ancient one.[44]

Again and again both in Shakespeare and in Corneille we are surprised at some speech or act of someone. We ask ourselves: "Why did this character say—or do—that?" Has the author blundered, or are we lacking in perception? In the case of Shakespeare, except in his very early or very casual work, we can be certain that the fault is ours if the arresting detail seems—and even never ceases to seem—wrong.[45] But we cannot have a similar assurance of iner-

[44] We have remarked the covert love-making of Rodrigue and Chimene—in acting nobly before each other—throughout their ordeal, and the amazing multiplicity of factors involved in the transfer of Pauline's love from Severus to Polyeucte. For one further illustration of this lifelike complexity in Corneille's treatment of character, let us note the mingling of several motives which can be found in even so small a detail as Chimene's choice of Don Sancho to be her champion. Her main reason for it—probably her only conscious reason—is that, as he reminds her, she has promised him this honor. But the reason which Leonora and the Infanta impute to her, that she knows he will be no match for Rodrigue, may well have influenced her, too, though subconsciously. (She must have been conscious immediately, or the next instant, of the *fact* that he could not win the duel; but she would not have been false to her self-imposed task by deliberately choosing him *for that reason*.) Still another very possible unconscious reason influencing her choice may have been the resentment which she must have felt in her heart towards Don Sancho for telling her, earlier, what she did not wish to hear, that she is indeed obligated to take vengeance, and for being eager to kill Rodrigue for her and thinking that he, forsooth, can do so. She will show him whether he can or not! And how much was it this resentment, and how much just a desire to be rid of his importunities as soon as possible so that she might surrender herself to her grief, and how much an instinctive grasp at the only help which had been offered her, that caused her to give him her promise in the first place?

[45] Nothing could be more unexpected, or more revelatory when its whole import is grasped, than his "Yet Edmund was beloved,"

rancy in Corneille, and the very challenge of the hazard thus involved in criticising him is not without its fascination. With him, what seems botch-work may be precisely that instead of some unfathomed subtlety, yet it is really a subtlety so often that one does not feel altogether safe in pronouncing it botch-work in any instance. Perhaps his fitfulness of inspiration is, in some measure at least, another result of his conforming to literary fashion and ceasing to depict life in accordance with his own observation and instinctive sympathies. There is certainly no botch-work in the *Cid,* or even in *Horace.*

Why was Corneille, with all his genius, so much more than Racine a victim of his environment? Racine was no less sensitive to criticism than he—was, indeed, more deeply wounded by censure or by lack of appreciation, if the testimony of their contemporaries can be trusted—and began to write when the influence of romanesque conventions was far stronger than in Corneille's youth. The answer is to be found in part in the younger dramatist's unquestionably surer taste and greater capacity for self-criticism. We have seen that Corneille's creative instinct, with its keen sense of reality, was at times his master rather than his servant,[46] perhaps in unconscious rebellion against the constraint

---

perhaps the most wonderful brief utterance in all drama. Even in so poor a play as *All's Well that Ends Well,* Shakespeare's sense of character consistency does not fail him: it is not an accident that the scene of coarse badinage between Helena and Parolles, in the like of which none of his other heroines ever engages, was assigned to one whose later conduct, though traditionally acceptable to his (male) public, would not have been that of any woman of any real refinement in any period of history.

[46] E.g., his portrayal of Nicomedes as the over-confident soldier unversed in intrigue, rather than as the hero equal to any situation —the sort of figure needed to secure the maximum sympathy of an audience.

which his compromises placed upon it. We have observed in him also a perverse fondness, quite absent in Racine, for complication—he took pride in exhibiting his skill in it—and for melodrama; this was doubtless partly innate. But still more important was a difference in their education. Racine's largely shaped his superior literary taste; and it furnished him with models of excellence in drama—such as Corneille did not have—to keep him from straying too badly from the path of true art.

Corneille's education did not give him Racine's knowledge of Greek. His chief acquaintance among the ancient classical dramatists was with the Latin Seneca, whose admiration for gigantic energy even when directed to criminal ends he echoed, and whose rhetoric he imitated all the more readily because his own legal training (as well as his native mental endowment and temperament) made it—and hair-splitting distinctions, and reasoning carried to the point of casuistry—natural to him. Racine had from boyhood worshipped at the shrine of Sophocles and Euripides; their surviving master-pieces were for him the quintessence of greatness in tragedy, guiding stars towards which his ambition led him. It is, consequently, his peculiar distinction that, beginning his career in the trammels of a dramatic convention as frustra-tive of great achievement (because envisioning a very un-real, artificial world) as ever hampered a playwright, he nevertheless got free of them—and rose above them—to an extent to which no one else, so enmeshed at outset, ever did. Corneille, on the other hand, has the sad distinction of being the greatest dramatist both actually and potentially who could not escape from the toils of similar circumstances and was enwound and dragged down by them.

CHAPTER II
TRISTAN L'HERMITE: *LA MARIANE*

IN his *Manual of the History of French Literature,* Brunetière states that among the tragedies which were written between 1640 and 1660 the *Saint Genest* and *Venceslas* and *Cosroès* of Rotrou, the *Saül* and *Scévole* of Du Ryer, and the *Mort de Sénèque* and *Mort de Crispe* and *Mort du Grand Osman* of Tristan l'Hermite, though "much below" *Horace, Cinna, Polyeucte, Pompée, Rodogune,* and *Héraclius* (he will not add *Théodore* and *Pertharite*), are "still of a certain rank." [1] Such an estimate is thoroughly characteristic of traditional criticism of French-classical plays and playwrights: all but the very poorest of the tragedies of Pierre Corneille are, as a matter of course, put on a quite different plane from that occupied by even the best work of his minor contemporaries, and not enough discrimination is evinced in regard to either his dramas or theirs. This is strikingly like the English attitude in the early years of the nineteenth century towards Shakespeare and the minor Elizabethans.

The great American authority on seventeenth-century French drama, Henry Carrington Lancaster, made his own estimate a full generation later. "While Rotrou," he says, "was quite inferior to Corneille in invention, Du Ryer as a poet, and Tristan in the structure of plays, they succeeded at times in producing tragedies that rival *Pompée, Théodore,*

---

[1] *Op. cit.* (authorized Eng. trans.), New York and Boston, 1898, p. 155. Brunetière probably classifies *Don Sanche* and *Nicomède* as heroic comedies rather than as tragedies, for he does not mention them.

and *Héraclius,* if not *Rodogune.* . . . . Three plays of Rotrou, *Saint Genest, Venceslas,* and *Cosroès,* Du Ryer's *Scévole,* and Tristan's *Sénèque* and *Osman* are among the most striking tragedies composed by minor authors of the century." [2] But this dictum, surely, goes at once too far and not far enough. Invention was indeed Rotrou's weakest point, poetry Du Ryer's, and construction Tristan's; but each of these men was in nearly all respects inferior to Corneille at the height of his powers—a fact which is not implied by Lancaster's statement. On the other hand, some of the dramas mentioned—they are of widely different degrees of merit— quite as much surpass *Pompée* and *Rodogune,* it seems to me, not to mention the wholly unsuccessful *Théodore,* as they are themselves surpassed by *Horace* and *Nicomède;* and at least one should be seen to vie with *Cinna* if we appraise at no more than its true worth that traditionally exalted play.

It is an interesting and impressive fact, however, that despite the difference in attitude of Lancaster and Brunetière towards the work of the lesser French-classical dramatists, their opinions as to what are the most notable tragedies immediately following the appearance of the *Cid* are so nearly identical. Agreement is even closer than it seems at first sight; for Lancaster failed to include *Saül* in his list of good plays only because he was not then considering Biblical dramas, and he has elsewhere said that "it deserves to be ranked among the five or six leading tragedies composed by the rivals of Corneille." [3] The one real difference in judgment between him and Brunetière is in regard to *la Mort de Crispe,* which is praised by Lanson, but which Bernardin, the chief authority on its author, esteemed even less than did Lancaster.

[2] *A History of French Dramatic Literature in the Seventeenth Century,* Part II, pp. 530, 532.

[3] *Op. cit.,* Part II, p. 350.

Whether Tristan l'Hermite be represented on the roll of
honor by three dramas or two, the place of these is near its
bottom, not its top. And yet the fact that two or three of
them should be on it at all is impressive, for his total output
was meager in comparison with that of Rotrou or Du Ryer.
The importance of his work is beyond all proportion to its
bulk. He it was who, in the period when the example of
Pierre Corneille was dominant, first wrote tragedies of a
somewhat different type, with simple rather than complex
action and with characters controlled by the emotions rather
than by the intellect and will—thus pointing the way for
Quinault and through him for Racine. Even in his subjects
he anticipates the great man in whose plays the technique
which he inaugurated found its full and final development:
la Mort de Sénèque (1643-1644), with its Roman setting in
the time of Nero and its portrait of that emperor, suggests
Britannicus; la Mort de Crispe (1644), like *Phèdre,* tells of a
queen's incestuous love for her step-son, who himself loves
someone else, and of his resulting death and the queen's suicide; *la Mort du Grand Osman* (1646-1647) precedes
Bajazet in finding its theme in contemporaneous Turkish history. Tristan's departures from the regnant conventions of
pseudo-classical tragedy are bolder than Racine's, alike as
regards his subordination of incident to the study of character, his realism of utterance, and his concern for "local color."

That his achievement was comparatively trivial was due
to sheer ineptitude. He lacked the talent and the good taste
to maintain constantly a high standard of style, though his
verse was often mellifluous and his imagery striking. There
have been few more incompetent dramaturgists. *La Mort de
Sénèque* has two ill-combined threads, the proscription of
Seneca and the failure of the conspiracy of Piso—neither
of them properly developed.[4] *La Mort de Crispe* is as flimsy

---

[4] This tragedy is a mere succession of historical scenes, not a

of structure as it is weakly written; too many important things happen between acts and are hardly more than implied; the play is not a well-knit fabric but a loose bundle of scenes. *Osman* is interesting quite as much for the opportunity it affords one to imagine what it would have been in the hands of Racine as for the imperfect excellence which it possesses.

A study of this last play gives a good idea of its author's abilities and shortcomings. It deals with the overthrow of the sultan Osman by his disaffected subjects. He quells one outbreak but falls victim to a second, which would not have occurred so soon or been so formidable but for the enemies he wins himself by disgracing the daughter of the mufti. This girl, nameless throughout, is a character of great

---

dramatic action at all, for the exposure of the conspiracy does not result from anything within the compass of the play. Yet the only opportunity for drama lay in the subject of the conspiracy; apart from it, the death of Seneca has none. For wealth of characterization, however, *la Mort de Sénèque* is almost unparalleled in minor French-classical tragedy. True, the figure of Seneca himself is somewhat marred by conscious posing, as also is that of his wife; but several of the conspirators are clearly depicted with remarkably few strokes; and Nero, Poppaea, and Epicaris are notable creations. Nero, instead of a conventional monster, is made a real human being, clever at inquisition, essentially cruel, cowardly, and hypocritical, but not without traces of conscience. Tristan boldly departs at times from the elevated language alone deemed appropriate in French-classical tragedy, to give Epicaris the speech natural to a courtesan and to put in the mouth of Nero and Poppaea expressions which they would have acquired from their disreputable associates. How self-revealing is Poppaea's mocking cry when Epicaris is carried in, broken by the torturers, "La voici qui paraît en triomphe portée" ("Here she comes, borne like a conquering hero"), and Nero's heartless comment, "Des gens trop curieux l'ont un peu maltraitée" ("Some prying folks have been a bit rough with her") ! Formless as it is, and largely frustrate in its totality, *la Mort de Sénèque* probably contains in its best scenes the finest work that Tristan ever did.

possibilities. She has seen the youthful sultan riding at the head of his troops, and has fallen violently in love with him; to bring herself to his notice, she has bribed someone to drop a flattering picture of her in his presence and to extol her charms to him, and the stratagem has been successful in arousing his interest. The first act is concerned with the threat of sedition and with Osman's eagerness, even at such a time, to acquire the new object of his desires; on the whole it is not badly done. The second act should have commenced with a scene between the daughter of the mufti, just brought to the palace by the Sultan's orders, and her confidante, in which her secret love for Osman, her ruse with the picture, and her present state of mind, rapturously hopeful of the result of her awaited meeting with him, would be revealed. It is easy to divine how Racine would have handled this. But in Tristan's play the Sultan's sister, who opened the first act with a foreboding dream, opens the second act also, by reiterating her anxiety and being once more reassured by her brother, so that much of the same ground is traversed all over again; and when at length the daughter of the mufti does appear, and Osman, discovering that she fails to equal her portrait in beauty and is not to his taste, rejects her, we are unable to appreciate the situation. We behold her humiliated pride but do not guess her wounded, baffled love, for of that love and its efforts and its anticipations we have been told nothing. And when do we finally learn the complete story of it? Not when she plans vengeance; not even when in Act III her indecision reveals her real feelings towards Osman. She does not give a full account of her love, from its inception, until the middle of the last act, when the uprising has succeeded and she encounters the dethroned monarch and offers to save him!

Another major flaw in this tragedy is the failure to make it clear whether right is mainly on the side of the Sultan or of the insurrectionists. Yet though *la Mort du Grand Osman* could have been a far better play without such faults, we must not overlook the fact that it is praiseworthy in some degree as it stands; it is not actually ruined by its blemishes. Indeed, a real and highly distinctive effect is achieved by its method of presentation: the treatment of the heroine's love-history employs the retrospective technique of Ibsen's *Rosmersholm;* and the failure to fix our sympathies in the revolt makes us observe it altogether objectively. Thus in Act IV, Osman's speech to the rebels and Orcan's in answer are very well handled. The Sultan is a Turk in his mixture of cruelty and ferocity with heroism. A good touch is the overweening self-confidence which he exhibits after he has subdued the first uprising. But his sister is allowed to drop out of the play after having taken a somewhat important part at its opening; and we are not even told what is her fate![5] There is much that is brilliant in *Osman;* realistic details of the oriental setting are introduced to an extent which no other French dramatist of the seventeenth century ever troubled himself to equal for the sake of "atmosphere"; the haughty young despot and the daughter of the mufti (compared by Bernardin to Racine's Hermione, as being like a preliminary sketch of her[6]) are finely conceived and as finely portrayed; but the author's almost incredible mismanagement vitiates the whole.[7]

[5] Moreover, she lacks personality. Her maids are better done, brief as are their roles; the old tutor is neatly drawn in a few lines; the chief mutineers have characteristics distinguishing them from each other.

[6] *Un précurseur de Racine, Tristan l'Hermite, sieur du Solier,* pp. 485 ff.

[7] The conclusion of the play is especially impressive. After the Sultan has refused all the overtures of the girl who has loved and destroyed him, and he has gone out to meet his fate, and a messenger has reported the gallant end he has made, the daughter of the mufti again takes possession of the scene. She declares that Osman is not dead:

Now, this combination of notable excellences and not less notable blunders is exactly the sort of thing we expect to find in Elizabethan rather than French-classical dramas. In both his merits and his defects, Tristan often seems an Elizabethan transplanted to French soil. One remembers that he went to England in 1634 and probably spent several

---

Il nage dans mon sang; il court dans mes esprits, . . .
Il subsiste en mon cœur; mais il faut qu'il périsse:
Il mourra sur-le-champ, cet aimable inhumain,
Qui ne pouvait mourir que d'un coup de ma main—

(He swims through my veins, he roves 'mid my thoughts, . . .
He lives in my heart; yet needs must he perish.
He shall instantly die, this cruel one beloved,
Who could only be slain by a blow of my hand.)—

and she stabs herself, not with the single deft and decorous blow customary on the seventeenth-century French stage, but with maniacal fury, three times in rapid succession.

The generally acute Bernardin calls the lines quoted "ridiculous"—a *"trait détestable"* (*op. cit.,* p. 491). This is conventional pseudo-classical criticism at its narrowest and most unimaginative worst. *"Il nage dans mon sang"* and *"il court dans mes esprits"* are indeed figures of speech unusual to the verge of grotesqueness, but they are as vivid and forceful as they are bold. The entire passage is true to life and of great emotional and dramatic power; if it had occurred in some English play of the time of Shakespeare, it would be highly praised.

The real fault in what Tristan has written here is to be found in the lack of harmony between such figures of speech and so banal a phrase as *"cet aimable inhumain";* this juxtaposition is very jarring, but it is surely to the author's credit rather than to his discredit that he sought here, as on other occasions in other ways, to escape from the rigid bonds of pseudo-classicism. That such an effort was frequent with him, is one of the things that make him an interesting person. And if he comes perilously close to the comic when, at the beginning of this outburst of the daughter of the mufti, someone takes her literally and asks in astonishment if Osman can indeed be still alive, that misunderstanding is as natural, as true to life, as are the wild fancies themselves of the hysterical girl.

months there; he might easily have witnessed plays in London or at the court of Charles I. The English dramatists of the same century to whom he is most analogous are Webster and Ford—not, of course, as regards Webster's atmosphere of gloom or the preoccupation of both with horrible subjects, but because of his weakness at plotting, his interest and skill in characterization, his emotional power, and the fitful inequality and very limited amount of his work. *La Mort de Sénèque,* with its invertebrate structure and its subtly psychologized portrait-gallery of figures, recalls Ford's *Perkin Warbeck,* as its scene of Epicaris' resourceful defense of herself with "innocence-resembling boldness" before Nero recalls the trial of Vittoria in *The White Devil* of Webster; and Tristan's best play, like Webster's most famous one. depicts the doing to death of a lovely and noble woman, who faces her doom unafraid though pitifully alone, and it bears the further resemblance to *The Duchess of Malfi* that in each drama the martyrdom of the heroine is concluded before Act V, which is entirely devoted to the remorse and retribution that ensue.

For, earlier than *Sénèque* or *Crispe* or *Osman,* and even a few months prior to the date of the *Cid,* Tristan wrote a tragedy which was little less acclaimed than the *Cid* itself, and which none of his subsequent productions ever matched in either popularity or merit. Unlike *Osman* and *Sénèque,* his *Mariamne* (1636), or *la Mariane,* is not unworthy to be grouped with the very best work of Rotrou and Du Ryer.

The story of Herod and Mariamne, related by Josephus, has been the theme of many dramas. Of course, incomparably the finest of them, and one of the really great plays of the world, is the *Herodes und Mariamne* of Hebbel; yet it is safe to say that the subject has never been reduced more rigorously to its essential elements or supplied with emotions

of more vehement intensity than by the pen of Tristan.[8] Just
as it is Bosola who fills the largest place in *The Duchess
of Malfi* instead of the Duchess herself, for whom it is named
and who is the "sympathetic" figure, in like manner Herod
and not its titular heroine is the central character in this
Mariamne. The entire play is built around him, to exhibit
the uncontrolled, furious, warring passions that possess him

[8] Less than a generation before, Alexandre Hardy had written
a *Mariamne* which is very similar to Tristan's throughout; but Bernardin has shown (*op. cit.,* pp. 321 ff.) that the similarity of the
two dramas is often the result of their having the same source rather
than of direct imitation. Critics have generally disparaged one play
in favor of the other; Bernardin and Lancaster prefer Tristan's;
Rigal, Saintsbury, and Tilley prefer Hardy's. If a comparison must
be made between them, it may be said with fairness that Hardy's
tragedy is superior in specifically dramatic qualities, Tristan's in
poetry and emotional power. Tristan pays more attention to local
color, as might be expected; he does not, indeed, dispense entirely
with allusions to classical mythology, which Hardy uses so abundantly, but a small sprinkling of these is not out of place on the lips
of the hellenistic Herod, and they are interspersed with a number
of references to things-Jewish. Tristan's first act is probably, and
his second and fifth acts are certainly, better than Hardy's; but
Hardy's third act is much the stronger, and so is his fourth, which
is wholly different from Tristan's. Bernardin is doubtless right in
saying that Tristan secures a more natural climax by making Herod's
belief in his wife's infidelity follow and quite overshadow his belief
that she attempted to kill him; but the final straw against the Queen
in Hardy, her defiance of Herod in the prison, is itself a not unnatural thing to seal her doom, and this prison scene which occupies
Hardy's fourth act maintains the suspense and the emotional grip
of the action more satisfactorily than does the corresponding part
of the other play. After all, the likeness between these two *Mari-
amnes* is little greater than that between Euripides' *Hippolytus* and
Racine's *Phèdre,* and Tristan's drama can be considered on its own
merits without introducing any question of its indebtedness or superiority to its predecessor, just as *Phèdre* can be (and frequently is)
considered without reference to the *Hippolytus,*

and sweep him on to the judicial murder of the woman who
is their object, and his subsequent paroxysms of remorse.[9]
Such concentration makes somewhat for monotony, but it
also makes for unity and for a plot structure so simple that
even Tristan could not seriously mar it.

The first act opens with Herod starting up from his couch
with a shout of dismay at the dream which has troubled his
slumbers.[10] He has beheld the long-drowned body of his
victim, Aristobulus, the brother of Mariamne, amid circumstances of peculiar horror. To his brother Pheroras and his
sister Salome, who come at his outcry, he relates his vision,
which leaves both of them aghast though the former
argues at somewhat too great length against the significance
of dreams before he hears this one. They feel, like Herod,
that it is a warning of imminent disaster; but the King now
recovers his self-possession. "What Fate hath written cannot be erased," he says.

> Il faut bon gré, mal gré, que l'âme résolue[11]
> Suive ce qu'a marqué sa puissance absolue:
> De ses pièges secrets on ne peut s'affranchir,
> Nous y courons plus droit en pensant les gauchir.
> L'homme à qui la Fortune a fait des avantages,

[9] In the first performances of this drama, the role of Herod was
taken by the famous actor Montdory, who scored a sensational triumph in it. So vehement was his rendition of this tempestuous role
that he eventually suffered an apoplectic stroke while playing it.

[10] An ominous dream is a detail which Tristan introduces again
and again in his plays, but here it is very effective and that is doubtless why he persisted in repeating its use.

[11] Willing or not, the resolute soul must needs
Do that which its omnipotence hath bidden.
One cannot 'scape from out its secret toils;
We run into them straighter, trying to shun them.
The man whom destiny hath made to prosper

Est comme le vaisseau sauvé de cent orages;
Qui sujet toutefois aux caprices du sort,
Peut se perdre à la rade, ou périr dans le port.

He can see nowhere about him anything to dread, unless
it be such a catastrophe as will overwhelm the entire world.
His seat on the Judean throne is secure, with no rival claim-
ants left alive. Augustus and the imperial Court are his
friends. No neighboring State is a menace to him, such are
his prowess and his power.

Je n'avais pas quinze ans lorsque je pris les armes,[12]
Lorsque j'allai chercher la mort dans les alarmes,
Et si dès ce temps-là mon bras par mille exploits
Domptait les nations, et soumettait les rois.
   Que j'ai fait de combats, et gagné de batailles,
Que j'ai surpris de forts, et forcé de murailles.
Dans un champ spacieux, quand le fruit de Cérès
Des ses tuyaux dorés enrichît les guérès,
On ne voit guère plus de javelles pressées,
Que j'ai vu contre moi de piques hérissées,

Is like the ship saved from a hundred storms,
Which, subject still to the caprice of chance,
May founder in the roadstead or the port.

12 Not fifteen years were mine when I took arms
And went to seek out death 'mid war's alarums;
And since that time, my hand with many a deed
Hath subdued nations and made kings bend low.
   What combats I have fought, what battles won!
What fortresses surprised and ramparts carried!
Upon a spacious plain, when Ceres' harvest
Enriched the plowlands with its golden blades,
One scarce hath seen more of dense swathes than I
Have seen opposed to me of bristling spears

Qui volaient en éclats partout où je donnais,
Dans la brûlante ardeur dont je les moissonnais.

Only in his own home is he unhappy, where all the heat of his heart's passion cannot melt the coldness of Mariamne, his wife.

> Pourquoi me parut-elle avecque tant de charmes,[13]
> Tant de rares vertus et de divins appas,
> Pour entrer dans ma couche, et pour ne m'aimer
>   pas?
> Faut-il que deux moitiés soient si mal assorties?
> Qu'un tout soit composé de contraires parties?
> Que je sois si sensible, elle l'étant si peu?
> Que son cœur soit de glace et le mien soit de feu?

His brother and sister chide him for his weakness in doting thus on one who is unresponsive—who is, actually, his enemy. This last, Herod will not believe. That his queen really loves him was proved, he thinks, when formerly she saved both his crown and his life; her coldness springs from her purity; her pride befits her descent from the kings who were his masters. "Indeed, she speaks as though all of us were her slaves," replies Salome, bitterly, "and we have to smile and endure her slanders"; and then she goes on to tell him that Mariamne calls him the land's oppressor and the

---

Which flew in splinters everywhere I smote
In the fierce ardor wherewith I did reap them.

[13] Why showeth she so many charms to me,
So many virtues, such divine attractions,
To share my couch and still to love me not?
Can two parts of one whole accord so ill,—
One whole be made of parts so contrary,—
I feel so keenly and she feel so little,—
Her heart be frozen and my heart all flame?

murderer of her nearest kindred and offers countless incite-
ments to the populace to revolt, until Herod, though unwilling to credit these reports which have come through
servants, is so far impressed as to send for his wife and bid
the carrier of the summons observe well her demeanor on
receiving it.

The scene at the opening of the second act (this play, like
the *Cid,* was written before convention prescribed a single
setting throughout) is the apartments of the Queen. She is
discovered with her lady-in-waiting, Dinah, who vainly seeks
to persuade her to conciliate Herod, urging the constraint
of her position and the presence everywhere of spies that
serve the malice of Salome. "Although my body be captive,
my soul is not," cries Mariamne. "Shall I shame my noble
birth and belie my heart by fawning upon a savage who did
not spare the white hairs and priestly office of my father,
nor yet my brother in his radiant bloom of youth? Ever do
they rise before me, blood-boltered and piteous, reproaching
me that I sleep beside their murderer. Let fire consume me,
ere I clasp him again!"—"These wrongs are past and should
be forgotten. Will you let them blight your best and loveliest
years? After all, the King loves you."—"Loves me? I am
only his possession. When he went to Rhodes in peril of his
head, he left orders with Sohemus for my death in the event
of his."—"Oh, monstrous! I no longer wonder at your feelings. But for your own sake and your children's, dissemble.
You cannot refuse to go to him."

"I will go—to tell him that he is an assassin, a villain, and
a traitor, and that I will endure him no more!" answers
Mariamne; and at that instant they observe Salome, standing in the doorway.

Dinah is terrified, but not so the Queen. "Come closer;
you will hear us better," she says to her foe; and a long,
acrimonious colloquy ensues between the sisters-in-law—on
either side a series of brief speeches of one or two lines each,

in rapier-play dialogue where swords are sharp with sarcasm and envenomed by deadly hate. At its close, Mariamne departs to beard Herod, as others dare not—"Because they fear death, and I do not fear it," she declares.

> Vous ne lui direz rien qui lui puisse déplaire,[14]
> Il aime tout de vous jusqu'à votre colère,

the other calls after her; and Mariamne rejoins before passing from sight:

> Et moi qu'il a rendue un objet de pitié,[15]
> J'abhorre tout de lui, jusqu'à son amitié.

Now comes to Salome the chief cup-bearer, whom she has suborned to charge the Queen with having tried to poison Herod. The man has thought of the dangers he would incur by such an accusation, knowing well how a glance, a tear, or a fond memory might rekindle in a flash his master's love for Mariamne; but Salome reassures him with the promise of aid at every step, and tells him that their intended victim herself works for them, by her present defiance of the King, and that this very moment, when he will be exasperated by her behavior, is the time to carry out their plan.

So it indeed proves. Act II, scene ii, begins with Herod thrusting Mariamne out of his chamber, beside himself with rage at her upbraidings and at her refusal to accord him marital relations. "Was I wrong?" he asks Salome, when she enters and inquires the cause of his anger.—"Wrong, in-

---

[14] Thou wilt say naught to him which can displease him.
He loves thee wholly—even thy very anger!

[15] And I, whom he hath made a thing for pity—
I hate him wholly, even his affection.

deed: to have borne with her so long. She will yet strike at you in some way."—"I know her feelings now and will protect myself against her."—"I am not sure that you can," replies Salome; "a vindictive woman is very ingenious";— and just at that moment the cup-bearer makes his appearance, saying that he brings news of a plot against Herod's life. He tells his story in a whispered conversation apart with his master, after which the King, greatly shaken, commands that Mariamne be brought to him at once.

Her trial is depicted in the third act. It is in the presence of the assembled council, but Herod entirely dominates it. He assumes the Queen's guilt from the outset; and when she treats the accusation against her as a ridiculous pretext of his to destroy her, and, declaring that he has given her ample grounds for treachery to him were she disposed to it, flings in his face his murder of her father and brother, he cuts short the proceedings, demands justice upon her, and over-awes one judge, who is loath to pronounce the death-sentence. "Go on, go on, cruel monster; do not soften!" exclaims Mariamne. "In killing me you will do me a service that I much prefer to your love. I would owe you thanks if you cut off my head: in heaven I shall wear a brighter, happier crown, which no base usurper can tear from me."

But the thought of her little children, who will too likely be ill-treated after her death, brings tears to her eyes, and at the sight of those tears the anger of Herod vanishes. His change is perhaps a trifle too abrupt to seem altogether natural, but it might be made convincing by the interjection here of silent acting. He will pardon her, he says to himself; only may she cease to treat him with contumelious pride, which else, some day, must bring them to their graves. He sends the members of the council from the room, and addresses his wife in the phrases of a wooer. To punish her would be to punish himself; she need only confess and regret her intended crime.—"This is but a trap you set for me," she answers. "It is not necessary for your purpose. My people all are gone; I beg to follow them."—"What!" cries Herod, "you seek my death afresh? Contrary to me as you are, our souls are linked inextricably. My life depends on yours."—"And my life," Mariamne retorts, "it would seem, depends on yours! such is the tenderness of your careful love!"—"What do you mean?"—"Did you not plan my death when you feared the justice of Augustus?"

The revelation that she knew of this fell design comes like a thunderbolt to Herod. So this was the cause of her hatred! Sohemus betrayed the secret to her! It must be that Sohemus loves her! With an access of jealousy as incredibly sudden, as ill-founded and fierce, as that of Leontes in *A Winter's Tale* (and hence the worst flaw, perhaps, in the play), he is convinced forthwith that she has been her informant's mistress; he orders the immediate arrest of Sohemus and of the Queen's eunuch, who must have been her accomplice. Even when his rage finds utterance in conventional phrases, the sense of its fervent violence is not lost:

> Tu m'as mis dans les fers, tu m'as mis dans la
>   flamme,[16]
> Tu m'as percé le cœur, tu m'as arraché l'âme,
> Mais ne te flatte pas de cette vanité,
> D'avoir fait tant de maux avec impunité.

Mariamne disdains to defend herself. "Believe all that you say, all that you think. . . . You can rob me of life, not innocence." She is sent to prison, and Sohemus is brought in. He admits contritely that he disclosed the orders given

---

[16] Thou threw'st me in chains, threw'st me in burning flame,
　　Stabb'dst my soul, torest my heart out of my breast;
　　But flatter not thyself with this vain thought,
　　That thou couldst do with safety so much evil.

him, but he is aghast to find what more he stands accused of. His shrift is brief. Offered mercy if he will tell all, he protests that he is not guilty of so unthinkable a crime as daring to love the Queen, and that she is greatly wronged by such suspicions.—"Let this maker of fine speeches be slain!" roars Herod. "Is the eunuch here, too? . . . Horror of nature, scorn of heaven itself, monster incapable of sense, vile reptile! I placed the rarest treasure in your charge; you aided the robber of it. You served to further my utmost hurt. You drew the curtains and kept watch when in my bed Sohemus slaked his love!"—"Sire, God can make your Majesty realize my fidelity."—"Fidelity, wretch? Drag him away and torture him to death!"

It is thus, at a rapidly mounting tempo, that the third act closes with a climax of blind rage and cruelty. The fourth represents the interval which must elapse before Mariamne's execution. It is divided into three scenes. The first of these depicts Herod in that interval, with his recent outburst of passion over and with time to think. He feels that he has been providentially saved from death, but he beholds his life laid in ruins.

> Ah! que je suis piqué de ce cruel affront,[17]
> J'en ai la rage au cœur comme la honte au front,
> Et de quelque façon que ma rigueur la traite,
> Jamais ma passion n'en sera satisfaite.
>   Cependant le désir que j'ai de me venger,
> Va mettre mon salut dans un autre danger,

[17] Ah, how I suffer at this cruel outrage—
Wrath in my heart and shame upon my brow!
And with whatever rigor I may treat her,
My fury never will be satisfied.
    Yet my desire now to avenge myself
Must needs expose me to another danger.

Je m'aigris contre moi lorsque je la menace,
Ma perte est enchainée avecque sa disgrace;
Je puis bien m'assurer qu'éteignant ce flambeau
Je ne verrai plus rien d'aimable ni de beau;
Bien que l'on me console, et qu'on me divertisse,
Mon âme en tous endroits portera son supplice,
A toute heure un remords me viendra tourmenter,
Un vautour sans repos me viendra becqueter.
    O cieux! pourquoi faut-il qu'elle soit infidèle!
Vous deviez la former moins perfide ou moins belle,
Et les traits de sa grâce, ou ceux de sa rigueur,
Ne devaient point trouver de place dans mon cœur;
Je ne devais point voir au fort de ces misères,
Mes pensées divisées en deux parties contraires.
    Je voudrais que mon nom fût encore inconnu,
Ne me voir point au rang où je suis parvenu,
Etre encore à monter au temple de la gloire,
Etre encore à gagner la première victoire;

I strike at mine own breast in threatening her.
My own destruction is bound up with hers.
I can be sure that, if I quench that light,
I shall see naught else lovable or lovely.
Howe'er I be consoled, howe'er diverted,
My heart will carry its anguish everywhere;
At every hour remorse will torture me,
A vulture come to tear me without cease.
    O God, why did she have to be unfaithful!
Less treacherous or less fair thou shouldst have formed her.
Her shafts of charm or else of cruelty
Ought not to have found lodgment in my breast;
Nor should I have beheld, at misery's peak,
My thoughts divided in two adverse factions.
    I would that I were still of name unknown,
Did not stand in the station I have reached,
Had still to clamber up to glory's temple,
Had still to gain my earliest victory,

Me trouver en l'état où j'étais en naissant,
Et que ce cœur ingrat se trouvât innocent.

In a revulsion of feeling, he may yet spare Mariamne;
and the concern of Salome and Pheroras is to prevent this.
They tell him that his fervent love for her only makes her
offense the blacker; such ingratitude is more wicked than
even murder or unchastity. When he flinches at the prospect of slaying one so beautiful, they speak of her inward
foulness. He wavers still; he is not sure now of her adultery,
for Sohemus expired protesting their innocence; a long
imprisonment would punish her better than a swift death.
Salome pretends to weep; let him obey his impulse, then,
and permit his wife to destroy them all. She and Pheroras
so beset the King with their arguments against mercy that
he cannot answer them: Mariamne's plots will not always
fail nor Heaven always work miracles to thwart them; . . .
if he loved her so much, he should not have taken action at
all; . . . if she tried to poison him when she was indulged in
every way, what will she do after the humiliation to which
he has subjected her? . . . only half-crush an enemy and
one exposes oneself to vengeance; . . . remember Hyrcanus,
her father, whom no kindly treatment could turn from his
hate; . . . if Augustus should die while yet she lives, she
could raise the populace in revolt.—"Well, kill her, kill her,"
assents Herod, at last quite overborne; and her fate is determined.

A brief scene ii shows Mariamne in prison. She still looks
on death as a release, and expresses her feelings in a soliloquy
written not in alexandrine couplets but in stanzas, in which
it was the custom in early French tragedies to couch an

Could find myself e'en as I was at birth,
So be it this ingrate heart might be proved guiltless.

emotional monologue at some point in the course of a play.
There are five such *stances* here; this is the last one:

> Auteur de l'univers, souveraine puissance,[18]
>   Qui depuis ma naissance,
> M'as toujours envoyé des matières de pleurs,
> Mon âme n'a recours qu'à tes bontés divines.
>   Au milieu des épines,
> Seigneur, fais-moi bientôt marcher dessus des fleurs.

Then the jailer comes to deliver her to execution. He is
distressed, but she is glad to go.

The third scene is episodic in that it is quite unnecessary
to the plot, but is entirely legitimate in that it heightens the
pathos of Mariamne's end. Its setting is a street along
which she must pass to her doom. Her mother, Alexandra,
enters. The elder woman is bitter enough at heart about her
daughter's fate, as her words to herself reveal; but more
powerful than her grief or anger is her fear lest Herod should
entertain suspicions also of her; to avert this danger she intends to hide her feelings and actually denounce and curse
Mariamne on her way to the scaffold, so as not to seem her
accomplice, and for that horrible purpose she takes a convenient post. She has not long to wait. The victim approaches,
unafraid of death as ever, as ever regretting only her little
children, whom she must leave behind her. She prays for
them; she apostrophizes the tiger who has condemned her
and to whom she gives all her blood to drink, but who cannot blot her honor as he blots out her life; then she sees

[18] O sovereign Power, Creator of the earth,
        Who, ever since my birth,
    Hast sent me fortune whereof tears are bred,
    My soul turns only to thy grace divine.
        Lord, may it soon be mine
    To go from midst life's thorns, on flowery fields to tread.

Alexandra and asks leave to go to her a moment for an eternal farewell and a last kiss. Her words to her mother are all meant to comfort her.

> Madame, on me contraint de changer de demeure,[19]
> Mais j'en vais habiter une beaucoup meilleure,
> Où les vents ni l'envie, avecque leurs rigueurs,
> N'excitent point d'orage en l'air ni dans les cœurs,
> Où sans aveuglement on connaît l'innocence,
> Où la main des tyrans n'étend point sa puissance;
> Où l'âme pour le prix de sa fidelité,
> Goûte en repos la gloire, et l'immortalité.

When, instead of the expected embrace, she receives a flood of imprecations, her constancy does not desert her. "You will live as one innocent and I shall die as one guilty," is all that she answers; and she goes out to death, leaving the wretched Alexandra herself almost dead with self-loathing.

The remorse, the anguish, the madness of Herod fill the whole of the final act. He is already cursing his jealousy when it opens; even now Mariamne is being led to execution unless treason is afoot—nay, already her beauty is no longer in the world. He will learn her fate, and if it is not yet consummated he will avert it. Then one of his men, Narbal, comes to announce that the headsman has done his work, and at these tidings Herod falls instantly, as though struck by lightning. On his recovery of his senses, he breaks

---

[19] Madam, I am constrained to change my home,
But I am going to dwell in one far better,
Where no fierce wind nor malice quite as fierce
Stirreth up storms in air or human hearts;
Where innocence is known to eyes unblinded;
Where the fell hand of tyrants hath no power;
Where, for its steadfastness' reward, the soul
Tasteth fair fame and immortality.

into a lamentation which, when interrupted, is resumed again and again and does not really end until the end of the play itself. There is nothing else quite like it in French-classical tragedy. Conventional phrases are indeed not absent, but they are jostled by imagery such as one expects to find rather in Seneca or the Elizabethans. There is power in the very monotony of the monstrous, disordered, ever-reiterated passion.

"Hath Mariamne swelled the ranks of death?" Herod begins.

> Ce qui fut mon soleil n'est donc plus rien qu'une
>   ombre? [20]
> Quoi? dans son orient cet astre de beauté,
> En éclairant mon âme a perdu la clarté?
> Tu dis que Mariamne a perdu la lumière,
> Et le flambeau du monde achève sa carrière?
> On le vit autrefois retourner sur ses pas
> A l'objet seulement d'un funeste repas,
> Et d'une horreur pareille il se trouve incapable,
> Quand on vient devant lui d'éteindre son semblable.
>   Astre sans connaissance, et sans ressentiment,
> Tu portes la lumière avec aveuglement!
> Si l'immortelle main qui te forma de flamme,

[20] Is that which was my sun, then, but a shadow?
Still in its eastern sky this orb of beauty
That lights my soul hath lost its light? Thou sayest
That Mariamne hath lost the light of day,
And the world's torch yet moveth through the heavens?
Men saw it once turn back upon its path
For the mere sake of an accursed feast,
And now it finds it cannot have like horror
Though it hath seen its counterpart extinguished!
    Day-star that knowest naught and feelest naught,
It is all blindly that thou givest light!
If the immortal hand that formed thee of flame,

En te donnant un corps t'avait pourvu d'une âme,
Tu serais plus sensible au sujet de mon deuil,
De ton lit aujourd'hui tu ferais ton cercueil,
Et par tout l'univers ta lumière éclipsée
Etablirait l'horreur qui règne en ma pensée.

He begs the faithful Narbal to tell him in detail the story
of what he cannot believe, yet cannot doubt; and Narbal
complies.

Alors que dans la tour on la vint avertir,[21]
Qu'un rigoureux arrêt la pressait d'en sortir,
Le funeste récit de sa triste sentence,
Ebranla tous les cœurs, mais non pas sa constance;
Car bravant ses malheurs, elle fit assez voir
Que ce choc furieux n'avait pu l'émouvoir.
Elle n'exprima point des sentiments timides,
Ses yeux restèrent secs parmi cent yeux humides,
Et des rayons de joie éclairants ses appas
Firent voir que la mort ne lui déplaisait pas.

In shaping thee had with a soul endowed thee,
Thou wouldst be more responsive to my suffering,
Wouldst make thy bed thy sepulcher, and establish,
By thy eclipse, throughout the universe
The selfsame horror that now reigns in me!

[21] When warning had come to her in the tower
That a stern doom would force her exit from it,
The dread recital of the fate decreed her
Shook every heart, but not her constancy.
For, scorning her ill fortune, she made it clear
That this fierce shock had not the power to move her.
She nowise uttered timid sentiments;
Her eyes were dry among so many weeping;
And joyful glances that lit up her charms
Showed well that death was not displeasing to her.

Après qu'elle eut fait part de quelques pierreries,
A ses filles d'honneur qu'elle a le plus chéries,
Et qu'en les embrassant, elle leur eut enjoint
De ne la suivre pas, ou de ne pleurer point :
Elle tourna ses pas, et plus gaie et plus belle,
Où l'échafaud dressé prenait de deuil pour elle.
Jamais on ne la vit dans un plus noble orgueil,
On lisait sur son front le mépris du cercueil.
Jamais reine Amazone avecque plus de gloire
Ne parut triomphante après une victoire ;
Le peuple en la suivant, se fondait tout en pleurs,
Admirant sa constance, et plaignant ses malheurs.

He goes on to relate how nobly she bore her mother's curses.
He tells of her demeanor upon the scaffold (it is here represented as somewhat too saint-like, more that of a Christian
martyr than of the haughty Maccabean queen, and to that
extent out of character), her last prayer and death. Herod's
agony bursts forth afresh :

Avoir ôté la vie à des beautés si rares,[22]

When she had made bequests of certain jewels
To those she loved best of her maids of honor,
And when she had embraced them and enjoined them
Neither to follow her nor to shed tears,
She bent her steps, more gay, more fair than erstwhile,
Whither the scaffold mournfully was waiting.
None ever saw her show a nobler pride.
Upon her face was written scorn of death.
Never more glorious appeared a queen
Of the Amazons in victory and triumph.
The people following her all burst out sobbing,
Awed by her courage, pitying her misfortune.

[22] To have deprived of life such loveliness—

O rigueur inconnue aux cœurs les plus barbares!
Un Sarmate inhumain ne pourrait l'exercer,
Un Scythe sans horreur ne pourrait y penser.
Quel fleuve, ou quelle mer sera jamais capable
D'effacer la noirceur de ce crime exécrable?
Quelle affreuse montagne, et quel antre écarté
Pourront servir d'asile à mon impiété?
Trouverai-je un réfuge au centre de la terre,
Où mon crime se trouve à couvert du tonnerre?
Où je me puisse voir sans peine et sans effroi,
Où je ne traîne point mon enfer après moi?

He seizes Narbal's sword and tries to kill himself, once,
twice; hardly can Narbal restrain him. He calls upon the
downtrodden Jewish people, the witnesses of his crimes, to
slay him and avenge their queen; but they are too craven to
rise against him, he says, and hence he devotes them to the
wrath of heaven.

Témoins de sa bassesse et de ma violence,[23]
Cieux qui voyez le tort que souffre l'innocence,
Versez sur ce climat un malheur infini.

Oh, cruelty unknown to the cruelest hearts!
A barbarous Sarmatian could not do it;
A Scythian could not think of it unquailing.
What river or what sea can ever wash
The blackness of this horrid crime away?
What savage mountain or what lonely cavern
Can be the asylum of my impious soul?
Will I find in earth's midmost depths a refuge
Where my sin may have shelter from the thunder;
Where I can hide with neither pain nor fright;
Where I shall not drag my hell after me?

[23] Observer of their baseness and my crime,
O heaven, that seest the wrong done innocence,
Shed on this land misfortunes infinite;

Punissez ces ingrats qui ne m'ont point puni.
Donnez-les pour matière à la fureur des armes,
Qu'ils flottent dans le sang, qu'ils nagent dans les
　　larmes,
Faites marcher contre eux des Scythes, des Gelons,
Et s'il se peut encor des monstres plus felons,
Qui mettent sans horreur en les venant surprendre,
Et leurs troupes en sang, et leurs maisons en cendre;
Qu'on leur vienne enlever leurs enfants les plus chers,
Et qu'une main barbare en frappe les rochers;
Qu'on force devant eux leurs femmes et leurs filles,
Que la peste et la faim consomment leurs familles;
Que leur Temple orgueilleux parmi ces mouvements,
Se trouve renversé jusqu'à ses fondements.
　　Et si rien doit rester de leur maudite race,
Que ce soit seulement des sujets de disgrâce,
Des gens que la fortune abandonne aux malheurs;
Qu'ils vivent dans la honte et parmi les douleurs;

　　Punish these slaves who have not punished me;
　　Let them be objects of thy chastisements;
　　Make them to float in gore, to swim in tears;
　　Send Scythians and Geloni marching 'gainst them,
　　And if 'tis possible yet more cruel monsters,
　　Who have no qualms, taking them unawares,
　　In blood to leave them, and their homes in ashes;
　　Grant that their dearest babes may be borne off
　　And dashed to death on rocks by barbarous hands,
　　Their wives and daughters raped before their eyes,
　　Famine and pestilence devour their households,
　　And their proud Temple, amid these disasters,
　　Be overthrown even to its foundations.
　　　Should aught remain of their accursed race,
　　May they be only objects of disgrace,
　　People whom Fate abandons to misfortune.
　　Make them abide in shame and amid sorrows.

Qu'ils se trouvent toujours couverts d'ignominie,
Qu'on les traite partout avecque tyrannie,
Que sans fin par le monde ils errent dispersés,
Qu'ils soient en tous endroits, et maudits et chassés,
Qu'également partout on leur fasse la guerre,
Qu'ils ne possèdent plus un seul pouce de terre,
Et que servant d'objet à votre inimitié,
L'on apprenne leurs maux sans en avoir pitié.
Faites pleuvoir sur eux de la flamme et du souffre,
De tout Jérusalem ne faites rien qu'un gouffre,
Qu'un abîme infernal, qu'un palus plein d'horreur,
Dont le nom seulement donne de la terreur.

But ever he recurs to the same theme at last:

Mariamne est donc morte, on me l'a donc ravie,[24]
Et pour mon désespoir on me laisse la vie?
O mort! en mes ennuis, j'implore ta pitié
Viens enlever le tout dont tu pris la moitié.

Let them find always naught but ignominy.
Let them be everywhere oppressed, and wander
Forevermore, scattered, o'er all the world.
Let them at every turn be cursed and hounded,
And everywhere alike be warred upon,
No longer own a single inch of earth,
And, as the objects of thy execration,
Receive no pity when their woes are told of.
Rain fire and brimstone down upon their heads.
Make all Jerusalem naught but an abyss—
An abyss only, only a sink of horror,
Of which the very name alone is fearsome.

[24] Is Mariamne dead, then—snatched from me—
And am I left alive still to despair?
Death, in my woe I beg for thy compassion.
Come and take all, where thou hast taken half!

After this paroxysm his faculties are beclouded; Pheroras
and Salome, who now enter, find that he no longer realizes
what has taken place, and he is anxious to see Mariamne.
When reminded of her death, he launches at once into renewed lament.

> Quoi, Mariamne est morte? o destins ennemis! [25]
> La Parque l'a ravie, et vous l'avez permis?
> Vous avez donc souffert cette triste aventure,
> Sans imposer le deuil à toute la nature?
> Quoi? son corps sans chaleur est donc enseveli,
> Et l'univers n'est point encore démoli?
> Vous avez donc rompu l'agréable harmonie
> Que vous aviez commise à son divin génie,
> Vous avez donc fermé sa bouche, et ses beaux yeux,
> Et n'avez point détruit la structure des cieux?
> Cruels dans cette perte, à nulle autre seconde,
> Vous deviez faire entrer celle de tout le monde,
> Enlever l'univers hors de ses fondements,
> Et confondre les cieux avec les éléments,
> Rompre le frein des mers, éteindre la lumière,

[25] What! Mariamne dead? Oh, hostile Powers!
Fate snatched her hence, and ye have let this be?
Ye have permitted, then, this sad event
Without requiring that all nature mourn?
What! her cold body hath been buried, then,
And still the world is not annihilated?
Have ye, then, shattered the fair harmony
Which ye had given to her soul divine?
Have ye, then, stopped her mouth—closed her bright eyes—
And not destroyed the fabric of the skies?
Cruel in this wreckage, second to none other,
Ye should have begun that of all the earth,
Swept the whole universe from its foundations,
Shuffled the heavens with the elements,
Broken the curb of the seas, snuffed out the light,

Et remettre ce tout en sa masse première.

He drives his brother and sister from him in terror, and turns to those who he feels were his true friends and Mariamne's—to Narbal and to Thares, the captain of his guard. They must help him mourn and commemorate her; she shall have a temple like a goddess, and a feast established in her honor. But his mind again suffers derangement; he again asks for the Queen, again comes to himself and again is racked with torment, prays to her in heaven for pardon, and at length sinks insensible to the ground. Over his prostrate form, Narbal speaks the final lines, that sum up his tragedy:

> O Prince pitoyable en tes grandes douleurs! [26]
> Toi-même es l'artisan de tes propres malheurs,
> Ton amour, tes soupçons, ta crainte et ta colère
> Ont offusqué ta gloire, et causé ta misère:
> Tu sais donner des lois à tant de nations,
> Et ne sais pas régner dessus tes passions.
> Mais les meilleurs esprits font des fautes extrêmes,
> Et les rois bien souvent sont esclaves d'eux-mêmes.

One is reminded of the "Cut is the branch that might have grown full straight," at the close of Marlowe's *Doctor Faustus*.

And reduced all to its original chaos.

[26] O Prince,
Piteous in thy great sorrows! lo, thou art
Thyself the architect of thy misfortunes.
Thy love, suspicions, fear, and anger have
Dimmed thy fair fame and caused thy miseries.
Thou canst administer laws to many nations,
Yet knowest not how to reign o'er thine own passions.
But rarest spirits oft commit great crimes,
And kings are often slaves unto themselves.

CHAPTER III

DU RYER AS A WRITER OF TRAGEDY

PIERRE DU RYER, according to Reynier, deserves
an honorable place beside Rotrou[1]—as, inferentially,
does no other contemporary of Corneille's prime. Lanson
calls him a "bad writer" (*mauvais écrivain*) [2] but means it
in the narrower sense, that his style was poor. Even about
this there are differences of opinion; Reynier does not agree,
nor does H. C. Lancaster in his monograph on this dramatist,[3] though it would seem that subsequently he changed
his opinion, for in his great *History of French Dramatic
Literature in the Seventeenth Century* he says: "It is unfortunate that Du Ryer's gift of expression was too limited
to bring out his genuinely dramatic talents." [4]

[1] In Petit de Julleville's *Histoire de la Langue et de la Littérature
française,* vol. iv., p. 384.

[2] *Esquisse d'une Histoire de la Tragédie française,* New York,
1920, p. 75.

[3] "The tragedies and late tragi-comedies are clear, often eloquent,
if at times verbose. Never entirely free from *préciosité* and technical
carelessness that shows itself in padded lines and conventional rimes
and phrases, Du Ryer, by his large study of the classics, did so much
to free himself from these faults that M. Reynier can assert with
truth that he wrote with a precision rare among his contemporaries.
Antithesis, which may become paradox, repetition of words, brief
comparisons, abstract terms, neat single lines expressing a general
truth are characteristic of his style. He possesses the qualities of an
orator rather than those of a poet, the swelling phrase, the maxim,
the power of generalization, occasionally the subtlety and love of
debate. In reading him we cannot fail to think of Corneille, whose
clearness, vigor, and rapidity he has to a lesser degree, while with
him he lacks grace and appeal to the senses." (*Pierre Du Ryer,
Dramatist,* Washington, 1913, pp. 168-169.)

[4] Part II, p. 772.

If not fluent, this playwright was at least original and forceful. More than either Rotrou or Tristan l'Hermite he gives us the sense of having a strong personality and a robust mind. In his very style there is individuality; it is dis-- tinguished by the rhetorical device of syntactic parallelism employed with a frequency unapproached by any of his fel- low dramatists. So far from having been turned by the *Cid* from romanesque tragi-comedies to tragedies, as was former- ly thought, he appears to have preceded the *Cid* by some months with his *Lucrèce*,[5] a tragedy on a classical theme, which together with Mairet's slightly earlier *Sophonisbe* pointed the way for Corneille's Roman plays. Here already in *Lucrèce* we find evidence of Du Ryer's incisive and in- dependent mentality, in passages which are not the conven- tional utterance of the figures of French tragedy. When a minion of "Tarquin" (as Sextus Tarquinius is called in this play) tells Lucretia that her husband is infatuated with a mistress, she bids her outraged female attendants to reflect that in such troubles,

> On irrite toujours celui dont on se plaint, [6]
> Et qu'il est difficile au plus noble mérite
> D'arrêter de l'amour dans les cœurs qu'on irrite.
> La plainte la plus juste a cela de fatal
> Qu'elle achève d'éteindre un amour conjugal,
> Elle endurcit au mal un cœur opiniâtre,
> Le rend de son péché beaucoup plus idolâtre,

[5] See Lancaster, *Hist. of Fr. Dram. Lit.*, Part II, p. 69.

[6] One always angers him whom one complains of,
And that one with the finest qualities
Can scarcely preserve love in hearts one angers.
E'en the best justified complaint hath fatal
Power to extinguish conjugal affection;
It will confirm a stubborn heart in evil,
Make it more wedded to its fault by far,

> Et chasse incessamment le repos souhaité,
> Qu'un silence discret eût sans doute arrêté.

And when "Tarquin" urges her to repay her husband's infidelity in kind, she answers:

> Et quand même l'honneur y pourrait condes-
>   cendre,[7]
> Mon inclination me le viendrait défendre.

This most natural of reactions in a normal chaste woman has found all too little expression in literature, but Du Ryer seizes on it at once as the essential thing in his heroine's feelings on such an occasion.

The same clear, strong intellect later produced, in his *Esther* (1642), the following passage, remarkable from the pen of a dramatist in seventeenth-century France:

> . . . enfin quelle flamme et quels malheurs éclatent [8]
> Quand deux religions dans un état combattent?
> Quel sang epargne-t-on, ignoble ou glorieux,
> Quand on croit le verser pour la gloire des Dieux?
> Alors tout est permis, tout semble légitime,
> Du nom de piété l'on couronne le crime;
> Et comme on pense faire un sacrifice aux Dieux

And ever drive away the peace one seeks,
Which discreet silence would have surely grasped.

[7] And even if honor could consent to this,
My inclination would still keep me from it.

[8] Truly, what flames break out, and what great mischiefs,
When two religions in one State contend!
What blood doth any spare, of churl or lord,
When for the glory of the gods one spills it?
Then all is sanctioned, all appears legitimate,
Crime with the name of piety is crowned,
And, as when sacrificing to the gods,

Qui verse plus de sang paraît le plus pieux.

And the idea expressed in this passage from his *Thémistocle* (1646-1647), however unpopular in our own immediate times, which have witnessed two world-wars with all the intense nationalism and patriotism that naturally are associated with them, was at least a notable conception for a man of Du Ryer's times:

> Je sais qu'une âme faible à ce mot de patrie[9]
> Se laisse transporter jusqu'à l'idôlatrie,
> Et qu'elle croit devoir par un ordre fatal
> Et sa mort et sa vie à son pays natal.
> Vain honneur, vain respect, qui rend l'âme servile.
> Cette amour du pays n'est qu'une erreur utile,
> Qu'une ruse d'état nécessaire aux états
> Puisque sans son secours ils ne fleuriraient pas.
> Mais ce n'est pas ainsi qu'un grand cœur se resserre,
> Il ne se borne pas par un morceau de terre,
> Et comme il naît au monde où ses faits sont oüis
> Il croit que tout la monde est aussi son pays.
> Ainsi toute le terre également chérie

He seems the most devout who sheds most blood.

[9] I know that weak men let themselves be carried
To sheer idolatry by the phrase "my country,"
And that they think they must, by a fixed mandate,
Give for their native land their lives, their death.
Vain reverence, which makes the soul a slave!
Such love of country is a useful error—
No more—a politic deception which
The State requires because it cannot prosper
Without this. But a great soul thinks not thus.
It is not bounded by some bit of land;
Born in the world wherein its deeds are bruited,
It deems the whole world hence to be its country.
So to a noble spirit all the earth,

A l'homme magnanime est une ample patrie,
Comme aux astres les cieux, comme l'air aux oiseaux,
Comme à chaque poisson tout l'empire des eaux.

Lucrèce, printed in 1638, was never republished and has
had less fame and fewer readers than it deserves, in comparison with Du Ryer's other tragedies. It is well constructed,
compact, and peopled with rather well-drawn characters—
though there is no inner strife in the soul of any of
them (the dramatic conflict is wholly external, between
them) and though the heroine's belief of the slander concerning her husband is too ready and, under the circumstances, quite stupid. On the whole, this play seems to me
distinctly superior to his subsequent *Alcionée* or *Thémistocle,*
if not to his *Esther,* though all of these have appeared in
several editions and hence are better known.

Whether he would have continued to work in the field of
tragedy thereafter, or would have returned forthwith to his
previous field of tragi-comedy, if Corneille had not produced
the *Cid,* it is impossible to judge; but the fact remains that
whereas before the *Cid* Du Ryer had written only one tragedy, one comedy, one pastoral, and seven tragi-comedies, he
wrote after the *Cid* five tragedies and five tragi-comedies.
Yet he was still quite as much a leader as a follower—even in
relation to the chief dramatist of the age.

It has been remarked that his next tragedy, *Alcionée*
(1637), takes the Infanta out of the *Cid* for its heroine.
Its princess, Lydia, is indeed beset, like the Infanta, by
the opposed promptings of her pride of rank and her love

Equally cherished, forms his native land,
As to the stars the heavens, to birds the air,
To every fish the whole of ocean's realm.

That these sentiments are not sincerely felt by the character who
expresses them, does not make them any less striking.

for a man not of royal blood; but the man, an invincible warrior, has joined her country's enemies when denied her hand, and has swept all before him until her father has promised her to him if he would return to his allegiance. This he has done, ridding the realm of its foes; but when he claims his reward, it is refused him, and being now without allies or support, he kills himself. Not only does Lydia call to mind Corneille's princess; the frequent discussion of political questions in this drama anticipates his work of a few years later. But the theme of a lover's disaster anticipates the tragedies of Racine, and is developed in a plot simpler than any other in French-classical tragedy before Racine's *Bérénice*. *Alcionée*, however, is very un-Racinian in its stiff, crude handling of the psychological drama which is its subject. The passion that brings the hero to his death never finds words of real warmth. Little impression is conveyed of the alleged struggle within the breast of Lydia: in soliloquy she speaks frigidly, with mechanical balance, of her "love" and her "hate" for Alcyoneus, both in the same breath; but such descriptive analysis of her feelings is not supplemented elsewhere by lifelike representation of the speech and actions of a divided heart. No doubt that is partly due to the fact that this early playwright's hand was unpracticed in such refinements; but the inadequacy of *Alcionée* may also have been due in part to his striving for verisimilitude, commendable in itself but here untempered by any proper awareness that a dramatist must compromise between the claims of realism and his audience's need to understand. Thus the exposition is faulty; there is never any clear statement about Alcyoneus' turning against his invader-comrades and defeating them. Naturally, neither the King nor his daughter would dwell on that, and the other characters happen only to allude to it; Du Ryer did not trouble himself to introduce this information deliberately. The disclosure of Lydia's real feelings towards Alcyoneus is very belated; the realistic conduct of prior scenes did not call for it, and the importance of enlightening the audience was evidently not considered. Yet *Alcionée* was greatly admired when first presented, and for a long time afterwards.

A point which with a modern audience would especially need preparation and explanation, then needed none. When understood, it is now in its very strangeness, its historical importance, and its vivid portrayal, the most interesting thing in this play: the arrogant irresponsibility of Lydia and her father, their unblushing refusal to consider themselves bound by any pledge extorted from them, no matter how solemnly sworn to, or given under what desperate circumstances. To people of the seventeenth century, and to Frenchmen even of the eighteenth, when kings believed that they ruled by Divine Right, this was a familiar fact about them; and it was largely the recognized impossibility of trusting the word of kings that sent Charles I of England to the headsman's block and Louis XVI of France to the guillotine. It may be doubted whether literature contains anywhere a more convincing depiction of the mental attitude of self-exalted, perfidious royalty than we find in *Alcionée*.

Du Ryer's last tragedy, *Thémistocle,* is generally considered his weakest, and with reason. Its plot is not unified. Themistocles, an exile at the Court of his erstwhile foe, the King of Persia, first faces the charge of being a spy there; against this he successfully defends himself in Act III in a formal speech before the King—a scene with little relation to anything in the two previous acts, which are occupied chiefly with presenting the attitude of the several characters towards each other. The last half of the play develops and dispels a new danger to the hero: if he disdains the King's favor by refusing to lead the Persians against his own countrymen, he may be put to death. This new crisis in his fortunes is handled more effectively, with accumulating pressure upon him not to sacrifice himself for the ungrateful land of his birth; but

when old loyalties finally triumph in him, it is revealed that
the King was only testing his character, after all!

Thémistocle has, moreover, many faults of detail. As in
Cinna and *Polyeucte,* a shift in our interest and sympathy is
required of us by the author; these are aroused at the outset
by the attractive character of Roxana, who loves Themistocles
devotedly, and not until the second act is well advanced is the
"heart-interest," regarded in those days as indispensable,
initiated between him and the far less likable Palmis, a
princess quite as feline as most of the other "heroines" of
French-classical tragedies.[10] Roxana practically fades out of
the action. The sentiments of Palmis' mother, Mandane,
towards Themistocles are transformed by information whose

[10] E.g., II, iii-iv, where she says:

> Ce Grec est-il jugé? . . .
> L'a-t-on puni, Roxane, ou bien m'a-t-on vengée? . . .
> Son crime est de plaire à mes yeux;
> Et le caprice est tel de mon coeur misérable,
> Que plus ce Grec me plaît, plus je le crois coupable.
>
> . . . .
>
> Un banni dans un coeur où doit être un monarque!
> Efface, efface-en jusqu'à la moindre marque,
> Et pour venger ton coeur d'un sentiment si bas,
> Voi tomber Thémistocle, et n'en soupire pas.

> (Hath this Greek been tried? . . .
> Hath he been punished, or have I indeed,
> Roxana, been avenged? . . .
> His crime is to be pleasing in my sight,
> And my unhappy heart's caprice is such,
> The more this Greek attracteth me, the more
> I deem him culpable. . . .
> (*To herself*) An exile in a heart where a king should be!
> Blot out, blot out the least sign of him from it;
> And, to avenge thy breast for such base feelings,
> Behold him fall, without a single sigh.)

There is a scene (IV, i) between Palmis and her unloved suitor,

source does not appear in the play and is very vaguely indicated. The action of *Thémistocle,* indeed, abounds in loose ends and is badly cluttered throughout.

At least this drama does not lack movement. In its own day, it doubtless held the interest of its audience. It contains some good situations and arrestive turns of thought, and its characters seem more genuinely to experience their alleged emotions than do those in most of Du Ryer's tragedies. No small part of our poor opinion of it is probably due to its depiction of Themistocles as feeling and speaking like any love-sick swain of pastoral romance—an incongruity especially offensive to us in such a well-known historical figure. The gallantry fostered by the Hôtel de Rambouillet, which marred the work of Corneille after *Polyeucte,* is regnant here; Julius Caesar, it will be recalled, is treated in the same way in his *Pompée.* We should better excuse such conformity to transient fashion, however, than Themistocles' constant references to himself as *"un misérable"* and in other, similar terms of unmanly self-pity.

Esther is interesting for its anticipation of Racine's lyrical drama of the same name. There is little similarity between the two plays, however, except that which necessarily arises from their having a common source. Racine's treatment of the Biblical narrative is almost naively simple and straightforward; it greatly excels Du Ryer's tragedy in poetic beauty and religious fervor, but is much less dramatic. Du Ryer has complicated his plot by making Haman an unsuccessful wooer of Esther, and his hatred of Mordecai springs not only from that Jew's persistent refusal of obeisance to him but also from the fact that Mordecai had opposed his suit for Esther's hand and was the person who had brought her to

---

Themistocles' pretended friend Artabazus, that is one of the most comical of the many unintendedly ridiculous scenes in the romanesque plays of the seventeenth century.

the King's notice. As further complications, Du Ryer introduces the figure of Vashti and, guided by the Vulgate, represents Haman as having been the leader of the conspiracy
against the King which Mordecai formerly had exposed.
But this play, as well as Racine's, follows the Book of Esther
at the expense of dramatic unity. Like *Thémistocle,* it has two
successive themes: the triumph of the heroine over Vashti,
and her frustration of the murderous designs of Haman
against her people. The first of these is treated in Act II and
the greater part of Act III, the second in the rest of Act III,
in Act IV, and in Act V. Act I serves as an introduction to
both of these subjects, but particularly to the second one.

By far the best portion of the play is that dealing with
the contest between Esther and Vashti for the King's favor.
It may be questioned whether Du Ryer has done better work
anywhere than in some of its scenes. His Vashti is all pride
and bitterness. She will be content with nothing but "the
throne or the tomb." Especially galling to her is the fact
that she is being supplanted by a woman with beauty but not
high birth. To Haman she gives free expression to her feelings:

> Pour craindre et pour trembler de quoi suis-je
> coupable? [11]
> Un roi capricieux, bizarre en ses projets,
> Donne de grands festins aux peuples ses sujets;
> Et pour faire éclater et la fête et sa grâce,
> Il veut que je me montre à cette populace,
> Comme si prodiguant ses biens de toutes parts,

[11] What am I guilty of, to fear and tremble?
A temperamental king, of strange devices,
Gives a great banquet to his subjects, and,
To signalize his feast and graciousness,
Would have me show myself unto these people,
As if, to squander on all men his blessings,

Il voulait la repaître avecques mes regards.
Hé bien! j'ai refusé de plaire à son caprice,
J'ai refusé ma vue au peuple son complice;
J'ai voulu conserver la majesté des rois.
En quoi cette action blesse-t-elle les lois?

AMAN.

Mais elle offense un roi que peu de chose offense.

VASHTI.

D'un monarque aveuglé ne prends point la défense.

AMAN.

Vous deviez à ses vœux accorder ce plaisir.

VASHTI.

J'ai satisfait, Aman, à son lâche désir,
Puisqu'il ne me faisait une loi si cruelle,
Qu'afin de m'obliger de paraître rebelle,
Qu'afin que mon refus, qu'il avait souhaité,

He fain would feed them with the sight of me!
Well! I refused to indulge his whim—refused
To be a spectacle to the rabble with him.
I would preserve the majesty of sovereigns.
How does my conduct violate the law?

HAMAN.

But it offends a king who finds offense
In little things.

VASHTI.

Defend not a blind monarch!

HAMAN.

Thou shouldst have done his pleasure, as he asked thee.

VASHTI.

Haman, I satisfied his base desire;
For he demanded this cruel thing of me
Only that he might make me seem rebellious,
Only that my refusal, which he hoped for,

Donnât quelque couleur à sa brutalité;
Car enfin a-t-il fait le choix d'une princesse,
Pour lui faire remplir la place que je laisse?
Non, non, tu le sais bien; mais de tous les côtés
Ayant fait assembler les plus rares beautés,
Comme s'il affectait et sa honte et ma peine,
Que sa brutalité vous choisit une reine;
Parmi tant de beautés, que ne fit-il un choix
Qui me put condamner quand je l'accuserais?
Mais la brutalité, sans respect des couronnes,
Affecte le plaisir, et non pas les personnes.
Une fille de peuple! et vous l'avez souffert!
Une fille du peuple! Ah! ce penser me perd,
Ce penser me remplit de fureurs et de rages.
Démons assez puissants pour venger tant d'outrages,
Si l'on me préférait le sang de quelques rois,
Constante en mon malheur, je me consolerois.
Mon plus grand mal n'est pas de quitter la couronne;

Might furnish grounds to excuse his bestial conduct.
For hath he now made choice of any princess
To fill for him the place that I am leaving?
Nay, thou know'st well he hath not; but having brought
Together from all sides the fairest women,
As if he sought both his shame and my anguish,
When like some brute he chose a queen for you,
'Mid so much beauty why did he not choose
One who could prove me wrong if I should blame him?
But swinishness, with no respect for crowns,
Seeks pleasure, and not persons of distinction.
A daughter of the people!—and ye have suffered it!
A daughter of the people!—ah, to think
Of that distracts me, fills me with rage and madness.
Ye demons able to avenge such insults,
If some king's child had been preferred to me,
I would bear all bravely and console myself.
My greatest woe is not to lose the crown;

Un sage quelquefois la fuit et l'abandonne:
Mais le plus grand des maux dont je sente les coups,
C'est de céder le trône à de moindres que nous.

She appears at the ceremony of the installation of Esther
as queen, and challenges the King to state why she has been
discarded. The contrast is effectively drawn between her outraged dignity and the sweet humility of the Jewish maid, who
answers Ahasuerus' words of welcome thus:

Sire, c'est en esclave, et non en souveraine,[12]
Que j'approche d'un roi qui me regarde en reine;
Et pour toutes beautés, ô monarque puissant,
Je n'apporte à vos pieds qu'un cœur obéissant.
Je ne me considère au trône d'un empire,
Que comme une vapeur que le soleil attire,
Et dont le corps léger ne s'élève si haut,
Que pour s'appesantir, et retomber bientôt.
Bien que le nom de reine, et grand et vénérable,
Puisse assouvir un cœur de gloire insatiable,
Je ne l'estime pas, ce nom si glorieux,

A wise man sometimes flees it or resigns it.
But the greatest of the woes whose shafts I feel
Is to give way to someone baser born.

[12] Sire, as a slave, not as a sovereign, I
   Approach a king who looks on me as Queen;
   And all my beauty, which I bring, great monarch,
   Unto thy feet, is an obedient heart.
   I deem an empire's throne but as a vapor
   Raised by the sun, whereof the buoyant cloud
   Rises so high only to gather weight
   And soon sink back. Although the name of Queen,
   Great and revered, çan satisfy a heart
   Athirst for grandeurs, I would not esteem it,
   This glorious name, for raising us to a station

Pour nous mettre en un rang ou nous devenons
    Dieux;
Mais pour ce qu'en rendant ma fortune parfaite,
Il me rend d'un grand roi la première sujette,
Et qu'en me faisant voir les biens que je vous dois,
Il m'apprend d'autant mieux à respecter mon roi.

In the acrimonious scene between Vashti and the King,
Esther herself interposes at length to plead the cause of her
rival:

Ah! Sire, regardez d'un œil plus pitoyable[13]
Une grande princesse, une princesse aimable,
Et ne m'élevez point à des prospérités
Qu'elle puisse accuser de ses calamités.
Pourrais-je bien jouir, sans remords et sans peine,
D'une félicité qui ruine une reine?
Quelque bien qui succède à nos ambitions,
La grandeur est funeste à ces conditions.
Regardez ma bassesse, et de quelle distance
Du trône où vous régnez s'éloigne ma naissance;

Where we become as gods, but for the fact
That when it crowns my fortunes, it doth make me
A great king's foremost subject, and that when
It makes me see the blessings that I owe him,
It teaches me to reverence him the more.

[13] Ah, sire! look with an eye more full of pity
On a great princess, on a lovable princess,
And raise me not unto an eminence
Whereby she can blame *me* for her disasters.
Could I enjoy, without remorse or pain,
A blissful lot whereby a queen met ruin?
Whatever good is granted our ambitions,
Greatness is dreadful under these conditions.
    Think of my low estate and by what distance
My birth divides me from thy throne of empire;

Vous direz que le ciel qui peut tout ici bas,
Nous éloigna si fort pour ne nous joindre pas,
Mais d'un autre côté regardez la puissance
D'où cette grande reine a tiré sa naissance;
Vous verrez que le ciel qui la veut soutenir,
Ne vous rendit égaux qu'afin de vous unir.
Considérez en elle, et le sang et la grâce;
La faire choir du trône et me mettre en sa place,
C'est au trône du jour porter l'obscurité,
C'est chasser de l'autel une divinité,
Et par un changement aussi nouveau qu'étrange,
C'est y mettre en sa place une idole de fange.
Ah! Sire, pour la reine, ah, Sire, pour Esther,
Faites votre justice à même heure éclater,
Nous rendant toutes deux où le ciel nous adresse,
La reine à sa grandeur, Esther à sa bassesse.
Tout l'honneur que je cherche, et que j'ai prétendu,
C'est de céder le trône à qui le trône est dû.

Thou'lt say that heaven, all-powerful here below,
So widely sundered us to prevent our union.
But on the other side, think of the greatness
From which this noble queen derives her birth;
Thou'lt see that heaven, which wishes to uphold her,
Hath made you equal only to unite you.
Consider in her both royal blood and grace.
To cast her down and set me in her place
Is to bring darkness to the throne of light
And from a shrine drive a divinity
And, by a change as new as it is strange,
Put there instead an idol made of clay.
Ah, for the Queen's sake! ah, for Esther's sake!
Show, show thy justice, sire, this very hour.
Replace us both where heaven bade us be:
The Queen in high, Esther in low degree.
The honor I seek, all I aspire unto,
Is to yield her the throne to whom 'tis due.

A clever touch, that saves her from over-saintliness, is her flash of resentment (for which she immediately apologizes) when the haughty Vashti greets this unselfish plea with the most withering scorn:

VASHTI.[14]

Belle et charmante Esther, épargnez-vous la peine,
A ma confusion, de défendre une reine;
Ne me secourez point dans un sort si douteux;
Le secours d'une esclave est un secours honteux.
Hé, que me servirait, où je suis méprisée,
La faveur d'une esclave en reine déguisée?

ESTHER.

Au moins à faire voir qu'en sa captivité
Cette esclave garda sa générosité:
Et qu'en vous remettant un sceptre qu'on lui donne,
Sa générosité mérite une couronne.
Pardonnez ce transport à mon ressentiment;
Un unjuste mépris l'excite justement.

[14] VASHTI.
Fair, charming Esther, spare thyself the trouble
Of coming, to my embarrassment, to a queen's
Defense. Lend me no aid when so uncertain
Is Fate. Aid from a slave is shameful aid.
Ah, what would serve me, where I am disdained,
The favor of a slave disguised as queen!

ESTHER.
At least 'twill show that in her lot as captive
This slave preserves her generosity,
And that, in giving back a scepter given her,
Her generosity deserves a crown.—
Pardon me this display of indignation.
My being unjustly scorned provokes it justly.

VASHTI.

Déjà la vanité s'empare de votre âme,
Mais enfin, qu'êtes-vous?

ESTHER.

Ce que je suis, Madame,
Telle que d'un grand roi l'ordonnera l'arrêt,
Esclave s'il le veut, et reine s'il lui plaît.

Lancaster says that Esther is bewildered by the treatment
which she receives from Vashti.[15] I can see no trace of bewilderment here.

Unfortunately, there is nothing in the latter part of the
play comparable to these scenes. Mordecai's exhortation of
Esther (IV, i) not to abandon herself to the enjoyment of
her regal greatness, but to use it to save her people as heaven
had obviously intended or else to fear heaven's vengeance,
has been praised, but such admonishing of her is entirely
uncalled for; there has been no previous indication that her
attitude is wrong—indeed, quite the contrary—and hence
the harangue is pointless except to enable Du Ryer to write
an impressive speech. No more than Racine does he succeed
in tying Haman's enforced honoring of Mordecai into the
plot; with him as with Racine it is an unassimilable episode
introduced because it is a famous feature of the Bible story.
The discovery of Haman's part in the old conspiracy against

VASHTI.
Vanity doth possess thy soul already.
But really, what art thou?
ESTHER.
That which I am,
Madam: whatever a great king decrees.
A slave if so he wills; Queen if it please him.

15 *Pierre Du Ryer, Dramatist,* p. 110.

the King is merely ascribed to "the Jews" without informative details or any such stress as its importance deserves. Yet Du Ryer's *Esther,* in spite of its structural defects, is one of the better plays of its times.

Of his two tragedies yet to be discussed, which are now considered his best, one, *Saül* (1640), was in his own day the least popular of all, whereas the other, *Scévole* (1644), enjoyed then and long afterwards a success unmatched by anything else that he wrote. The comparative failure of *Saül* is easy to understand. Dealing with the fate of the Hebrew monarch, King Saul, it is a decidedly meritorious study of a man verging upon melancholia, who is possessed by a "fixed idea" that he is doomed and who thereby involves himself the more hopelessly in disaster, from which he struggles in vain to extricate his sons at least; thus it essentially is a one-role play, and it is lacking in movement and variety.

The first act, indeed, though not notably good, is fairly adequate as an opening act to introduce what should follow. It displays Saul haunted by a sense of heaven's irrevocable wrath against him, especially indicated by the silence of God's oracles; when assured by Jonathan that the enduring loyalty of his subjects is proof to the contrary, he tries to take heart, but is immediately confirmed in his gloom again by the news of the disaffection of Jerusalem; when David is pointed out as the one sure help that will save him, the report comes that David is with the invading Philistines, and Saul's diseased mind at once takes this for a certainty and elaborates upon it. But the second act is quite bad. Its picture of the unfortunate monarch sunk yet deeper in his melancholy, tormented by dreadful imaginings and inconstant of purpose, is well drawn, and no doubt the vacillations of such a man would be as patternless as they are here portrayed, but for effective drama they must be marshaled by the author to some sort of climax; and they are not. Most of the act is taken up with the question of recalling David, which is reopened by Saul's daughter

Michal, who is David's wife. Her insistence results in her father angrily giving her, wife though she is, to his bad-counselor, Phalti; but later the arguments of Jonathan win Saul's reluctant consent, after which the curtain falls. When it rises again, we learn that the King has changed his mind once more and David is not to join him. This decision, then, which is one of the two that seal the fate of Saul, is made between Acts II and III instead of being the climax of a dramatic scene on the stage. His other fatal decision, to seek from the powers of darkness through necromancy the knowledge which he could not obtain from holy priest or prophet, is reached early in Act II; it should instead conclude that act together with his resolve to have none of David, and should be bound up therewith. There can be little doubt that it is this rambling, unorganized second act of *Saül,* following as it does a first act which itself has barely enough movement and incident, that makes the drama as a whole seem somewhat ill-developed, dull, and monotonous. For the rest of this play is really excellent.

When, in Act III, the Witch of Endor raises the ghost of Samuel at Saul's command, we come to the first, and indeed the most, genuinely dramatic scene in the play. It is well prepared for by Jonathan's protests, the King's own hesitancy to take a step so heinous, and the realistic portrait of the obliging, frightened practitioner of black magic; furthermore, the wild, "romantic" setting of night and country-side and cavern's mouth, as presented to the imagination if not to the eye of an audience, was a transfer from tragi-comic to tragic drama, daring at even that early period of decorous French classicism. Jonathan argues plausibly against the value of any revelation of the future by infernal agents:

Croit-on que les démons sachent le cours des armes,[16]

[16] Is it thought that demons can foresee the fortunes

Les succès des combats et les événements
D'où dépendent nos maux et nos contentements?
Quel rayon de clarté, montrant nos aventures,
Les ferait pénétrer dans les choses futures?
Si tout ce qui doit être en tout temps, en tout lieu,
Enfin si l'avenir est seulement en Dieu,
Pense-t-on que l'enfer, ce lieu plein de blasphème,
Sache ce qui se fait dans le sein de Dieu même?
C'est un lâche penser que nous devons bannir,
Les démons seraient Dieux s'ils savaient l'avenir,
Ou parmi les tourments cette engeance mutine
Partagerait au moins la puissance divine.
Quand même les démons volant par l'univers
Verraient de l'avenir les secrets découverts,
Eux qui sont des humains les plus grands adversaires,
Leur annonceraient-ils des succès salutaires?
S'ils annoncent le bien, c'est un appas fatal
Qu'ils sèment sous nos pas pour nous conduire au mal;

Of war, th' outcome of battles, and the events
On which depend our woes and our contentment?
What ray of light that shows what will befall us
Enables them to divine things to come?
If all that shall be in all times, all places,—
In short, the future,—is in God's hands alone,
Can it be that hell, the place of blasphemy,
Knows that which passeth in the breast of God?
That is a vile thought which we ought to banish.
If devils knew the future, they would be gods,
Or midst their torments that rebellious brood
Would at least share with God his power divine.
And even if they, stealing through the cosmos,
Could see laid bare the secrets of the future,
Would those who are man's greatest enemies
Announce to us results that would be helpful?
If they tell good things, 'tis a lure they spread
Before our feet to lead us into evil.

S'ils annoncent les maux, l'horreur et le tumulte,
C'est pour désespérer celui qui les consulte,
Et par le désespoir dont son cœur est pressé,
Le conduire au malheur qu'ils avaient annoncé.

But when Samuel's ghost appears, there is no doubt that its pronouncements of doom, which rise impressively to a climax, are authentic, and Saul's fortitude deserts him at last.

L'OMBRE.[17]

Si le ciel te poursuit, si le ciel t'abandonne,
Crois-tu trouver ailleurs l'appui de ta couronne?
Penses-tu qu'un esprit dépouillé de son corps
Puisse aux arrêts du ciel opposer ses efforts?
Songe qu'un Dieu vivant te tira de la poudre,
Pour te mettre en un rang où l'homme tient la foudre;
Songe qu'il t'éleva dans un trône adoré,
Où tes vœux plus hardis n'eussent pas aspiré;
Mais songe en même temps à la méconnaissance
Dont Saül trop ingrat a payé sa puissance;

If they tell bad things, horror and confusion,
'Tis to make desperate him who doth consult them,
And by the madness which besets his heart
To bring him to the ills they have foretold.

[17] THE GHOST.

If heaven pursues, if heaven abandons thee,
Thinkest thou to find elsewhere thy crown's support?
Deem'st thou a spirit divested of its body
Hath power to oppose the will of heaven?
Remember that a living God once raised thee
Out of the dust, to set thee in that station
Where a man wields the thunderbolt; remember
That he did set thee on a throne of worship
To which thy boldest prayers did not aspire;
And then remember the ingratitude
With which the thankless Saul repaid his bounty.

Souviens-toi que le ciel est ennemi du mal,
Et que tu fus ingrat quand il fut libéral :
Souviens-toi des forfaits qui souillèrent ta vie,
Et tu verras l'horreur dont elle est poursuivie.
Pense à ce peuple saint par tes lois égorgé
Pour avoir contre toi l'innocent protégé,
Pour avoir fait trouver dans l'enclos de sa ville
Au malheureux David la faveur d'un asile.
Pense combien de fois ma voix t'a menacé,
Et pour voir l'avenir regarde le passé.
Le ciel te commanda, tu te montras rebelle ;
Tu lui donnas ta foi, tu lui fus infidèle ;
Et ta rebellion, et ton manque de foi,
Ont allumé les feux qui vont choir dessus toi.
Tu vas tomber du trône, et quoique l'on conspire,
David persécuté va monter à l'empire,
Ce David, cet objet à toi seul odieux,
El l'amour éternel de la terre et des cieux,

Recall that heaven is the foe of evil,
And that thou wert ungrateful when 'twas generous.
Recall the crimes with which thy life is stained,
And thou wilt see how vengeful heaven must loathe it.
Think of the sinless ones thy hest hath slain
Because they shielded innocence from thee,—
Because within the circuit of their city
The hapless David found a kind asylum.
Think of how many times my voice hath warned thee,
And to foresee the future, scan the past.
Heaven laid commands on thee; thou wast rebellious :
Thou pledgedst thy faith thereto; thou wast unfaithful :
And thy rebellion and thy faithlessness
Have lit the fires that shall descend upon thee.
Thou from thy throne shalt fall, and, do thine utmost,
The persecuted David shall mount thither—
That David odious to thee alone
And ever the beloved of earth and heaven—

Ce David de tes maux le souverain remède,
Que ton peuple inspiré demandait pour ton aide,
Ce David repoussé par d'injustes efforts,
Entrera glorieux au trône d'où tu sors,
Et les rois apprendront par ta chute effroyable
Que qui règne en tyran doit périr en coupable.

Saül.

Je reçus la couronne afin de la quitter;
Le ciel me la donna, le ciel peut me l'ôter.

L'ombre.

Mais ce n'est pas assez au ciel qui t'abandonne
D'arracher de ta tête une illustre couronne.
Il livrera les tiens aux mêmes ennemis
Que son bras tout-puissant t'a si souvent soumis;
Il veut que ta défaite et ta pompe étouffée
D'un roi ton adversaire honorent le trophée;

David, the one sure healer of thine ills,
Whom thine own people were inspired to ask for
To be thine aid—yes, David, driven from thee
By thine injustice, shall most gloriously
Assume the throne from which thou shalt descend,
And kings shall learn by thy dread overthrow
That he who reigns a tyrant, needs must die
For his sins' sake.

Saul.
I gained the crown to lose it.
Heaven gave it to me; heaven can take it from me.

The Ghost.
But still 'tis not enough for heaven, which
Abandons thee, to snatch away thy crown.
It will deliver thee to those same foes
Whom its all-powerful arm so oft hath bowed
To thee. It wishes thy defeat and ruin
To exalt a king who was thine adversary.

Il veut, il veut, encore ennemi de tes jours,
Qu'une effroyable mort en termine le cours.

SAÜL.

Hé bien, nous périrons; ce m'est une victoire
Que de perdre la vie aussitôt que la gloire.

L'OMBRE.

Mais ne présume pas, monarque infortuné,
Que par tant de malheurs ton tourment soit borné.
En donnant à tes jours une fin déplorable,
Le ciel te fait sentir la peine d'un coupable;
En te privant d'un trône où tu vivais sans loi,
Le ciel te fait sentir le châtiment d'un roi;
Mais pour comble d'horreur, de peine et de misère,
Le ciel veut t'exposer au supplice d'un père,
Et par un même coup il veut punir en toi
Un père, un criminel, un misérable roi.

It wishes still, still hostile unto thee,
To end thy life's course with a fearful death.
SAUL.
Well, I shall die, then. 'Tis for me a victory
To end my life together with my glory.
THE GHOST.
Do not suppose, however, hapless monarch,
That even these many ills are all thy woes.
In bringing thee to a deplorable end,
Heaven makes thee undergo the penalty
That is a sinner's due. In robbing thee
Of a throne whereon thou livedst lawlessly,
Heaven makes thee undergo the punishment
That is a bad king's due. But for a climax
Of horror, of anguish, and of misery,
Heaven wishes to expose thee to a father's
Pangs, and by one same blow to punish in thee
A sire, a criminal, and a wretched king.

Ne crois donc pas laisser à ta race naissante
Du trône que tu perds ou la gloire ou l'attente;
Ne t'imagine pas revivre en tes enfants
Que tu vis tant de fois revenir triomphants:
Mais sache, malheureux, que ce sont des victimes
Que tu verras tomber sous le faix de tes crimes.
Avant qu'une autre nuit obscurcisse les cieux
Sache que tes enfants périront à tes yeux.

SAÜL.

Hélas! voilà le coup dont l'atteinte me tue. [*Il tombe.*

Act IV declines considerably from this high standard,
but still preserves an adequate amount of interest. It is devoted to the efforts of Saul to keep his children from sharing
his fate. He bids Michal to fly to David, thus reversing his
high-handed action in bestowing her upon Phalti, and attempts to send his sons on errands that will take them away
from the impending battle. But Jonathan refuses to go;
and when the Philistines attack, the others throw themselves
into the fight and Saul and Jonathan rush to join them.

Though less animated than Act III, the fifth act rises
to perhaps even greater heights. Its scene, like that of Act
III, is picturesque far beyond the usage in French-classical
tragedy, showing the skirts of a battlefield, from which the

Think not to leave, then, to thy budding offspring
The honor or expectation of the throne
Thou losest; dream not thou shalt live again
In sons whom thou hast seen so oft return
In triumph; but know, thou wretch, that thou shalt see them
Fall, 'neath the burden of *thy* crimes, as victims.
Before another night makes dark the skies,
Know that thy sons shall die before thine eyes.

SAUL.

Alas! that is the blow that overcomes me. [*He falls.*

army of Israel is streaming in flight. Two of the King's sons
lie dead near at hand, and Jonathan presently appears, fatally
wounded. All of his thoughts are of his father: when in de-
lirium he sees Saul in mortal danger, he cries to his armor-
bearer to go to the rescue; and when Saul at length does approach, Jonathan attempts to hide, so as not to distress him.
The defeated monarch is himself badly wounded; he espies
the bodies of his dead sons, and afterwards Jonathan, whose
death-scene is one of the finest passages by any of the minor
French-classical dramatists. Indeed, in its simplicity, poignancy, and naturalness it is genuinely classical, without ad-
mixture of any elements of French pseudo-classicism, to a degree that can hardly be matched outside the work of Racine,
if even there. It actually calls to mind the famous scene between Theseus and his dying son which concludes the *Hippolytus* of Euripides and except, of course, for being immeasurably inferior poetically, is not altogether unworthy
of comparison with it.

SAÜL.[18]

. . . O toi que ton courage aussi bien que mon sort,
Avecques tant d'horreur, précipite à la mort!
O toi pour qui mon cœur fut capable de craindre,
Dois-je ici, Jonathas, te blâmer ou te plaindre?
Voulais-je t'imposer d'infructueuses lois?
Devais-tu préférer ton courage à ma voix?
Mais pourquoi te blâmer dans ce commun naufrage

---

[18] SAUL.
. . . O thou whose bravery no less than my fate
So horribly hath hurled thee to thy death,—
O thou for whom my heart could be so anxious,
Should I now, Jonathan, blame or pity thee?
Were the commands I sought to give thee needless?
Shouldst thou have heard thy courage, not my voice?
But wherefore blame thee in this common shipwreck

D'avoir moins écouté ma voix que ton courage?
Si le ciel te poussait, pouvais-tu m'écouter?
Si le ciel te poussait, pouvais-je t'arrêter?
Ha! mon cher Jonathas, c'est toi que je dois plaindre,
Et c'est le ciel . . .

JONATHAS.

Ha, Sire!

SAÜL.

Il faut donc se con-
traindre.
Hé bien, sans murmurer supportons nos malheurs,
Bienqu'on ait murmuré pour de moindres douleurs.
O père malheureux!

JONATHAS.

O fils plus déplorable
De ne pouvoir aider un père misérable!
Mais, Sire, sauvez-vous, ainsi soulagez-moi;

For having heard my voice less than thy courage?
If heaven urged thee on, how couldst thou hear me?
If heaven urged thee on, how could I stay thee?
Dear Jonathan, 'tis thou whom I should pity;
'Tis heaven . . .

JONATHAN.

Ah, nay, sir!

SAUL.

Then I must be patient.
Well, let us bear our ills without a murmur,
Though men have murmured at less weighty sorrows.
O hapless father!

JONATHAN.

O yet more wretched son
Who cannot aid a father in his anguish!
But sire, save thyself; thus comfort me.

L'état n'a rien perdu s'il ne perd pas son roi.
Ne pouvant vous servir par ma main impuissante,
Que je vous serve au moins par ma voix languissante;
Peut-être que le ciel satisfait et content,
Veut pour votre salut vous donner cet instant.

SAÜL.

Songer à mon salut, quand je perds un empire!
Quand le ciel me poursuit, quand Jonathas expire!

JONATHAS.

Ma mort est honorable aussi bien que mes coups.
Voulez-vous l'adoucir? ha! Sire, sauvez-vous!

SAÜL.

Un roi qui n'a plus rien à perdre que la vie,
Ne peut trop tôt en perdre, et l'usage et l'envie.

JONATHAS.

Un roi qui se voit libre, et qui porte un grand cœur,

Nations lose nothing till they lose their king.
Since with my strengthless arm I cannot serve thee,
Let me at least with my last accents serve thee.
It may be, heaven with anger satisfied
Offers to thee this moment for thy safety.

SAUL.

What! Think of safety when I lose a kingdom,
When heaven pursues, when Jonathan is dying?

JONATHAN.

My death is honorable, like my wounds.
Wouldst thou fain sweeten it? Ah, save thyself!

SAUL.

A king who hath naught more to lose but life
Cannot too soon lose that nor its desire.

JONATHAN.

A king who still is free and great of heart

Est toujours en état de vaincre son vainqueur.
Sauvez-vous!

SAÜL.

Tout s'oppose au salut de ton père,
La terre, les enfers, et le ciel en colère;
Ce corps même, ce corps, que tu voudrais sauver,
Ce corps qu'à l'ennemi tu voudrais enlever,
Ce corps percé de coups, et que la force laisse,
S'oppose à son salut par sa propre faiblesse.

JONATHAS.

Achas, rappelle Abner, et qu'il vienne au secours.
Ha, Sire!

SAÜL.

Ha! ce moment a terminé ses jours;
Il est mort, ils sont morts, déplorables victimes!
Et ce qui plus me gêne, ils sont morts par mes crimes.
Enfants infortunés, je ne vous pleure pas

Ever may conquer those who conquered him.
Save thyself.

SAUL.

All forbids thy father's safety,—
The earth and hell and heaven in its wrath.
This body itself, this body which thou wouldst save,
This body which thou wouldst bear off from the foe,
This body pierced with blows, whose strength departeth,
Forbids his safety by its own great weakness.

JONATHAN.

Achas, call Abner, bid him come to help!
Oh, sir . . .   [*He falls back, dead.*

SAUL.

Ah me! this moment ends his life.
He is dead, *they* are dead, unhappy victims—
Dead, what is worse, by reason of my crimes!
Children ill-starred, I do not weep for you

Pour avoir ressenti les rigueurs du trépas.
Hélas! de vos vertus votre mort est un gage;
Elle est digne de vous et de votre courage.
C'était pour le pays que vous deviez périr,
Et c'est pour le pays qu'on vous a vu mourir.
Donc cette mort est belle, et vaut mieux que la vie;
Elle n'est pas à plaindre, elle est digne d'envie,
Et telle que des rois heureux et triomphants
La pourraient souhaiter pour leurs propres enfants.
Non, je ne me plains pas de voir dessus la terre
Votre sang répandu par le sort de la guerre,
Mais si le désespoir s'empare de mon cœur,
S'il chasse me raison, s'il se rend mon vainqueur,
C'est parce que je vois que de votre ruine
Mes forfaits seulement ont été l'origine,
Et que par un malheur, qui passe les plus grands,
Le châtiment du père a perdu les enfants.
Epouvantable arrêt du ciel inexorable,

For having tasted of the pangs of death.
Alas, your death bears witness to your manhood;
'Tis worthy both of you and of your courage.
'Twas for your country that ye should have died,
And 'tis for her that men have seen you die.
This death is lovely, then—worth more than life.
'Tis not to be lamented, but desired,
And such that happy and victorious kings
Could well have wished it, too, for their own sons.
Nay, nay, I do not mourn to see your blood
Lie spread out on the ground by chance of war;
But if despair doth seize upon my heart,
Drive reason from my mind, and conquer me,
It is because I see that of your ruin
My crimes alone have been the origin,
And that by the most huge of all misfortunes
A father's punishment hath slain his children.
Fearful the sentence of relentless heaven,

Qui perd trois innocents pour punir un coupable,
Et qui pour m'accabler sous un plus rude poids,
Semble au moins affecter d'être injuste une fois!
Pitoyables objets, ce matin mes délices,
Puisque le ciel le veut maintenant mes supplices,
M'est-il au moins permis d'espérer seulement
D'avoir en nos malheurs un même monument?
Grandeur toujours à craindre, et toujours désirée,
Grandeur partout funeste, et partout adorée,
Charmante illusion qui flattes, qui séduis,
On te suit, on te cherche, et voilà de tes fruits.

                         [*Il montre ses enfants.*

  Quiconque en un empire a de la confiance,
Qu'il considère en moi sa fatale inconstance,
Qu'il juge si d'un roi le destin est si beau,
Le matin dans le trône, et le soir au tombeau,
Et le soir si détruit, qu'à l'instant qu'il succombe
A peine seulement attend-il une tombe;

Which kills three guiltless youths to smite one sinner,
And which, to crush me 'neath a crueler weight,
Seems once, at least, to do what is not justice!
  Pitiful objects, my delight this morning,
Since ye by will of heaven are now my torment,
Is it at least permitted me to hope
That we may have in death one sepulcher?
Ah, greatness always dangerous, always longed for,
Everywhere fatal, everywhere adored,
Winsome illusion, flattering and seducing,
Thou'rt courted, sought, and lo, thy fruits are these.

                         [*He points to his sons.*

  Whoever in a kingdom hath his trust,
Let him, in me, consider how it passeth.
Let him judge if a king's lot be so fair.
Morn finds him on the throne, eve in the tomb,
Yea, so brought low that when he yields his life
He scarcely even doth expect a grave;

A peine seulement peut-il pour son repos
Espérer que la terre enveloppe ses os.
O ciel, quand vous donnez la grandeur souveraine,
Montrez-vous votre amour, ou plutôt votre haine?

The Philistines now draw near, and the King, too weak from his wounds to die fighting, falls on his own sword.

Neither an inept second act nor a too static quality as a whole can keep *Saül,* with such a third and a fifth act and such sobriety and truth in its depiction of human emotions in general, from ranking among the very best plays by the contemporaries of Corneille and Racine.

Whereas *Saül* appeared after *Alcionée* and before *Esther,* *Scévole* appeared after *Esther* and before *Thémistocle*—probably in 1644. This was only three or four years after Corneille's *Horace* and *Cinna;* and now Du Ryer palpably imitated them and sought to rival their great success, and that of *Pompée* in 1643, with a Roman play of his own; for like *Horace, Scévole* is full of the martial spirit and patriotic ardor of early Rome, and like *Cinna* it depicts a good monarch's clemency to those who have conspired against his life and abounds in discussions of political principles. Its imitation of Corneille is at once a source of strength and weakness in it. No other tragedy of this author is so well constructed, so vigorous, or so full of action. But also being, as an imitation of another author's work, one remove further from life than the others, it is more conventionalized and has a less firm grasp on reality than Du Ryer exhibits when at his best.

Its story is, of course, the familiar one of Mucius Scaevola,

---

He scarcely even can for his repose
Hope that the earth will clasp and hide his bones.
O heaven, when thou conferrest regal state,
Is it thy love thou showest or thy hate?

who tried to assassinate the Etruscan king, Lars Porsena, and thus raise the siege of Rome and spare her from having the exiled King Tarquin forced upon her again—how this Roman patriot failed in his endeavor but, when threatened with a cruel death, showed his contempt for tortures by thrusting his right hand into the flames and letting it be consumed, with the result that he was pardoned by his admiring foe. A "love-interest" is concocted by the introduction of Brutus' daughter, Junia, who has been captured by the besiegers. Scaevola loves her, and so does Porsena's son Aruns, whose life Scaevola had previously saved—a complication to afford opportunities for contending emotions and displays of generosity—and Porsena, too, is absurdly represented as loving her, in conformity with French-classical dramatic conventions, according to which everybody who possibly can must be in love. Junia herself secretly loves Scaevola, but both of them are quick to believe the worst of each other—again like French-classical lovers in general. When she finds him disguised in Etruscan armor, she promptly thinks he is so from cowardice (though surely it would not have been wrong of him to try to preserve his life for further usefulness to his country!) ; when she opposes the plan to kill Porsena, he at once concludes that her motive is ambition to become Queen, though the motive of gratitude for Porsena's kind treatment of her (if not the more important motive of wishing to serve Rome's interests better by another course) is plain to see. When Junia tells him that he will risk his life ineffectually, he answers:

> Mais nous en tirerons tous deux de l'avantage ;[19]
> Moi de mourir pour Rome en homme de courage,
> Et toi, de ne voir plus un amant obstiné

[19] Nay, we shall both derive advantage from it:
I dying for Rome's sake like a brave man,
And thou seeing no more a stubborn lover

Que cent fois à la mort tes yeux ont condamné.
Si je n'ai pu gagner ton amour poursuivie
Par les plus beaux travaux qui signalent ma vie,
Laisse-moi, comme en proie à des maux inoüis,
Mériter par ma mort l'amour de mon pays.

"Unexampled woes"! One would think, to hear him, that no other man had ever been unsuccessful in his wooing! And when Aruns finds that his former rescuer not only has tried to slay Porsena but is loved by Junia, he soliloquizes:

Quoi, je puis l'excuser, quand je le considère[20]
Ainsi que l'ennemi du destin de mon père;
Et je ne puis le voir sans haine et sans effroi,
Lorsque comme rival il se présente à moi?

for the conventions of French-classical tragedy do not conceive it natural that to love the same woman may breed a generous instead of a malignant rivalry between honorable men. *Scévole,* says Gustave Reynier, is a work *"purement classique."* [21] It would seem that some French critics are so accustomed to pseudo-classicism in their old "classical" dramas that they cannot recognize it.

At times, the resounding rhetoric of Corneille's Roman

Whom thy cold glance so oft hath doomed to death.
If I could never win thy love, which I
Sought by the fairest deeds that mark my life,
Let me, a prey to unexampled woes,
Deserve my country's love by dying for her.

[20] What! can I pardon him when I regard him
Thus as the enemy of my father's fortunes,
Yet cannot see him without hate and fear
When I perceive him as my rival here?

[21] In Petit de Julleville's *Histoire,* vol. iv, p. 385.

tragedies becomes in the hands of his imitator a bombast amid which unreality has free scope. The turgid description of Horatius at the bridge can be defended as contributing to Porsena's admiration for Rome, which is one of his reasons for raising the siege at last, but its details are grotesque: the victorious Etruscans would never have delayed so long their attack on him, nor would they have assailed him merely with darts instead of rushing upon him in a body at once, and the climax of absurd exaggeration is reached in the statement that the missiles showered upon him as he swam the Tiber served as a wind to waft him faster. Scaevola paints for Junia a highly colored picture of the dire straits to which beleaguered Rome has been reduced by famine, requiring his desperate venture against Porsena:

Il faut ou que demain soit la fin de ses jours,[22]
Ou bien qu'elle reçoive aujourd'hui du secours.
Tarquin ne combat plus pour une ville entière;
Il combat seulement pour un grand cimetière,
Tant le destin de Rome est triste et malheureux.
La famine y produit tout ce qu'elle a d'affreux.
Il n'est rien de funeste en toute la nature,
Que la nécessité n'y change en nourriture.
Bref, le peuple de Rome emploie à se nourrir
Tout ce qui peut aider à le faire mourir.

[22] Tomorrow needs must be the end
Of her, if she receives not aid today.
Tarquin no longer fights now for a city;
He fights now for a great necropolis,
So sad and hapless is the fate of Rome.
Famine there causeth its most dread results.
Nature hath no fatality wherein
Necessity doth not find nourishment.
In brief, the Roman people use for food
All that can help to make them die. And thus

Aussi voit-on partout des images tragiques
Et de malheurs publics et de maux domestiques.
Là, le fils chancelant de faiblesse et d'ennui,
Mettant son père en terre y tombe avecque lui;
Ici, l'enfant se meurt d'une mort triste et lente,
Sur le sein épuisé de sa mère mourante;
Et la mère qui voit ce spectacle inhumain,
Se meurt en même temps de douleur et de faim.
Enfin on voit partout la mort, ou son image;
Chacun la porte au cœur, ou dessus son visage;
Et telle est ta patrie en cette extrémité,
Qu'elle semble un séjour de spectres habité.

But when Porsena spares his life, he in his gratitude reveals that three hundred Roman youths, scattered through the Etruscan camp, have awaited the result of his effort and will each *in turn* try to succeed where he has failed. The author has not observed the contradiction involved between the representation of Rome's last remaining day of life and these successive, methodical, almost leisurely attempts to kill Porsena. There is, of course, a still more serious fault in their disclosure by Scaevola; though this is part of the original story, Du Ryer stultifies the play by

---

Everywhere tragic spectacles are seen
Of public misery and private woes.
There the son, tottering with distress and weakness,
While burying his father, falls beside him.
There the babe dies a piteous, lingering death
Upon his dying mother's breast, drained dry—
And she, beholding this cruel sight, herself
Dieth at the same time of grief and hunger.
One seeth everywhere death or death's image;
It is in every heart or countenance;
And such is thy dear land's extremity,
It seemeth but a dwelling place for ghosts.

introducing it. For the whole emphasis throughout has been on the Romans' suppression of self in the interests of Rome; and here Scaevola tries to pay his personal debt to Porsena by betraying, while there is yet no prospect of peace, the plans of his countrymen which, he himself has said, alone can save her!

A recital of these very serious defects makes it difficult to present afterwards in just perspective the great merits of this drama. Du Ryer has hardly portrayed any other character with such vividness and such economy of effort as the exiled King Tarquin, embittered, savage, arrogant, doubting the gods and their justice, and so churlish that he eventually alienates the temperate, magnanimous Porsena, who is almost equally well drawn. When the heroism of Horatius is glowingly described, Tarquin only interrupts with the impatient query,

Quoi? l'on n'a pu l'abbattre? [23]

and when Porsena is dismayed by unfavorable omens, this "atheistic" king exclaims:

Donc vous vous figurez qu'une bête assommée[24]
Tienne notre fortune en son ventre enfermée,
Et que des animaux les sales intestins
Soient un temple adorable où parlent les Destins?
Ces superstitions et tout ce grand mystère
Sont propres seulement à tromper le vulgaire.

[23] What! could none strike him down?

[24] Dost thou conceive, then, that a slaughtered beast
Holdeth our fortunes hidden in his belly,
And that the foul entrails of animals
Are a fair temple where the Fates are heard?
These superstitions and all this great mystery
Are fit to cozen the common folk alone.

To make his play acceptable in monarchial France, Du Ryer cleverly perverts history and represents the Romans distinguishing between tyrants like Tarquin and upright sovereigns, and abhorring only the former.

The scene in which Junia, after she has found that she cannot wean Porsena from support of the banished king, finally permits Scaevola to proceed with his task and, sending him as she believes to death, confesses her love for him, is well managed and genuinely moving. When he fails and is brought before Porsena, his defiance of his outraged captor is expressed in some of the most striking lines of the play:

PORSENNE.[25]

. . . Quel es-tu, malheureux?

SCÉVOLE

Je suis Romain, Porsenne,
Et tu vois sur mon front la liberté romaine.
J'ai d'un bras que l'honneur a toujours affermi,
Tâché, comme ennemi, de perdre l'ennemi;
Et maintenant qu'un sort plein d'horreur et de blâme,
M'expose à la fureur que j'allume en ton âme,
Je n'ai pas moins de cœur pour souffrir, pour mourir,
Que j'en ai témoigné pour te faire périr.

[25] PORSENA.
. . . Who art thou, wretch?
SCAEVOLA.
I am a Roman, Porsena.
Thou seest Roman freedom in mine aspect.
I with an arm which honor ever strengthened
Attempted, as a foe, to slay a foe;
And when a horrible and shameful fate
Exposes me to the anger that I kindled
Within thy soul, I have a heart as fearless
To suffer and to die as I displayed

J'avais conclu ta mort, ordonnes-tu la mienne?
J'y cours d'un même pas que j'allais à la tienne.
Enfin je suis Romain; et de quelques horreurs
Que tu puisses sur moi signaler tes fureurs,
Le propre des Romains en tous lieux invincibles,
C'est de faire et souffrir les choses impossibles.
Frappe, voilà mon cœur; mais ne présume pas
Par mon sang répandu te sauver du trépas.
D'autres cœurs que le mien forment la même envie;
D'autres bras que le mien s'arment contre ta vie;
Et mille transportés d'un courage aussi fort,
Recherchent comme moi la gloire de ta mort.
Résous toi donc, Porsenne, à ce péril extrême,
De donner chaque instant des combats pour toi-même,
Et d'avoir l'ennemi tôt ou tard ton vainqueur,
Toujours dans ton palais, et proche de ton cœur.
La jeunesse romaine, à la foudre semblable,

To take thy life. I had decreed thy death;
Wilt thou not order mine? I shall go thither
With the same step wherewith I went to slay thee.
For I am Roman, and with whatsoever
Doom thou canst manifest thy wrath against me,
Ever unconquerable is Roman spirit.
It is the spirit to do and to endure
Impossible things. Strike, then. Here is my heart.
But do not think to save thyself from death
By shedding *my* blood. Other hearts than mine
Will have the same thought. Other hands than mine
Will arm themselves to slay thee. And with fervor
Of courage no less great, a thousand others
Will seek like me the glory of thy death.
  Make up thy mind, then, Porsena, in thy peril
To battle every moment for thy life,
And to have foes, thy conquerors late or soon,
Everywhere in thy palace, nigh thy heart.
The youth of Rome, like lightning swift to strike,

Te déclare par moi cette guerre effroyable,
Ne forme des desseins que contre ton salut,
Et de ton cœur sanglant fait sa gloire et son but.
Ne redoute donc plus nos puissantes armées,
A ta confusion si souvent animées,
Mais que chaque Romain t'inspire de la peur
Puisque chaque Romain ne bute qu'à ton cœur.
Si ma main ne t'a pas la lumière ravie,
Ce n'est pas que les Dieux prennent soin de ta vie,
C'est qu'ils veulent, ces Dieux qui combattent pour
    nous,
Que tu sentes la crainte auparavant les coups.

And when his barbarous self-punishment is reported by the astonished, shaken monarch, Junia becomes possessed by the same ardor, and the resulting scene works up to a truly fine climax:

JUNIE.[26]

Juge par ce grand coup, et par ces grands desseins,

Declare through me this fearsome war against thee;
They have no purpose save to kill thee. They
Find in thy heart's blood their one goal and glory.
Then dread no more our army's might, so often
Aroused to thy confusion, but let every
Roman with fear inspire thee, because every
Roman has no aim but to stab thy heart.
If *my* hand hath not reft the light from thee,
'Tis not because the gods protect thy life,
But 'tis because these gods, who fight for us,
Desire thee to feel fear before thy death-blow.

26 JUNIA.

Judge from this great act and from this high purpose

Combien te doit coûter la haine des Romains.

PORSENNE.

Quoi! partout de l'audace?

JUNIE.

Et partout des exemples
De grandeur, de vertu, digne même des temples.

PORSENNE.

Mais dignes des enfers, et d'un sort plein d'horreurs,
Si je laissais agir mes trop justes fureurs.
Certes, par tes discours tu m'as bien fait paraître
Que tu n'ignorais pas l'attentat de ce traitre.
Ingrate, et dans l'instant que tes vœux et son bras,
Cruels également, poursuivaient mon trépas.
Je voulais noblement réparer tes ruines,
Et te donner un sceptre, à toi qui assassines.

How much the Roman people's hate should cost thee.

PORSENA.

What! boldness everywhere?

JUNIA.

And everywhere
Examples of greatness and of manhood, worthy
Of honoring with shrines.

PORSENA.

Nay, worthy of hell
And of a fate full to the brim with horrors.
If I should give free scope to righteous rage,
Thy words past doubt have shown me that thou wert not
Ignorant of this traitor's foul attempt,
Ungrateful woman; and at the very time
When *thy* prayers and *his* arm, equally cruel,
Sought my death, I was trying honorably
To build again thy fortunes and to give
A scepter to thee, who wouldst murder me!

JUNIE.

Oui, tu m'as présenté ces biens et cet honneur,
Où l'ambition même établit son bonheur ;
Mais sache qu'en mon cœur la qualité de reine
Est beaucoup au dessous de celle de Romaine.
Si tu m'as fait un bien, c'est par la liberté
Dont tu caches l'horreur de ma captivité. . . .
J'ai voulu te payer, mais ton aveuglement
T'en a fait refuser le noble payement . . .
Pourquoi par un discours inspiré par les cieux,
T'ai-je représenté les Tarquins odieux ?
Pourquoi t'ai-je voulu, favorable ennemie,
Arracher d'un parti fertile en infamie ;
Et qui ne méritant que des maux éternels,
Fait de ses partisans autant de criminels ? . . .
Mais enfin connaissant que tes mauvais destins
T'attachaient pour te perdre au crime des Tarquins,
Moi-même secondant leur haine découverte,

JUNIA.

Yes, thou hast offered me this gift, this honor,
Wherein ambition bases all its joy;
But know that to my heart the estate of queen
Is much below that of a Roman woman.
If thou a kindness didst me, 'twas in masking
The horror of a captive's lot with freedom. . . .
I tried to recompense thee, but thy blindness
Made thee refuse my noble payment for it . . .
Wherefore did I, with words inspired by heaven,
Picture to thee the infamy of the Tarquins?
Why did I seek, as thy well-wishing foe,
To win thee from a cause most infamous
And worthy of eternal evils, which
Makes all its partisans the same as criminals? . . .
But finally seeing that thine evil star
Linked thee, for thy destruction, with the Tarquins,
I myself seconded the hate it showed.

J'ai poussé le grand cœur qui courait à ta perte;
Je n'ai plus retenu son bras trop malheureux
D'avoir manqué de faire un acte généreux;
Je n'ai plus empêché son illustre colère
D'exécuter un coup si grand, si salutaire;
Car j'appelle les coups salutaires et grands,
Qui poussent aux enfers les amis des tyrans.

PORSENNE.

Ingrate à mes faveurs, tu diras les complices
Si ce n'est par douceur, au moins par les supplices.

JUNIE.

Contente tes fureurs et tes ressentiments.
Ma vertu veut paraître, invente des tourments.
Ce Romain a brûlé sa droite triomphante;
S'il n'en frappe ton cœur, au moins il l'épouvante;

I urged that great heart on, which fain would slay thee.
No more did I restrain that brave arm, now
Hapless in having failed in a brave deed.
No more did I prevent its noble anger
From dealing so great and so benign a blow;
For I call blows "great" and "benign" which hurl
To hell the friends of tyrants.

PORSENA.
                              Thou, ungrateful
For all my favors, shalt declare to me
The names of the accomplices, if not
As a result of kindness, as a result
At least of tortures!

JUNIA.
                    Gratify thy frenzy
And thy vindictiveness. My constancy
Would fain be shown, imagineth new torments.
That Roman burned his right hand, and thus triumphed.
If he stabbed not thy heart, he terrified it

Et moi, pour enchérir par dessus ses efforts,
Je verrai mettre en cendre et ma main et mon corps.

PORSENNE.

Tu veux donc me forcer?

JUNIE.

Tu veux donc me contraindre?

PORSENNE.

Songe que je le puis, et que tu dois le craindre.

JUNIE.

Je ne crains point les maux, les fers, et la rigueur,
Qui peuvent faire voir la force de mon cœur.

Of all the tragedies of the seventeenth century written in
deliberate imitation of Corneille, *Scévole* was the best and
the most successful. It more nearly catches the tone and spirit
of Corneille's Roman dramas than does any other. These facts
and its comparative fame among the plays of Du Ryer
would tend to create an impression that in tragedy he was
primarily a disciple of Corneille. Rather was he himself a
pioneer. In *Saül* and *Esther* he struck off independently;

At least. And I, to outdo his efforts, I
Will see my hand and body both made ashes.

PORSENA.

Thou wishest, then, to make me act?

JUNIA.

Thou wishest,

Then, to constrain me?

PORSENA.

Recollect that I
Can do so, and that thou shouldst fear I will.

JUNIA.

I fear no evils, chains nor tortures rude,
Which can exhibit my soul's fortitude.

Saül especially is an original contribution to tragic drama. *Scévole* stands apart from the rest of his work, with somewhat different faults and merits. In spite of its success he apparently did not care to do anything more of the sort. He went back instead to his earlier field of tragi-comedy, upon which his one subsequent tragedy, *Thémistocle,* verges. Perhaps that field was really more congenial to him, however inferior his achievements in it.

For tragedy is necessarily concerned with strong emotions, and the tragedies of Du Ryer are, save in very rare passages, austerely cold. Of an equally prolific Elizabethan dramatist, Middleton, it has been said that he might almost have rivaled Shakespeare in some respects but for "a fatal coldness of personal temper." [27] This would seem to define Du Ryer's chief defect, aside from his lack of poetic ability— which might perhaps be conceived also to spring, in final analysis, from the same incapacity for emotional fervor. Hence, despite his genuine originality of mind, his intelligence, and his instinct for realities, he did not go beyond the best of his fellow minor dramatists. Middleton found in collaboration with the crude but romantic William Rowley the warmth of human feeling needed to supplement his own gifts and enable him to produce better work than he could do unaided. But Du Ryer never had a Rowley.

[27] *William Shakspere,* by Barrett Wendell, New York, 1894, p. 412.

CHAPTER IV
COSROES: ROTROU'S BEST PLAY

O F all the tragedies written by the minor dramatists of
the Age of Corneille, Rotrou's *Venceslas* (1647) had
the greatest success on the stage. It alone of them was acted
as late as the third quarter of the nineteenth century. Its
performances at the Comédie Française between 1680 and
1857 totaled 227, "a record surpassed by no tragedy of
Rotrou's contemporaries except by seven of Corneille's";
and in evidence of its popularity more than thirty editions of
it appeared between 1648 and 1907.[1]

Among the productions of its author it traditionally shares
first honors for excellence with but one rival and equal.
The most prolific dramatist of his times, and hence customarily writing in haste, Rotrou was little more than a
facile adapter of foreign plays until the very last part of his
too brief career. Neither his amusing comedy, *la Sœur*
(1645), nor his charming tragi-comedy, *Laure persécutée*
(1637), which, with its naively accretionary plot and its
winsome girl-heroine, calls to mind the work of the early
Elizabethan Robert Greene, contains enough original matter to entitle it to a place beside *Venceslas,* in the opinion of
most French critics. That eminence, they have accorded only
to *le Véritable Saint Genest* (1645), and indeed, to the
average well-educated Frenchman of today, and thus to the
world at large in so far as it knows of Rotrou at all, he is the
author of *Saint Genest* and *Venceslas.*

But *Saint Genest* does not really deserve such distinction.
It has enjoyed it partly because of being a convenient martyr-

---

[1] H. C. Lancaster: *A History of French Dramatic Literature
in the Seventeenth Century,* Part II, p. 550.

play to compare and contrast with Corneille's *Polyeucte,* and still more because of the undue importance attached in France to style; it contains Rotrou's best and most characteristic poetry. French criticism recognizes, of course, that *Saint Genest* is exceedingly loose in structure. Its hero and namesake, the head of a troupe of actors in the days of the Roman emperor Diocletian, is converted to Christianity, and in the midst of a Court performance of a play about Christian martyrs, suddenly departs from his lines, testifies to his new-found faith, and thereby himself wins martyrdom. Not only is a large part of the action devoted to the play-within-the-play, but there are gratuitous glimpses of the life of a dramatic company (purely French, nowise Roman) and of the affairs of the Emperor's family. However unassimilable structurally, these excrescences are rather interesting in themselves: nor is the drama damned by its lack of any such struggle over the fate of its protagonist as we find in *Polyeucte;* our interest in *Saint Genest* lies in the suspense arising from our ignorance of just how and when the fatal revelation that the hero is a Christian will be made—an altogether weaker interest but still a genuine one.

The really vital defect in this tragedy is the nature of the play which is represented as being performed before the imperial Court. We cannot possibly imagine that such a play, unmistakably pro-Christian in tone, should have been given in the presence of Diocletian and Maximian, who were trying to stamp out Christianity. If, instead, that religion had been held up to ridicule and obloquy in the enacted drama, only slightly so at first but increasingly until, when a passage was reached where Genest had to show it or its disciples in a most unfavorable light, he had cast aside his role and declared his own convictions with fearless vehemence, a powerful effect would have been achieved. But Rotrou, it must be supposed, was of too timid piety to write blasphemies, even for the pur-

pose of refuting them later, and therefore his martyr-play
has little convincingness or value.

Yet *Venceslas* does not stand alone among the dramas of
Rotrou. It does not, rightly appraised, even stand highest.
That position belongs to *Cosroès* (1648), the last tragedy
which he wrote—a work strangely neglected by most critics,
though Lancaster did consider it second only to *Venceslas*
and Hémon and Reynier seem to rank it first, as did Person.

Venceslas contains perhaps Rotrou's finest single act and
in the figure of Prince Ladislaus his most impressive study
of a single character—one which anticipates Racine in its
depiction of a soul ravaged by frenzies of love and hate.
But it is not really a good play. It creates a striking dramatic
situation, and then fails to work out on its merits the problem
thus posed. King Wenceslaus of Poland has two sons, Ladislaus and Alexander, and a daughter, Theodora. Ladislaus,
the elder prince, is of a fiery, passionate temper; he chafes at
his aged father's retention of the throne and at the favor
enjoyed by the Duke of Courland, who has led to victory the
army which he himself had wished to command. In his
enforced idleness he has become infatuated with Cassandra,
the Duchess of Königsberg, who cannot endure him because
he tried to seduce her before offering honorable marriage,
but who loves and is loved by his younger brother. Fearing
opposition, she and Alexander have concealed their feelings
for each other under the pretense that it is the Duke of Courland who wooes her and whose suit Alexander furthers in
seeing her. Consequently, each time the Duke is about to ask
Wenceslaus, as the reward of his services, for the hand of
the princess Theodora, whom he worships in secret, Ladislaus, thinking he will ask for Cassandra, furiously interposes,
and on learning at length that Cassandra is to be wedded surreptitiously that very night, steals to her home and stabs
his rival there in the dark, not knowing it is his own brother.

Now comes the great act of the play. It opens before the

following dawn, and first reveals Theodora, terrified by an ominous dream and by finding the apartment of Ladislaus empty. Then he himself appears, supported by a friend; he has been wounded in the midnight encounter, and is fainting and dazed. He confesses his deed to his sister, and later to his father, who has risen early and comes upon him unexpectedly. "I have killed the Duke," he declares; and at that moment the Duke enters, announcing that Cassandra implores instant audience with the King. With reeling brain, Ladislaus cries:

O justes cieux! [2]

M'as-tu trompé, ma main? me trompez-vous, mes yeux?
Si le duc est vivant, quelle vie ai-je éteinte?

Cassandra speedily ends the mystery; she brings the news that it is the young prince who has been murdered, and she knows the murderer and asks of King Wenceslaus vengeance for his son upon his son. Here, in the quandary of the king and father, who is the sworn dispenser of justice yet owes his realm an heir,—who has lost one of his two sons and is therefore called upon to lose the other also,—is a subject of rare power. One of the several possible solutions of the dilemma is the one which Rotrou fumbled at. The King can preserve for the land its needed future ruler and for himself his remaining son, and yet still maintain the sovereignty of the law, only by putting Ladislaus above the law—that is, by abdicating in his favor. He can do this the more readily because he has reason to believe that the young man's evil courses have been the result of his inactivity

[2] O ye just heavens! My hand, hast thou deceived me?
Mine eyes, do ye deceive me? If the Duke
Is living, what life was it that I quenched?

and will terminate when his restless energy has outlet and scope, that he is capable of reigning ably, and that his present predicament has sobered him and awakened. his true manhood.

But Rotrou has botched that solution. The issue devolves properly upon Wenceslaus and the Prince—and no one else —and should be settled in view of the considerations of ethics and expediency involved. But in the play the decision of the King is determined—is indeed forced—by the intrusion of factors quite external to the problem itself. The Duke, to whom he has promised any reward whatsoever that he might desire, asks, not for the hand of Theodora, but (by her orders) for the pardon of Ladislaus. Theodora begs for it. Cassandra, persuaded by her, withdraws all demands for vengeance. Finally the populace rise in favor of the Prince. Wenceslaus could not punish him, if he would.

Moreover, the regeneration of Ladislaus is not depicted as sufficient to make such a solution satisfactory. He acknowledges that death is what he deserves, and he faces the prospect of it with commendable fortitude, but his acquiescence in the doom which threatens him springs less from a suitable detestation of his crime than from the fact that Cassandra desires it; his passion for her still dominates him. When elevated to the throne, he instantly renews his efforts to gain her hand; and by the ghastliest of artistic blunders it is with this act of supreme effrontery, in which he hopes to profit by his brother's murder and which leaves us with the suggestion that he is precisely the same unchanged and unchastened man as ever, that the play ends— Cassandra recoiling in horror at the thought of marriage with her lover's assassin, and the King assuring them that time will reconcile her to such a step! It is a palpable copy of the final scene of Corneille's *Cid*—but with every moral factor that justifies that ending, condemning this one—and the French critics of those days apparently saw no difference be-

tween the two, or rather raised clamorous protest against
Corneille and none that we know of against Rotrou! After
all, Cassandra's lover was not actually married to her! and
hence, they probably reasoned, she had no such obligation to
him as Chimene had to her father; inflexible prescriptions of
formal relationships, without regard to the facts of circumstances or feelings, constituted their entire code.

There is a further imitation of the *Cid* in the role of Theodora, who, like Corneille's Infanta, hesitates between her love
and her reluctance, as a king's daughter, to wed a subject.
Her treatment of the Duke is extremely shabby, by our
standards. Even when Ladislaus in the end gives her to him,
she has not the grace to admit that the union accords with her
own wishes; and earlier, when she supposes that it was he
who was the victim of the Prince, she chides herself for regretting the death of one who she believes loved Cassandra
instead of her. An amiable princess, truly!

But indeed the whole secret of the Duke's affections is so
handled as to constitute another major fault in this drama.
It is absurd that he should think, each time Ladislaus forbids him to name as his reward the object of his desires, that
the Prince is aware that he would ask for Theodora and is beside himself with rage on this account; for the Duke is openly
pretending to woo Cassandra (a pretense which must deceive
Ladislaus like everybody else), whereas he has hidden from
all the world his love for Theodora. Anyone would realize
that the Prince imagines he will ask for Cassandra, and calls
him presumptuous not for aspiring to wed Ladislaus' sister,
but for daring to be Ladislaus' rival and ask for the lady
whom Ladislaus himself seeks to wed. It is also unreasonable
that the Duke should not recognize that Theodora too may
be deceived by his feigned attentions to Cassandra; but he
never views her conduct in the light of that possibility. And it
is ridiculous, when the Prince has interposed a second time
and then stalked off defiantly, that the now angered Wences-

laus does not command the Duke to resume his interrupted petition and say who it is that he loves; everything that has gone before makes it inevitable that he would be ordered to do so then and there. In these misunderstandings and postponings, on which the course of events largely depends, we see a dramatist's arbitrary manipulation of his characters for convenience in shaping his plot.

Now, though *Cosroès* has no act which is the equal of the fourth act of *Venceslas,* its merit is much better sustained throughout, and its entire first half is of a really notable excellence. True, in the latter part of Act III and in Act IV it deteriorates, chiefly because of the intrusion here of the unnecessary and conventional figure of Narsea; but Act V returns to something like the standard of the first two and a half acts. And though this play does not possess the emotional intensity of *Venceslas* nor any figure so vivid and vital as the Prince, it is written with naturalness, imaginative competence, and restrained power, and is peopled with well conceived and clearly presented characters.

Cosroès, moreover, furnished the model for the better drama of a greater man, the *Nicomède* of Corneille. That is perhaps a reason for the neglect it has suffered: *Nicomède* treated a very similar situation with a brilliancy that eclipsed its predecessor. Yet *Cosroès* itself has enough merit to deserve some little fame, and it contains, indeed, important elements not included in *Nicomède*—grim elements which are its very heart, and which require for it, in contrast to the other play, a tragic ending.

Like Prusias in *Nicomède,* the king here, Chosroes of Persia, has married twice, and by his second wife, Sira, has a son, Mardesanes. But as in *Nicomède,* there was also a son by the first marriage, Siroes, the rightful heir to the throne; and (still as in *Nicomède*) his step-mother hates him and seeks to bend the will of her doting husband to set her own child in his place. The parallel is too close to be attributable to

chance, especially since Rotrou's play appeared in 1648 and
Corneille's late in 1650 or early in 1651. But Sira is impelled
quite as much by hate of her step-son as by love for her son;
and Chosroes is no semi-comic Prusias but a man sinking
deeper and deeper into madness through the gnawings of remorse because he gained his crown by overthrowing and killing his predecessor, his own father. How else, in these circumstances, can Siroes prevent the loss at once of his heri-
tage and of his life than by overthrowing and killing *his*
father?

The first scene of the play is a quarrel between Siroes and
Sira—a one-sided quarrel, however, for the young man answers his step-mother's abuse respectfully though with
dignity, until she finally says, "I will die, traitor, or my son
shall reign!" Then he instinctively lays his hand on his
sword, and at that moment Mardesanes enters. "He tried to
murder me," the Queen declares, before storming out. Siroes
protests his innocence of the charge, and the two princes
discuss the situation with amicable frankness. "Do not be
disquieted by my mother's zeal for me," the younger begs.
"You and I are at one about this matter. I would not have
a scepter that is rightly yours, nor the cares and dangers of
its usurped possession."—"Your mother will win it for you
without your connivance; then, when it is in your grasp, you
will find supreme power too sweet to refuse it, just as you
now find sweet your newly acquired command of the Persian
army."—"But I *will* refuse it," insists Mardesanes.—"Since
you say so, I must trust you. But remember: if you ever do
betray that trust, be sure to kill me, for it will then be my
life or yours."

Seeing the great Persian noble, Palmiras, now approach,
Mardesanes takes leave of his half-brother. "You do ill to
yield place to me," mutters Palmiras, gazing after him, "just
as you did ill to take my command of the army from me.
That was Sira's work, in long-sought revenge for my op-

position to the King's marriage with her." He turns to
Siroes. "Be warned by my fate, Prince, and forestall your
ruin while you still can."

But Siroes is sunk in meditation, as he walks back and
forth, revolving in his mind the Queen's last words:

"Mais je périrai, traître, ou mon fils régnera.[3]
Qu'ai-je à délibérer après cette menace?
Quoi! Mardesane au trône occupera ma place!
Et l'orgueil de sa mère, abusant à mes yeux
De l'esprit altéré d'un père furieux,
Par l'insolent pouvoir que son crédit lui donne,
Sur quel front lui plaira fera choir ma couronne!
Quel crime ou quel défaut me peut-on reprocher
Pour disposer du sceptre et pour me l'arracher?
Ma mère, ma naissance, en êtes-vous coupables?
D'un sort si glorieux sommes-nous incapables?
Veut-on, après vingt ans, jusque dans le tombeau
Souiller une vertu dont l'éclat fut si beau?
Non, non, le temps, ma mère, avecque trop de gloire
Laisse encor dans les cœurs vivre votre mémoire;

[3] "I will die, traitor, or my son shall reign."
After this threat, what have I still to ponder?
Yes, Mardesanes will sit on the throne
Instead of me! and his proud mother will
Before mine eyes beguile my father's mind,
Which madness hath impaired, and by the power
Her influence o'er him giveth her, will set
My crown upon the brow where she desires it!
What crime or what defect is mine, that one
May snatch my scepter and bestow it elsewhere?
My birth, my mother, is there blame in them?
Are we unfit to fill a glorious station?
Would any, after twenty years, besmirch
E'en in the tomb a virtue once so fair?
Nay, nay, my mother, time with too much honor
Still keeps thy memory living in men's hearts.

C'est un exemple illustre aux siècles à venir,
Que la haine respecte et ne saurait ternir.
Mon crime est seulement l'orgueil d'une marâtre,
Dont un fils est l'idole, un père l'idolâtre.

He prays heaven to protect him in his rights; but Palmiras
counsels action. "Do not ask divine aid when you can aid
yourself. Friends will rally to you on every side. Weariness
of our unending war with Rome, the soldiers' preference for
me as their leader, the memory of the previous king's death,
the wrongs and humiliations suffered by this satrap and
that, your splendid youth, Chosroes' madness and Sira's
domination of him, all conspire in your behalf. Understand
that if you are deprived of the succession you will be killed
forthwith; the Queen would not dare to leave you alive."

The whole essence of this drama is contained in the lines
that follow.

Siroès, *rêvant.*[4]

Laisser ravir un trône est une lâcheté,
Mais en chasser un père est une impiété.

Palmiras.

Que, pour vous l'enseigner, lui-même il a commise.

For centuries it will be a thing illustrious
Which hate shall reverence and cannot stain.
My sole crime lies in having a proud step-mother,
Who loves her son, and whom my father worships.

[4] Siroes (*thoughtfully*).
To let one's throne be stolen is craven, but
To drive one's father thence is impious.
Palmiras.
Which he, to teach thee how, himself hath been!

SIROÈS.

Par son exemple, hélas! m'est-elle plus permise,
Et me produira-t-elle un moindre repentir?

PALMIRAS.

Vous ne l'en chassez pas, puisqu'il en veut sortir,
Ou que votre marâtre, à mieux parler, l'en chasse,
Pour y faire à son fils occuper votre place.

SIROÈS.

Il m'a donné le jour.

PALMIRAS.

Il donne votre bien.

SIROÈS.

Mais c'est mon père enfin!

PALMIRAS.

Hormisdas fut le sien,

SIROES.

Alas! doth his example justify me
Better, and shall it cause me less repentance?

PALMIRAS.

Thou dost not drive him from the throne, since he
Desires to leave it, or since thy step-mother,
To speak more accurately, drives him from it
So that her son shall occupy thy place there.

SIROES.

He gave me life.

PALMIRAS.

He gives away thy birthright.

SIROES.

Yet 'tis my father.

PALMIRAS.

Hormisdas was *his* father;

Et, si vous agissez d'un esprit si timide,
Gardez d'être l'objet d'un second parricide.
Qui n'a point épargné le sang dont il est né
Peut bien n'épargner pas celui qu'il a donné.

SIROÈS.

O dure destinée, et fatale aventure!
J'ai pour moi la raison, le droit et la nature;
Et, par un triste sort, à nul autre pareil,
Je les ai contre moi si je suis leur conseil.
Du sceptre de mon père héritier légitime,
Je n'y puis aspirer sans un énorme crime:
Coupable, je le souille; innocent, je le perds;
Si mon droit me couronne, il met mon père aux fers;
Et de ma vie, enfin, je hasarde la course,
Si mon impiété n'en épuise la source.
O mon père! ô mon sang! ne vous puis-je épargner?
Ne puis-je innocemment ni vivre ni régner?
Et ne puis-je occuper un trône héréditaire

And if thou art so faint of heart, beware
Of being the victim of his second crime.
He who spares not the blood from which he sprang
May well not spare that which proceeds from him.

SIROES.

O bitter destiny! O cursèd fortune!
Upon my side are reason, right, and nature;
And by a sad fate, like no other's, they
Are 'gainst me, if I follow their advice.
Though lawful heir unto my father's scepter,
I cannot hope to have it, save by crime.
Guilty, I stain it; innocent, I lose it.
If my right crowneth me, my sire must wear
Chains; and I risk my life if I do not
Impiously quench the source from which 'twas mine.
O father, mine own blood, can I not spare thee?
Can I not innocently either live or reign?
Can I not sit on our ancestral throne

Qu'au prix de la prison ou du sang de mon père?

But at this moment Pharnaces, another nobleman, enters, saying it is reported in the camp that the King intends to crown Mardesanes before the army; and Siroes hesitates no longer. So ends the first act. Quotation cannot do justice to it, for its excellence is not to be savored in isolated passages but lies rather in its high quality as a whole—most of all in the conduct of the action and in the exhibition and interplay of the characters. The same is equally true, or even truer, of the second act.

This shows Chosroes in one of his fits of madness:

> Quoi! n'entendez-vous pas, du fond de cet abime,[5]
> Une effroyable voix me reprocher mon crime,
> Et, me peignant l'horreur de cet acte inhumain,
> Contre mon propre flanc solliciter ma main?
> N'apercevez-vous pas, dans cet épais nuage
> De mon père expirant la ténébreuse image
> M'ordonner de sortir de son trône usurpé,
> Et me montrer l'endroit par où je l'ai frappé?
> Voyez-vous pas sortir de cet horrible gouffre,
> Qui n'exhale que feu, que bitume et que soufre,

Save by my sire's imprisonment or death?

[5] What! Hearest thou not from the depths of yon abyss
A fearful voice reproach me for my crime,
Picture the horror of that monstrous deed
To me, and 'gainst mine own breast urge my hand?
And canst thou not espy in yon thick mist
The shadowy image of my dying father,
Who orders that I quit his throne usurped
And shows to me the place where fell my blow?
Seest thou not, issuing from yon dreadful chasm
Which belches fire and sulphur and bitumen,

Un spectre décharné qui, me tendant le bras,
M'invite d'y descendre et d'y suivre ses pas?
O dangereux poison, peste des grandes âmes,
Maudite ambition, dont je crus trop les flammes,
Et qui pour t'assouvir ne peux rien épargner,
Que tu m'as cher vendu le plaisir de régner!
Pour atteindre à tes vœux, et pour te satisfaire,
Cruelle, il t'a fallu sacrifier mon père.
Je t'ai d'un même coup immolé mon repos,
Qu'un remords éternel traverse à tout propos.
Il te faut de moi-même encor le sacrifice,
Et déjà dans le ciel j'ois gronder mon supplice,
Et son funèbre apprêt noircir tout l'horizon.

He recovers his sanity, and sadly confesses that he cannot put aside the recollection of that deed of which all his realm and rule remind him. "Then cast off their burden," Sira urges. "I will thus be a queen no longer, but your good is more precious to me than everything else in the world. And we do not really cease to reign when our flesh and blood reigns in our place." She invokes the solar deity to witness that it is not ambition for her son that makes her advise

A fleshless ghost stretching an arm to me,
Who bids me to descend there, following him?
O deadly poison, malady of great souls,
Cursèd ambition, unto which I hearkened
And which, to glut thyself, canst stop at nothing,
How dearly hast thou sold me kingship's joys!
To achieve thine aims and give thee satisfaction,
Cruel voice, I had to sacrifice my father.
With the same stroke I sacrificed my peace,
Which endless remorse thwarts at every turn.
There still remains to sacrifice myself
To thee, and in the skies I hear already
The rumblings of the storm that will fall on me,
And its approach makes all the horizon dark.

the bestowal of the crown on him rather than on Siroes, but regard for the best interests of Chosroes alone. The claims of primogeniture are of doubtful validity while the King still lives; he can depute his power to whomever he pleases. He would find Mardesanes the safer depository, the more pliant instrument. Ruling only through sufferance, her son would rule according to Chosroes' desires. Siroes, on the other hand, with his own rights to the throne, would no sooner attain it than he would wish to rule as he pleased; Chosroes might presently seem a vexatious clog to his activities, and Sira could fear the worst from him, especially as on that very morning he had drawn his sword against her and only the arrival of Mardesanes saved her life.—"O gods!" exclaims Chosroes. "What do you tell me?"—"I was not surprised. He hates me because you love me. What, then, could I expect from his enthronement? But raise Mardesanes to the supreme station and he will faithfully make your comfort and your will his one concern. I know him; he is the child of our love; I dare to stake my life on his loyalty."
Chosroes hesitates no longer.

> Par les pleurs que je dois aux cendres de mon père,[6]
> Par le char éclatant du dieu que je révère,
> Par l'âge qui me reste, et qu'il éclairera,
> Mardesane, Madame, aujourd'hui régnera!

he declares. To no avail the attending captain of the guard objects that this decision is fraught with danger; he is bidden to hold his peace, and, for a precaution, to arrest Siroes. "On your head be it to obey."—The captain unwillingly goes out.

---

[6] Now, by the tears I owe my father's ashes,
By the bright chariot of the god I worship,
By the old age still left me, which he lights,
Madam, this day shall Mardesanes reign!

Mardesanes enters, and Chosroes informs him of what is intended. He, too, objects. "I am yours utterly; I could have no greater wish or honor than to be the prop of your old age. Give me the power that wearies you, but keep your rank. If you must resign both rank and power, give them to Siroes. They are his by law."—"A father's mandate is the highest law," says Chosroes.—"Vain is my mother-love for a child without the heart to govern!" exclaims Sira.

Mardesanes answers:

> D'un sang assez ardent n'animez pas les flammes;[7]
> J'ai tous les sentiments dignes des grandes âmes,
> Et mon ambition me sollicite assez
> Du rang que je rejette et dont vous me pressez.
> Un trône attire trop, on y monte sans peine;
> L'importance est de voir quel chemin nous y mène,
> De ne s'y presser pas pour bientôt en sortir,
> Et pour n'y rencontrer qu'un fameux repentir.
> Si j'en osais, Seigneur, proposer votre exemple,
> De cette vérité la preuve est assez ample.
> Ce bâton, sans un sceptre, honore assez mon bras.
> Grand roi, par le démon qui préside aux Etats,
> Par ses soins providents, qui font fleurir le vôtre,

[7] Rouse not the fires of one who lacks not ardor!
I have all feelings that befit great souls,
And my ambition summons me full loudly
To the station I refuse and thou'dst force on me.
Too much a throne allures; one mounts it gladly;
But one should scan the road which leads one to it,
And not press on thereto only to leave it
Soon and to find there naught save great repentance.
If I might dare, sire, to name thy example,
The proof that I speak truly, would be ample.
   Enough my hand by this baton is honored
Without a scepter. Great king, by the Genius
That watches over States; by all his cares

Par le sang de Cyrus, noble source du nôtre,
Par l'ombre d'Hormisdas, par ce bras indompté,
D'Héraclius encore aujourd'hui redouté,
Et par ce que vaut même et ce qu'a de mérite
La reine, dont l'amour pour moi vous sollicite,
De son affection ne servez point les feux,
Et, sourd en ma faveur, une fois, à ses vœux,
Souffrez-moi de l'empire un mépris salutaire,
Et sauvez ma vertu de l'amour d'une mère.
Songez de quel périls vous me faites l'objet,
Si votre complaisance approuve son projet.
Les Grecs et les Romains, aux pieds de nos
    murailles,
Consomment de l'Etat les dernières entrailles,
Et, poussant jusqu'au bout leur sort toujours vain-
    queur,
En ce dernier asile en attaquent le cœur.
Des satrapes mon frère a les intelligences,
Et cette occasion, qui s'offre à leurs vengeances,

Which make thine prosper; by the blood of Cyrus,
The noble source of our blood; by the ghost
Of Hormisdas; by thine own unconquered arm,
Which Heraclius stands in dread of, still;
And by the worth and merit of the Queen
Herself, whose love solicits thee for me,
Minister not to the fires of her affection,
And, deaf for my sake once unto her prayers,
Permit in me a wise disdain of empire;
Save from a mother's love my rectitude!
    Thou makest me the target of what perils
If thy consent approveth her design!
The Greeks and Romans even to our walls
Will the whole body of the State devour,
And with their fortunes thus triumphant always,
In this last refuge will attack its heart.
My brother has the good will of the satraps,
And the occasion offered them for vengeance

Donne un pieux prétexte à leurs soulèvements,
Et va faire éclater tous leurs ressentiments.
Un Palmiras, enflé de tant de renommée,
Démis de ses emplois et chassé de l'armée;
Un Pharnace, un Saïn, dont les pères proscrits
D'une secrète haine animent les esprits,
Peuvent-ils négliger l'occasion si belle,
Quand elle se présente, ou plutôt les appelle?
Si l'ennemi, le droit, les grands, sont contre moi,
Au parti malheureux qui gardera la foi?
Par qui l'autorité que vous aurez quittée
Sera-t-elle, en ce trouble, ou crainte, ou respectée,
Si pour donner des lois il les faut violer?
En m'honorant, Seigneur, craignez de m'immoler.

But the absolute command of Chosroes constrains him
to accept the crown; he only prays that the consequences of
his elevation may fall on him alone.

Siroes now comes in. He has heard what is afoot, and
reminds Chosroes and Sira that he but recently, at the cost
of wounds, had saved the life of their son in battle. "You

Supplies for their revolt a pious pretext
And will make all their enmity burst forth.
Can a Palmiras, swollen with his renown,
Dismissed from office now and from the army,
A Pharnaces, a Saïn, in whose breasts
Hate burns because their fathers were proscribed,
Neglect so rare an opportunity
When it presents itself, nay, cries out to them?
If the enemy, justice, and our great men
Are all against me, to my luckless cause
Who will stand loyal? The authority
Which thou wilt have laid down, will be by whom
Feared or respected in this time of strife
If I must break the law when I dispense it?
Beware lest thou, in honoring me, destroy me.

have informed us of this quite often enough already," says
the Queen; "and our debt to you for it, if it ever happened,
was counterbalanced by your attempt upon my life today."—
"I made no such attempt."—But Chosroes refuses to listen
to Siroes' assertion of innocence, and enjoins him to bow
to the order which has been issued concerning him.

"What is this order?" Siroes asks the captain of the
guard, who enters as the others go out.—"To arrest you,
Prince, as I value my head. But I will not arrest you. I lay
my head and my office at your feet. It is time to wrench
from your step-mother's clutches the realm which calls to
you and worships you."—"Come; let us loose the lightning,
then," says Siroes.

Act III finds Sira exulting over the triumph, as she thinks,
of her designs. To an audience which has just beheld their
miscarriage at the end of the preceding act, her jubilation to
Hormisdate, her attendant, is full of the keenest dramatic
irony. Warned that her success may be short-lived (for Persia, if at first surprised into acquiescence, will presently refuse to let its laws be overridden and its rightful prince wear
chains), she seeks to use Hormisdate to forestall sedition.
"You have a brother, Artanasdes; greatness lies today within your grasp and his," she tells her. "Let him take this
dagger and this poison cup to Siroes in prison, and if Siroes
will not choose one of these two offered means of death,
himself kill him."—Hormisdate conceals her horror and
feigns to be persuaded.

The thunderbolt poised above the Queen's unwitting head
now falls. Sardaric, the captain of the guard, enters.

SIRA.[8]

Votre ordre, Sardarigue, est-il exécuté?

***

[8] SIRA.
Hath the charge given thee, Sardaric, been performed?

SARDARIGUE.

Non, Madame, à regret j'en exécute un autre.

SIRA.

Quel?

SARDARIGUE.

De vous arrêter.

SIRA.

Quelle audace est la vôtre!

Moi, téméraire?

SARDARIGUE.

Vous.

SIRA.

De quelle part?

SARDARIGUE.

Du roi.

SARDARIC.

Nay, I perform another with regret,
Madam.

SIRA.

What?

SARDARIC.

To arrest thee.

SIRA.

How audacious

Thou art! Me, rash man?

SARDARIC.

Thee.

SIRA.

For whom?

SARDARIC.

The King.

SIRA.

Imposteur! Cosroès t'impose cette loi?

SARDARIGUE.

Cosroès n'a-t-il pas déposé la couronne?

SIRA.

Qui donc? est-ce mon fils, traître, qui te l'ordonne?

SARDARIGUE.

Votre fils m'ordonner! en quelle qualité?

SIRA.

De ton roi, de ton maître, insolent, effronté!

SARDARIGUE.

Siroès est mon roi, Siroès est mon maître:
La Perse sous ces noms vient de le reconnaître.

SIRA.

Dieux!

SIRA.

Impostor! Chosroes lays this charge on thee?

SARDARIC.

Hath Chosroes not resigned the crown?

SIRA.

What, then?

Is it my son who thus commands thee, traitor?

SARDARIC.

Thy son command me! In what capacity?

SIRA.

That of thy king, thy master, insolent dog!

SARDARIC.

Siroes is my king; he is my master.
Persia hath just acclaimed him with these titles.

SIRA.

Gods!

Nowhere may she look for assistance. Her threats of dire revenge if Fortune again should turn are heard with a shrug; Siroes comes in, attended by Palmiras and guards, and bids her have done with pride and bow to his authority as he formerly bowed to hers.

Sira.[9]

Perfide, après ma place en mon trône usurpée!

Siroès.

Après ma place au mien justement occupée.

Sira.

Vôtre, un père vivant, et pendant que je vis?

Siroès.

Mien, quand vous prétendez y placer votre fils.

Sira.

Si le sceptre est un faix que le roi lui dépose?

Siroès.

Si la loi de l'Etat autrement en dispose?

---

[9] Sira.
Traitor, my place usurped upon my throne!
    Siroes.
Rightfully taking my place on my own.
    Sira.
Thine, while thy father lives and while I live?
    Siroes.
Mine, though thou seekest to set thy son thereon.
    Sira.
When the King lays the scepter's load on him?
    Siroes.
When the land's laws consign it otherwhere?

SIRA.

Le roi n'étant point mort, vous n'avez point de droit.

SIROÈS.

Quittant le nom de roi, c'est à moi qu'il le doit.

SIRA.

Il croit servir l'Etat par cette préférence.

SIROÈS.

L'Etat de l'un et l'autre a fait la différence.

Palmiras interposes, and reminds Siroes that it is not becoming to bandy words with people under arrest. The firmest foundation for a throne is the blood of foes, he continues when Sira has been led away; a monarch must use his power drastically at first. Victory is now in Siroes' hands; only the fall of two heads is needed to ensure its permanence.

But the new sovereign still shrinks from extremities against his father. "Though a king, I yet feel myself a son," he protests.—"A son, forsooth! Yes, you are the son of a sire who no longer feels himself a father, knows no son except Mardesanes, and puts him in your place to cheat you of it!"— "Reason assents to your logic; but what a destiny is thrust upon me!" exclaims Siroes.

Je regrette d'un père ou la perte ou la fuite,[10]

SIRA.
The King not being dead, thou hast no rights.
SIROES.
He owes me the King's title when he doffs it.
SIRA.
He thinks to serve the nation by his preference.
SIROES.
The nation hath decided differently.

[10] I sorrow for a father's death or flight,

> Mais ce regret n'en peut arrêter la poursuite.
> Hors du trône, mes jours n'ont plus de sûreté :
> Tout mon salut consiste en mon autorité ;

and when Palmiras has gone out to inspect the city, he cries in an anguished revulsion of feeling:

> Que tu m'aurais, ô sort, dans un rang plus obscur,[11]
> Fait goûter un repos et plus calme et plus pur!
> Les pointes des brillants qui parent les couronnes
> Figurent bien, cruel, les soins que tu nous donnes,
> Et ce vain ornement marque bien la rigueur
> Des poignantes douleurs qui nous percent le cœur.

He now beholds Narsea approaching—Narsea, his betrothed;[12] Narsea, the supposed daughter of Sira by the Queen's former marriage with Sapor, King of Armenia. She has not appeared hitherto, and would seem to have been added as an afterthought, to supply "love-interest"—

> Yet though I sorrow, still must I pursue him.
> Save on the throne, my life no more is safe.
> All my security lies in my reigning;

[11] Would thou hadst given me, Fate, a lowlier rank
And let me taste of peace more calm and pure!
Cruel goddess, the bright stones that crowns are set with
Symbolize well the cares thou givest us,
And such vain ornaments show well the hardness
Of those sharp griefs with which thou stabbest our hearts.

[12] "It is not clear whether she is the hero's fiancée or his wife," says Lancaster (*op. cit.,* Part II, p. 553). The words addressed to her in IV, iii, "Par votre hymen futur je vous crois souveraine" ("I deem thee, because of thy coming marriage, my sovereign") should make it clear enough, even if we do not accept the lines which appear in Act I in one of the two early editions of this play, in which Siroes says that he and Narsea are secretly in love.

or perhaps was invented to fill space, for Rotrou could seldom stretch his treatment of a single theme to occupy five whole acts. In any case, her introduction so late and to so little purpose is a serious blemish in the play. Moreover, there is something frigid and artificial in the scenes in which she figures; the conventional language of gallantry makes its appearance with her; and her story, which later transpires, is a very hackneyed one. But though unnecessary to the plot, she does serve the function of showing yet another distressing complication which may result from such violence to family ties as the *coup d'état* of Siroes entails.

For she comes in order to learn what position she now occupies. Can Siroes love her and expect to wed her, and yet have imprisoned her mother?—"I imprisoned her as I did my father," he answers. "Empire and safety compelled me."—"Is empire worth this inhumanity?"—"Ask *them* that question. Do I owe anything to one who would arrest me? Must I thank him for life who would take mine? You will have to choose between Sira and me: me, who love you and whom she would send to the scaffold if she could!"— "But have you not the power, now, to prevent this?"—"I will indeed prevent it," he assures her, grimly. "I dare not risk the chance of a counter-stroke against my still new authority."—"Then kill me also!" she cries, "you, that must take no risks! Might I not strike to avenge my mother? Could I endure her murderer as my husband or share a power cemented by her blood?"

The sight of Narsea's anguish is too much for Siroes. "Take the guards and do with Sira as you will," he says. "It means my death, but no matter."—"Then I will die with you. But truly, I will watch over you well and be your shield; and I promise you life, the throne, and myself."

The fourth act is largely concerned with Narsea. Artanasdes tells Siroes of being suborned by the Queen to effect his death in prison, and shows him the deadly cup and the

dagger which she supplied for that purpose. When Siroes
exclaims against this wicked woman, whose life he has just
granted to her daughter, Artanasdes says that the Queen is
not Narsea's mother and hence can be dealt with as she deserves. The story which he then relates to Siroes is the
time-worn, over-worked tale of children exchanged in their
cradles. The infant Narsea, just after Sira married Chosroes,
died of a sudden attack of convulsions, and Hormisdate, who
was her nurse, rushed with the news to Artanasdes, in terror
of the Queen's wrath. She found him at the house of Palmiras, who substituted his own infant daughter for the dead
child. Narsea is the daughter of Palmiras.

The captain of the guard now appears and tells how the
whole army rose in revolt when Mardesanes was proclaimed
king before it. It is at this moment bringing him and Chosroes there as prisoners. Shall they be led in?—Siroes cannot
yet steel himself to look upon his father. He commands that
they be held in the adjoining room and, struggling to restrain his tears, goes out in the opposite direction. Narsea
enters, on her way to release Sira from prison; but Palmiras
at this moment comes with orders to the contrary. The
lengthy scene between him and Narsea is rather absurd: he
takes much more time in declaring that she has no cause
for concern and no comprehension of his relationship to her,
but that he cannot stop now to explain matters, than would
have been required to enlighten her. Then he decides that he
will do so; and then, before he can, Artanasdes rushes in with
the news that Palmiras is needed at once to prevent the filial
compunctions of Siroes from ruining everything, and he
accordingly hastens away, leaving Artanasdes the task of informing Narsea of her real identity.

In Act V the prisoners are brought one by one before
Siroes. The Queen will not stoop to beg for mercy, nor
will she abate her venomous hatred of him.

La pointe de mes traits a tourné contre moi;[13]
Et, par où j'ai voulu mettre un fils en ta place,
Je te mets en la mienne et m'acquiers ta disgrâce.
J'ai fait plus; j'ai tenté, pour le coup de ta mort,
Par le bras d'un des miens, un inutile effort;
J'ai, si tu l'as ouï, souhaité ma franchise
Pour, de ma propre main, en tenter l'entreprise.
Ne t'en étonne pas, le jour m'est à mépris;
J'ai juré de périr ou voir régner mon fils,
Et, si la liberté m'était encore offerte,
J'en emploîrais pour lui tout l'usage à ta perte.
Est-ce assez? les témoins sont ici superflus.
Mon procès est bien court, prononce là-dessus.

Siroes offers her the choice between the same dagger and cup of poison that she had meant for him. She thanks him and chooses the poison, which will taste sweet since she cannot have his blood. She makes only one request: that her son shall die before her, so that she may be assured he will not have the disgrace of being subject to his enemy.

For Mardesanes, Siroes feels pity. His whole crime was a mother's overweening ambition. But Mardesanes is no

13 The shafts I aimed at thee have turned against me;
And by those means by which I hoped to set
My son in thy place, I have in mine own
Set thee and wrought my fall instead of thine.
I have done more; I tried without avail
To deal thy death-blow by my servant's hand.
I have (or knowest thou this?) desired my freedom
That I myself might then attempt the deed.
Be not astonished; life do I disdain.
I swore to die or see mine offspring reign,
And still, if liberty were granted me,
Would use it to achieve for him thy ruin.
Is this enough? Witnesses here are needless.
My trial is soon ended. Pronounce sentence.

longer the modest, circumspect youth of Act I. Since
then, he has been king for a brief moment, and according to
the notions about the psychology of kingship, which were
current among French seventeenth-century dramatists, the
assumption of sovereignty has an instantaneous and electrical
effect; indeed, it quite transforms a man. Mardesanes, as
little as the Queen, will conciliate his captor.

> J'ai trop de votre orgueil pour me soumettre à vous.[14]
> L'instant que j'ai tenu la puissance suprême,
> Et que j'ai sur ce front senti le diadème,
> M'a donné, comme à vous, des sentiments de roi,
> Qui ne se peuvent perdre et mourront avec moi.
> Ayant pu conserver, j'eusse eu peine à vous rendre
> Le sceptre, que, sujet, j'ai hésité de prendre.
>
> .   .   .   .
>
> On ne peut mieux tomber du trône qu'au cercueil.
> L'ardeur de commander trop puissamment convie,
> Pour me la faire perdre en me laissant la vie;
> Un cœur né pour régner est capable de tout;
> Je n'excepterais rien pour en venir à bout,
> Pour accomplir en moi les desseins de ma mère.

> [14] I have thy pride too much to bow before thee.
> The instant when I held the regal power
> And felt the diadem upon my brow
> Gave me, like thee, the spirit of a king,
> Which ne'er will leave me, but will die with me.
> Only with sore pain could I have restored
> The scepter to thee, if I might have kept it,
> Which, when a subject, I was loath to grasp.
>
> .   .   .   .
>
> From the throne one falls best into the tomb.
> The zest of governing lives in me too strongly
> To let me lose it while my life is left me.
> One born to reign is capable of all things;
> I would not stop at aught to gain that end,
> To bring to pass my mother's plans for me.

He wants no terms with one that has risen against his king
and father, whom he would avenge if he could. His defiance
at length angers Siroes, and he is led out to execution.

Now at last it is Chosroes' turn to know his fate. Siroes,
who has hitherto avoided and deferred the issue, must now
at last come to a decision about him. And the resolution of
Siroes breaks down utterly.

> A mon père, inhumains, donnez un autre juge,[15]
> Ou dans les bras d'un fils qu'on lui souffre un refuge.
> O toi, dont la vertu mérita son amour,
> Ma mère, hélas! quel fruit en as-tu mis au jour!
> Que n'as-tu dans ton sein causé mes funérailles
> Et fait mon monument de tes propres entrailles,
> Si je dois ôter l'âme et le titre de roi
> A la chère moitié qui vit encor de toi!
> Régnerais-je avec joie? et, bourreau de mon père,
> Aurais-je ni le ciel ni la terre prospère?
> Pour cimenter mon trône et m'affermir mon rang,
> Tarirais-je la source où j'ai puisé mon sang?
> Aurait-on de la foi pour un prince perfide
> Dont la première loi serait un parricide?

[15] Give my sire, savage lords, another judge,
   Or let him in a son's arms find a refuge.
   O thou whose virtue merited his love,
   Mother, alas! what fruit thou borest to light!
   Why heldest thou not my funeral in thy side
   And gavest me not thy womb for monument
   If I must take his life and rank of king
   From the dear other half yet left of thee?
   Would I reign blithely? Would either heaven or earth
   Favor one's own sire's executioner?
   To prop my throne and make my station firm,
   Would I exhaust the source whence flowed my being?
   Who will keep faith with a perfidious prince
   Whose first decree hath been a parricide?

Non, non, je ne veux point d'un trône ensanglanté
Du sang, du même sang dont je tiens la clarté.
J'ai cru la passion aux grands cœurs si commune,
Et, contre la nature, écouté la fortune;
J'ai fait de ma tendresse une fausse vertu;
A l'objet d'un Etat, mon lâche sang s'est tu;
.Mais, au point qu'il lui faut sacrifier un père,
La fortune se tait, et le sang délibère.

He kneels humbly before Chosroes. "I am no tyrant," he
declares, "nor my father's judge. I would rather lose all than
reign by crimes. Take back your scepter. Do not resign it at
my expense, but rule over your children in peace."—"These
words to me, after your treatment of Mardesanes and the
Queen? Revoke their death! Restore them to me!"—
"Guards, follow him and do whatever he orders!"
In vain Palmiras points out that Siroes will thus destroy
himself as well as all those who have been his loyal friends.
But now it is learned that the reprieve came too late. Mardesanes, to escape the ignominy of the headsman's stroke, had
already snatched a dagger and stabbed himself; Sira had
drunk from the poisoned cup; and Chosroes, finding them
so, has drained the rest of it. The curtain falls with Siroes
rushing out "to save a sire or die with him," and the others
following to protect their new king from his own frenzy.
Thus the tragic sequence of a son maddened with remorse by

No, no, I do not want a throne befouled
With blood, the very blood whence I took life.
Trusting that passion common in great spirits,
I against nature heard ambition's voice
I deemed my tenderness of heart false virtue;
With sovereignty the stake, my heart was silent;
But when a father must be sacrificed,
Ambition speaks no more and sonship counsels.

a father's death that he has caused, is to be continued . . . perhaps indefinitely.

Such, then, in so far as a mere outline and brief extracts can give some idea of it, is Rotrou's *Cosroès*. Even quite aside from the part dealing with Narsea, it is of course not a great play. It continually re-states, rather than develops, the dilemma of Siroes, its theme. Yet except for Narsea it would be an excellent play; and despite her it is unquestionably a good play. There is perhaps no other tragedy by a minor French dramatist of the seventeenth century that is of superior or even equal merit.

CHAPTER V

THE TRAGEDIES
OF THOMAS CORNEILLE

IT is a fact well known to students of literature that the
writer whose work is most typical of some school or
period is frequently not its greatest genius—for genius is
highly individual—but some lesser figure. Such a man, in
French drama of the seventeenth century, was Thomas Corneille.

This younger brother of the great Pierre Corneille wrote,
at one time or another in his long career, almost every sort
of play that was in vogue. He wrote comedies after the
Spanish manner and after the French; he wrote romanesque
tragedies, Corneillian tragedies, Racinian tragedies, spectacle plays, and operas. The present study is limited to his
tragedies.

Of these, not only are there three kinds, but no single
play or pair of plays stands out, at once characteristic and
superior, as in the case of all the other minor tragic
dramatists of the period. The compiler of an anthology of
French "classical" tragedies by the lesser writers could not
be wrong in selecting Mairet's *Sophonisbe,* Tristan l'Hermite's *Mariane,* Rotrou's *Venceslas* and *Cosroès,* Du Ryer's
Saül and *Scévole,* Quinault's *Astrate,* Campistron's *Andronic*
and *Tiridate,* La Fosse's *Manlius Capitolinus,* Crébillon's
Rhadamiste et Zénobie, and Voltaire's *Zaïre;* but anyone
would find trouble in choosing not more than two tragedies
to represent Thomas Corneille adequately. *Ariane* and *le
Comte d'Essex* do have a certain measure of fame denied
to the rest: they held the stage much the longest, were frequently included in old editions of the dramas of his illustrious brother, and are commonly thought to be his best

plays; but they stand apart, forming a little group of their own, less representative of his work in general than anything else that he wrote.

Of all the productions of this author, *Timocrate* enjoyed the greatest immediate success—the greatest, indeed, of all dramas in the whole seventeenth century, if tradition may be trusted. We are told that it was acted in two theaters simultaneously, and that it had a "run" of nearly six months, then unprecedented, with some eighty consecutive performances (three a week, as was the custom in that day)—until the public knew its lines by heart, and it was finally withdrawn only at the instance of the actors themselves, who feared they would forget the rest of their repertory! In its influence it was Thomas Corneille's most important play; for whether or not it was the first romanesque tragedy, a claim which has been disputed, it at least, with its enormous popularity, set the fashion for this type of drama, which engaged so large a share of his subsequent labors and those of Quinault, Boyer, and other playwrights.

The fantastic absurdities of *Timocrate,* some account of which has already been given in the Introduction to this book (pp. 13-14), must not blind us to the fact that to a public uncritical of such things, and even enamored of them, it must have been irresistibly appealing. The delighted audiences, steeped in the high-flown novels of adventure and preposterous gallantry then all the rage, who first beheld it were unaware that Timocrates, king of Crete and attacker of Argos, and "Cleomenes," the chief support of that city, were the same man; only one of the original spectators is said to have divined this. In the first act they heard of the heroic deeds of the stranger "Cleomenes"; they observed his modest but manly bearing in the council, where he alone spoke temperately; they learned that he dared to love the princess Eriphyle herself, to whose hand two allied kings and the subject prince Nicander also aspired, and who was promised by the Queen of Argos to whoever should make Timocrates her prisoner. Then throughout the second act they were confronted with all the refinements of gallant love after the most approved fashion; their sympathies were further enlisted in "Cleomenes'" behalf when they discovered that the Princess loved him, despite herself; they must have been amused, though not exactly as we would be today, by her pique at his having advised that she should be given in marriage to the invader, who demanded her as his bride; they doubtless relished her cleverness in avoiding the unwelcome suit of Prince Nicander; and even while they thrilled to "Cleomenes'" apparently selfless devotion, they heard from his own lips an account of the magnificent impressiveness of this Timocrates, so feared and hated, and were left with the prospect of a duel to the death between these two heroic champions—in which Eriphyle, momentarily at least, was willing to be the prize of the unknown soldier of fortune, should he prevail.

The third act is a triumph of suspense, as repeatedly the aspect of battle changes with the arrival of fresh tidings: first Thrasiles, the chief lieutenant of Timocrates, is captured and the Cretans give ground; next the tremendous prowess of Timocrates himself is manifested, the two allied kings fall before his hand, then he takes Nicander prisoner, then with bewildering magnanimity releases him; all seems lost; "Cleomenes" has disappeared, his fate unknown; and then— presto! "Cleomenes" enters with the news that he has captured Timocrates; and he claims the hand of the Princess and now declares himself to be of a birth which would not forbid such a union! It is a most effective climax to end this act, but still the play does not flag. The Queen has vowed the death of Timocrates if he should fall into her clutches, and Nicander cannot bear to see his generous captor thus immolated, and plans to release him; but the supposed royal prisoner refuses to escape, and it is rumored that he is not really Timocrates. The other prisoner, Thrasiles, denounces him as an impostor. "Cleomenes," however, reiterates that Timocrates has indeed been delivered into the hands of the Queen, and tries to persuade Eriphyle to accord pity and pardon to the hapless king of Crete; but having failed in this attempt and being again beset with charges of fraud, he demands to be confronted with Thrasiles, who on seeing him is aghast and speechless. "I myself am Timocrates," he tells the dismayed Queen, "and hence you unquestionably have Timocrates in your power. Take your vengeance on me, as you have sworn to do; but first marry me to your daughter, as the same oaths require of you." And the curtain falls on Act IV.

Though the pace of the fifth act is somewhat more leisurely, the situation that has been created is developed with no loss of interest. The efforts of Eriphyle to save the life of Timocrates occupy its earlier scenes. The populace will not come to the aid of their former idol; they fear the anger of the gods if the Queen's dreadful vows to slay her captive are not fulfilled. Nicander declines to interfere, when Eriphyle appeals to him with a directness which is in refreshing contrast to the usual behavior of the heroines of French "classical" tragedy in regard to their lovers. She then says she will prevent the death of Timocrates by refusing to wed him, their marriage no less than his execution being necessary to the discharge of her mother's oaths. But Timocrates insists that all shall be done as promised; he is happy to be the husband of Eriphyle before the world, however briefly; and he is still happier to discover that she loves him even when she knows who he is. The Queen is torn between her affection for "Cleomenes" and her long hatred for the King of Crete; she wishes she had not committed herself so irrevocably. Such is the predicament when news comes that the enemy are masters of Argos; Nicander has opened the gates to them, to repay his debt to Timocrates and to release the Queen from a dilemma which obviously distressed her. (He explains that he has concealed his intentions from Eriphyle in order to punish her for thinking that she needed to incite him to do what honor required of him!) The Queen is truly thankful to be queen no longer; and Timocrates will marry her daughter and rule the united realm of Crete and Argos.

If this drama derives from the romances of La Calprenède and Mlle de Scudéry, it also derives from Pierre Corneille's *Rodogune* and *Héraclius*. Like them, it has an involved plot and effective stage situations. But Thomas Corneille possessed no share of the poetic genius of his great brother. His lines are commonplace and colorless, and at times unprecise or even ambiguous in meaning. The characters of *Timocrate* are conventional figures, without distinctive individuality. Eriphyle perhaps comes nearest to being a real person: the same frankness which she displays with Nicander in Act V is exhibited earlier when, on hearing it rumored that the prisoner supposed to be Timocrates is not he, she goes straight to her "Cleomenes" and says to him:

> Parlez; et dût ma gloire en demeurer ternie,[1]
> Je vous en croirai seul, est-ce une calomnie?

This is quite unlike most heroines of romanesque drama, "who spend their time asking themselves if their dignity is preserved." [2]

Thomas Corneille wrote many other plays of the type which he established in *Timocrate*. They are characterized by similar complexity of subject matter, problems of identity, preoccupation with gallant love, and—this is the true,

[1] Speak! and though my fair fame should thence be stained,
    I shall believe thee only: is it slander?

[2] *Philippe Quinault*, by Etienne Gros, p. 486: ". . . *qui passent leur temps à se demander si leur dignité est sauve.*"

distinguishing mark of the dramas which we call "romanesque," for those of Quinault have comparatively simple plots—a complete absence of "local color," even of the meager sort attainable in seventeenth-century France. The names of the dramatis personae might be well known to history or legend, the names of the places involved might be clearly indicative of Asia, or classical Greece or Rome, or the Gothic Dark Ages; the real setting in every instance was the world of extravagant romance and gallantry as imagined by Madeleine de Scudéry. But interspersed among these effusions—*Bérénice* (not about the same person as Racine's *Bérénice*), *Darius, Pyrrhus, Persée et Démétrius, Antiochus, Théodat, la Mort d'Achille,* and *Bradamante*— he produced eight soberer, more serious tragedies, six of which were in evident imitation of his brother's work and hence are called "Corneillian." Whatever the relative merit of the other two of those eight, these six plays, taken together, constitute a solid corpus of achievement which must be considered his principal and most characteristic contribution to tragic drama.

True, in every instance their author is patently the author of *Timocrate:* gallant love holds a larger place in them than in most of the tragedies of his brother, between which and his own romanesque plays they are a sort of cross; and like the romanesque plays they exhibit that ability to invent striking if melodramatic situations, of immense effectiveness on the stage, which was Thomas Corneille's greatest gift as a dramatist. Reynier says that none of these plays "can be compared with *Cinna,* with *Rodogune,* or with *Nicomède,* which are the works of Pierre Corneille that they most nearly resemble." [3] This statement is true as regards *Nicomède* and in less degree *Cinna,* and as regards *Rodogune* in respect to poetry or as *Rodogune* has been tra-

[3] Translated from his *Thomas Corneille,* p. 143.

ditionally appraised; but, style aside, the real superiority of *Rodogune* to some of them may well be challenged. Indeed, one could argue not unplausibly that even *Timocrate* is, apart from the quality of the verse, a better play than *Rodogune*. For if *Rodogune* builds up to a tremendous climax in the last act, its preceding acts are admittedly none too good and its long preliminary exposition is quite bad, whereas the whole of *Timocrate* is excellent "theater"; and if the "Cleopatre" of *Rodogune* is an impressive stage villainess and the characters in *Timocrate* are mere lay figures, at least none of the latter is botched with irreconcilable contradictions like Rodogune herself or exasperates us like Antiochus. Now, when a case can thus be made out even for *Timocrate,* no instinct of bardolatry should beguile one into disdaining Thomas Corneille's better dramas in comparison with his great brother's minor work.

Yet as to which is the best of the younger dramatist's Corneillian tragedies, there is no agreement among critics. Lancaster preferred *Stilicon,* Saintsbury *Camma* and *Laodice,* and Reynier *la Mort d'Annibal,* while the second-best according to Lancaster is *Camma* and according to Reynier is *Laodice.* Reynier's reason for assigning a primacy to *la Mort d'Annibal,* however, was the characteristically Gallic one that he considered its style much better than that of the others. Poetry can adorn and improve a good play; it cannot make a play good.

Everyone, though, would recognize that the earliest of this group of dramas, *la Mort de l'empereur Commode* (1657), is the poorest of them. It is singularly ill-made, for the work of so capable a playwright. Too much of it (almost all of the first two acts) deals with two pairs of young lovers. The obligatory scene of an attempt to stab the Emperor is omitted; this incident, about which no very clear indication is ever given, occurs between acts—and so does the turning of Flavian, the captain of the guard, against his master and the discovery through him of Commodus' written orders to put all the other principal characters to death, which is the crisis of the plot. The fifth act is little more than a series of conversations, with scant tension; the Emperor is poisoned off-stage, and when he finally enters, his concealment of his sanguinary plans has no dramatic effect because the audience is aware that he is a dying man, and he leaves the stage before he dies. Thomas Corneille did few better pieces of characterization, however, than his portrait of the tyrant, and most scenes in this play are quite effective and as near to reality as was possible in the mannered drama of that day; there are frequent historical references and a fair amount of factual background.

Lancaster's preference for *Stilicon* (1660) is easily understandable. It has the best theme of any of the Cornellian plays of its author—the theme of a great man becoming a traitor because of ambition for his son, and only bringing about his son's death thereby—a theme on which a great tragedy could be written. Doubtless the moral struggle in the heart of the protagonist, which should be chiefly stressed in such a tragedy, would be difficult to depict when the time of the action is limited to a single day, as in classical drama generally; however, it at least might be presented in retrospect. Racine, we may be sure, would have so presented it; Thomas Corneille has not. The gigantic potentialities of his subject were in no wise exploited by him. When Stilicho, the mainstay of the Roman Empire and for many years the loyal servant of the Emperor Honorius (who has taken Stilicho's daughter for wife and empress), first appears, his treason has long been determined, his plans are laid, and no qualms assail him. Between this scene and the one in which he stands at last with ruined hopes and ruined life, his conspiracy is made the subject of melodrama, showing his resourcefulness in meeting every difficulty that arises from the premature discovery that some plot is afoot against the Emperor, and thus creating interest and suspense. It is good melodrama. There are several very striking scenes and one fine situation, characteristic of the author's craftsmanship, when it becomes clear to Honorius that either Stilicho or Stilicho's son Eucherius must be guilty, and Stilicho contrives to throw suspicion entirely on his son that he himself may be left free to act. For Eucherius to have foiled the plot in the end, as Lancaster asserts and reiterates that he did,[4] would have been an excellent touch, but in point of fact Honorius is indicated rather to have been saved by his wife: she stationed in the Emperor's apartments a strong body of loyal guards, who rushed to his aid when the conspirators burst in, and though Eucherius exhibited the prowess invariably ascribed to young heroes in French-classical tragedies, and died gallantly in defending his sovereign, it is hardly conceivable that his efforts would have been successful without the help of these guards, who, on the other hand, might have been adequate without him. Melodrama is left behind and genuine tragedy takes its place only with Stilicho's bitter cry thereafter:

> Pour élever mon fils au rang où je vous voi,[5]
> J'ai trahi vos bienfaits; j'ai violé ma foi;
> J'ai démenti mon sang, j'ai pris le nom de traître,
> J'ai porté le poignard dans le sein de mon maître,
> J'ai souillé lâchment la gloire de mon sort;
> Cependant, cependant, seigneur, mon fils est mort.

---

[4] *A History of French Dramatic Literature in the Seventeenth Century,* Part III, pp. 438, 439.

> [5] To raise my son to where I see thee throned,
> I have ill paid thy boons, been false to thee,
> Belied my blood, acquired the name of traitor,
> Stabbed with a dagger at my master's breast,
> And basely soiled the glory of my lot;
> And now, and now, my lord, my son is dead.

The first act of *Camma* (1661) is occupied with presenting love-complications even more intricate than usual in French-classical tragedies. Sinorix, who had some claims to the throne of Galatia, secretly loved Camma, the newly wedded

---

There would have been abundant space to develop the tragic possibilities of this subject, but something much worse than melodrama unfortunately takes up a very sizable part of the play. The love of Eucherius for Placidia, the Emperor's sister, is well related to the main action; for it is her outrageous treatment of him that incites his father to treason; but the words, the ideas, and the behavior of this irritating pair are actually more romanesque, more remote from life, than anything in *Timocrate*. There is hardly another youth in the dramas of Thomas Corneille, if indeed anywhere in French-classical tragedy, who can but "sigh and die" at the cruelty of his heart's mistress so abjectly as Eucherius; and Placidia would be equally difficult to match among "proud" heroines for sheer perversity and dislikableness. Unlike many of the princesses in these plays who disdain to wed anyone but a sovereign, she has not the excuse of being a queen in her own right or the heir to a throne; and she at least could have refused Eucherius' suit firmly without the spiteful contempt which she continually exhibits towards him. When he tries to please her by furthering a royal marriage for her, she is not only miffed, like Eriphyle under analogous circumstances in *Timocrate,* that her lover is willing to give her up—a favorite situation with Thomas Corneille—but also furious that she should owe anything to *him.* She reasons in circles, and dishonestly. She can allege the most amazing motivations: she says that she treats Eucherius with such scorn because she hopes that on this account her brother will reward his great merits by sharing the Empire with him, to make him a fit husband for her; she says that Eucherius cannot have conspired to gain the throne in order to win her, because a love for *her* could never prompt anyone to do anything bad! It is hard to imagine that this woman would confess to her confidante that she loves him, though by French-classical convention one tells one's confidante everything; it is utterly incredible that she would confess it to Eucherius himself, not when she believed him falsely accused of treason—then the confession would have been natural, and good psychology—but when she has decided finally that he is guilty of it!

wife of Sinatus, its king. A bargain was struck by which he
was to wed Hesione, Sinatus' daughter by his first wife;
but Sinorix poisoned Sinatus, got himself made king in his
stead, and proceeded to pay court to the widowed queen,
threatening the now rejected Hesione with exile unless she
would marry Sostrates, his best friend, who alone (so he
believes) shares a knowledge of his crime. But Camma also
knows of it—just how, remains in some doubt—and it is
she whom Sostrates really loves, and she loves him and
tries to persuade him to avenge her husband's murder for
her. And Hesione thinks that she herself is loved by Sostrates—as Sinorix and everybody else but Camma think—
and she says she will marry him if he will avenge her wrongs
by killing Sinorix,[6] but not otherwise, for she will not give
up her hopes of reigning; and Sostrates refuses to be false
to his friend and king for the sake of either the woman he
loves or the woman he is believed to love.

This complicated state of affairs is developed with a good
deal of tension and suspense in the subsequent acts, with
again a fine theatrical situation when Camma attempts to stab
Sinorix in the back and Sostrates, entering at that moment,
stops her. Sinorix turns and sees them struggling, as the
dagger falls to the floor; and he does not know which of

---

[6] Here, as in *Pertharite*, we find a notable anticipation of *Andromaque;* there had been another close parallel in *la Mort de l'empereur Commode*. Racine was doubtless acquainted with all three
of these plays to which his indebtedness has been suggested, but
the resemblance of *Pertharite* to *Andromaque* is much the most
striking; for in both of them, as in neither *Camma* nor *Commode,*
the rejected woman loves the man whose death she demands, and
the person whom he threatens to kill if another woman will not
marry him is that other woman's little son. Hence the traditional
view that *Pertharite* was the source of the similar situation in *Andromaque* is decidedly the most probable; other parallels between
these several plays are less significant and more easily attributable
to coincidence.

them is his would-be assassin and which was his rescuer. Sostrates takes the blame to shield Camma; and she lets him take it, that she may have further opportunities for vengeance;[7] and Hesione imagines that Sostrates was trying to kill Sinorix for *her*, and claims a share in the attempt. One is reminded of Pierre Corneille by the unexpected, ingenious turns of reasoning ascribed to the dramatis personae —and also by the inhumanity which characterizes their decisions.[8]

The final act is marred by the especial prominence here of romanesque clichés of thought and conduct. Sostrates raves about his tortures of disappointed love to his successful rival, Sinorix, with no restraining impulse whatever of self-respect. He declares to Camma that his death will be a deserved retribution for his crime of having made her stoop to love him! He also expresses to her the absurd idea, in line with conceptions current in seventeenth-century French drama, that the mere name of "husband" must so dominate her imagination that she will not be able to take her intended vengeance on Sinorix but must love ere long this murderer whom she now hates. She does take it, however, by poisoning the nuptial cup from which she and Sinorix both drink before the ceremony; and she will not prevent the deadly effects to herself because she wants to die, too, since she has had to submit to this marriage to attain her ends. As may be inferred from the foregoing, *Camma* is

[7] Cf. in *Stilicon*, Stilicho's making suspicion rest on his son, Eucherius.

[8] Thus Camma now resolves to requite Sostrates doubly by wedding Sinorix: she can thus save Sostrates' life, he having saved hers, and at the same time will punish him for having thwarted her revenge! And Hesione, on her part, refuses the opportunity offered her to save Sostrates by marrying him, because to do so would lessen her chances of gaining the throne, though she never doubts that it is for her sake that he is about to die.

impaired by the fact that not one of its characters arouses sympathy.[9]

Maximian (1662), like *Stilicon*, deals with the unsuccessful plot of a distinguished man to kill one of the later Roman emperors—again his daughter's husband—and usurp the throne; but it is generally regarded as inferior to *Stilicon*. No one has ever thought it the best of these "Corneillian" tragedies. Yet for the first four acts it gives promise of being precisely that, and Thomas Corneille never did better work than is to be found in it. Its juxtaposition of excellences and defects reminds one of an Elizabethan play.

Maximian is not an appealing character like Stilicho. He does not conspire for the sake of a son, but to regain the imperial power which his co-emperor, Diocletian, forced him to resign at the same time that Diocletian resigned his own. But he is a far more impressive figure than Stilicho— one of the most impressive to be found anywhere in French-classical drama—with his ruthless will, his craft and daring, and his monstrous web of villainy, in the weaving of which no tie is sacred to him. He has betrothed his daughter Fausta to the young Roman general Severus, and they love each other; but he forces her to wed the Emperor Constantine while her lover is fighting Constantine's wars, and then, when Severus returns victorious, excuses himself with a false tale that the Emperor tyrannically compelled him to agree to this marriage, and broaches the subject of his plot (undertaken in revenge for that compulsion, he says) with the prospect of Severus' winning Fausta if it is successful. He also makes use of the distress of another eminent young man, Licinius, who loves the Emperor's sister, Constance; she loves Licinius, too, but Constantine is determined to marry her to Severus, for whom he knows

---

[9] Sinorix is a somewhat unusual if not altogether satisfactorily presented villain, with sharp pangs of conscience.

that the Empress Fausta still grieves, and of whom he is hence madly jealous.

It is in vain that Severus reveals Maximian's treasonous designs to Fausta, hoping that she may be able to save her husband without bringing death upon her father. It is in vain that one of the conspirators tells Constantine of the existence of the plot, and in vain that this man's chief comrades are arrested. No one knows Maximian is the real head of the conspiracy except his agent Martian, Fausta, and Severus; and Martian, when seized, declares that Licinius is. Maximian is even thought to be another intended victim of it. And when Severus, seeing no alternative, does at last denounce him, Maximian convinces the Emperor of his innocence and of the guilt of Severus and Fausta, gets Severus led off to prison, and then, when left alone with the heart-broken Fausta, defies her to testify against him— for she would be no more believed than Severus was! Act IV closes with him thus triumphant.

So far, all has been handled uncommonly well, in comparison with the usual degree of artificiality which characterizes the tragedies of the period and of this particular author. It is true that the young men disappointed in love are sure they will die; and when Constantine tells Constance that he will kill Licinius if she does not consent to marry Severus, she informs her lover that she will probably have to do so, and Severus that if she does so, it will be against her will, but she never tells either of them of her brother's ultimatum to her! That dear device of romanesque drama, an uprising of the populace for the sake of their favorite, appears in *Maximian* as it does, indeed, in half of the author's Corneillian tragedies. Yet in general the conduct of this play is less conventional, the psychology and behavior of the characters are more lifelike, than in any previous tragedy by Thomas Corneille.[10]

[10] In these respects there is no deterioration even in the fifth act.

But having brought Act IV to a brilliant conclusion, the author proceeds to wreck a play hitherto much superior to either *Stilicon* or *Camma*. He violates alike consistency of characterization and the most obvious principles of good dramaturgy. It is inconceivable that the arrogantly confident Maximian of the close of Act IV should immediately afterwards feel such anxiety about what Severus could do, for which he had just shown his disdain, as to take the risk involved in stabbing him in prison, and should entrust the

---

A notable feature of *Maximian* is that it almost entirely dispenses with the stereotyped role of the confidant: one speaks seven lines in Act I; another's lines and fragments of lines in Act II amount to about another seven; and that is all. Moreover, this drama would be hard to parallel among the tragedies of its day in having lengthy scenes in which a number of characters take an active part. French-classical tragedies are essentially a series of duologues or triologues; especially is this true with Racine. But in *Maximian* five characters are of dramatic importance in III, v, and again in IV, iv. And in the latter scene something occurs that is perhaps unique in these French dramas in which misunderstandings and half-understandings play so large a part: in the midst of an involved, badly tangled situation, a character (Severus) speaks out and makes a succinct but adequate statement of all the important facts, as one might in real life. As an ironic commentary, it may be significant that he is not believed!

Thomas Corneille again gets excellent stage effects. Fausta's unexpected announcement, when matters are most confused, that *she* will see to the Emperor's safety (III, vi) is one of them, though in view of his jealous distrust of her, Constantine's willingness to place or leave in her hands the power to do so is barely credible, even as a consequence of heart-sick bewilderment. But the most frequently used device for the enhancing of dramatic effect in this tragedy is the presence, during almost every display of Maximian's wiles, of someone who is known by the audience to be aware of his villainy and hostile to it. This is the chief source of dramatic interest left in the fifth act, where he exhibits all his former cleverness and effrontery—in ignorance that Constantine has learned the whole truth about him.

escape of Martian (which does not seem to have been necessary) and therewith all his own fortunes to a man whom
he completely misjudges and who betrays him. It is this
man, one Valerius, who by that betrayal decides the whole
outcome of the tragedy; yet Valerius does this between
acts, never appears on the stage, and had never even been
mentioned earlier! As we have seen, it is not the first time—
nor will it be the last—when Thomas Corneille relegates
crucial details to the intervals between the acts. A propen-
sity for doing so was his besetting sin as a shaper of plots,
the capacity in which he was in general most competent. The
ill success of *Maximian* was probably due more, however,
to another defect, in which merit was mingled. Severus and
Fausta are quite "sympathetic" figures; their fate is too
piteous to have place in a tragedy of which they are not the
subject; and the preservation and good fortune, at their
expense, of Constantine, who has acted so shabbily, could
not be a palatable conclusion.

There is no similar wealth of characterization in *Laodice* (1668). Its dramatis personae are colorless and conventional, except for the title role, which was evidently
patterned after the "Cleopatre" of *Rodogune*. Laodice, the
dowager queen of Cappadocia, has contrived the death of
five of her six sons, that she may not have to surrender the
crown, in which she finds all her joy. She tried to kill also
the sixth, Prince Ariarathes, who was held at Rome as a
hostage. This little child disappeared, and she believed him
dead; but she pretended that she was sure he was still living,
and used him as an excuse for not allowing her daughter,
Arsinoë, to marry and reign. The truth was that Ariarathes
indeed lived; the Romans had hidden him that he might be
reared in safety; and when he reached manhood they allowed him to go to Cappadocia under the name of "Orontes,"
to enter the service of Laodice and see if he could not win
her affection while his identity was unknown to her. In

this aim he succeeded—only too well: by his prowess, ability, and devoted service he rose to the highest station possible for one supposed to be a commoner; but the love which the Queen came to feel in secret for this handsome and assiduously attentive young hero was not motherly.

That is the situation at the opening of the play, and instead of being concealed from the audience, as in *Timocrate*, the essential facts are presented early, with a great gain in dramatic effectiveness. Of course there must be a love-affair for "Orontes"-Ariarathes; it is supplied by the presence of Axiana, the Princess of Cilicia, who was destined to be the bride of Prince Ariarathes, if he lived. "Orontes"-Ariarathes loves her, and she loves "Orontes" and hopes in her heart that Ariarathes will never appear, though of course she feels that disparity of birth is a barrier between her lover and herself. Rome is sending an ambassador to Cappadocia, ostensibly to select a husband for Arsinoë from several princely candidates for her hand and for the sovereignty which they expect to accompany it, but really to proclaim the identity of Ariarathes and set him on the throne. Laodice has other plans: she herself will give a master to her subjects, who are tired of being ruled by a woman; she will not be the vassal of her daughter or of her daughter's husband, prescribed by Rome; she herself, instead of Arsinoë, will wed; she will wed the popular "Orontes" before the Roman ambassador can arrive, feigning that she does so because she knows that her son will soon make his appearance and she can trust none but "Orontes" to surrender the crown to him willingly when he reveals himself. And now, like a thunderclap, comes the news that Aquilius, the Roman ambassador, is at hand, and that he brings the long-lost Ariarathes with him. In reality, this "Ariarathes" is an impostor who claimed to be the Prince, and whom Rome has pretended to believe and has sent to Cappadocia to be unmasked and punished there, but he will serve as an excellent instrument by which the true Ariarathes can test everyone concerned. To the latter's horror, Laodice wishes "Orontes" to murder her supposed son for her; when he refuses, she offers her hand to one of the ambitious native princes, if he will serve her will. This confederate encompasses the death of the counterfeit Ariarathes; the Roman ambassador with his escort arrives; the true Ariarathes is revealed; the evil Queen Laodice kills herself; and her son will marry Axiana.

All this is the familiar material of French pseudo-classical tragedy. In fact, *Laodice* might perhaps be selected as the most thoroughly representative specimen that can be found of that literary type. Yet it is, I believe, despite its hackneyed subject-matter and undistinguished characterization, the best of its author's Corneillian tragedies, and with only one exception the best tragedy, indeed, that he wrote. Its melodramatic plot is well managed, and the interest in what is really "a good story" is sustained throughout. Though Ariarathes is a quite conventional young "hero," he is not a ridiculous one, and that is more than can be said of most of his breed. He is positively fatuous only in his persistence in believing, towards the end of the play, that some kind of arrangement can yet be devised for affectionate association between himself and his monstrous mother, with her incestuous passion for him. *She* knows that none can. It is an unusually acute touch, in an age when characters in plays too often acquire or discard emotions with grotesque immediacy—and a daring touch in an age so quick to censure anything unseemly—that when she learns that the youth with whom she has fallen in love is her own son, she cannot, though horrified at herself, instantly cease to feel the sort of attraction towards him that she has been accustomed to feel. Would that this dramatist, and others, showed everywhere as much sense of psychological realities! . . . Axiana is the conventional princess, with heart divided be-

tween pride of birth and love for one who seems hopelessly
beneath her, but perhaps none of her sisterhood is so little
disagreeable and so little unreasonable as she; actually, she
is not unattractive. Like Eriphyle with "Cleomenes" and
like Placidia with Eucherius, she is much vexed with her
"Orontes" for his readiness to see her marry a king,[11] but
if Thomas Corneille has made use of this situation too frequently in his plays, he at any rate has never made of it so
amusingly human and so little offensive an episode as here.
And his peculiar talent for situations of great theatrical
effectiveness is manifested in *Laodice* less melodramatically,
in scenes of a less superficial dramatic power, than ever
before.

There are two of these. The first is the scene in which
Laodice solicits her unknown son to kill her supposed son.
There it is not merely that, as Ariarathes demolishes one
after another her specious reasons for refusing to give up
the throne to its rightful heir, she perforce reveals gradually
to the horror-stricken youth the real depth of his mother's
depravity. This is much; this is of the genuine substance of
tragedy; but it is not all. For just as when Shakespeare's
Portia pleads with Shylock to be merciful, it is not really
to save Antonio that she is pleading, but to save Shylock
himself from the doom beneath which she must crush him
if he proves to be unredeemably wicked, so is it here not
Laodice's intended victim but Laodice herself whose fate is
at stake and in whom her son vainly tries to find some
spark of goodness, as their dialogue works up to its powerful, inexorable climax:

[11] Here as in *Timocrate* the king is really the same man as her
lover; but in *Laodice,* unlike *Timocrate,* the audience is aware of
this fact, and the scene is on that account much more piquant.

ARIARATE.[12]

... Pour rompre un projet à ses jours si funeste,
Souffrez qu'il s'abandonne à l'espoir qui lui reste,
Et que, pour vous fléchir, ce prince infortuné
Vous oppose par moi le sang dont il est né.
Croyez, en m'écoutant, que c'est lui qui vous prie,
Qu'en regardant sa mère il la cherche attendrie,
Et qu'enfin à vos pieds il vous dit par ma voix,
"Accordez-moi la vie une seconde fois,
Je vous suis odieux. Mais, quoi? Qui vous anime?
Etre né votre fils n'est pas un si grand crime.
Daignez lui faire grâce en faveur d'un respect
Que jamais rien de moi ne vous rendra suspect,
Prenez-en pour garant la foi sincère et pure
Qu'à la face du ciel ma tendresse vous jure,
Cette foi que jamais les plus durs changements ..."

---

[12] ARIARATHES.

... To make thee lay aside a purpose
So deadly to him, grant that he may cherish
The hope which still is his, and that this hapless
Prince may through me oppose thee with the ties
Of blood that birth has given him. Believe,
In hearing me, that it is he who pleads,
That he would fain soften his mother's heart,
And that he kneels and through my voice says to thee:
"Give life to me a second time. I know
Thou hatest me. But what inspires thy feelings?
To be thy son is not so great a crime.
Consent to pardon it since I so revere thee
That thou shouldst never be suspicious of me.
Take for thy warrant the true, pure loyalty
Which my love pledges thee in the face of heaven,
That loyalty which no vicissitudes ..."

Laodice.

Lorsqu'il s'agit de trône, on se fie aux serments?
Ne vous y trompez point, quand il se pourrait faire
Qu'à ce fils comme à vous le crime pût déplaire,
Qu'une vertu pareille eût pour lui même appas,
Dans ce qu'il sait de moi, je ne m'y fierais pas.
Je dis plus. Quand j'aurais une entière assurance
Qu'il dût laisser toujours le trône en ma puissance,
Toujours comme sujet me soumettre son sort,
J'aurais la même ardeur à poursuivre sa mort.
Pour en tenir l'arrêt et juste et légitime,
Il suffirait de voir qu'il fait grâce à mon crime,
Et que je périrais si, par un noble effroi,
Il ne refusait d'être aussi méchant que moi.
Ainsi, je ne puis voir cette mort assez prompte,
Ne fût-ce que pour voir un témoin de ma honte.
C'est par là que son sort est toujours combattu,

Laodice.

With thrones at stake, does one put faith in oaths?
Do not deceive thyself: though it should be
That crime was odious to him, as to thee,—
That virtue had for him the same attraction,—
With what he knows of me, I would not trust
Myself in his hands. Nay, if I should have
Complete assurance that he would leave the throne
Always in my possession, and would always
Be my submissive subject, I would feel
Still the same ardor to achieve his death.
To make my ordering it just and lawful,
'Twould be enough to see that he forgave
My crime, and that I needs would die if he,
Because of noble fears and scruples, did not
Refuse to be as wicked as myself.
Therefore I cannot see him dead too soon,
Though he were but a witness of my shame;
Therefore I always must attempt his life,

Je dois craindre son crime, ou haïr sa vertu.

The other great scene is, of course, that in which Laodice discovers that "Orontes" is her son. Its emotionalism is more violent, more obvious, less subtle; it is not nearly so fine a scene. But early in the course of it occurs a brief passage that is nothing short of remarkable. Laodice has entered, beaten at last since her plot had struck down the false instead of the real Ariarathes, and content to accept the little kingdom of Lycaonia, which the Romans have granted her—content because she expects to wed "Orontes" and reign with him there. The dramatist has already shown the softening effect on her, in some degree, of the young man's noble nature: though at first furious with him for having declined to commit murder for her, she has presently loved him all the better for it. Now she tells him it is because of him that she will no longer seek her son's death. "By virtue," she declares, "you have torn me from crime's ways." She explains that the reasons of State policy which she has alleged for marrying him, and which no longer exist, were largely pretenses, and that she loves him passionately—then she stops short and asks the cause of his evident consternation. He tells her that he must reveal a secret which will confound her equally and make her hate him. And thereupon she says:

Vous aimez donc ailleurs, et l'hymen d'une reine[13]
Ne vaut pas que pour elle on brise une autre chaîne;
La constance en amour est digne d'un héros.

I needs must fear his crime or hate his virtue.

[13] Thou lovest, then, elsewhere; and to wed a queen
Is not worth breaking other bonds for her.
Such constancy is worthy of a hero.

Into what tantrums would not the average "heroine" of French-classical tragedy have gone if she had thought she had a rival who was preferred to her! But this most wicked of evil queens has come so to love "Orontes" for his virtues that her first reaction to a fancied discovery which would crush all her hopes is an affectionate, indulgent appreciation of his nobility in being faithful to a prior love at the expense even of a throne. There is nothing else like this in the drama of the period—not even in the great Corneille or in Racine. One cannot help wondering whether Thomas Corneille actually intended so marvelous a touch. But at any rate, it is in his play.

Though la Mort d'Annibal (1669), whatever the superiority of its verse, is decidedly less good than Laodice, it continues the diminution of romanesque elements that is discernible in the Corneillian tragedies of this author after Camma, however often he still wrote other plays of the purely romanesque type. It is his own version of his brother's Nicomède, with the action put a little earlier, while Hannibal yet lived, a refugee at the Court of King Prusias of Bithynia; it has some of the same dramatis personae as Nicomède and some different ones. Prusias, Nicomedes, and Flaminius reappear; and there is again an Attalus who is Nicomedes' rival in love, but instead of being the younger son of Prusias, this Attalus is the brother of Eumenes, king of Pergamus, whose supposed death seems to give him the crown. But it is no Armenian queen, but Elissa, the daughter of Hannibal, that these young men love—and Thomas Corneille makes old Prusias in love with her, too! All the plot turns on their rivalry. Elissa loves Nicomedes, but is resolved to marry only as will best serve her father's interests; Hannibal, as in Pierre Corneille's drama, has taught Nicomedes the art of war, and he is very fond of his pupil, but Attalus would seem better able, as a reigning king, to further his eternal enmity against Rome if made his son-in-law.

Flaminius manipulates Prusias and Attalus until the former delivers Hannibal into the hands of the Romans because he thinks the latter is about to do so. Nicomedes rescues his master; but the great Carthaginian has already taken poison to avoid captivity, and, as Prusias has been killed in the fighting and Attalus been carried off a prisoner by Flaminius, in death Hannibal gives his daughter to his rescuer.

After the first act, which is thoroughly romanesque, being devoted to the disclosure that every important character in the play is in love with Elissa except her own father and Flaminius, and to the problems arising in consequence, there are a number of good scenes in *la Mort d'Annibal*, developed with dignity and naturalness, and written with a vigor, clarity, and concision which, as Reynier pointed out, can hardly be paralleled in any other play of its author. Once more (in II, i) we find a striking realistic departure from the romanesque convention; the heroine is actually represented as refusing to admit to her confidante that she is in love (though she is) when her confidante taxes her with it. Moreover, the historical background, though depicted less vividly than in *Nicomède,* is evoked with an amount of detail that is unique in the work of Thomas Corneille.

The fundamental weakness of this tragedy is that its half-dozen principal characters are all about equally prominent, and thus none is prominent enough. Nicomedes plays the smallest part of any, and is a rather colorless figure, merely the usual young hero of romance; he is conventionally sure of dying if Attalus wins Elissa, though he himself advises her to accept his father. The real intentions of Attalus towards the Romans, who have befriended him, and towards Hannibal, to whom he gives his word that he will be hostile to them, are left most unsatisfactorily doubtful until Flaminius at last forces his hand. The trump card of the wily Roman is the discovery that Eumenes still lives and hence Attalus is not king of Pergamus; the plot to a considerable extent turns on this fortuitous fact, extraneous to the action and reported between Acts III and IV. And the earlier scenes of the fifth act, in which both Prusias and Attalus successively come to Elissa, while her father is being seized, to tell her that they could not prevent this catastrophe and to assure her that they will protect her—and incidentally to make love to her—are rather inept and are implausibly handled.

Of this author's two tragedies classified as "Racinian," only the one about Ariadne should be so called.[14] I have

---

[14] Even in this play Lancaster does not consider Racine's influence certain. He points to Thomas Corneille's *Camma* and *Stilicon* as dramas with simple subjects and to his romanesque *Persée et Démétrius* as another tragedy in which pity is the chief emotion, and says, "It is, of course, possible that the example of *Andromaque* may have encouraged him to treat such a subject and that the simplicity and pathos of *Bérénice* may have influenced his structure and his presentation of Ariadne, but the facts hardly warrant the confident assertions of M. Reynier and M. Lanson" (*op. cit.,* Part III, p. 599); and again that Ariadne's "appealing character and the simplicity of the plot have made some critics suppose that the tragedy was written in imitation of Racine, but there is no proof that this was the case" (*op. cit.,* Part V, p. 82).

Now, actual proof of the influence of one literary work on another is almost impossible except when indebtedness is admitted by the author himself or when there are long, striking parallel passages. Coincidence *may* account for almost any resemblance, but probabilities may be established which preclude "a reasonable doubt." Thomas Corneille's *Ariane* was written the year after *Bérénice,* when Racine was at the height of his fame; it is much simpler in plot than *Camma* or *Stilicon,* or than any other play of that period but *Bérénice;* like *Bérénice* it deals, without violent action, with the piteous disappointment of a loving woman's serenely trustful hopes of marrying the man she loves; like *Bérénice* its dramatis personae consist of three major characters and their respective confidants, except that in *Ariane* the fact that the heroine loses her beloved to another woman necessitates the additional

already, as in the case of *Timocrate,* had occasion to speak
of this play in the Introduction to the present volume (pp.
15-18). *Ariane* (1672) shares with *le Comte d'Essex* (1678)
the honor of having been the most frequently and longest
acted of all French tragedies by the minor authors of its
period, and it is generally considered the best tragedy of
Thomas Corneille. With this judgment, however, I cannot
concur.

A very clever parody many years ago of the once popular,
saccharine novels of Robert W. Chambers was given the sub-
title: "A Story of Love and Absolutely Nothing Else." A
similar sub-title would be appropriate for *Ariane.* In Du
Ryer's *Alcionée* love is opposed by pride of royal blood, in
Timocrate as in *Romeo and Juliet* by hereditary feud, in
Quinault's *Astrate* by the duty of vengeance, in Racine's
Bérénice by State policy. In *Andromaque* love imperils the
life of a child, in *Phèdre* the most sacred family ties. But
Ariane is a tragedy about love and absolutely nothing else.
Love is the sole concern of all the important characters, and
the love of none of these is hindered or thwarted except
by some other love.

Now love does not need to be of subordinate interest in

---

presence of her rival; and in both plays the heroine has an unsuccessful lover, who is one of the major characters. If all this be
sheer coincidence, it is a truly remarkable coincidence. Moreover,
there is a clenching piece of evidence which Lancaster seems to
have overlooked: love in *Ariane* is represented as arising, not from
esteem as in Pierre Corneille and in all the previous work of his
brother, but from sheer fatality as in Racine; that such is the nature
of love is stressed again and again throughout the play. (Contrast
relevant statements of Oenerus, Theseus, and Phaedra in Act I of
Ariane with those of Placidia regarding Eucherius in *Stilicon,* II,
i, and Axiana regarding "Orontes" in *Laodice,* I, ii. The only expression of conventional Corneillian, as opposed to Racinian, love
to be found in *Ariane* is put significantly in the mouth of Ariadne
when she is speaking insincerely to Oenarus in IV, ii.)

a tragedy as Pierre Corneille maintained, but it cannot be—
it never has been in any impressive drama—the only interest. A play in which no one thinks of anything else is
almost certain to lack dignity. The omnipresent jargon of
gallantry which assails the ear in the opening scenes of
Ariane may in itself be accepted by us intellectually as characteristic of the period in which it was written (though it
is most unacceptable to our taste), but the impression which
it gives of an artificial society, occupied only with love-
affairs, does not belong to great drama or even to good
drama. When a lover on seeing his beloved can exclaim to
himself, *"O trop charmante vue!"* we feel we are in a world
unfit for good drama.

Though Phaedra's qualms at the enormity of the wrong
being done her sister, and her doubts of Theseus' fidelity to
her after his unfaithfulness to Ariadne, are well pictured,
the appeal which this play has had for both readers and
theater-goers has been almost wholly due to the sympathy
aroused by the plight of its heroine. No loving woman ever
deserved better or was more shamefully betrayed by those
of whose loyalty she was so sure. Her complete confidence
in Theseus, which enables her to view without anxiety his
apparent interest in other young women and which makes
her fondly excuse his coldness towards her on the ground
that it is unbecoming of a hero to be demonstrative, is at
once touching and lovable. Her scenes with her sister and
with Theseus exhibit again Thomas Corneille's skill in
creating dramatic situations, and are very effective. But at
the moment when she should be most appealing in her distress and helplessness, when she learns that Theseus loves
someone else, the author turns her into a vengeful Fury,
who artfully attempts to discover who her rival is, in order
to kill her, and who loses none of her bloodthirstiness when
she finds that it is her own sister. Such murderous rage is
in accord with French pseudo-classical tradition, which

assumes it to be characteristic of every jealous woman; but, except perhaps to audiences habituated to that tradition, her frenzy, as well as her total want of self-respecting reticence when in the fifth act she loudly bewails her woes to all the world, is decidedly unattractive and a blot on the play. Both afford great opportunities for emotional acting, but they make her a much less poignant figure than she would otherwise be.[15]

[15] In fairness, it should be said that Ariadne's sudden display of ferocious wrath is not, as Bernadin declares (in Petit de Julleville's *Histoire de la Langue et de la Littérature française,* vol. v, p. 140), a departure from the author's previous portrayal of her. There have been several earlier passages to prepare us for it. When she first suspects her lover's perfidy, without waiting for it to be confirmed she cries (II, vii):

> Son sang devrait payer la douleur qui me presse.
> C'est là, ma sœur, c'est là, sans pitié, sans tendresse,
> Comme après un forfait si noir, si peu commun,
> On traite les ingrats; et Thésée en est un.
> Mais quoi qu'à ma vengeance un fier dépit suggère . . .

> (His blood must pay me for the grief that wracks me.
> Thus, thus, my sister, without love or pity,
> After a crime so monstrous, so exceptional,
> Ungrateful men are treated, and Theseus
> Is one of them. But whatsoe'er a fierce
> Resentment may suggest for my revenge . . .)

and in the third act she speaks of the *"rage"* and the *"colère"* which she feels. Of course the very end of this act suggests clearly her sanguinary purpose:

> M'en voir trahie! Il faut découvrir ma rivale. . . .
> Mais si d'un autre amour il se laisse éblouir,
> Peut-être il n'aura pas la douceur d'en jouir:
> Il verra ce que c'est que de me percer l'âme.
> Allons, Nérine, allons; je suis amante et femme:
> Il veut ma mort, j'y cours; mais avant que mourir,
> Je ne sais qui des deux aura plus à souffrir.

> (To see myself betrayed so! I must needs

In dramatising the well-known story of Queen Elizabeth and the Earl of Essex, Thomas Corneille followed in the footsteps of La Calprenède, whose *Comte d'Essex* was one of the three or four best tragedies written in the interval between the *Cid* and *Horace*. Unlike La Calprenède, he did not represent Elizabeth as an old woman, such as she really was at the time of the action, nor did he make use of the apocryphal incident of the ring which could have saved the life of her favorite. The Essex of his play has done great deeds and won mighty victories; he is hated by Cecil, Raleigh, and other powerful nobles, whose selfish schemes he opposes. The Queen is infatuated with him, but he is un-responsive because he secretly loves one of her ladies-in-waiting, who returns his love but who feels that he is courting ruin for her sake and accordingly, to save him from himself, consents to wed the Duke of Ireton. Essex learns

---

> Discover who my rival is. . . .
> But if he lets himself be fascinated
> By a new love, perhaps he will not taste
> The sweetness of it. He will see what 'tis
> To stab me to the heart. Come, come, Nerina;
> I am a woman and in love. He wishes
> My death; I hasten to it; but ere dying,
> I know not which will have the most to suffer.)

Yet Lancaster, also, finds in her desire for vengeance in the fourth act a new element of Ariadne's character "that is not shown else-where," though he points out that it serves the dramatic purpose of making her partly responsible for her fate by frightening Phaedra, hitherto restrained by pangs of conscience, into fleeing with Theseus forthwith (*op. cit.*, Part III, p. 600). Reynier in his discussion of this play simply ignores the fourth act altogether, the phase of Ariadne's nature with which it deals being inconveniently at variance with his sympathetic description of her! And indeed, the fact is that behind all unsound criticisms regarding her vengefulness lies the sound instinct that, though repeatedly indicated as one of her traits, it does accord ill with the rest of them.

of their impending marriage and, in a desperate effort to stop it, leads a mob against the palace, where the ceremony is being performed. He fails; his mad act has every appearance of being an attempt to seize the throne; his foes accuse him of this and also of treasonable correspondence with the Irish rebels; and without exposing the Duchess to the Queen's jealous rage he cannot reveal the truth which would clear him of the graver, better attested charge. Elizabeth is willing to forgive all if he will only confess his guilt; but when he insists that he is innocent of any wrongdoing, she lets him be arrested, tried, and sentenced to death. Even now she will pardon him if he will confess. He refuses to dishonor himself by owning to crimes that he has not committed; nor will he accept a pardon for them. In vain the Duchess of Ireton tells the Queen what is the real explanation of his conduct. Elizabeth has set her heart on his humbling himself before her, and declares that she will not intervene in his behalf unless he will "save her face" by furnishing her with an excuse for clemency; and he will not. With matters thus at a deadlock, the enemies of Essex, fearing lest he may escape them, hurry his execution through without waiting for the Queen's signature to authorize it.

One might maintain with some justice that such an outcome, not depending on Elizabeth herself, is no proper solution of the dramatic conflict between her and Essex. This, indeed, appears to be the chief defect in the play. True, it may be said that she invited that outcome when in obstinate pursuance of her cherished purpose she still left the Earl under the shadow of the executioner's axe after she had learned that he was guiltless; and that though she did finally declare, too late, that she would free him unconditionally, all her previous conduct indicated that she would never actually have brought herself to do so, but would have changed her mind after every such resolve—an indecision which must have cost him his life eventually, more or less

as it does at once in the play. Such rebuttal is inadequate; a
feeling that the conclusion is somewhat unsatisfactory will
not down. Yet in spite of this flaw, *le Comte d'Essex* is
Thomas Corneille's best tragedy—is, indeed, one of the
best tragedies written by any minor dramatist of the seventeenth century.

In this play, at last, there is none of that specific, distinctive flavor of *Timocrate,* which persists not only through all
the Corneillian dramas of this author but in *Ariane* also;
the romanesque elements, of which *le Comte d'Essex* like
all other French-classical tragedies has some share, are
merely those that any of them might possess. There is a
solidity, a sobriety, an air of reality about this play which
may or may not derive from the fact that its subject matter
is taken from English history of no distant date, but which
in any case is gratefully apparent. There is here a minimum
of gallantry for such a theme in that day. The characters
are complex, and their psychology is sound. Indeed, the
second-greatest fault in *le Comte d'Essex* results from the
realism of their portrayal; they (Elizabeth especially) go
over and over the same ground, as tortured people who do
not know too clearly their own minds are wont to do—
which, as we have seen in the instance of Du Ryer's Saul,
does not make for the orderly, effective progress of a dramatic action. The Duchess in her weakness, fear, and love,
is excellently drawn. The depiction of Elizabeth has been
commended by all critics; she, as they point out, is a
Racinian heroine in her intense emotions and fluctuating
impulses, though nothing could be more characteristically
Corneillian than her desire to love and be loved by Essex
without hope of marriage, which their inequality of station
forbids. And finally there is the figure of the Earl.

Reynier, who has made inexcusable errors of fact about
this play[16] just as we have seen that he did about *Timocrate*

16 E.g., concerning Essex's attack on the palace: "Elizabeth at

and *Ariane,* considers Essex an *"insupportable"* character, offensive because of his boundless self-esteem. Lancaster appears to agree in some measure with this opinion.[17] Certainly the Earl is all too proud; but other characters in the play testify to his great services and enormous value to his queen and country, other heroes of French-classical dramas have been outspoken as regards their own importance, and there is nothing unusual in one of them thinking that posterity will take note of him. And though it is true that Essex wantonly insults his enemies and considers his arrest, or at any rate his conviction and punishment, impossible, his death is not really a consequence of the overweening pride which makes him first incredulous of danger and afterwards unwilling to stoop at all to avert it. Critics seem to have overlooked the chief factor in his fate, a factor which is something so human and yet so little treated elsewhere in literature that this tragedy would be notable for the portrayal of it if for no other reason.

Essex is the willing victim of his own bitterness of heart. He dies to satisfy his savage desire to hurt those who love him but have wronged him and hurt him—to make them suffer, as he can because they love him. The woman whom he adores has presumptuously taken it upon herself to decide what is best for him and to act on her decision (without his knowledge or consent and against his fervent wishes) in regard to that about which he cares most in the world; "for his sake" she has crucified his feelings and hers, to put herself irrevocably beyond his reach. In his helpless rage and despair he wants to prove that she has not fur-

---

first refuses to think him guilty; she begs him to explain what he was attempting to do; she is ready to believe anything he tells her." (Translated from his *Thomas Corneille,* p. 171.) Every one of these statements is the exact opposite of the truth.

[17] *Op. cit.,* Part IV, p. 150.

thered his interests but has ruined his life; he wants her
sacrifice of their happiness to be vain; and he wants her to
know that it will be vain.

> Si vous m'aviez aimé,

he says—that, of course, is to wound her—

> vous auriez par vous-même[18]
> Connu que l'on perd tout quand on perd ce qu'on aime,
> Et que l'affreux supplice où vous me condamniez
> Surpassait tous les maux dont vous vous étonniez.
> Votre dure pitié, par le coup qui m'accable,
> Pour craindre un faux malheur, m'en fait un véritable.
> Et que peut me servir le destin le plus doux?
> Avais-je à souhaiter un autre bien que vous?

To complete his bitterness, he is accused and convicted of
foul treason; the Queen, whom he has served so well, believes him guilty; she and his country, too, which he has
served no less, will let him die by the hand of the headsman.
He has no wish to live, with such wrongs and with future
prospects so black. He spurns the suggestion that he should
seek a more honorable end on the field of battle:

> Quand contre un monde entier armé pour ma défaite [19]

----

[18] If thou hadst loved me, thou wouldst of thyself
Have known that when one loses one's beloved,
One loses everything, and that the anguish
To which thou wert condemning me surpasses
All those misfortunes which dismayed thy soul.
Thine unkind pity, with a crushing blow,
Through fear of a calamity imagined,
Gave me a real one. What can now avail me
The fairest fortune? Had I the desire
For any other blessing than thyself?

[19] Though 'gainst a whole world armed for my defeat

J'irais seul défier la mort que je souhaite,
Vers elle j'aurais beau m'avancer sans effroi,
Je suis si malheureux qu'elle fuirait de moi.
Puisqu'ici sûrement elle m'offre son aide,
Pourquoi de mes malheurs différer le remède?

Le crime fait la honte, et non pas l'échafaud;
Ou si dans mon arrêt quelque infamie éclate,
Elle est, lorsque je meurs, pour une reine ingrate
Qui, voulant oublier cent preuves de ma foi,
Ne mérita jamais un sujet tel que moi.
Mais la mort m'étant plus à souhaiter qu'à craindre,
Sa rigueur me fait grâce, et j'ai tort de m'en plaindre.
Après avoir perdu ce que j'aimais le mieux,
Confus, désespéré, le jour m'est odieux.
A quoi me servirait cette vie importune,
Qu'à m'en faire toujours mieux sentir l'infortune?

To no avail does the Duchess beg him to preserve, in pity
for her if not for himself, the life which he had once laid

I were to go alone in search of death,
I vainly would approach it without fear;
Such is my misery that 'twould flee from me.
Since here it surely offers me its aid,
Why not take now the remedy of my woes? . . .

The crime, and not the scaffold, makes the shame;
Or if my doom brings any infamy,
It falls on an ungrateful queen, who could
Forget a hundred proofs of my devotion
And ne'er deserved a subject such as I.
But since I find death more to be desired
Than feared, her harshness is a favor to me,
And I have been wrong in complaining of it.
When I have lost that which I loved the best,
Confused and in despair, I find existence
Hateful. What serves it me, this irksome life,
Save better to acquaint me with misfortune?

at her feet; he is careful to make her realize that by her high-handed course she has brought him to this plight and is responsible for his death:

> Des mes jours, il est vrai, l'excès de ma tendresse[20]
> En vous les consacrant vous rendit la maîtresse:
> · Je vous donnai sur eux un pouvoir absolu,
> Et vous l'auriez encor si vous l'aviez voulu.
> Mais, dans une disgrâce en mille maux fertile,
> Qu'ai-je à faire d'un bien qui vous est inutile?
> Qu'ai-je à faire d'un bien que le choix d'un époux
> Ne vous laissera plus regarder comme à vous?
> Je l'aimais pour vous seule; et votre hymen funeste
> Pour prolonger ma vie en a détruit le reste.
> Ah! madame, quel coup! Si je ne puis souffrir
> L'injurieux pardon qu'on s'obstine à m'offrir,
> Ne dites point, hélas! que j'ai l'âme trop fière;
> Vous m'avez à la mort condamné la première;
> Et refusant ma grâce, amant infortuné,

[20] 'Tis true that my love's fervor dedicated
  My life to thee and made thee mistress of it.
  I gave thee utter power over it,
  And thou wouldst have that still, hadst thou so wished.
  But now in this disaster fraught with woe,
  What can I do with a possession useless
  To thee? What can I do with a possession
  Which thy selection of a husband lets thee
  No more regard as thine? I treasured it
  For thy sake only; and thy fatal marriage,
  To make my life be longer, hath destroyed
  Whate'er remained of it. Ah, what a deed!
  If I cannot endure the insulting pardon
  Which so insistently is offered me,
  Do not say, madam, that I am too proud.
  Thou wert the first who did to death condemn me;
  And I, a hapless lover, refuse mercy

J'exécute l'arrêt que vous avez donné.

            Ah! qui vous perd n'a rien à conserver.
Si vous aviez flatté l'espoir qui m'abandonne,
Si n'étant point à moi, vous n'étiez à personne,
Et qu'au moins votre amour moins cruel à mes feux
M'eût épargné l'horreur de voir un autre heureux,
Pour vous garder ce cœur, où vous seule avez place,
Cent fois, quoiqu'innocent, j'aurais demandé grâce.

That he wishes also by his death to bring shame on his ungrateful sovereign and country, and to cause them regret and remorse when they realize his innocence too late, is not so explicitly set forth; yet I think it is clear enough that this motive, also, influences him. Of course the whole idea of making others sorry by permitting harm to oneself is somewhat childish; but there is more or less of the child still left in every man. In Essex, the erstwhile creator of romanesque tragedy achieves the undeniably real and the latently universal.

Le Comte d'Essex deserves a more extended treatment than can be given it in this study of the tragedies of Thomas Corneille. Yet even so good a single play is of less importance in our estimate of him than is the impressive sumtotal of his work in the tragic vein, possessing as it does an

---

And carry out the doom dispensed by thee.

            Ah, the man who loses thee
Has nothing to preserve! If thou hadst flattered
The hope which now I lack; if, though not mine,
Thou still wert no one's; and if thy love at least
Had been less cruel to *my* love and had spared me
The horror of seeing someone else possess thee,
To save this heart for thee in which thou only
Hast place, I would a hundred times, though guiltless,
Have asked for mercy.

average of merit that cannot be approached in a comparable number of tragedies by any other minor French-classical writer except Du Ryer. With his lack of poetic gift, his skill in plot-construction and stagecraft, and the variety and volume of his output, he is most naturally comparable to Philip Massinger among the Elizabethans. Massinger, though not a genuine poet, wrote much better verse—good rhetoric, at least, and always clear in meaning. The average quality of his plays was doubtless higher. But Thomas Corneille, despite all his romanesque convention, had a truer insight into character, and on occasion he made use of it—with better results in *le Comte d'Essex* than Massinger ever achieved.

CHAPTER VI
QUINAULT'S *ASTRATE*

ONE of the books that should but doubtless never will be written could best, both for piquancy and accuracy, be entitled *The Comical History of French Classical Tragedy*. It would of course be addressed to the educated general public, not to scholars; and it might well be almost a "best-seller." The potential amusingness of its subject matter is very great. French-classical tragedy from the first was tinctured with the absurdities of pastoral romance, with its sighing lovers and artificial conventions of speech and conduct, and the subsequent influence of the pseudo-historical romances only increased the artificiality and the absurdity.

One could almost say that in some part that book has been written already, though not in the popular vein nor with the object of arousing mirth—nor in English. Etienne Gros's huge monograph on Quinault[1] might well furnish no small portion of it. And a volume devoted to Quinault is indeed the most natural place in which to look for such material; for he, more than any other dramatist, is naturally to be associated in our minds with romanesque tragedy and tragi-comedy, where we find all the extravagances of the pseudo-historical romances themselves.

Thomas Corneille unquestionably gave vogue to the type —if he did not actually create it—with his *Timocrate*. But he wrote other kinds of tragedies, too; and even in his romanesque dramas he shows the influence not only of *le Grand Cyrus* and *Clélie,* but also of his illustrious brother. The same may be said of Boyer and others, but not of Quinault. Of humbler origins than any of his fellow playwrights,

---

[1] *Philippe Quinault, sa vie et son œuvre.*

and serving in childhood and youth as valet to Tristan l'Hermite, who launched him on his literary career, he presently became a protégé of the nobles and especially of the great ladies of *précieuse* society. It was the favor of these that he sought, writing what he knew would please them most; and so long as he won their plaudits he was well content. Clever, discreet, ingratiating, and affable, he went his way, taking no part in the literary quarrels and controversies of which the period was full, undisturbed apparently by the attacks made upon him and his pinchbeck plays, and leaving his defense to others. Boileau criticised him savagely; De Visé charged him with plagiarism in the case of his admired comedy, *la Mère coquette;* he seems to have replied to neither.[2] In his tragedies—and tragi-comedies—love is the supreme good; the hero is the slave of love, and will sacrifice his reputation, his life, or his country to it; all the characters, regardless of historical names and setting, are poured into the moulds established by the romances and the drawing-rooms.

In *la Mort de Cyrus* (1658-1659) Cyrus the Great, the founder of the Persian Empire, sees Tomyris, Queen of the Scythians, leading her troops against him, and instantly falls in love with her. Mindless of his responsibilities as king and commander, he lets his army be routed and himself be taken prisoner. He is told that he is to be executed, but when offered a chance to escape, he chooses to die rather than not be near his beloved. This amazonian queen of a savage people in turn falls in love with him, and writes in her *"tablettes"*

---

[2] His lowly antecedents and his success in climbing above them must have rendered him the more likely target of malice, jealousy, and scorn; and no doubt he felt that for such a one as he a patient silence when abused was the wisest policy. His behavior was in striking contrast to that of other French tragic dramatists of the seventeenth century. Often these were over-sensitive, envious, and waspish, comparing very poorly with the Elizabethan dramatists as men. There were two impressive exceptions, however, among them: Rotrou and Thomas Corneille.

dainty, subtle verses about the turmoil in her heart. Eventually he kills himself for her sake. The hero of *Amalasonte*
(1657) is accused of treason and could easily establish his
innocence; but he will not, because the woman he loves believes him guilty and to do so, would be to prove her wrong.
The hero of *Agrippa* (1662), one of Quinault's better plays,
when set upon by those whom his adored lady has incited to
kill him, does defend himself against them—but not very
vigorously at first, for he feels that his resistance to her
emissaries involves a lack of respect for her; he brings himself to seek safety only because he realizes that she would not
wish his death if she were correctly informed about him.

With all Quinault's absurdities, however, he has a light-
ness of touch that we do not find in Thomas Corneille, and
some genuine if not deeply-probing psychological insight.[3]
Delicacy is always the most notable of his virtues as a dramatist. Though his heroes are all of one same fantastic piece,
his heroines are individualized and rather well drawn. His
plots are less complex than those of *Timocrate* and most other
romanesque dramas, including much of the work of Pierre
Corneille. He is, in fact, an exponent and continuer of the
only other type of "classical" tragedy written in seventeenth-
century France besides the usual Corneillian sort: the type
originated by his master, Tristan l'Hermite, which found at
last its great author in Racine. Quinault, notwithstanding his
preoccupation with the romanesque, is the link between these
two more gifted men, carrying on, within the scope of his

[3] *Stratonice* (1660), perhaps his most characteristic play, is about
a prince and a princess who think themselves each disliked by the
other, while each really loves the other secretly; both of them are
ashamed and angered because their love is, supposedly, requited by
ill will, and they consequently feign the animosity which they do not
feel. In the case of the princess, this pretense is carried to truly outrageous extremes; but there are almost no limits to the spitefulness
customarily depicted, and accepted as "natural" and to be condoned, in romanesque "heroines."

limited abilities, the tradition of simplicity of theme, of emphasis on emotion rather than will and on love rather than on the heroic emotions, of verse which aims at smoothness and sweetness and poetic beauty rather than at impressive rhetoric, and of especial study of the heart of woman—a tradition which begins with Tristan, culminates in Racine, and is echoed in Campistron.

Astrate (1664-1665) shares with Thomas Corneille's *Timocrate* the distinction of being the most famous of purely romanesque dramas. It contains Quinault's best work by far, and almost if not quite his worst. It was this play in particular that Boileau unsparingly assailed. A summary of it, with quotations at some length, will give a good idea both of it and of Quinault.

After reigning fifteen years—so we learn from its expository scenes—a usurper of the throne of Tyre died and was succeeded by his daughter, Elissa, whom he had promised to Prince Agenor, the son of the man who had most helped him in his *coup d'état*. When ruled only by a woman, the populace were ready to revolt in favor of their legitimate sovereign, who had been held in prison all these years along with his two eldest sons, but Elissa saved her crown by promptly putting the three of them to death. There was one other son, but he disappeared in infancy, when his father was deposed; the hopes of those still faithful to the royal line are now centered in him, and it is rumored that he will soon come forward to claim his rights.

Meanwhile, Prince Agenor at the head of Elissa's army has been defeated twice by the forces of Syria, and she and her kingdom, as well as Agenor's life, have been saved only by the prowess of a young soldier, Astrates. This Astrates has fallen desperately in love with the Queen, but feels that with no other status than that of the son of a nobleman, Sichaeus, his passion is necessarily hopeless.

The play begins with a chance meeting—in an antechamber

of the palace where the action is located throughout—between
Astrates and Agenor, each accompanied by the usual "confidant." Seeing that Astrates tries to avoid him, the Prince
asks for an explanation. Astrates' confusion at a reference
to Agenor's impending marriage betrays his feelings, and
Agenor charges him with loving Elissa. He replies:

Puisque, jusqu'à vos yeux, mes feux ont éclaté,[4]
J'aime, je le confesse, avec témérité:
J'aime en dépit du sort, dont l'aveugle puissance
De moi jusqu'à la reine a mis trop de distance:
J'aime, malgré l'hymen, de qui les nœuds sacrés,
Pour vous unir demain, sont déjà préparés:
J'aime, malgré l'horreur de perdre ce que j'aime;
Et, pour dire encor plus, j'aime, malgré moi-même.
Mais, malgré votre hymen, mon destin et mes soins,
Malgré tous mes efforts, je n'en aime pas moins.

He thus without a vestige of dignified reserve "undrapes
his heart," be it noted, not only to his fortune-favored
"rival" but in the presence of two other men besides. Further self-exhibition follows:

Pour combattre, en secret, le mal dont je soupire,[5]

---

[4] Since to thine eyes my love's flame is displayed,
I love most rashly, I confess. I love
In spite of Fate, which sets, with her blind power
Too great a gulf betwixt the Queen and me.
I love despite the holy bonds of marriage
That will tomorrow join you, now awaited.
I love despite the pangs of losing her
I love—nay, more, I love despite myself.
But with thy marriage, my lot and my distress,
And all my efforts, I still love no less.

[5] To cure the malady that makes me sigh,

Je me suis dit cent fois tout ce qu'on peut se dire :
Tout ce qu'on peut tenter, je l'ai fait jusqu'ici ;
Du moins mon faible cœur se l'est fait croire ainsi,
Mais, s'il faut dire tout, contre un mal qui sait plaire,
On ne fait pas toujours tout ce que l'on croit faire ;
Et pour se reprocher un crime qu'on chérit,
Pour peu que l'on se dise, on croit s'être tout dit.

On Astrates' departure, Agenor's confidant expresses amazement that the Prince should leave such boldness unpunished, but Agenor points out that vain love itself is this lover's worst punishment, that the present unsettled condition of the realm makes it unadvisable to take any action against him now, and that a statesman must know how to dissemble his feelings. Agenor truly has need of this knowledge when Sichaeus brings him a message from the Queen postponing—not for the first time—their marriage ; and he indeed plays his part well, acquiescing in a further delay instead of seizing the crown forthwith as Sichaeus advises him to do. This old nobleman, one of the most loyal adherents of the last legitimate king, is artfully trying to create dissension between those wielding the usurped power ; having unsuccessfully urged Agenor to turn against Elissa, he warns her in the next scene not to trust the too-ready obedience of that prince.

"If I must have a lord and master, I want a worthy one," the Queen tells him.—"I am glad. Some neighboring king

---

Within my heart a hundred times have I
Told myself all that one can tell himself.
I have done all ere now that can be done.
At least my weak heart makes me think I have.
But, to be frank, against so sweet a sickness
One does not always do as much as he
Believes he does ; and to condemn wrongdoing
Which one loves dearly, howsoever little
One says, he deems he has said everything.

who could lend you support . . ."—"No. I, who can make a king, need not seek for one. My choice is your son."—"My son! O gods!"—"Why, what is the matter?"—"I am overwhelmed, madam. But this is not to your interest. Agenor, slighted thus, will be dangerous."—"Agenor forfeited all possible claim to me when he lost the battles that nearly cost me my throne. Another rescued it and gave it to me anew, not stained with wrong as formerly, but won by a hero's sword." —"I love my son dearly, but this is not a fitting marriage. He has no scepter of his own to bring you."—"He has purity (*vertu*) and that is what I stand in need of," says Elissa, and in her lines that follow there is a note of reality and sincerity not found before in this play. Crime gave her father the crown, she continues, but she herself has been worse than he, for her first act on becoming queen was to put to death the old king and his two sons. She has done this deed with horror, but she had no choice, she declares; it was their lives or her life, then; now there is the threat of the third, unknown son—the last, true heir to the throne—and he too must die. Fate, she says bitterly, has robbed her of conscience and linked her inextricably with crime. She bids Sichaeus send Astrates to her.

In the second act Elissa hears the response of the oracle of Jupiter Ammon, which she has consulted about her new danger. Its words are ominous, but she refuses to be frightened by them, for such prophecies are often fulfilled only because of the terror which they inspire. Agenor enters; he tells her that since evidently she does not want him for her husband, he will release her from all obligations towards him and leave her free to choose whom she wishes—and then promptly withdraws. His generosity makes her feel the more deeply indebted to him, though she does not quite believe him sincere. She confesses to her confidante that not merely need of Astrates' aid, nor even appreciation of his services, chiefly influences her choice; she loves him. She knows that he loves her, too; but she would be offended, or ought to be, if he forgot his respect and spoke to her of his love; though she is a woman, it is for her, as a queen, to speak first. When he now appears, she tells him that she has been informed of his presumptuous passion, which he admits in typical romanesque style:

> ... cette ardeur aveugle a sur moi tant d'empire,[6]
> Que, dussé-je en périr, je ne sais pas trop bien,
> Si je pourrais vouloir que vous n'en sussiez rien.
> J'ai bien jugé toujours, quoi que je pusse faire,
> Que je vous aimais trop, pour m'en pouvoir bien taire:
> Mais quelqu'affreux péril qui me dût alarmer,
> J'aurais bien du regret d'avoir pu moins aimer.
> D'un crime si charmant mon cœur insatiable,
> En voudrait, s'il pouvait, être encor plus coupable:
> Et, si je l'ose dire, aime mieux consentir
> A tout votre courroux qu'au moindre repentir.

Then she reveals to him (rather attractively, for such scenes are Quinault's especial forte) that her heart is his. But when she asks him what she ought to do after Agenor's magnanimity, he argues that, for the sake of her *"gloire"* and her interest alike, she should marry the Prince! She is not pleased, naturally, by this advice from Astrates and tells him that

> [6] ... this blind ardor hath such power o'er me
> That, though it meant my death, I am not sure
> That I could wish thou knewest nothing of it.
> I have deemed always that, do what I might,
> I loved thee so much I could not conceal it;
> Yet, needed I to fear the dreadest fate,
> I would be sorry if I could love thee less.
> Insatiable for such sweet sin, I fain
> Would be, if possible, still guiltier of it,
> And—dare I say this?—sooner would consent
> To bear thy wrath than in the least repent.

he deserves to see her follow it, but her manner when they part encourages his highest hopes.

Radiant with these, he comes again to the palace at the opening of Act III, with important news for Elissa about the conspiracy against her. What follows is the most comical, perhaps, of all the unintentionally comical scenes in French pseudo-classical tragedy. At the door to the Queen's apartment, Corisbe, her confidante, stops him. The Queen has forbidden entrance to all.—"May not an exception have been intended in my case?" Astrates asks her.—"No. To be frank, the order was given particularly for you."—"For me?"—"Maybe I shouldn't tell you anything more. Evils unknown are more easily borne."—"Better the most fearful blow than this uncertainty!" protests the now frantic young man.—"Well, then, you were no sooner gone than she had Agenor come; and in case you returned wanting an immediate audience, she commanded me to let you know that she is with the Prince and cannot see you."—"She sees my rival and forbids me her sight!"—"Wait; you have heard nothing, yet. She received him with the highest favor. She has given him the royal ring itself."—"Alas! My recent moment of bliss makes this the more terrible. Otherwise I would have been prepared for misfortune. My bitterest despair comes from having hoped."—"It comes from your too conscientious advice," Corisbe tells him roundly. "That was heroic of you, no doubt; but heroism is not always what love wants. To lose your happiness thus is more a virtue of a hero than of a lover. You ought not to talk quite so well against your own interests."—"I never dreamed I could persuade the Queen, at least not so easily. I wanted to show her that one who loved truly would give up all for his loved one's sake, but I thought she would feel the same way and follow my example instead of my advice!"

At this moment Agenor appears from within. "Here he is," Corisbe warns Astrates in a hurried aside. "Control yourself, and think . . ."—"Alas, am I in any state to think!" the distracted lover cries; and, quite unable to contain himself, he rushes straight up to the Prince.

> Come on, come on, my lord! gloat over me.[7]
> See the dread punishment of my presumption;
> And drink in, with long draughts, the matchless
>   pleasure
> Afforded by a rival's lorn despair.

"I should indeed be wrong to complain of the Queen," replies Agenor, placidly, displaying the royal ring. "At least this token justifies me in venturing to think so. But you have no grounds to complain of her either. You love; you are beloved. Is there anything sweeter to a lover's heart?"

"Enjoy your triumph! Insult a wretched man! Corisbe has told me all!"

"Let *me* tell you what happened after the last that Corisbe saw. The Queen tactfully explained to me that you had won her heart; but in recognition of the magnanimity of my attitude, and to soften her rejection of me, she wished, at least, that it might be as a gift from me that you should be made happy, and therefore she gave me this ring of authority. She did not doubt that, after what she had said, my generosity would be displayed in a great effort to crown your love."

Astrates is in ecstasy. "Ah, even thus far, my lord, wouldst thou be generous?"

"I cannot conceive a loftier purpose," Agenor tells him.

---

[7] Venez, venez, seigneur, jouir de ma disgrâce,
   Voir, l'affreux châtiment de mon aveugle audace,
   Et goûter, à long traits, le plaisir sans égal,
   Qu'on trouve au désespoir d'un malheureux rival.

Honor incites me to this noble act;[8]
Its countless charms strongly attract me to it;
But love, still stronger, will not let me do it!

Astrates recoils with incredulous horror. "And this is
love—love, whose mighty power should be strong enough
to conquer even itself?"

"Though self-conquest is heroic, to be happy is sweet," answers the imperturbable Agenor. "It is wrong for lovers to
be too generous."

"But you promised to waive your claims!"

"Love's promises are valueless. Love cannot betray its
own interests or surrender a happiness within its reach."

"And you call yourself 'in love,' my lord?" exclaims Astrates, in fine scorn. "Is it thus that one shows love!—thus
that a great heart would burn with love's flame!"

Agenor, we can imagine, shrugs his shoulders. "What
would you have? Each man has his own way of loving. *You*
love as a hero; for my part, I freely admit, I am weaker.
But I have never been ashamed of that sort of weakness."

"Yours is too flagrant to be excused!"

Another shrug, doubtless. "The Queen, though, found it
excusable. Yes, she was much vexed at first, and was surprised like you, when I would not give her up. But I was
able to make my peace with her; 'my great love' was my excuse. In short, she is going to marry me, and seeing you
jealous does not make me any the less happy."

"Reckon your good fortune above all others; mine, since
I am loved, is at least as good as yours." Thus does Astrates
clutch at some consolation in his despair. "Despite your name

[8] A cet illustre effort la gloire me convie;
La générosité m'y fait voir mille appas;
Mais l'amour plus puissant ne me le permet pas.

of 'husband,' it is not for me to be the more jealous of the two. Hapless though I am, the Queen loves me;

> And since thou knowest (and from her own lips)[9]
> That in thy marriage the love she feels for me
> Withholds her heart from what she offers thee,
> This prize thou lackest, whereof I deprive thee,
> For all thou gainest avenges and consoles me.
> This prize alone gives lovers joy in love.
> I keep from thee more than thou robb'st me of.

"Leave to me the delights which are accorded me"—one can almost see Agenor give the end of his little mustache an elaborately casual twist as he speaks the words—"and you may enjoy in peace these supernal fancies of yours."

> Since holy wedlock places in my arms,[10]
> Just as I wish, the Queen and all her charms,
> And since, no idle scruples troubling me,
> Before thy very eyes shall I, serene,
> Possess all this (the while with raptures keen
> My senses prove to me that I am happy),

[9] Puisque vous le savez, et par son aveu même,
Que, malgré votre hymen, l'amour en ma faveur
De ce qu'elle vous offre a séparé son cœur,
Ce bien qui vous échappe, et que mon feu vous vole,
De tout votre bonheur me venge et me console;
Ce bien seul des amants fait les félicités,
Et je vous ôte en lui plus que vous ne m'ôtez.

[10] Tandis qu'un nœud sacré, propices à mes souhaits,
Va mettre entre mes bras la reine et ses attraits;
Que sans m'embarrasser d'un scrupule inutile,
Je vais être à vos yeux le possesseur tranquille,
Et vais enfin, au gré de mes transports pressants,
M'assurer d'être heureux sur la foi de mes sens,

Console thyself, remembering that the Queen
At heart gives up thy love unwillingly.
Taste this sweet triumph; tell thyself indeed
That my good fortune beside thine is naught;
And be ingenious to beguile thy pain,
Conceiving joys in victory so vain.
I am quite willing! A remnant left of friendship
Still makes me see with pity thy distress,
And I, assured of my real blessings, yield
A fancied blessing easily to thee.
Thus shall we both alike contentment know:
Thou thinking thyself happy, I being so.

"No! The truth is, we are both miserable," cries Astrates, and thereupon he challenges the Prince to a duel! Agenor haughtily orders his arrest. But the captain of the guards arrests the Prince instead. The Queen was only testing him, and the royal ring is taken from him and given to Astrates. "Let us go," Agenor says to the guards. "Spare me, in the misfortune that crushes me, the unendurable sight of my triumphant rival."

And then, after this ludicrous episode, an abrupt change occurs in the play. Except for a few *précieuse* or extravagant phrases of gallantry, one can no longer laugh at it. Its sub-

---

Pour vous en consoler, songez qu'au fond de l'âme
La reine, avec regret, s'arrache à votre flamme.
Goûtez ce doux triomphe; imaginez-vous bien
Qu'auprès de votre sort tout mon bonheur n'est rien;
Et par les faux appas d'une victoire vaine,
Soyez ingénieux à flatter votre peine;
J'y veux bien consentir. Un reste d'amitié
M'oblige à voir encor vos maux avec pitié;
Et, sûr d'un bien solide, il ne me coûte guère
De vous abandonner un bien imaginaire.
Ainsi, chacun de nous se tiendra satisfait;
Vous de vous croire heureux, moi de l'être en effet.

ject matter becomes that of real drama, rising to a genuinely great issue. The somewhat thin, insipid, cliché-filled, facile, mellifluous style of Quinault is doubtless inadequate for this and leaves much to be desired—Boileau's gibe, that he could not say even "I hate you" except with tender sweetness, is famous—yet, nevertheless, no small pathos and tension are achieved. It is as though romanesque drama found here its apotheosis; for its invariable, central, all-absorbing, and irresistible factor, love as conceived in the romances of the day, here rises to a sort of grandeur by its potency when faced with truly tragic situations. The theme of the play henceforth—from almost exactly its halfway point, right on to the end—may be said to be the victory of such love over every other human impulse or obligation, and at last even over love itself. To a very considerable extent the characters and their problems "come alive"; one can surrender oneself to their story and largely accept for the moment their psychology, code, and viewpoint.

Astrates is rushing away to throw himself rapturously at the feet of the Queen, when Sichaeus stops him. "All your hopes have been fulfilled," says Sichaeus; "you can be the husband of Elissa if you wish. But are you really willing to marry a woman stained with the slaughter of our rightful kings?"—"Yes, for I loved her before that; I shuddered at the deed, but my love found excuse for it."—"But do you not at least fear to involve yourself in the retribution that is about to descend upon her?"—"No. The plot against her has been discovered."—"Discovered?" Sichaeus cries, recoiling. —"Yes; I know who several of the conspirators are," says Astrates, and mentions three names.—"But these men are our friends!"—"What is friendship beside love?"—"My son, I see I must tell you who is their chief. It is I, I whose loyalty to our kings has been ever steadfast. I have collected strength against the usurper. I alone know the identity of the true prince, who shall avenge his father and brothers

and wield again their scepter. You will destroy me, my son,
if you speak and reveal what now you know."—"And I destroy the Queen if I do not speak."—"Can you hesitate between us? I trust your filial virtue."—"Trust nothing from
a lover who fears for the life of his beloved. Abandon the
rebels; ask the Queen for pardon, and she will grant it for
my sake."—"Betray my oaths, my prince, and my friends?"
exclaims Sichaeus. "I have sworn to avenge my murdered
lord and to crown his son. The Queen or I must die. You
must choose between us."

This is an excellent climax, to which Quinault has worked
up with undeniable effectiveness, and his formerly absurd
hero rises to it worthily. "Between you and the Queen I will
not take sides, except to defend you each in turn, with my
life, against the other. Just now it is she who is in danger,
and I go to her aid. When I have shielded her from your attacks, I will come to you and either save you or die with
you."

Scarcely less dramatic than this final scene of the third
act, is one near the opening of Act IV—after a brief scene in
which Sichaeus gives his lieutenants the signal to begin the
revolt before Astrates' revelations can thwart his purpose.
To him comes Astrates, full of joy; the Queen has pardoned
them all, at her lover's request; only the unknown survivor
of the royal line must die, that she and the land may have
peace, for between him and her there can be no reconcilement.
"Do not surrender him," says Astrates; "name him but to
me, and with my single arm I shall prove whether his vengeance or my love, that so oppose each other, shall prevail."
—As all who know the ways of French romanesque tragedy
will have realized from the beginning, Astrates himself is
this true heir to the throne, this hereditary enemy of Elissa.
He recoils from the irrefutable proofs of his identity, which
Sichaeus now gives him. "Why was that secret not hidden
from me forever," he demands, "or why was it not told me

before my love took root?"—"I dared not disclose it till your revenge was assured," Sichaeus replies, "and I did not anticipate your unfortunate love, of which I learned only today."—"Why did you yourself have me save the Queen from the Syrians, who had taken up arms to avenge the blood which she had shed?"—"That was only their pretext. They are our enemies from of old; they really sought conquest, and had they achieved it, we would have rid our land of them much less easily than of her. Vengeance for your father belongs to you alone."—But the very thought of vengeance horrifies Astrates. "If I could only be *your* son!" he cries.— "You are the King's son. The proof of it is clear."—"No matter; in pity's name, be my father always!"—A not uneloquent appeal which the inexorable Sichaeus makes to him falls on deaf ears; he espies Elissa approaching, and answers a final "Consider who you are!" with a sudden grotesque lapse into the jargon of gallantry, of which the earlier acts were full:

Hélas! qui que je sois, à cet aspect charmant,[11]
Je ne me connais plus, et ne suis plus qu'amant,
Tout mon devoir s'oublie aux yeux de ce que j'aime.

But it is not gallantry that lies ahead, though some phrases still may smack of it. Sichaeus has gone out, baffled. Astrates and Elissa face each other at last, with every yet-remaining mask or veil to be stripped off before they part again; this, even more than the immediately preceding dialogue between Astrates and Sichaeus, is the "obligatory scene" of the play:

[11] Alas! whoe'er I be, at her sweet sight
I know it not and am a lover only.
All duty is forgot in her dear presence.

Elise.[12]

Hé bien! mon ennemi vous est-il découvert?
Nul espoir contre lui ne peut-il m'être offert?
Doit-il m'ôter le sceptre et la vie . . .

Astrate.

Ah, madame!

Elise.

Je vous trouve interdit! qui trouble ainsi votre âme?
Tout votre soin pour moi n'a-t-il rien obtenu?

Astrate.

Hélas! votre ennemi ne m'est que trop connu.

Elise.

En l'état où je suis, c'est peu de le connaître;
Peut-être de ces lieux est-il déjà le maître?
On vient de m'avertir que le peuple en fureur
Se soulève, s'attroupe et s'arme en sa faveur;

---

[12] Elissa.

Well, hath thy search disclosed my enemy?
Is there no hope to offer me against him?
Must I be reft of throne and life . . .

Astrates.

Ah, madam!

Elissa.

I find thee stunned. What troubles thus thy heart?
Has all thy care accomplished nothing for me?

Astrates.

Alas! I know thy enemy all too well.

Elissa.

As I now stand, to know him avails little.
Is he, perchance, already master here?
I have just heard the populace in fury
Hath risen, gathers, and takes up arms for him,

Et qu'un gros de soldats, joint à la populace,
En soutient la révolte, et redouble l'audace.
J'ai vu même à ce bruit la frayeur s'emparer
De ceux en qui j'ai cru devoir plus espérer;
Tout cherche à me trahir, tout me devient funeste;
Et, si j'ai quelqu'espoir, c'est en vous qu'il me reste:
Mon ennemi, sans vous, est sûr de m'accabler.

ASTRATE.

Non; n'appréhendez rien; c'est à lui de trembler.
L'état où mon amour l'a déjà su réduire,
Ne lui peut désormais permettre de vous nuire.

ELISE.

Quoi! contre ses efforts, vous pourriez m'assurer?

ASTRATE.

Je puis même encor plus, je puis vous le livrer.

While many of the soldiers, joining it,
Aid its revolt and give it greater boldness.
I even have seen fear at this rumor seize
On those in whom methought I most could trust.
All would betray me; all would be my foes.
If I have any hope, it lies in thee.
My enemy, but for thee, is sure to crush me.

ASTRATES.

Nay, feel no fear. It is for him to tremble.
The pass to which my love e'en now hath brought him
Does not enable him henceforth to harm thee.

ELISSA.

What! Thou couldst make me safe 'gainst all his efforts?

ASTRATES.

I can do even more. I can deliver him
Into thy hands.

ELISE.

Me le livrer vous-même! ô ciel! se peut-il faire
Que j'aie un bien si doux par une main si chère?
Et que le plus mortel de tous mes ennemis,
Par un amant aimé, me soit enfin remis?
Ce temps presse à ma haine; offrez donc, sans attendre,
Ce sang fatal qu'il faut achever de répandre:
De cette heureuse mort hâtons-nous de jouir.

ASTRATE.

Hé bien, madame! hé bien! il faut vous obéir;
Et pour tarir ce sang qui vous est si funeste,
En montrer à vos yeux le déplorable reste.
Ce dernier fils d'un roi par votre ordre égorgé;
Ce fils par son devoir à vous perdre engagé;
Cette victime encore à vos jours nécessaire;
Ce malheureux vengeur d'un misérable père,

ELISSA.

      Deliver him into my hands!
Ah, heaven! can it be contrived that I
Should have so sweet a gift from one so dear,
And that the deadliest of all my foes
Should in my power be placed by him I love!
The time is ripe for ruthlessness. Then show me,
Without delay, this blood that must be spilled,
And let us hasten to find our joy therein.

ASTRATES.

So be it, madam; so be it. I must obey thee,
And to exhaust this blood so baleful to thee,
Must point out its forlorn last residue.
This last son of a king slain by thine order,
This son whom duty bindeth to destroy thee,
This victim necessary for thy life,
This sad avenger of a wretched father,

D'une maison détruite et d'un sceptre envahi;
Enfin, cet ennemi tant craint et tant haï,
Dont nous cherchions la perte avec un soin extrême,
Qui l'eût pu croire? Hélas! Madame, c'est moi-même.

ELISE.

Vous! O ciel! Vous, Astrate!

ASTRATE.

En vain pour me flatter,
J'ai fait ce que j'ai pu pour tâcher d'en douter.
Sichée en me montrant ce que je frémis d'être,
S'il en eût cru mon cœur, m'eût laissé méconnaître:
Mais de ce sort affreux ignoré jusqu'ici,
Il ne m'a, malgré moi, que trop bien éclairci.
Je vois que ce revers comme moi vous accable;
Que votre âme, à ce coup, n'est pas inébranlable.

ELISE.

Si j'ai cru l'être, Astrate, et me l'étais promis,

A house obliterated, a throne usurped,—
In fine, this enemy so feared and hated,
For whose destruction we have spent such toil:
Who could have dreamed? alas, 'tis I myself.

ELISSA.

Thou! O God! Thou, Astrates!

ASTRATES.

All pretenses
Are vain. I did the best I could to doubt it.
Sichaeus proved me what I quailed at being.
If he had judged me aright, he would have left me
In ignorance; but not knowing my dire plight,
Too well he made all clear against my wishes.
I see that thou art overwhelmed, like me;
That *thy* soul, at this blow, is not unshakable.

ELISSA.

If I have thought and sworn it was, Astrates,

Je ne vous comptais pas parmi mes ennemis.
Je me vantais à tort d'un courage invincible,
D'une âme à la terreur, au trouble inaccessible.
L'ingénieux courroux du ciel plein de rigueur,
N'a que trop bien trouvé le faible de mon cœur.
J'aurais bravé mon sort, s'il ne m'eût point trompée;
Je ne m'en gardais pas par où j'en suis frappée.
De ce piège des dieux, qui se fût défié?
Mon cœur, était, sans doute, assez fortifié
Contre tous les dangers qui menaçaient ma vie;
Il ne l'était que trop contre un peuple en furie,
Contre les dieux vengeurs, les destins en courroux;
Mais il ne l'était pas contre l'amour et vous.

ASTRATE.

De l'amour et de moi que peut craindre votre âme?
Contre votre ennemi vous pouvez tout, madame;
Vous vouliez le connaître, et je vous l'ai montré;
Vous cherchiez à le perdre, et je vous l'ai livré.

I did not then count thee among my foes.
I boasted wrongly of a dauntless courage,
A spirit unmoved by terror or confusion.
The ingenious wrath of unrelenting heaven
Hath found too well the weakness of my heart.
If it had not betrayed me, well might I
Have challenged destiny. But I kept no guard
Where I was smitten. Who would have suspected
This snare set by the gods? My heart was steeled
Indeed against all dangers threatening me—
Only too well against a frenzied people,
Against avenging deities, angry Fates—
But it was not steeled against love and thee.

ASTRATES.

From love and me, what has thy heart to fear?
All power is thine, madam, against thy foe.
Thou fain wouldst know him; I have shown him to thee.

N'épargnez pas mon sang dans ce malheur extrême;
Vous en avez besoin, il me pèse à moi-même;
Il coulera sans peine, et tout vous est permis;
Il est coupable assez de nous faire ennemis.
Trop heureux, s'il vous laisse en paix au rang su-
    prême . . .

ELISE.

Ne me reprochez pas d'aimer le diadème.
S'il m'a pu tant coûter d'injustice et de soin,
C'etait pour vous l'offrir, l'amour m'en est témoin.
Je n'ai fait cependant rien qui ne vous trahisse;
Le ciel, contre mes vœux, tourne mon injustice;
Et tout ce que pour vous j'ai commis de forfaits,
Au lieu de nous unir, nous sépare à jamais.

ASTRATE.

Ainsi, madame, ainsi, pour avoir su vous plaire,

Thou soughtest his blood; I offer it to thee.
Spare not to shed it in my misery.
To thee 'tis needful; me it weigheth down.
'Twill flow forth without pain, and 'tis all thine.
Its guilt is great in making us be foes.
Too happy would I feel if by its loss
Thou shouldst be left in peace with power supreme . . .

ELISSA.

Do not reproach me that I love a crown.
If I have bought it by so much injustice
And cares so many, 'twas that I might give it
To thee, be love my witness! But I have done
Nothing, the while, that was not treason against thee.
Lo, heaven hath made my sins defeat my wishes,
And all the crimes that for thy sake I wrought,
Far from uniting, sunder us forever.

ASTRATES.

So, then, by finding favor in thy sight,

C'est donc moi qui vous fis sacrifier mon père,
Répandre tout le sang qui m'avait animé,
Et je fus parricide à force d'être aimé.

ELISE.

Vous vous justifierez, en immolant ma vie;
Et serez innocent, quand vous m'aurez punie.
Vous devez vous venger et même me haïr:
Votre sort vous l'ordonne . . .

ASTRATE.

Hé! lui puis-je obéir?
Vous, un objet pour moi de haine et de vengeance!
Et vous me condamnez à cette obéissance!

ELISE.

J'avouerai ma faiblesse, Astrate, et qu'en effet
J'ai peine à vous presser d'obéir tout à fait.
Ne suivez qu'à demi ce devoir trop funeste;
Sauvez-m'en la moitié, je suis d'accord du reste;

'Tis I who made thee sacrifice my father,
Shed all the blood of those who gave me life—
Yes, was a parricide through being loved.

ELISSA.

To slay me is to vindicate thyself.
Thou wilt stand innocent when I am punished.
Thou shouldst avenge thy wrongs and even hate me.
Thy destiny so bids . . .

ASTRATES.

Can I obey it?
An object, thou, of hate and vengeance for me?
And thou condemnest me to this obedience!

ELISSA.

I shall confess that I am weak, Astrates.
'Tis hard to urge thee to obey entirely.
Discharge but half of this too cruel duty.
Save me from part of it; I will accept the rest.

J'y consens sans regret; vengez-vous: mais, hélas!
Astrate, s'il se peut, ne me haïssez pas.

ASTRATE.

Ah! j'obéirai trop pour peu que j'obéisse!
Et comment voulez-vous qu'un amant vous punisse?
Non, non; le ciel veut bien voir trahir son courroux,
Puisqu'il prend un vengeur si faible contre vous:
C'est pour vous épargner qu'en mes mains il vous
    livre,
Qu'il m'impose un devoir que je ne saurais suivre;
Et s'il avait voulu vous perdre absolument,
Il ne s'en fierait pas au devoir d'un amant.

ELISE.

C'est par vous toutefois qu'il veut que je périsse;
Un oracle l'assure, il faut qu'il s'accomplisse;
Les dieux me l'ont trop dit, pour en oser douter.

I yield, unforced; avenge thyself; but, oh,
Astrates, if 'tis possible, do not hate me!

ASTRATES.

Ah, I obey too much, if I obey
At all! And how wouldst thou that one who loves thee
Shall punish thee? Nay, nay, 'tis heaven's will
To see its anger foiled, since it hath taken
So strengthless an avenger 'gainst thee. 'Tis
To spare thee that it puts thee in my hands
And sets for me a task I cannot do.
If it desired thine absolute destruction,
It would not have relied on one who loves thee.

ELISSA.

Yet 'tis through thee that it would have me perish.
So saith an oracle; so must it be.
Too much the gods have told me, to dare doubt it.

ASTRATE.

L'Amour est le dieu seul qu'il en faut consulter,
Et sa voix dans mon cœur, s'expliquant sans obstacle,
Vous répond du contraire et vaut bien votre oracle.
C'est le dieu qui me touche et me connaît le mieux;
Fiez-vous plus à lui qu'à tous les autres dieux.
S'ils menacent par moi vos jours et votre empire,
Ils se sont abusés, j'ose les en dédire:
Je prétends vous sauver en dépit des destins.

The captain of the guard rushes in with news that the insurrection is sweeping all before it, and Astrates goes to aid in the Queen's defense. It is the end of Act IV.

There is nothing in the rest of the play that reaches this standard. But, for Quinault, the whole of the fifth act is remarkably strong and real. It begins with Elissa and her confidante. Confronted with the immediate prospect of death, she yet is happy—happy that her lover defends her in spite of everything.[13] Her one fear is for him; and to save him from the peril he incurs for her, she is determined to die by

ASTRATES.

Love is the only god to be consulted,
And in my breast his voice outspokenly
Gainsays thee and outweighs thine oracle.
'Tis he who moves my heart and knows me best.
Trust more in him than all the other gods.
If they through me threaten thy life and throne,
They are deceived; I dare to contradict them.
I mean to save thee even in spite of Fate.

[13] It is a point in Quinault's favor that, in contrast to romanesque heroes like Timocrates, who without a qualm fight against those loyal to them, Astrates is carefully represented as first trying to appeal to the insurrectionists to desist and drawing his sword against them only when they refuse to listen to him and continue their attacks on the palace.

her own hand. Sichaeus and his triumphant companions enter; she is told that her final hour has come, and that Astrates,
his sword broken, is held a prisoner. Elissa thinks only of
him and asks, as a last request, that he be carefully protected
from suicide after her death; with the permission of Sichaeus
she withdraws to kill herself. Now Astrates, breaking away
from his captors, bursts into the room. He pleads for her
life; but Sichaeus is adamant and will not make public
Astrates' identity until she is beyond rescue. Afterwards the
young king may slay him if he likes; his work will have been
done.—"If she dies, I will follow her in death," declares
Astrates. "Cruel man, do you fear to shed my blood when
you do not fear to tear out my heart?"—"I am not without
pity; but do you, my lord, think that it is right to spare the
Queen?"—"Granted, if you will," says her lover, "it is a
crime to spare her! I take that crime, however terrible, upon
myself. I absolve you from it. I, your king, command you!"
—Sichaeus, for the first time, wavers, and when Astrates,
changing to a tenderer tone, beseeches him "in the name
of your son that I so loved to be," he yields and orders Elissa
to be brought in. She comes, but she has already taken poison.
"My love has softened this too loyal subject," Astrates tells
her, "vanquished his sense of duty, seduced his zeal."—"But
did your love," she asks, fondly, "think to seduce mine also?
No, no; love, when it is great, may seduce all and van-
quish all, except love itself. Justice demanded my death of
you, and when our mutual love makes you forget this for
my sake, I must needs remember it for you. . . . Thus I expiate my offense and bring peace to the contention within
your breast. You can love me without sin after my death.
Nothing is left me to live for, now. The throne was dear to
me, and you were dearer still. Life in obscurity with you
would have been sweet; but with neither a throne nor you,

what is life to me!" She dies, and Astrates falls in a death-like swoon as the curtain descends.

After *Astrate,* Quinault underwent in some degree the influence of Racine. His *Pausanias* (1668) imitates *Andromaque,* though not very successfully; his *Bellérophon* (1670-1671) is, in a rather undistinguished way, his best tragedy as a whole, with a portrait in its Stheneboea of a passionate, unscrupulous woman quite along Racinian lines.[14] He then permanently forsook dramatic composition to write librettos for the operas of Lully—just as, in the period of Elizabethan drama, Ben Jonson in the latter part of his life devoted himself for a number of years to the composition of Court masques. Now at last Quinault found his proper vocation. All the qualities, good and bad alike, which had marked his plays—his metrical facility, his conventional saccharine verses, his prettiness of fancy, and the delicate artificiality of his stage world—were entirely appropriate in opera. It is said that his collaboration with Lully was the most satisfactory partnership that has ever existed between a composer and his librettist. But their operas have long been forgotten; and, thanks to a great critic's spleen, such dubious immortality as Quinault may have is as the author of *Astrate.*

[14] It has frequently been said that this play furnished suggestions for Racine's *Phèdre,* notably for its hero's love, its heroine's jealousy, and the fact that its hero wounds the monster that he encounters—none of which details are in the *Hippolytus* of Euripides or the *Phaedra* of Seneca. I must confess myself unimpressed by these similarities of *Phèdre* to *Bellérophon.* For when was there any heroine of French-classical tragedy not jealous if she had a chance to be? When was any young hero in French-classical tragedy not in love with somebody, and when did he ever fail to exhibit "prowess"—if there was a chance for it—before being killed? Without any "source" for these details, Racine would have been absolutely certain to invent them.

CHAPTER VII
RACINE'S APPRENTICESHIP

IN 1660, when Racine was twenty years old, he wrote a tragedy called *Amasie,* which was never acted and has not been preserved. What its theme was, we do not know. Lancaster has suggested that it may deal with Amasiah, King of Judah, the son of the Joash of *Athalie.* "If this could be established," he says, "it would make an interesting connection between Racine's first play and his last." He continues, however: "But it seems highly improbable that a young dramatist in 1660 would have sought to make his début in a play drawn from the Bible." [1]

The improbability appears somewhat less if we take into consideration the fact that Racine had been educated by Jansenists, at Port Royal and indeed even earlier. One so piously reared, whose mind was steeped in the Scriptures, might not unnaturally find in them his first idea for a play. But N. M. Bernardin was inclined to derive *Amasie* from the romance *Scanderbeg* (1643) .of d'Urbain Chevreau, "in which the princess Amasie is in a position between the loving Eleazar and the fierce Mustapha almost identical with that of Bajazet between the sensitive Atalide and the jealous Roxana." [2]

The youthful Racine seems to have undertaken two other dramas of which we possess not a single line, one on the love affairs of Ovid, the other on the Greek romance of Heliodorus, *The Loves of Theagenes and Chariclea,* which had

[1] *A History of French Dramatic Literature in the Seventeenth Century,* Part IV, p. 51, note 2.

[2] Translated from his chapter on Racine in Petit de Julleville's *Histoire de la Langue et de la Littérature française,* vol, v, p. 78.

been one of his favorite books in his adolescent years. We do not know whether he finished either play, but their nature reveals a predilection already for amatory subject matter, which indicates that even then he was no disciple of the great Corneille. And his own comment when *Amasie* was rejected by the company at the Marais theater makes that fact evident: "I am afraid that actors at present care only for rhodomontade, provided it comes from a great author." Indeed, he first phrased it "from *the* great author." Clearly, his taste from the very beginning was for simplicity of style. *Les Amours d'Ovide* and *Théagène et Chariclée*, if not *Amasie* too, suggest that he may, however, have been in these lost works an imitator of Quinault, who was at that time very popular. But when we next come to his first extant play, *la Thébaïde* or *les Frères ennemis*, we find that here he follows, as best a young man of twenty-four can in this year of 1664, in the footsteps of Euripides, whose *Phoenissae* is its principal source.

The significance of this choice of material has not, I think, been sufficiently remarked upon. Perhaps it has been passed over because Racine says in his preface to the play that the subject was suggested to him by certain *personnes d'esprit*. But this preface was written in 1676, when he was at the very peak of his career, and reveals him decidedly apologetic about *la Thébaïde*. He asks more indulgence for it than for his other plays: he was very young when he wrote it; some verses of his fell by chance into the hands of these *personnes d'esprit*, and they urged him to write a tragedy and proposed this subject. Racine's word cannot be trusted in regard to sources, as too many misrepresentations attest.[3] He well

---

[3] E.g., he does not admit his indebtedness to Corneille or any other contemporary in *Andromaque*, or to Seneca in *Phèdre;* and he tells two somewhat different stories, neither of which seems to be accurate, about his source for *Bajazet*.

knew that *la Thébaïde* was inferior work, and he would have
all the more excuse for it if, when he wrote it, he were not
only youthful but also merely trying to carry out the ideas
of others. The fact is that he grew up a better Greek scholar
and a greater lover of ancient Greek literature than any other
dramatist of the seventeenth century, was a fervent admirer
of both Sophocles and Euripides, and had just before this
time been annotating Pindar and the *Odyssey* with the keenest relish. He needed the impulsion of no one but himself to
direct him to Antigone (his "Thebaness") for a heroine and
to the fratricidal strife of Eteocles and Polynices (his "hostile brothers") for plot-material.

The time had been when the themes of surviving Greek
tragedies had frequently served the needs of French playwrights. Garnier and other sixteenth-century dramatists had
reworked them; and in the sixteen-thirties there was a decided vogue of these themes—as witness the *Médée* of Corneille, the *Antigone* and *Iphigénie* of Rotrou, and several
other plays. But between 1645 and *la Thébaïde* there had
been only one tragedy based on a Greek subject, the *Œdipe*
of Corneille, which appeared in 1659. Yet the first drama
that Racine produced was in source Greek; and out of his
total of nine secular tragedies, four were Greek. Except
Alexandre and possibly *Bajazet,* all of them were either
Greek or else products of his bitter rivalry with Corneille;
whenever he followed his own taste, he followed his Attic
masters.[4] So strongly was he influenced by his early reading
and the literary ideals which this formed in him!

Just how, in *la Thébaïde,* did he follow his Attic masters?
No dramatist can achieve success without paying some

---

[4] Let us note also his three projected tragedies on Iphigenia in
Tauris, Alcestis, and Oedipus, of which his retirement deprived us.
And when he took up his pen again, many years later, to write
Biblical plays, he approximated the form of Greek drama as closely
as possible.

regard to the tastes of his audience, and no writer is entirely uninfluenced by current ideas and literary fashions. In 1663-1664 the tide of romanesque tragedies was still at full flood. Thomas Corneille had made them the rage with his *Timocrate* in 1656. Quinault and Boyer had followed him in writing this type of play; Pierre Corneille had compromised with it. The other most famous example of it, *Astrate,* was to appear in the winter of 1664-1665. Under the circumstances, *la Thébaïde* could not but contain a love-affair. But the fact is that the love between Haemon and Antigone was a detail of the Greek story itself. Racine only played it up and brought them on the stage together. Any dramatist of the nineteenth or twentieth century, finding it in his source, would have done the same. The only difference was that Racine made his lovers talk in the sole way he knew which would have been acceptable to his immediate audience—that is, like the lovers in seventeenth-century French romances and romanesque dramas. Therefore this play has been said by some to be reminiscent of the work of Quinault, just as others have thought it reminiscent of Corneille because the rival brothers and the ambitious Creon talk of political matters somewhat in the way in which Corneille's men of affairs talk of them. But, really, it is hard to see how a dramatist in that day could have written more closely in imitation of classical tragedy than Racine did here—for the first four acts.[5] It would appear that he had attempted, with his head full of the surviving Greek dramas, to reweave the threads of the Theban legend so as to make a new play that would vie with the ancient dramatists in their own manner, and had incorporated in this play only as much of what smacked of his own times as it was inevitable that he would have.

[5] True, he borrowed freely from the *Antigone* of Rotrou, but that play itself belongs to a time (1637) when the conventions of French pseudo-classicism were not yet completely established.

That ubiquitous figure of French-classical tragedy, the confidant, is found here only in the persons of Olympia and Attalus, whose roles are brief; and they, except the latter in his scene with Creon in Act III, play the part of the classical "messenger" quite as much as that of confidant.[6] The rhetorical nature of many speeches is perhaps no more Corneillian than Senecan. The weakness of *la Thébaïde*—for the first four acts, at any rate—springs less from pseudo-classical convention than merely from youthful ineptitude. Racine had not yet attained to the insight into character and to the mastery of the language of passion that were to signalize his later work. And there are numerous flaws in detail; for example, he introduces a description of the legendary self-sacrificial death of Menoeceus, though this cannot be very moving because that youth is not one of the dramatis personae.

In concluding his play, he quite spoiled it. Evidently he wished it to be as tragic as possible, and mistakenly supposed that to do so involved making it tragic for everyone concerned. Into the one remaining act after the death of Eteocles and Polynices he could not possibly crowd the whole famous story of Antigone's martyrdom. He could have represented her instead, however, as committing suicide because her brothers and her lover were dead. (If he had not represented Haemon as having already died, she would have lived for him—or else their love would have seemed of little strength, belying their scenes together.) But why should Creon die, the ruthless Creon, whom ambition ruled? Now, Racine could indeed imitate true classicism; but when thrown back on his own powers of invention his mind invariably ran in the groove of pseudo-classicism. And thus he consequently

[6] The conventionality of Attalus as confidant, however, is especially marked in his being made the recipient of Creon's confidences with which he is evidently not in sympathy.

devised: Creon will be reduced to despair, ready to take his own life at the final curtain, by the death of Antigone; he has loved Antigone, silently, all along! Why, of course! for in pseudo-classical tragedy everybody must be in love with somebody, and love must be at least a factor in everything.

There has been little preparation earlier in the play for this turn of the plot. Creon's secret passion for Antigone is not really disclosed till Act V is more than half over; there is only a brief hint of it previously. It does not harmonize with the rest of his portrayal; it demands a twelfth-hour change in our conception of him. Neither it nor his conventional despair at its frustration is at all convincing.

For a first-play, la Thébaïde was reasonably successful; but Racine would not be satisfied with anything less than unqualified success immediately achieved. His next drama, Alexandre le Grand, was carefully designed to win precisely this.[7] Its ultimate source of inspiration seems to have been Corneille's la Mort de Pompée, which his contemporaries perversely regarded as a masterpiece.[8] Pompée deals with one

---

[7] That to do so now, and make himself a prominent figure once for all, was his besetting purpose, is proved by the well-known facts connected with this play. He gave a reading of it before a group of notables before putting it on the stage. He dedicated it to the young king Louis XIV himself, drawing a fulsome parallel between him and Alexander. He placed it with Molière's company and then, being dissatisfied with their acting of it, gave it, without a word to them, to the rival troupe of the Hôtel de Bourgogne, who put it on in competition with Molière's company. Thus Racine sacrificed alike the principles of fair dealing and a friendship which ended, naturally, then and there. The play itself sacrificed his already-formed literary ideals. Truly, in this great bid for fame its author spared nothing and nobody!

[8] Did Racine himself always so regard it, even to the end of his own career? Judged by the standards of his fully matured genius, it should have been anathema to him; yet when he delivered his eulogy of his great rival in 1685, he named as Corneille's chefs-d'œuvre the Cid, Horace, Cinna, and Pompée, omitting Polyeucte.

of the two great conquerors of antiquity, Julius Caesar, whom it depicts, however, largely in the role of a gallant lover, like some hero in *Clélie* or *le Grand Cyrus,* and whom it does not bring on the stage till the third act of the play. Racine's new "tragedy" deals with the other great conqueror of antiquity, Alexander, depicts him mainly in the role of a gallant lover, and does not bring him on the stage till the third act. *Pompée* is full of the conventional language of romanesque love, and so is *Alexandre. Pompée* begins with a discussion as to whether the approaching Caesar should be placated or opposed, *Alexandre* with a similar discussion in regard to the approaching Alexander. The most admired scenes of this drama of Corneille's had been those dealing with Pompey's widow, Cornelia, who cannot help admiring Caesar but persists in hating him for having been the cause of her husband's death. Racine's Indian princess Axiana expresses the same conflicting sentiments about Alexander so long as she believes her lover, Porus, to be dead. But Porus, who is more prominent throughout the play than Alexander himself, does not really die in his resistance to the invincible Macedonian; and not only is that in accord with history but it also pleased the audiences of Racine's day, who saw the true lovers united in the end and Porus' base rival, Taxiles, alone killed. To the modern mind, however, until the eventual treachery of Taxiles, there is much that commends him more than Porus, a characteristic strutting "hero" of the period, who thinks of nothing but love and his *"gloire,"* never of what may be to the best interests of his subjects!

But *Alexandre* does not have the evocation of a historical background or the vitality of characterization that are rarely

---

This was in line with the consensus of critical opinion of that day. Did it also represent Racine's opinion? Or did he speak only in deference to the view generally held, rightly not wishing to be controversial on such an occasion?

absent from Corneille's work. With its lack of action or true human passion and its disproportionate concern with conventionalized "gallant" love, it is rather in the manner of Quinault. Obviously, this mere romanesque drama is inferior to *la Thébaïde*. Yet it shows a certain growth of Racine's powers. Its plot is of a genuinely classical simplicity, as are the plots of its author's later plays; it goes, already, far beyond even Quinault in this respect, to say nothing of the two Corneilles. As regards poetic ability, Racine is now little short of his full stature; his verse here exhibits in large measure all its distinctive qualities of exquisite clarity, euphony, and precision, its well-ordered arrangement of thoughts and discriminating choice of words. Truly eloquent, for example, is the reply of Porus when Hephaestion would have him perceive in others' fate the futility of his resistance:

> Que verrais-je, et que pourrais-je apprendre[9]
> Qui m'abaisse si fort au-dessous d'Alexandre?
> Serait-ce sans efforts les Persans subjugués,
> Et vos bras tant de fois de meurtres fatigués?
> Quelle gloire en effet d'accabler la faiblesse
> D'un Roi déjà vaincu par sa propre mollesse,
> D'un peuple sans vigueur et presque inanimé,
> Qui gémissait sous l'or dont il était armé,
> Et qui, tombant en foule, au lieu de se défendre,

[9] What would I see? What could I know
To make me bow 'neath Alexander so?
How without effort Persia was subdued,
And how your arms grew tired with shedding blood?
  What glory to o'ercome a king no less
Defeated by his own unmanliness,
A folk supine, almost inanimate,
Who groaned beneath their golden armor's weight
And, falling in heaps instead of showing fight,

N'opposait que des morts au grand cœur d'Alexandre?
Les autres, éblouis de ses moindres exploits,
Sont venus à genoux lui demander des lois;
Et, leur crainte écoutant je ne sais quels oracles,
Ils n'ont pas cru qu'un Dieu pût trouver des obstacles.
Mais nous, qui d'un autre œil jugeons des conquérants,
Nous savons que les Dieux ne sont pas des tyrans;
Et, de quelque façon qu'un esclave le nomme,
Le fils de Jupiter passe ici pour un homme.
Nous n'allons point de fleurs parfumer son chemin;
Il nous trouve partout les armes à la main;
Il voit à chaque pas arrêter ses conquêtes;
Un seul rocher ici lui coûte plus de têtes,
Plus de soins, plus d'assauts, et presque plus de temps
Que n'en coûte à son bras l'empire des Persans
Ennemis du repos qui perdit ces infâmes,
L'or qui naît sous nos pas ne corrompt point nos âmes.
La gloire est le seul bien qui nous puisse tenter,

With but the dead faced Alexander's might,
While the rest, dazzled by his deeds least grand,
Came and knelt, begging him to rule their land,
Heard in their fear who knows what oracles,
Deemed that a god could find no obstacles?
But we—we look on conquerors otherwise;
We know that tyrants are not deities;
And though slaves call him by what name they can,
The son of Jove here passes for a man.
We shall not with sweet flowers perfume his way;
He everywhere will find us armed, at bay,—
Will see his conquest at each step withstood.
A single rock will cost him here more blood,
More trouble, more assaults, more time, almost,
Than the whole empire of the Persians cost.
We hate such peace as made them die forgot.
The gold within our soil corrupts us not.
Only fair fame can tempt us; and for this

Et le seul que mon cœur, cherche à lui disputer.

Moreover, there appears at times in *Alexandre* a sense of human realities alien to the romanesque tradition. The intrusion of these realities may even jar—as when, amid the general preoccupation with *"gloire"* and with the personal feelings of sovereigns, the wantonness of Alexander's invasion of India is pointed out, and all the death and sorrow he brings to those who have done him no wrong. And it is not true of this Alexander that, as Babbitt and others have mistakenly averred, his sole object "in conquering the world is that he may lay his conquest at his lady's feet." [10] It was true, apparently, of the Julius Caesar of Corneille's *Pompée,* but Racine's soberer instincts saved him from that crowning piece of absurdity. Alexander *tells* Cleofile that his sole object is this; his emissary, Hephaestion, tells her the same thing; but neither of them states it as a fact to anyone else, and none of the other characters states it at all. It is a polite extravagance of courtship according to the conventions of the artificial society of seventeenth-century France. Cleofile herself knows well that it is nothing more than extravagant courtship; she does not for a moment believe it. Quite to the contrary, she says to her gallant wooer:

On attend peu d'amour d'un héros tel que vous:[11]
La gloire fit toujours vos transports les plus doux.

And when he promises that with new deeds of prowess he will make the remotest regions bow to her, she replies:

Alone my valor seeks to vie with his.

[10] *Racine's Phèdre,* ed. by Irving Babbitt, p. xv. Cf. also Mornet in his *Andromaque,* pp. 95, 209.

[11] From such a hero one expects scant love.
Glory is ever dear to thee above
All else.

Oui, vous y traînerez la victoire captive;[12]
Mais je doute, Seigneur, que l'amour vous y suive.
Tant d'Etats, tant de mers qui vont nous désunir.
M'effaceront bientôt de votre souvenir.
Quand l'Océan troublé vous verra sur son onde
Achever quelque jour la conquête du monde;
Quand vous verrez les Rois tomber à vos genoux,
Et la terre en tremblant se taire devant vous,
Songerez-vous, Seigneur, qu'une jeune Princesse,
Au fond de ses Etats vous regrette sans cesse,
Et rappelle en son cœur les moments bienheureux
Où ce grand conquérant l'assurait de ses feux?

In some ways, however, *Alexandre* is not better but worse
than the romanesque tragedies of Thomas Corneille and
Quinault. With popularity his supreme aim in this play,
Racine was doing violence here to his own conception of
drama (evidently held by him from the first) as these
dramatists were not doing it to theirs in their plays, and
consequently he was in the detached position of one engaged in a literary exercise; he could not enter into his
theme imaginatively and be worked by it instead of working
at it. Hence, doubtless, the inconsistency of his hero. This
Alexander says he invades India to pit himself against

12 Yes, thou wilt carry with thee victory;
   But, sir, I doubt if love will follow thee.
   The realms and seas that will between us lie
   Shall soon efface me from thy memory.
   When heaving ocean sees thee, far away,
   Complete the conquest of the world some day,—
   When thou beholdest earth's kings before thee kneel
   And all mankind silent and trembling,—still
   Wilt thou recall that in her distant land,
   Sir, a young princess mourns thee without end,
   Remembering in her heart what joy had moved her
   When this great conqueror swore to her he loved her?

Porus, the fame of whose prowess has reached his ears and made him eager to face the one rival worthy of his steel. But he offers Porus the alternative of peace on easy terms of submission, which would have prevented their test of each other in battle; and he is angered by Porus' decision to fight, which alone could give him that test! He even declares (ll. 1281-1285) after his victory that his adversary's resistance has been unforgivable and has earned his intense hatred, and that he ought to make an example of this stubborn foe; then, less than a hundred lines later and without ever having left the scene, he tells Axiana (l. 1370) that he has taken pains to save Porus' life, and in the end he overwhelms him with favors.[13]

Repeatedly throughout the play we find a similar imperfect grasp of the subject. Taxiles, who is Cleofile's brother, cannot be unaware, as he states that he is (without reason for deception), of why Alexander tries to be his friend. Moreover, in real life one may indeed not want to know the truth; but to say so as Taxiles does when she asks him if he can doubt the obvious fact that Axiana loves Porus, is as unnatural as it is to speak of oneself thus in the third person:

> Je tâchais d'en douter, cruelle Cléofile.[14]
> Hélas! dans son erreur affermissez Taxile.

---

[13] It is a curious touch that the feelings which Alexander on the one hand and Porus and Axiana on the other have for each other as adversaries are continually said to be "wrath" and "anger" and "hate" (*courroux, colère, haine*)—as though opposition in war were a matter for personal offense! Such feelings are understandable in Porus and Axiana towards the invader, but not in him towards them. This particular puerility was, so far as I know, peculiar to the young Racine; I cannot recall any other instance of it in French pseudo-classical tragedy.

[14] I tried to doubt it, cruel Cleofile.
Ah, confirm Taxiles in his mistake!

Pourquoi lui peignez-vous cet objet odieux?
Aidez-le bien plutôt à démentir ses yeux.

His exit a few minutes later, to leave Porus alone with
Axiana, has no motivation except the convenience of the
author. After the battle, he and subsequently Alexander
tell her in glowing terms about the exploits of Porus in
defeat—a fine way, forsooth, to turn her heart from that
hero to Taxiles as both these unnatural eulogists of her lover
are attempting to do. An enumeration of all the blemishes
which are to be found in this drama would, however, be an
endless task.

But Racine knew his immediate public. The taste of the
times was never better demonstrated than by the acclaim of
Alexandre, not only on its first appearance but in the sober
second thought of that generation. For them it was no mere
'prentice work but one of his masterpieces. Boileau praised
it, asserting non-existent differences between it and the
tragedies of Quinault. Even in 1672 Madame de Sévigné
wrote to her daughter, after *Britannicus, Bérénice,* and
Bajazet: "Racine will never surpass *Alexandre* and *Andromaque; Bajazet* is inferior to them."

There was one very large fly in the ointment of his first
triumph. Before *Alexandre* was produced he submitted the
manuscript of it—confidently, no doubt—to the illustrious
Corneille himself. And the elder dramatist told him that it
showed he had great talent for poetry but none for tragedy
—and this was the beginning of the long feud between
them. Critics have not ceased to be amused at Corneille's
egregious mistake. But though he perhaps should not have
judged so unfavorably a play whose worst faults were derived from his own *Pompée,* the fact is that, on the evidence

---

Why show him truths so odious, alack!
Help him, instead, not to believe his eyes.

he possessed, his appraisal was justified. No one could possibly have foreseen, from this romanesque effusion, that its author would next, and within two years' time, write *Andromaque!*

Alexandre concludes the period of Racine's apprenticeship in his art; thenceforth he wrote with a sure hand. Yet twice later he again broke ground in a new field. *Andromaque* was directly followed by his one comedy, *les Plaideurs,* an adaptation of Aristophanes' *Wasps.* It may well have been that the youthful lover of ancient Greek drama, having successfully imitated Euripides, wished to do the same with Aristophanes. But another consideration also, or instead, may have influenced him in undertaking this task. Though *Andromaque,* as we shall see in dealing with it, was a less great departure from the mannered type of tragedy written in those times than his subsequent plays were to be, in one respect it went beyond any of them in the direction of naturalness. There is a decided touch of the comic in the midst of its tragic passions and situations, as in real life. In the scene between Hermione and Orestes in Act II, her flare of anger at his unfortunate reference to the disdain of Pyrrhus, which wounds her, her spiteful retaliation with words which will hurt him in turn, his outburst under this goading, her pretended indifference to Pyrrhus, followed by her betrayal of dread lest he should marry Andromache —all have a strongly comic element. Comedy is no less inherent in the scene between Pyrrhus and Phoenix later in the same act, when Pyrrhus, who says he has put the ungrateful Andromache out of his heart, cannot stop talking about her, and especially when he wonders if she will be jealous if he weds Hermione. Again, in Act III there is a comic flavor in the situation where Andromache and Pyrrhus covertly observe each other and try to overhear each other's words while they talk to their respective confidants.

This lifelike mingling of tragedy and comedy, which seems to us entirely proper, indeed eminently desirable, and very effective in drama, was condemned by the rigid theories of French pseudo-classicism. Its appearance in *Andromaque* did not escape censure; and Racine, always hyper-sensitive to criticism, never repeated his experiment; but he may have felt that if everything comical was forbidden him outside of pure comedy, he would attempt this genre also. *Les Plaideurs,* however, was little admired by its first audiences, and he did no further work of that sort.

And of course *Esther,* his first "religious drama," was preliminary to the great *Athalie.* The break with the conventions of secular tragedy is here not yet so complete as *Athalie's* was to be; *Esther* dispenses with a love story and with the language of gallantry, but still makes use of confidants. More than any other French-classical tragedy it approaches *Athalie's* striking employment of background or "local color." Designed for amateur performance by young girls, its dialogue merely puts the essential facts of the Biblical story of Esther in the form of a play, without regard for dramatic unity and with little concern for dramatic effectiveness. Characterization is slight and simple, but the verse is of notable beauty and the choruses are very lovely—indeed, are preferred by many critics to those of *Athalie* itself. This little "play" owes its charm solely to its poetry, and its poetry makes it truly charming.

CHAPTER VIII

RACINE'S *ANDROMAQUE*

AS a memorable event in the history of the French stage, the first performance of *Andromaque* yields in importance only to that of Corneille's *Cid* and perhaps that of Victor Hugo's *Hernani*. The enthusiasm which Racine's play aroused was scarcely less great than the furor created by the *Cid;* the fashionable theater-goers of 1667-1668 could think of nothing but the Trojan heroine and her sorrows. In the nineteenth century *Andromaque* was acted more times than any other tragedy of its author.

Few dramas have achieved such continuous tension and so many startling effects with an equal economy of means. Each of the four major characters is ruled by a single emotion. Orestes loves Hermione to distraction, who in turn is infatuated with Pyrrhus, her betrothed, who has conceived an overmastering passion for his Trojan captive, Andromache, whose own heart is with her dead husband, Hector. Pyrrhus tells Andromache that he will kill her child if she will not marry him, and on her hesitation to take this step, to which her fears as a mother urge her, and from which her instincts as a devoted widow make her shrink, the action of the play depends. When she encourages Pyrrhus, he forsakes Hermione, who in wild frenzy of outraged pride and jealous love has to fall back upon Orestes, who thereupon is beside himself with joy and hope; when she repulses Pyrrhus, she drives him into the arms of the enraptured Hermione, who then disdains Orestes, who becomes frantic with rage and despair. Notwithstanding the decorous language and the smooth flow of the polished alexandrines in which they speak, the struggle of these tormented souls is nothing less than that of "wildcats in a red-hot iron cage." Unfriendly critics of French-classical drama have complained that it portrays types rather than individuals. But Orestes, Pyrrhus, and Hermione are living, individualized figures, were it only by reason of their appalling vileness, pettiness, and malevolence. Suffering makes them hateful. When it seems that Hermione is to wed Pyrrhus after all, Orestes plans to abduct her that she may not be happy while he himself is miserable. Pyrrhus, in announcing his decision to marry her, wantonly tortures Orestes; and later, when he has broken his word and is about to espouse Andromache instead, he cannot keep away from the woman he has betrayed. As for Hermione, her position is piteous, but she is no "sympathetic" victim of man's perfidy. The strain and agony of the situation in which she is placed have keyed her nerves to the snapping-point and brought out all the hardness and unloveliness in her nature. It was she who, before the play opens, incited Greece to demand the life of the infant Astyanax. In the face of all evidence and argument, she persists in regarding Andromache as her voluntary "rival," and hates her accordingly. She tries to hold Orestes that she may have someone in reserve if her hopes are finally defeated; but her claws are quick to wound him when he maladroitly says that Pyrrhus disdains her; and when she presently feels that her wedding is sure to take place, she dismisses him and his anguish from her mind with the impatient question, "Have we no theme, except his sighs, for cheer?" and in that hour of her seeming triumph, when Andromache implores her to save Astyanax, nothing could be more venomous than her sweetly-phrased refusal.

The character of Hermione is, in fact, the finest thing in the play; she may almost be said to "make" the play; Racine has done scarcely anything else so brilliant. She is one quivering compound of intense emotion, veering impulses, unreason, and vicious spite—utterly feminine and eternally real. Pyrrhus and Orestes, also, are in essence true to life, though in their case universal human nature is tricked out in the garments of a highly mannered, artificial civilization, as different as can well be imagined from that heroic and legendary age of Greece to which they properly belong. There is not much "local color" in the secular dramas of Racine; in this respect he followed the example of his fellow playwrights. Some of his characters, like Hermione, have few traits peculiar to people of his own land and times; some have many; but none of them has an appreciable number which are *not* those of seventeenth-century French men and women but are instead distinctive of the country and period in which the scene is laid. Taine and Benjamin W. Wells have pointed out that Pyrrhus' conception of love is "that of the *précieux* salons of Paris and of the courtiers of Versailles, with a certain decorum in its outward expression, with happily turned phrases, and insinuating attenuations that mask with a certain courtliness the fundamental brutality of his absolute power." [1] Orestes, indeed, is something more than a conventional young prince of the dramatist's own day who is disappointed in love; but that something more is not ancient but, strange to say, prophetically modern. As Jules Lemaître has shown in a very acute piece of critical writing, Orestes is an anticipation of the characteristic hero of the age of romanticism, a melancholy egoist who considers himself uniquely persecuted by heaven and hence a man apart, not subject to the same responsibilities as other men.[2] But his creator, unlike Chateaubriand, Hugo, and the elder Dumas, does not solicit our admiration for such a person; he represents him, rightly, as a potentially criminal weakling.

[1] *Racine's Andromaque,* ed. by Benjamin W. Wells, New York, 1899, pp. xi-xii.

[2] *Jean Racine,* by Jules Lemaître, pp. 147-150.

It is a commonplace of criticism that after the two plays of his novitiate, *la Thébaïde* and *Alexandre le Grand,* Racine attained to full stature of genius at a single bound and gave to his country a new type of tragedy, his own peculiar type, with simple plot, natural characters swayed by universal human passions, and (for the French-classical stage) a minimum of conventions;—that this type was at once originated and perfected in *Andromaque,* a masterpiece which stands on an essential parity with his very best subsequent work. The truth is somewhat less spectacular, as truth is wont to be. Others before Racine—notably Rotrou and Tristan l'Hermite—had portrayed with considerable success men and women mastered by genuine, passionate love; Tristan had used simple plots, with no more conventions than Racine and with far greater regard for certain kinds of realism. And, moreover, *Andromaque* has a larger share of the artificialities which then characterized French tragedy than can be found in any subsequent play of Racine.

This is true, for instance, as regards its preciosity of diction, marked by "an incredible abuse of the word *yeux*" [3] and such extravagances of the language of gallantry as the declaration of Pyrrhus that the flames of love with which he burns for Andromache are fiercer than the flames of burning Troy. Again, with each of the four chief characters—Andromache, Pyrrhus, Hermione, and Orestes—is associated a "confidant," one of those insipid, colorless figures peculiar to pseudo-classical drama, who have no personality of their own but exist solely to listen to their respective principals, to inform them, advise them, and sympathize with them, and to do their bidding. And the very dilemma of Hector's widowed wife, which is the mainspring of the action, owes its poignancy to feelings which are not of all time but of an age.

[3] "Eyes." We are familiar with a somewhat similar conventional use formerly of the word "glance" in English.

Andromache might, indeed, not unnaturally have found it very difficult to bring herself to wed Pyrrhus, because he was associated in her memory with the horrors of the sack of Troy. She alleges this obstacle once in a brief reference to it in the first act and once at length in an eloquent speech near the end of Act III. That it was what she felt she ought to feel, rather than what she did feel, and that she did not instinctively shrink from Pyrrhus for this or any other reason, is made sufficiently clear by the rest of the play. In the first place, as critics have frequently pointed out, she appeals constantly to his love for her in every way that she can without committing herself; she would find such a course intolerable if he really were repulsive to her. Furthermore, Pylades' report indicates that after the murder of Pyrrhus she mourns him with genuine affection; and this fact was brought out unmistakably in a scene which the author included in his original version of Act V but afterwards suppressed as dramaturgically defective. It was because of her belief that to wed again would be a disloyalty to Hector's ashes that she refused marriage with Pyrrhus even when it seemed the only way to save the son whom she had borne to Hector. The best that can be said for such a viewpoint is that it was in keeping with the ideas of the pastoral and gallant romances, with the notions of the salons of Paris, which are reflected in the drama as well as in the social life of the period. Natural, rational, sane, it is not. The more Andromache loved Hector, the more precious should the life of their child have seemed to her, and the more readily should she have sacrificed any personal repugnances with the feeling that by the preservation of that child she could be most truly loyal to its father.[4]

---

[4] Cf., in contrast, Euripides' beautiful portrait of Andromache in *The Trojan Women*. Faced with the prospect of having to be not Pyrrhus' wife in honorable marriage, but his mere concubine, she, too, shrinks from such a sequel to her dear union with Hector, but

When the issue presently becomes unescapable, the solution which Andromache finds for it is no less preposterous than was her attitude which drew its lines so sharply. She will consent to wed Pyrrhus, she tells her confidante, and will make him swear in turn to protect her son, and then, as soon as the marriage ceremony is over, she will kill herself. It never seems to occur to her that Pyrrhus may very probably, and reasonably, think that he is in no way obligated to keep a bargain of which she has kept only the letter, not the spirit at all; or that he, too, might keep only the letter of it and find a savage satisfaction in thus amply revenging his disappointed hopes—perhaps, for instance, by guarding the child "safely" in a tower, without food or drink, like Ugolino and his sons. It does not seem even to occur to her that Pyrrhus, who for her sake must become

---

is advised by Hecuba to make the best of the inevitable, so as to ensure her son's being well treated. Then she is told that the Greeks have decided to kill him. Her first, immediate words are: "Oh, I could have borne mine enemy's bed!" (G. Murray translation).

The "dilemma" of Racine's Andromache is taken straight from *Pertharite,* one of the most far-fetched and unnatural of Corneille's tragedies in the period of his degeneration as a dramatic artist. This and other parallels in the relations of four of its characters with each other to those of the four major characters in *Andromaque* were first pointed out by Voltaire. Like similarities can be found with Thomas Corneille's *Mort de L'empereur Commode* and *Camma,* as I have mentioned in the chapter on that dramatist. Lancaster, in his *History of French Dramatic Literature in the Seventeenth Century,* Part IV, pp. 54-55, has noted these and many more parallels between details in *Andromaque* and in earlier French pseudo-classical plays, and there are yet others. Daniel Mornet, in his *Jean Racine,* has tried to show that all Racine's plays draw heavily upon the work of his immediate predecessors, but he can assemble no such list of similarities in the case of any of the rest of them. The fact is that in *Andromaque* Racine took details right and left from these predecessors, and into this body of romanesque material breathed a fierce breath of life.

irrevocably embroiled with the whole of Greece, will not be thankful for merely being able to call himself her husband for a few minutes. In contrasting *Andromaque* with the extravagant dramas which immediately preceded it, Jules Lemaître selects as an example of their absurdities the rapture of the hero of Thomas Corneille's *Timocrate* when he finds that he will be wedded to the woman he loves and then be killed directly afterwards.[5] But almost the identical absurdity which Lemaître ridicules in *Timocrate* is to be found in *Andromaque!* In charging Cephissa, who will survive her, to see that Pyrrhus does not break his word, Andromache says:

> Fais-lui valoir l'hymen où je me suis rangée;[6]
> Dis-lui qu'avant ma mort je lui fus engagée.

At the end of the drama "all who gave way to passion have perished in body or in mind," observes Benjamin Wells; "Andromache alone remains, because she alone has not been passion's fool." [7] But soberly considered, Andromache might with justice be described in the phrase of Shakespeare's Thersites as "a fool positive."

And yet—so strangely wise is genius even when most perversely astray—the folly of Andromache is self-con-

[5] *Jean Racine,* p. 133.

[6] Make him appreciate
The marriage which I grant him. Tell him that
I was united with him ere I died.

In their point of likeness, the heroine of *Andromaque* is really more absurd than the hero of *Timocrate*. He, like many lovers but to a greater degree than they, *feels* extravagantly; she bases her plans on the *belief* that the man who loves her will feel thus, and thinks it only natural and right that he should!

[7] *Op. cit.,* p. x.

sistent. If any woman could be capable of one phase of it, she might perhaps be capable of it all. It all admits of a single explanation: that Andromache's mind deals almost entirely—as everyone's does to some extent—with words, which are but the names of real things, instead of dealing with the realities themselves. Pyrrhus wants to marry her; well, if she "marries" him, she satisfies his wish! She will have "kept her bargain" (the words of it); he will keep his. If, in spite of herself, she should live after the wedding (as in fact she does), Pyrrhus, alive or dead, is her "husband," and that makes her love him. She loved Hector and cannot bear to "be untrue to his memory"; it would be "untrue to his memory" to "wed another husband"; therefore she cannot "wed another husband"—circumstances make no difference. Her eventual decision, to marry Pyrrhus and then immediately take her own life, is not at variance with the rest; her suicide would punish and atone for her "disloyalty" to Hector in submitting to the ceremony, and she would be dead (she thinks) before she could begin to love Pyrrhus as "her husband." So bizarre a figure is not very convincing, yet is perhaps sufficiently plausible to be allowed in a drama; but to fill the role of the sympathetic heroine—that is another matter! The tragedy in which this character is presented in that role cannot rightly be accounted a genuine masterpiece and one of the great plays of the world; it is, rather, a superb, an astonishing *tour-de-force*.[8]

[8] Emile Faguet maintains stoutly, in his *Propos de Théâtre,* vol. i, pp. 333 ff., that Racine purposely represented Andromache as "passion's fool," and that he did not intend her "stratagem" to be regarded as a well-advised plan but merely as the utmost concession to which she can force herself for her son's sake, and one in the efficacy of which she believes because she wishes to believe in it. In answer it may be said: (1) that Cephissa's failure to point out the absurdity of Andromache's plan shows that Racine did not

think it absurd or expect his audiences to do so; (2) that her plan was in keeping with the fantastic conceptions prevalent in the upper-class seventeenth-century French society that read Madeleine de Scudéry's romances and went to plays like *Timocrate;* and (3) that even if Faguet's interpretation is correct, Racine has none the less blundered, for among people who are not saturated with the pseudo-classical tradition a "heroine" who is so foolish and self-indulgent and unmotherly will elicit irritation or disgust more often than such sympathy as the artistic effect demands for her.

CHAPTER IX

RACINE'S *BRITANNICUS*

AMONG the plays of Racine, *Britannicus* occupies a somewhat anomalous position. Though of very high merit poetically, as are all his important tragedies, it is perhaps the least notable of them in this respect; and aside from one or two fine passages such as Nero's description of his first sight of Junia, its poetry is more sententious and oratorical than is customary with Racine. The love interest is less dominant in it than usual; the political interest is unusually large; its general tone is unwontedly austere and masculine; and for all these reasons it is grouped with *Mithridate* as the most Corneillian of the works of its author.

From a purely dramatic standpoint it is Racine's masterpiece. Lacking the florid appeal of the romanesque tragedies of the period, *Britannicus* is one of those rare plays in which, the characters and the situation being what they are, the outcome could be nothing else than what it is—whereas if any factor were changed, the outcome would be changed. If Agrippina and Burrus had not been just the people they were, they would have reached an understanding and, between them, would have curbed Nero. He would not have broken from all restraint in any case, if Narcissus had not been a very Iago for infernal persuasiveness. If Junia had been more adroit, more courageous, less frank and less sweet-natured and less loving, she might have managed not to arouse Nero's jealousy or might have got Britannicus safely out of the palace, or else by defiance might have precipitated an equally tragic but somewhat different denouement. If the Emperor—but the suppositions could be continued indefinitely.

As a single instance among many of Racine's consummate craftsmanship in this play, we may note the scene in which Nero, concealed behind a curtain, listens to Britannicus and Junia. For tension, for terror, for sheer force and effectiveness, it can hardly be matched by any similar situation in all the dramas of the world. Even that in which Orgon hides under the table and hears Tartuffe reveal his true character pales beside it, and Sheridan's much-lauded screen scene in *The School for Scandal* is utterly trivial in comparison. No wonder Voltaire called *Britannicus* "la pièce des connaisseurs"!

In naturalness and comparative freedom from convention, an immense improvement is shown over *Andromaque*. Let us take, for example, the use of confidants. In *Andromaque* there is one for each important character. In *Britannicus,* on the other hand, Albina is the only specimen of these lay figures. If someone who had never read the play, but was familiar with French-classical tragedy in general, were to scan the list of its dramatis personae, he would no doubt suppose Burrus, the former tutor of Nero, to be the Emperor's confidant and Narcissus, the tutor of Britannicus, to serve in a like capacity for the young prince. But the fact is that both Nero and Britannicus confide in Narcissus, and he and Burrus are as thoroughly individualized characters, with wills and plans and purposes of their own, as anyone else in the play. And there is nobody at all to whom Junia can go for counsel or sympathy—and how poignantly effective is this very isolation of the helpless, friendless girl!

There is far less of preciosity in *Britannicus* than in *Andromaque*. Derived largely from Tacitus, it seems to catch something of the Roman historian's terse power. Whatever of Versailles and the salons does enter into this drama, as regards either language or sentiments, appears less incongruous in the setting of imperial Rome, itself complex and in some degree artificial, than in the world of Greek legend. The real Pyrrhus would forthwith have made Andromache his concubine willy-nilly; but the Nero of history, like Racine's emperor in the play, would probably have wanted Junia to dismiss the man she loved and become his wedded empress, for he later did, in fact, desire and marry Poppaea Sabina, the wife of Otho, and it was only a few years afterwards that Domitian, as Suetonius relates, took Domitia Longina from her husband and espoused her. Racine's Nero and Narcissus and the other characters in *Britannicus* still speak the jargon of gallantry now and then, but their thoughts and feelings are those of people in all ages—instead of merely those of a mannered Court society of the seventeenth century—and hence we are able to imagine the dramatis personae to be indeed the historical figures whose names they bear. The one exception is found in Britannicus himself; it apparently was next to impossible for Racine to draw an attractive picture of a young man who is in love. He succeeded in doing so after a fashion, though rather colorlessly, in the case of Xiphares in *Mithridate,* but Xiphares is older and more experienced than Britannicus and Hippolytus;—these, Racine's two most flagrant examples of the type, unfortunately are in his two best secular dramas! He meant to portray Britannicus as a high-spirited and pathetic youth; he did portray him as a *petit maître* who is at times unmanly or affected. Junia, on the other hand, is a lovely creation—of all Racine's women the least sophisticated and, unless perhaps Monime, the most appealing—with the simplicity, the directness, the sweet dignity, and the fresh, unstudied charm of young girlhood. Despite the pathos of her situation, the author somehow, by some miracle of delicate art too subtle to be analyzed, has made us feel that she was naturally of a merry disposition, as, in point of fact, his sources describe her to have been—*"festivissima omnium puellarum"*—and this only adds to the piteousness of the lot which is hers. Her love for Britannicus is that of the stronger for the weaker, protective and nourished on compassion; she has cheered and comforted and mothered like an older sister the unhappy boy who loves her.

But notwithstanding the title of the play, its central figures are Nero and Agrippina. Its theme is not the death of the unfortunate prince, except in as much as that is Nero's first plunge into crime; its real object is to depict this plunge—to exhibit the royal monster in the making. And Agrippina's ambition has been the chief moulding influence in her son's life, both directly and through his reaction of antagonism against it. She is, indeed, the more impressive character of the two, for she surpasses the Emperor in force of personality, intelligence, energy, and courage; and a legitimate alternative view of *Britannicus,* according to Racine himself, is that its subject is the final defeat of her long-cherished hopes. In order that the wickedness of Nero may stand out more strikingly, the darker aspects of her nature have not been emphasized by the dramatist, but their existence is not denied and at least a glimpse of most of them is permitted. In like manner the conception of the Emperor himself is, in the main, the traditional one, but not all its phases are equally stressed; that of virtuoso, which was perhaps dominant in him, is clearly revealed only once in the play, though then at a crucial point. Racine did not attempt, as a modern author might, to show Nero to be the perverse product of corrupting environment and circumstances; he represents him as a young man fundamentally cruel, vain, and vicious, whose predisposition to evil at length causes him to break from restraints hitherto imposed by his weakness and timidity.

The outcome of the struggle between the contending forces within him has been decided by the close of Act III, and the play really might end there. Nero has ordered the imprisonment of his rival and the detention of Agrippina under guard, and has threatened Burrus with arrest if he does not obey; the wild beast has been uncaged at last. The swiftly-ensuing murder of Britannicus might be taken for granted, as an assured sequel; its actual occurrence, even if included, could barely furnish material for one other act, at most. But inflexible convention in the Age of Louis XIV required that a tragedy should have five acts. The device by which Racine triumphantly solved the difficult problem of an intervening fourth act is a supreme achievement of dramatic art. Instead of writing an obvious "filler," he contrived a succession of scenes which yield in interest and power to no other part of the play. At the end of the act the wheel has come full circle and the situation is practically the same as at the beginning of it. But in its course something more has been given us than a mere sequence of theatrically effective dialogues spiced with the excitement of real or pretended fluctuations of purpose. Racine there epitomizes and causes to pass before our eyes in brief review, as it were, all the influences, good and bad alike, to which Nero has been subjected. Agrippina with her schemes and with her claims on him, Burrus with his rectitude, Narcissus with his insidious, flattering villainy—one after another is shown in contact with the young emperor, so that we can observe the solicitations of each and their effect upon him. It is interesting to note that Racine's problem in this act was much the same as Shakespeare's in the fourth act of *Julius Caesar,* and that Shakespeare, with his great quarrel scene between Brutus and Cassius, which alters nothing but which delineates character, met it in much the same way.

Not even a genius, however, could work two miracles in immediate succession. After having made something magnificent out of nothing, Racine was unable to go on and then make something altogether satisfying out of next to nothing. The last act of *Britannicus* is a little flat and perfunctory. It displays signs of abated inspiration, with several unconvincing details[1] and with scenes which are palpably devised to bridge the time between others of greater importance. Only in the meeting of Agrippina and Nero after the murder, when she charges him with it and foretells the course of crime that he will run, does the play once more attain to those heights on which it moved in the earlier acts. But if the conclusion does not add to the effect of what has gone before, it at any rate does not seriously impair that effect; and this drama in its entirety ranks an impressive third in greatness among the works of its author, surpassed only by the passion and power of *Phèdre* and the exalted, almost flawless beauty of *Athalie*.

[1] One is Agrippina's statement that Nero confided to her "Des secrets d'où dépend le destin des humains" ("Secrets on which depends the destiny of nations"). Surely, the mind of a Nero could have no great ideas or designs. But in the seventeenth century, when the doctrine of the divine right of kings was regnant, a monarch was popularly supposed to be a marvelous sort of person, whose thoughts were not like those of other men; and Racine has here momentarily lost his imaginative grip on his subject and limply conformed with the conventional notion, implicit in so many other plays of the period.

His grasp of his theme is again loosened in the long speech of Albina, just before the end of the play. She has entered in frantic haste, imploring immediate aid for Nero. But when asked what is the situation, instead of saying briefly: "Junia has escaped from the palace and found refuge with the Vestal Virgins. When Narcissus tried to stop her, the populace tore him to pieces. Nero is in despair. He may kill himself at any moment. Come quick!" she gives a leisurely, detailed account of what has happened, becoming for the time not a character but the stereotyped *Nuntius* of classical drama, who must deliver a lengthy and formal "messenger-speech"; and then when her narrative is completed, she abruptly begins to clamor again for instant action!

CHAPTER X

RACINE'S *BERENICE*

GUSTAVE MICHAUT'S book, *la Bérénice de Racine*,[1] appends a strange corollary to the well-argued conclusions of its first half. That first half is the really valuable part of his volume; it reveals the unsubstantial basis of the legend that Henrietta of England, Louis XIV's sister-in-law, suggested to Corneille and Racine that each should write a play on the story of Titus and Berenice, and offers an alternative explanation for the practically simultaneous appearance of Racine's tragedy and Corneille's dealing with the same subject.

It was at this time, says Michaut, that the feud between the two poets was bitterest. Their relations had first become strained when Corneille declared, after reading *Alexandre,* that Racine's proper field was not drama. With the sensational success of *Andromaque* Corneille's partisans, jealous of his eclipse, were heard belittling the achievement of his young rival, who, they said, could write a pretty play about love but had not the virile power and broad historical grasp of their own idol; such criticism led Racine to choose a theme from Roman history, and involving political motives, for his next tragedy and thus to vie with Corneille in his own peculiar domain; and when this play, *Britannicus,* encountered a disappointing reception, he laid the blame upon Corneille himself. Then, while his real or fancied wrongs rankled sorest within him, he must have learned, in some way, that his foe was at work upon the drama *Tite et Bérénice.* Here, Racine felt, was a subject which he could treat more successfully than Corneille. He would write upon it,

[1] Paris, 1907.

also; he would work with all possible speed and have his version of it completed as soon as the other one; produced at the same time, the two plays would decide by their respective fortunes who was the greatest tragic poet of France. Thus he would at once exalt himself and discomfit the man he hated. It is a matter of record that he did.

But Michaut does not stop with formulating this plausible hypothesis to account for the *Bérénice* of Racine. He maintains that if such a hypothesis be accepted, *Bérénice* becomes of capital importance among the works of its author. Its subject was taken by Racine because it was appropriate to his dramatic system,—because better than any other it gave him a chance to exhibit the theory of that system and to apply it effectively. That he should be victorious in the contest which he had initiated was imperative; for a new defeat, after *Britannicus,* would definitely relegate him to the second rank and confirm the supremacy of his rival; his whole future as a dramatist and the future of his conception of drama were at stake. Therefore is it not clear, says Michaut, that he mustered all his powers and made every effort of which he was capable, and that thus *Bérénice* must be the most carefully wrought, the most perfect, the most Racinian of the plays of Racine? [2]

It is indeed clear that on this occasion Racine must have tried his hardest to surpass Corneille; but the rest of Michaut's deductions are unwarranted and unreasonable. To surpass Corneille: that was Racine's object, whether he initiated their contest himself or was forced into it by the Princess Henrietta; and success, as Michaut rightly points out, was absolutely vital to him. Such being the case, he would surely use any methods that seemed most likely to accomplish his aim, even though they consorted ill with his literary ideals. In this play, above all others, he was attempt-

[2] *Op. cit.,* p. 137.

ing to win the plaudits of his immediate audience, not of posterity. It is, of all his plays, the one in which we should least expect to see him trying to exemplify his dramatic theory instead of trying solely to be popular; it is the one in which we should most expect him to compromise with current tastes and fashions, however little he relished them at heart. If, as Michaut thinks, he himself chose this subject for competition with Corneille,[3] he did so because he believed it one which he could handle in a way that would please the public better than Corneille could—and not because it was peculiarly suited to illustrate his conception of what a tragedy should be. A *pièce de combat* is not the place where one exhibits ideals and illustrates theories. The public to be courted is little concerned with such things.

It is not likely, then, that *Bérénice* should be the best embodiment of Racine's dramatic creed. As for Michaut's other contention, that it is the most perfect of his plays, this too is improbable, *a priori,* because of the haste of its composition and the objective it had. Michaut himself admits, a page or so earlier, that the subjects of pure passion, such as Racine found in his master Euripides, from which his rivalry with Corneille long diverted him, were better suited to his genius. But the merits of a drama should not be determined by *a priori* arguments of probability, but by an investigation of the drama itself.

"Your true Racinian of the inner circle sets *Bérénice* above all other plays," observes the author of a popular biography of Racine in English.[4] That alleged fact, even

[3] Léon Herrmann has argued (*Mercure de France,* vol. cciii, 1928, pp. 313-337) for the directly contrary hypothesis: that it was Racine who independently began a drama about Titus and Berenice, and that it was Corneille who tried to outdo and humiliate his rival. H. C. Lancaster demonstrates, however, in his *History of French Dramatic Literature in the Seventeenth Century,* Part III, pp. 573-575, that the probabilities are wholly on the side of Michaut.

[4] Mary Duclaux, *The Life of Racine,* New York, n. d.; p. 99.

if it be a fact, is of no critical importance. People who do not stop at intelligent appreciation of a writer, but form a cult to bow down and worship him, may be expected to be blind to his characteristic defects and perhaps actually relish them, or else they would not make a fetish of him; in consequence they are likely to feel especial admiration for those of his works in which these defects are most prominent. Thus the typical Dante cultist considers the *Paradiso* his masterpiece; scarcely otherwise explainable, it seems, was Quiller-Couch's amazing opinion that *The Tempest* is a more precious literary treasure than *Hamlet* or *Othello* or *King Lear* (or the *Odyssey* or the *Divine Comedy*); and a Wordsworthian shows marked partiality for such poems as "The Character of the Happy Warrior" and "She Was a Phantom of Delight."

Bérénice enjoyed a notable success when first produced, and in modern times Jules Lemaître in France and G. Lytton Strachey in England have praised it highly. The economy of its plot, whereby an entire drama has been made out of such meager material, and the easy, changing flow of its verse from colloquial simplicity to extreme poetic beauty are justly celebrated. On the other hand, neither the great Sainte-Beuve nor N. M. Bernardin, of later critics one of the best grounded in the dramatic literature of the seventeenth century, rated it among Racine's masterpieces, or even among his plays of the second rank with *Bajazet* and *Mithridate;* and more recently still, Pierre Brisson has expressed a rather poor opinion of it.[5] From the time of its original performance to the present day, it has been thought by many to possess too slight a theme—to be, indeed, an elegy in dramatic form rather than a tragedy. Such a view

[5] In his *Les deux visages de Racine,* Paris, 1944, pp. 71-90. A similar opinion is voiced in *The Classical Moment,* by Martin Turnell, pp. 188-191.

may be justified; but *Bérénice* has faults which are far worse than that. These faults are obscured by its traditional fame as a classic; but a candid examination will discover that, however congenial to that immediate public to which it was addressed, the characters and codes of conduct to be found in it are such as must greatly lessen its permanent appeal and thereby the estimate of its worth.

The effectiveness of the play depends primarily on our admiration and sympathy for its three principal figures, Titus, Berenice, and Antiochus. The tone and treatment throughout make it impossible that we should find artistic satisfaction in contemplating the anguish of these characters with ironical cynicism, as we are meant to contemplate the writhings of the weak or base dramatis personae in some plays of the modern naturalistic school. Berenice herself shows in her words of last farewell how the author intended us to regard the story which he put upon the stage.

> . . . servons tous trois d'exemple à l'univers[6]
> De l'amour la plus tendre et la plus malheureuse
> Dont il puisse garder l'histoire douloureuse.

The love of Titus and Berenice was, traditionally, one of the great loves of all time; as such it was known to Racine, and as such he made it the subject of his drama. Now a truly great love, a love which in its frustration fills us with a sense of human dignity and lofty pathos and piteous waste

[6] Let us all three
Unto the whole world an example be
Of the tenderest and the most unhappy love
That it can treasure the sad history of.

The verse translations in this and the next three chapters are taken from my *Racine's Mid-Career Tragedies*.

so that the tragic emotion is aroused, can proceed only from great souls—that is, from essentially noble souls.[7] There is material for very moving, powerful drama in the theme of two such lovers placed in circumstances which compel, on grounds of transcendent importance, their renunciation of each other. But the Titus and Berenice of Racine are emphatically not great and noble souls, and the moral issues which confront them are somewhat nebulous.

A man's choice between the claims of empire, to which his own worth and a nation's preference call him, and of a

[7] On this point H. C. Lancaster, to my surprise, has expressed his emphatic dissent. He writes: "Mr. Lacy Lockert in RR, XXX (1939), 26-38, points out the shortcomings of the three characters and holds that 'a truly great love . . . can proceed only from great souls—that is, from essentially noble souls.' As I disagree entirely with this dictum, I cannot accept the conclusions of his article. The appeal of Titus and Berenice, like that of Phèdre or of Eriphile, is the greater because their failings bring them nearer to average humanity."(*Op. cit.,* Part IV, p. 74, note 5.)

The "Eriphile" of Racine's *Iphigénie* is a very effective character in the unlovely part that she plays; but very few people, surely, would consider her an appealing figure. The heroine of *Phèdre* is indeed appealing, but she is far from being petty or ignoble or contemptible; and it is pettiness and baseness (not imperfection, not the possession of human failings even if they result in great wrongdoing) which are the opposite of nobility or greatness of soul.

As to whether noble feelings and greatness of soul are necessary in the characters *in such a play as Bérénice* if the proper tragic effect is to be had, we know the authoritative opinion of Racine himself, stated in his preface to this very drama: "It is not absolutely requisite that there should be blood and dead bodies in a tragedy; it is enough that the action should be great and the characters heroic; that one's emotions should be stirred and that one should feel, throughout, that majestic sadness which constitutes the whole pleasure of tragedy."

As to whether it is possible, or not, for an essentially petty or ignoble person to feel a truly great love, the answer should seem axiomatic. "Do men gather grapes of thorns, or figs of thistles?"

deeply beloved and deeply loving woman involves, in itself, no easy struggle. Some people today, if not in Racine's day, would sympathize with, and commend, a decision in favor of the latter alternative. But the dramatist throws added weight into that scale of the wavering balances. For five long years his Titus has assured Berenice that no considerations of State shall part them, and thus has encouraged her to let her love for him grow without restraint and without fear that his choice will one day be against her; only on his actual accession to the throne, with its sobering sense of responsibility, does his resolve weaken and change. We may well question whether Berenice is not correct in maintaining that a man who has so thoroughly committed himself has no right to draw back. Moreover, it may reasonably be argued that the obligation of Titus to employ his ability to serve the Roman commonwealth is vitiated or even quite canceled by the fact that he owes that ability entirely to Berenice; it was her love which inspired him to be no longer a profligate; the valor and benevolence of Titus are her creation, and *she* owes no debt to Rome, being a foreign queen—rather is Rome in *her* debt for the services which Titus has already rendered to his country.

It would have been easy for Racine to present more compelling grounds for the lovers' sacrifice. With scant departure from history he could, for example, have brought out the point that if Titus should renounce the imperial diadem it would fall to his brother Domitian, a monster like Nero, whose reign would cause untold suffering.[8] He

---

[8] In reality, Titus might have appointed some other heir, but the author could have assumed, as he does throughout *Britannicus* and as his audience would assume, that the succession was hereditary, just as it was in France. Yet even in that situation, so great a claim had Berenice upon her lover's loyalty that some of us would feel that the right thing for Titus to do was to put the question squarely before the Roman people whether they would accept him with

has not chosen, however, to do anything of the sort. On the contrary, it would seem that he has deliberately made the case for Berenice as strong, and the case for Rome as weak, as possible in order that he might show that even thus the claims of empire are paramount.[9] His opinion may not be our own, but we can understand it—at least in some measure. It is a corollary of the doctrine of the Divine Right of Kings, which was then current. If a monarch rules by divine right, he is God's chosen one for the task of ruling, and to decline that task would be to flout God's will—would be, in Dante's phrase, to make the great refusal, an act at once cowardly and impious.[10] But the divine call to the throne

---

Berenice or take another ruler, and if, in their prejudice against a queen and a foreigner, they chose the latter alternative, the consequences of their choice would justly be on their own heads. But a submission of the matter to the public would probably have resulted in a divided vote and the horrors of civil war.

[9] Titus even puts to himself the question, implying a negative answer (ll. 1003-1004) :

> Vois-je l'Etat penchant au bord du précipice?
> Ne le puis-je sauver que par ce sacrifice?

> (Do I see the State
> Tottering upon the brink of an abyss?
> Can nothing save it but this sacrifice?)

[10] Cf. the words of Titus himself (ll. 452-466) :

> . . . si je penche enfin du côté de ma gloire,
> Crois qu'il m'en a coûté, pour vaincre tant d'amour,
> Des combats dont mon cœur saignera plus d'un jour.
> J'aimais, je soupirais dans une paix profonde:
> Un autre était chargé de l'empire du monde;
> Maître de mon destin, libre dans mes soupirs,
> Je ne rendais qu'à moi compte de mes désirs.
> Mais à peine le ciel eut rappelé mon père,
> Dès que ma triste main eut fermé sa paupière,
> De mon aimable erreur je fus désabusé:

does not seem to have been looked upon merely as imposing the practical obligation to govern a State; it was viewed as something like a challenge to a man's own self-respect. With kingship was imagined to come a noble ambition to reign, which none but a dastard would disregard. Empire must be yielded only with life. Everything else must give way to it in importance.[11] Again and again Titus speaks of his *gloire,* which compels him to take the step he finally takes; *gloire* has indeed something of the sense of "duty" or "obligation," but not wholly nor alone that sense; it can better be rendered by "honor" or "glory" or "reputation"—often best by the old phrase "fair fame."

Now, if an author conforms to the moral concepts of his own age, he does reasonably well; but if he is true to moral

---

Je sentis le fardeau qui m'était imposé;
Je connus que bientôt, loin d'être à ce que j'aime,
Il fallait, cher Paulin, renoncer à moi-même;
Et que le choix des Dieux, contraire à mes amours,
Livrait à l'univers le reste de mes jours.

(... if I cleave to honor [*gloire*] finally,
Know that to conquer love meant inward fray
From which my heart will bleed for many a day.
I loved; I breathed my vows in peace unmarred.
Another had the cares of empire. Lord
Of mine own fate and free to feed love's fires,
I took no thought save of mine own desires.
But scarcely was my father to the skies
Called home than, when my hand had closed his eyes,
Of my fond error I was disabused;
I felt the charge that on me was imposed;
I knew that, far from being my love's thrall,
I must, Paulinus, soon renounce it all,
And that the gods' choice, thwarting my heart's will,
Gave to the world the life-days left me still.)

[11] Cf. in Rotrou's *Cosroès* the change in Mardesanes after he is made king.

concepts of permanent validity, he does still better—as he needs must do to achieve anything really great. If the moral concepts implicit in his work are not of permanent validity, his work is to that extent a thing of his own age, not of all time. There are, of course, different degrees of validity and of universality. The self-imposed task of Sophocles' Antigone does not seem to us a duty, but there is nothing evil in it— only nobility and love—and we can imaginatively conceive of her feelings about it and sympathize with them and with her. But the *gloire* of Racine's Titus makes him break his plighted word to a woman who loves him, and it is not so much duty to others as it is a pride which is dependent upon conformity to ideas now obsolete.

To make matters worse, the dramatist shows that Berenice herself cannot understand Titus's viewpoint.[12] She eventually appreciates some of the considerations by which he is constrained, but never his notion of *gloire;* it seems to be a concept which a sovereign fully grasps only after he is invested with sovereignty, and is hence a specimen not of universal morality but of that "private morality" which Lemaître condemns in the characters of Corneille in his decline and of all the other playwrights of the period except Racine.[13] That such is its nature is proved by the fact that Titus in his hour of deepest despair thinks of suicide as an honorable way out of his troubles. If his *gloire* were an in-

---

[12] Till she learns his decision from his own lips, she believes his *gloire* compels him to cleave to her. (N. B., 1. 908: "Il ne me quitte point, il y va de sa gloire."—"He will not leave me; he is honor bound.") Afterwards she says (1. 1103), "Hé bien! régnez, cruel; contentez votre gloire" ("Well then, reign, cruel man; satisfy thy *gloire.*"), and goes on to speak of his broken oaths to her and of his "injustice." It is hard for her to realize that he still loves her.

[13] Jules Lemaître, *Jean Racine,* pp. 131-134. Cf. also the same writer's article on Pierre Corneille in Petit de Julleville's *Histoire de la Langue et de la Littérature française,* vol. iv, p. 295.

telligible duty towards his country to discharge the task of
ruling it which has been committed to him, his suicide would
be no less a flight from that duty than his abdication would
be; it would have all the disadvantages of abdication and
none of its advantages; it would make both Rome and Berenice lose him, instead of only one or the other of them.
Plainly, then, either his *gloire* is an artificial "point of hon-
or," according to which it would be disgraceful to live without the crown if one has the opportunity to live with it;[14]

[14] Cf. ll. 1399-1406, where Titus says to Bérenice:

> Oui, Madame; et je dois moins encore vous dire
> Que je suis prêt pour vous d'abandonner l'Empire,
> De vous suivre, et d'aller, trop content de mes fers,
> Soupirer avec vous au bout de l'univers.
> Vous-même rougiriez de ma lâche conduite:
> Vous verriez à regret marcher à votre suite
> Un indigne Empereur, sans empire, sans cour,
> Vil spectacle aux humains des faiblesses d'amour.

> (Yes, madam; and I ought still less to say
> That I am ready now to put away
> The empire for thy sake, and follow thee;—
> To go, thy willing captive, tenderly
> To bide with thee on earth's remotest shores.
> Thou wouldst thyself blush at my craven course.
> Thou wouldst with sorrow see me following swift
> Upon thy footsteps, an unworthy emperor, reft
> Of realm and courtiers, an example base—
> To the eyes of mortals—of love's weaknesses.)

He exhibits the same conception earlier (ll. 1024-1026) in his self-
reproaches for his hesitancy:

> Ah! lâche, fais l'amour, et renonce à l'Empire:
> Au bout de l'univers va, cours te confiner,
> Et fais place à des cœurs plus dignes de régner.

> (Ah, coward! renounce the empire and take love!
> To the world's farthest bound go, hide amain,
> And yield thy place to souls more fit to reign.)

or else his impulse to kill himself is so pusillanimous and so silly that he appears abject instead of nobly "sympathetic" as his role requires him to be.

But indeed all three of the major characters in the play are anything but sympathetic—Titus and Berenice and Antiochus alike. When Titus resolves to break with Berenice, he shirks at first the final interview and leave-taking which common decency demands of him, and asks Antiochus instead to acquaint her with his decision. He is afraid, he says, that he will weaken if he sees her again; and the fact is that he has already shown himself too weak to make the necessary explanations to her when the right opportunity was

---

Titus, in fact, is sure that he cannot live long when separated from his beloved. He tells her (ll. 1122-1125):

Je n'aurai pas, Madame, à compter tant de jours.
J'espère que bientôt la triste renommée
Vous fera confesser que vous étiez aimée.
Vous verrez que Titus n'a pu sans expirer . . .

(Madame, I need but briefly count the time.
I hope that soon sad tidings will compel
Thee to admit that Titus loved thee well.
He cannot, thou wilt see, do aught but die . . .)

In that case his sacrifice of himself and Berenice will be of no real benefit to Rome. She interrupts his words with the very sensible question: "Ah! Seigneur, s'il est vrai, pourquoi nous séparer?" ("Ah, sire, if this be true, why part us?") Her logic is wasted, because it is not the good of his country which chiefly concerns Titus, but the figure he himself will cut. His *gloire* requires that, while life is his, he shall cling to the scepter which has been placed in his hand; how long he may do so, is as heaven shall dispose, but he can at least (ll. 1173-1174)

. . . laisser un exemple à la postérité,
Qui sans de grands efforts ne puisse être imité.

(Leave an example to posterity
Which nowise can be rivaled easily.)

offered him to do so. Then Antiochus in his turn comes presently to the conclusion that he is unwilling to be the bearer of such evil tidings to the woman he himself has in secret loved long and hopelessly. He reflects that it will cause him fresh pangs to behold, in her tears, the evidence of how much she loves another; so he plans to slip away without discharging the task entrusted to him or informing Titus that he will not discharge it, for "plenty of other people will come to apprise her of her misfortune"! This dastardly flight is forestalled by the chance entrance of Berenice herself. When he sees her, he cannot refrain from saying that he knows she is disappointed in not encountering Titus instead of him; he hints that there are very distressing things which he might tell her, but he will not tell them.

> D'autres, loin de se taire en ce même moment,[15]
> Triompheraient peut-être, et, pleins de confiance,
> Céderaient avec joie à votre impatience.
> Mais moi, toujours tremblant, moi, vous le savez bien,
> A qui votre repos est plus cher que le mien,
> Pour ne le point troubler, j'aime mieux vous déplaire,
> Et crains votre douleur plus que votre colère.
> Avant la fin du jour vous me justifierez.
> Adieu, Madame.

Berenice, already alarmed by the manner in which Titus has avoided her, now fears anything and everything. She

[15] Other men, far from keeping silent now,
Would triumph, perhaps, and boldly satisfy
This thine impatience with great joy; but I,
Trembling always, to whom, as well is known
To thee, thy peace is dearer than mine own,—
I dread thy grief more than thine anger; fain
Would I displease thee rather than cause thee pain.
Thou wilt approve my choice before this day
Ends. Farewell, madam.

protests that to leave her thus in terrified suspense is more
cruel than the ghastliest revelation could be. (This fact
should have been apparent to anyone!) She implores Antiochus to speak out, and finally, with entire justice, threatens
him with her eternal hatred if he will not. When, thus
constrained, he breaks the sad news to her in as kindly a
manner as possible, she refuses to believe him, declares it
all an infamous falsehood intended to cause dissension between her and Titus, and bids him, *even if he has not lied to
her,* never to come into her presence again. The more clearly
the situation is comprehended, the worse her conduct at
this moment is seen to be. She has always in long years of
trial found Antiochus a man of stainless honor who has
put self behind him in his unwavering devotion to her interests (for of course she knew nothing of his design to
flee from the task of enlightening her, and Racine obviously
did not mean this to be a baseness in him); she does not
really believe the outrageous charges which she flings in his
face, but only wants to believe them, as she admits to Phenice
a moment later; she is going instantly to Titus, she says, and
she might at least wait to learn the truth from his own lips
before making those charges. But no: what she has heard
stabs her to the heart; and in blind anger at her pain, and
in blind craving to assuage that pain (even by self-deception,
and by cruelty and injustice to the mortal who has seemed
most loyal to her) she strikes out at the unoffending messenger—"naturally," says Lemaître, and the tenderness with
which other critics treat her indicates that they share his
opinion. "Naturally," beyond doubt, if by "naturally" one
means in accord with the nature of some kinds of people. But
such an act is not natural to anyone whom it is possible
to admire or to sympathize with; for honorable men and
women do not lose all sense of rectitude and fairness, no
matter how dire the shock of anguish that assails them.

Shakespeare's Hermione would not have behaved like Berenice, nor would Racine's own Junia or Monime.

The one time in the play at which Antiochus appears genuinely to advantage is when he announces that he is cured of his love by such treatment, but it soon becomes evident that he is not. For the rest, he vacillates throughout between hope and despair. Titus, also, frequently wavers more or less in his adherence to what he believes to be the only right course for him; and there is a good deal of conscious pose in the things he says and does. As for Berenice, though she has been told by Antiochus that Titus is compelled to renounce her because of the Roman prejudice against queens and that he is half mad with helpless love and sorrow, she instantly concludes that if he leaves her he cares nothing for her. In Act V she at first refuses to see him again; and though she denies that she wishes heaven to avenge her upon him, she says that his own conscience will do so, and she repeatedly charges him with cruelty, indifference, and bad faith. A really great love tends to feel grief rather than anger if it thinks itself abused. But it also has more confidence in the beloved one than Berenice exhibits in Titus; though utterly unprepared for his decision and quite unable to see the rightness of it or to follow his arguments justifying it, she ought to believe him at least sincere, however tragically mistaken he might be—if hers were the love which is natural to the higher type of man or woman. Even before she hears that she and Titus must part, she is prone to find petty, personal explanations for what she cannot understand in her lover's conduct. When she comes to him in the second act and he shows constraint and perturbation and finally rushes from the room with stammered words about Rome and the Empire, she does not account for his strange behavior in the obvious way, though Phenice has warned her that hostile public sentiment remains to be reckoned with; she imagines instead that Titus has learned of Antiochus' love for her and that he is jealous—a conventional hypothesis which, as Voltaire pointed out, would be entertained by characters on the stage rather than by people in real life—and comforts herself with the conventional idea that if Titus feels jealousy, he loves her.[16]

"Conventional"—that word explains a large share of the blemishes of *Bérénice*. Not only was the view held by Titus of what befits a monarch the one which other French tragedies of the period would lead us to expect him to hold, but those tragedies frequently represent lovers as acting in a manner which today would be thought despicable. We have seen that in the eternal discussions of love and its manifestations with which the salons of the seventeenth century busied themselves, any ignoble feeling or impulse which might assail human beings in the grip of that passion was regarded as natural and therefore as legitimate—almost, even, as necessarily present in any love which is sincere—and that this point of view came by way of the romances into the convention-ridden, pseudo-classical drama of that age, and so dominated it that its heroes and heroines are often quite beyond the pale of more enlightened sympathies.

No other play of Racine's after *Andromaque* has so much

16 To some people today, Berenice's rebuke of Antiochus for declaring his love to her may seem another exhibition of the unamiable side of her character. But even today, for a man to tell a married woman that he loves her is regarded as an act of very doubtful propriety, and Racine's contemporaries evidently felt much the same way in the case of a woman who was betrothed. By drawing this parallel we can better understand the feelings of both Antiochus and Berenice throughout the first act; and it will be apparent that the Queen's behavior then was dignified and kindly—indeed, quite fine. Nor need we be surprised that when afterwards, in Act III, Antiochus comes again into her presence, she asks him somewhat sharply if he has not yet departed. She at that time fancies that Titus has been offended by the knowledge of his secret passion and its indiscreet avowal.

of the flavor of romanesque tragedy as *Bérénice*. Its very subject is, in essence, the one most frequently met with in the dramas of the two Corneilles, Quinault, and their fellows: a conflict between the claims of love and honor, or of love and the State. Each of the principal characters has a confidant, just as each does in *Andromaque;* nowhere else in Racine is the pairing thus complete and stiffly conventional. Of the three confidants in *Bérénice,* only Paulinus has the slightest individuality; Phenice is stupid even beyond the wont of confidants when she cannot imagine the reason for Titus's flight from her mistress, though it was she herself who insisted that the laws and feelings of Rome remained a serious obstacle. And in no other play after *Andromaque* is the conventional love-language of gallantry so jarringly in evidence.[17]

There is perhaps a reason for all this, quite beyond the exigencies of a contest with Corneille. More familiar than any other author of his times with the great tragedies of ancient Greece, Racine appears to have been actuated, throughout his career as a dramatist, by two ambitions: to write plays as nearly like those of Sophocles and Euripides as would be possible in seventeenth-century France, and to write plays that would be universally admired. *La Thébaïde* contains few pseudo-classical elements. Save for Creon's love for Antigone, it is a straightforward attempt to put the story of the children of Oedipus as told by Seneca and the Greeks into the form of a French tragedy; its faults are for the most part merely those of inexperience. It enjoyed a quite creditable success for a maiden effort, but nothing like the success that Racine had hoped for. Very well, he must have said to himself, if people did not care for what *he* preferred, he would show that he could give them

---

[17] There is actually more of such language in *Phèdre* than in *Bérénice,* but in *Phèdre* it is so used that somehow it is much less objectionable.

what *they* preferred; and he wrote the wholly romanesque *Alexandre,* which was extremely popular. He had now proved that he could win favor; perhaps he could win it also with something more nearly to his taste. In *Andromaque* he took a long stride towards naturalness and truth, and both city and Court hailed his daring experiment with the wildest delight. He then went still further in the same direction in *Britannicus;* but this tragedy, though it became after a few years one of the most highly esteemed of his works, was a failure when first presented, until it was saved by the praise which Louis XIV bestowed upon it. *Bérénice* was the next product of Racine's pen; it hence comes at a crucial point in his career.

Two courses lay open to him. He could continue resolutely in the vein of *Britannicus,* hoping that he might at length please the public with that sort of play, whether by more fortunate selection of subject or by educating his audiences to a better appreciation of true dramatic values, but in any event persisting in his own search for those values; or he could revert to the manner of *Andromaque,* in which case he would be certain to acquire fresh laurels. He chose the latter alternative. *Bérénice* has little less of pseudo-classical convention than has *Andromaque,*[18] and it scored a triumph. Thereafter, Racine again made progress away from the romanesque and towards a purer form of art, but this time slowly and cautiously, through *Bajazet* and *Mithridate* to an *Iphigénie* which in large part is of genuine classical inspiration, and thence, doubtless reassured by the applause that had greeted each step, to the transcendent achievement of *Phèdre.*

[18] This fact is remarked upon by Bernardin in his edition of *Bajazet* (*Théâtre complet de Jean Racine,* vol. iii, Paris, n.d.), p. 54, note 12: ". . . in *Bérénice* and *Bajazet,* Racine went back completely to romanesque tragedy, from which he had seemed to want to break away in *Britannicus";* but no one, apparently, has hitherto pointed out the reason for it.

CHAPTER XI

RACINE'S *BAJAZET*

N O single formula can wholly account for the work of a writer of genius. The most significant light is shed on Racine's by an envisagement of the conflict between the prevailing pseudo-classicism and his own Hellenistic inclinations in drama; but other factors, too, were of importance. Rivalry with Corneille, as Michaut (and Lemaître earlier) pointed out, influenced him; and it doubtless even determined his selection of the subjects of *Britannicus* and *Mithridate,* as well as that of *Bérénice,* and was responsible for some features of his handling of *Iphigénie.* Deltour is no less clearly right in his suggestion that almost every new play of Racine's was affected by the criticisms made of his last preceding play; [1] this is obviously true of *Bajazet.*

Bérénice lacks the substance of tragedy, insisted Saint-Evremond and the rest of the hostile faction. Accordingly, in his next drama, Racine sought blood and passion.

He found them in an almost contemporaneous theme— the only one he ever treated—supplied by actual events in Constantinople; these he dramatized with some alterations. Geographical remoteness, he felt, has much the same effect as remoteness of time in lending dignity to the characters of a play, separating them from the commonplace and trivial details of life familiar to the audience, and showing them in not their accidental but their essential human qualities. That such should be done in all tragedies was part of the regnant literary theory of his day, though in practice what all the dramatists of that period really did to a large extent

---

[1] *Les Ennemis de Racine au XVIIᵉ Siècle,* by F. Deltour, 7th ed., Paris, 1912. See especially pp. 385-386.

was to impose grotesquely their own artificial, transient fashions of speech and feeling and conduct upon the people of every country and age represented in their plays! Such unwitting grotesquery, however, is not nearly so apparent with Oriental as with ancient classical subject-matter; for though seventeenth-century France probably knew even less about the manners and customs of the Orient than about those of classical antiquity, most of us today have made a much greater advance in our knowledge of classical antiquity than in our knowledge of the East.

Racine was not the first to write a play dealing with recent Turkish history. A notable instance of its exploitation earlier was *la Mort du Grand Osman* by Tristan l'Hermite. In 1670, only two years before *Bajazet,* Molière had introduced Turkish scenes into his comedy, *le Bourgeois Gentilhomme.* Political events were especially directing public attention to the Ottoman Empire. *Bajazet,* therefore, was well precedented and timely.

With less striving after "local color" than Tristan, Racine achieved the atmosphere of the seraglio by a few deft touches[2] —an absolute minimum of effort necessary for that purpose. He well knew that costumes and stage properties could add whatever more the taste of an audience might at any time require.

Stated in its barest outlines, without details, the action of *Bajazet* appears eminently suitable for a "harem tragedy." The Sultan Amurath, while leading his army on a campaign, has left his favorite, Roxana, in power in the seraglio, where he holds in prison his younger brother, Bajazet, before putting him to death as Sultans usually put to death their

---

[2] Allusions to viziers, janissaries, slaves, mutes, expounders of the Moslem law, execution by strangling, the standard of the Prophet, the sacred gate, the secret exit opening on the Bosphorus, Solyman and his beloved Roxelana, etc.

near relatives who might overthrow them. Roxana conceives a passion for Bajazet which she is led to believe he reciprocates. She conspires with the discredited vizier "Acomat" (Achmet) to seize the throne for the young prince, with whom she expects to share it; but when she finds that a secret love exists between him and his cousin Atalide, their intermediary, and that these two have been hoodwinking her all the while for their own ends, she has him executed. She herself is killed by an emissary of Amurath, and Atalide commits suicide.

Such a story is not only appropriate to the setting; in essence it is dramatic and piteous. It is made all the more so by certain details in Racine's treatment of it: Bajazet and Atalide have been childhood playmates whose love is but the ripening of long and tender attachment; one item of the bargain arranged by Roxana and Achmet is that Atalide shall be the bride of the aging vizier; and the really tragic turn given to the situation is caused by Roxana's unexpected, eleventh-hour demand to be made not merely the favorite but the wedded wife of Bajazet if she saves him and helps him to the throne. Under such circumstances it would be only natural that the lovers should wish both to give and to receive, mutually, frequent comfort, encouragement, and reassurances—natural that they should sometimes be imprudent in communicating with each other, and that their secret should hence be suspected and presently discovered. It would not have been difficult to devise a dramatic action in which this course of events could be very sympathetically portrayed.

But Racine just prior to this time, as we have noted in the immediately preceding chapter, had passed through a crisis and made a decision. After *Britannicus* had met with only a tardily achieved success, he had chosen to return in his next drama to some such degree of compromise with pseudo-classicism as had proved so popular in *Andromaque;*

and the facile triumph of *Bérénice* was the result. Now, whatever might be the best way to develop the situation in *Bajazet* and to conduct the love of its hero and Atalide to exposure and disaster, undoubtedly the *easiest* way was to introduce into their difficult situation a factor eternally recurrent in French-classical drama: jealousy. And Racine took the easiest way.

It permitted him, since jealousy if once born is hard to extirpate and awakens to renewed life again and again, the sort of "pendulum-plot," as it has been called, that had gripped the audiences of *Andromaque*. Just as, in that play, Andromache by her indecision swings the intentions of all the dramatis personae—and therewith the prospective course of events—first in one direction and then in its opposite like a gigantic pendulum, so too in *Bajazet* Atalide's jealousy now masters her, now is overcome, and now masters her again, with consequent pendulum-like oscillations in the behavior of everyone else. No audiences in that day would lose sympathy with Atalide, however unreasonable and extreme her feelings. What people of later times and other countries, who had not been brought up on the *Astrée* or *Clélie* nor undergone the influence of the Hôtel de Rambouillet, might think of her could not enter into Racine's calculations.

Since the love of Bajazet and Atalide had grown out of their affection for each other as children, it had doubtless been tacitly understood between them rather than passionately avowed. In consequence, there is nothing surprising or censurable in Atalide's anxiety, at a time before the opening of the play, lest Roxana's great services to the Prince, combined with so much beauty and ardent love for him, might win his heart away from her. But Bajazet, so she tells her confidante, at length dispelled her fears; evidently he swore to her that he loved her and would love no other. When she learns of Roxana's resolve to exact marriage of him as the

price of his life and to let him die if he refuses to agree to it,
Atalide at first is sure that he will indeed refuse. She wishes
that she could see him before his interview with the Sultana,
and persuade him not to defy one in whose power he is. Then
abruptly all her jealous distrust and self-depreciation revive.

> Au moins si j'avais pu préparer son visage! [3]
> Mais, Zaïre, je puis l'attendre à son passage:
> D'un mot ou d'un regard je puis le secourir.
> Qu'il l'épouse, en un mot, plutôt que de périr.
> Si Roxane le veut, sans doute il faut qu'il meure.
> Il se perdra, te dis-je. Atalide, demeure:
> Laisse, sans t'alarmer, ton amant sur sa foi.
> Penses-tu mériter qu'on se perde pour toi?
> Peut-être Bajazet, secondant ton envie,
> Plus que tu ne voudras aura soin de sa vie.

She thereupon gives up all idea of trying to assist him in
the mortal peril in which she herself says that he stands unless the hypothesis created by her jealousy be true. She says
that it only "may" be true (*peut-être*) but she at once entertains it and acts as though it were a certainty. Such is her
behavior, when the life of one who loves her is at stake! How
petty and despicable her feelings are is shown by the very
manner of their expression.

Bajazet does recoil from the proposal which Roxana makes

---

[3] If I could even have prepared his face!
But, Zaïre, I can wait for him to pass.
I with one word, one glance, can give him aid.
Sooner than he should perish, let them wed.
His fate lies in Roxana's hands. I say
He will destroy himself! . . . Atalide, stay.
Leave, without fear, thy lover to his faith.
Thinkest thou that one for *thy* sake will choose death?
Bajazet well may meet thy wish to save him,
More careful of his life than thou wouldst have him.

to him and does incur her deadly wrath. Atalide, again in
terror for him, persuades him to placate the enraged woman
at any cost—to tell her whatever may be necessary to
avert his death. It is not easy to conquer his pride and
scruples, which make such a course repugnant to him; she
prevails on him only by declaring that otherwise she will
confess her love for him and her part in deceiving the Sultana, and so will die with him. Then, as soon as he has
obeyed her and accomplished what she has bidden him to
accomplish, jealousy again torments her and she reveals
to Zaïre that she intends to kill herself.

But it was solely by making Bajazet think that his dis-
sembling would save her life—by urging precisely this consideration—that she has prevailed on him to do violence to
his instincts and conscience. No wonder she does not trust
the faithfulness of his vows to her, being herself capable of
such bad faith! To her perfidy towards the man who most
deserves fair dealing from her, she adds a readiness to believe
the worst of him, accepting at face value the vizier's statements about the joy of Bajazet and Roxana in their reconciliation—though the slightest use of her intelligence at this
time would have reminded her that her informant, knowing
nothing of the true state of affairs, would not distinguish between a pretended feeling on the part of the Prince, such as
she herself had enjoined on him, and the real ecstasy of the
Sultana. She turns to Zaïre as soon as Achmet has left them:

Allons, retirons-nous, ne troublons point leur joie.[4]

. . . .

Tu vois que c'en est fait : ils se vont épouser.
La Sultane est contente ; il l'assure qu'il l'aime.

[4] Come; let us hence. Let us not mar their bliss.

. . . .

Thou seest that all is o'er : they are to wed.
Roxana is content ; he vows his love

Mais je ne m'en plains pas, je l'ai voulu moi-même.
Cependant croyais-tu, quand, jaloux de sa foi,
Il s'allait plein d'amour sacrifier pour moi;
Lorsque son cœur tantôt m'exprimant sa tendresse
Refusait à Roxane une simple promesse;
Quand mes larmes en vain tâchaient de l'émouvoir;
Quand je m'applaudissais de leur peu de pouvoir:
Croyais-tu que son cœur contre toute apparence,
Pour la persuader trouvât tant d'éloquence?
Ah! peut-être, après tout, que, sans trop se forcer,
Tout ce qu'il a pu dire, il a pu le penser.
Peut-être en la voyant, plus sensible pour elle,
Il a vu dans ses yeux quelque grâce nouvelle.

. . . .

Quand mes pleurs vers Roxane ont rappelé ses pas,
Je n'ai point prétendu qu'il ne m'obéit pas.
Mais après les adieux que je venais d'entendre,

To her. But I do not complain thereof.
I myself wished it. Yet wouldst thou have thought,
When to be true to me just now he sought
To sacrifice himself with heart suffused
With love—yes, when for my sake he refused
To the Sultana a mere promise—when
I tried to stay him with my tears in vain
And yet was pleased they had so little might—
Wouldst thou have thought, I say, that now, in spite
Of all this show of tenderness, he could e'er
Find so much eloquence in wooing her?
Ah, perhaps after all 'twas not too hard
To make his feelings and his words accord.
Perhaps the more he looked on her, the more
He saw new charms and yielded to their power.

. . . .

When I recalled him to Roxana, I
Had no intention he should not comply.
But after the farewells I lately heard

Après tous les transports d'une douleur si tendre,
Je sais qu'il n'a point dû lui faire remarquer
La joie et les transports qu'on vient de m'expliquer.

Here we see her indulging in the same unworthy fancies
about her devoted lover, with complete disregard of all that
has been said between them. When he himself enters, she reproaches him tearfully. Thus she destroys both him and herself. He tries to assure her that he has given no promise of
any kind to Roxana, who with eager credulity has taken all
for granted on his first efforts to propitiate her; but Atalide
remains deaf to his protestations, and he says he will no
longer continue the odious deceit which he has practised
for her sake. But—and this is a vital defect in the play—
their tragedy does not proceed inevitably from what has
taken place in this scene. Atalide might again have come to
her senses and brought him to his—and after that, since he
was going immediately to head the insurrection, any further
emotional veerings on her part would not have mattered—
but *by sheer chance* it is exactly at this moment, before she
can utter a word of remonstrance to him, that Roxana enters and is so rebuffed by his coldness that her fatal suspicions are aroused. These are presently confirmed by the hackneyed stage device of the discovery of a letter from Bajazet
to Atalide, but even then the outcome is decided by a purely
fortuitous time-sequence; for Achmet, learning of the situation, forms a rescue-party which breaks into the seraglio,
and it is mere chance that they reach Bajazet just after instead of just before his death. True, suspense is in this way

---

And the sweet grief wherewith his heart was stirred,
Surely he need not have shown openly
Such rapture as was just described to me.

maintained to the end, but it is the suspense not of genuine tragedy but of melodrama.[5]

But this play was already seriously marred beyond mending, in any case. Sympathy for some of the characters, as we have observed in our consideration of *Bérénice,* is an essential in tragedy of the best type; and no one who is not under the spell of the French-classical tradition can sympathize with an Atalide or feel any real concern about what happens to her. Her monologue of self-condemnation before taking her own life cannot have the pathetic effect on us that Racine intended. And his Bajazet, no Turk save in name but rather a French gallant, who can love this Atalide and is weak enough to react to her moods regardless of the consequences to himself or to her or to those who have espoused his cause —he, too, forfeits our sympathy.[6] In these characters Racine

---

[5] In this denouement the usual pseudo-classical stereotypes of conduct are not absent. Bajazet must defend himself against his executioners and display his prowess, like other pseudo-classical "heroes," before being killed. Atalide must commit suicide after an appropriate speech, like other pseudo-classical "heroines"—and, really, there was not much else that she could decently do as a sequel to her previous behavior and its results. Zaïre wishes to die with her mistress, and Osmin has expressed a similar wish to die with Achmet when he supposed Achmet would die, like other pseudo-classical confidants. Racine's invention was here strictly in the romanesque groove.

[6] I have already pointed out (see Introduction, p. 21, especially) that among critics and scholars who write of seventeenth-century French plays, a large number even in modern times do fall into the habit of accepting, while they write of them, the ethical code of pseudo-classical drama, in which jealousy was looked upon with indulgence and sympathy. Some (e.g., Lemaître and Geoffrey Brereton) would have us see Atalide as innocent and dove-like—as wholly piteous, commendable, and lovable. Stressing the scenes in which her fears for Bajazet make her urge him to save his life at whatever expense to her, Brereton passes as quickly and lightly as possible over the ones which exhibit her jealousy and bad faith

appears to have gone too far even for the taste of the century following his own, if we can judge by so staunch a French-classicist as La Harpe, who wrote of the crucial dialogue between this precious pair:

"It is in this scene that one realizes more clearly than ever how weak and false is the motivation of the plot, which the author has based upon the jealousy of Atalide and the faint-heartedness of her lover. It is inconceivable that the conclusive details into which Bajazet has just gone should make so slight an impression upon Atalide that he would think himself obliged to risk everything and lose everything. The very just confidence in him which she has shown in the second act makes it impossible that in the third she should doubt his veracity, in the face of every appearance of truthfulness. This is the first fault.

"The second, which is much more serious, is the puerile despair (not to mince words) that costs Bajazet his life. He ought to have said to her: 'In the crisis we are in, it is a

with her lover. (Cf. his *Jean Racine,* London, 1951, pp. 177-178.) He could not have dwelt on these scenes with the same emphasis as on the others without ruining the picture he tries to paint of Atalide. It is hard to believe that he would have viewed her with the same tenderness if she had been a figure in any literature except that of France in its "classical" period, in which he had immersed himself. Sarcey, not thus immersed but a practical dramatic critic, voiced (in his *Quarante Ans de Théâtre,* Paris, 1900, vol. iii, pp. 185-186) the natural feelings of even a French audience in the nineteenth century—and surely in the twentieth also—when witnessing this play:

"You cannot imagine the impatience of the public in the third act, when all is supposed to be settled, when Bajazet has given for the second or third time his word to Roxana and to his minister Achmet, and then suddenly, because he has just heard the plaints of that little blockhead (*pécore*) of an Atalide, he changes his mind and leaves everybody in consternation. . . . How do you expect me to be interested in this exalted ninny (*majestueux dadais*) and his whining sweetheart (*plaignarde de maîtresse*)?"

question not of persuading you, but of saving your life as
well as my own. Thank heaven, I have promised nothing,
and I am on the point of accomplishing everything. Another moment, and I shall have it in my power to repay
Roxana in the manner that I choose, and to crown Atalide,
and this without being either ungrateful to the one or unfaithful to the other.'

"If he talked thus, he would talk like a man. When one
considers that nothing less is at stake than the life of such a
friend as Achmet, than the fate of Atalide, of Bajazet himself, and of the empire, one is obliged to admit that refinements of delicacy and insane compliance are alike the exact
reverse of tragedy, because they are the reverse of good
sense. . . . A prince who in this situation sacrifices everything
to such attenuated scruples of love is not only no hero and
still less a Turkish hero, but in no way deserves to have anyone die to serve him." [7]

What interest the play does possess is to be found in the
figures of Achmet and Roxana, which are among Racine's
greatest creations. And this is no small interest, though of
a lower, less moving kind than that in which sympathy is involved; it is the interest that any superb portrait excites,
and the interest—combined with quasi-admiration—stirred
by the spectacle of a cool, capable intellect at work or of vol-
canic, unleashed passions. For such excellence as can be attained where sympathy is lacking, *Bajazet* is comparable
among tragedies to *The Alchemist* of Ben Jonson among
comedies—the finest Elizabethan play by anyone but Shakespeare, and a play which misses greatness only by that lack—
though sympathy with someone is not so important in comedy as in tragedy.

Achmet is one of Racine's few really striking male char-

[7] Translated from the footnote where it is quoted in N. M.
Bernardin's *Théâtre complet de Jean Racine,* vol. iii, *Bajazet,* pp.
91-92, note 7.

acters; Roxana is an achievement surpassed only by Phaedra, Hermione, and perhaps Athaliah among his women. Both have been adequately discussed by a number of critics; an understanding of neither presents any serious difficulty. Here, at last, are genuine Orientals.

The vizier is adroit, resourceful, indefatigable, untroubled by scruples and impervious to the influence of any emotion except pride—which has been sorely wounded when the Sultan deposed him from his command of the army and, heading it himself, took the field without him. It is this mortal offense and his knowledge that it merely preludes his "liquidation" that impel Achmet to plan a revolt which would seat Bajazet on the throne.

> Je sais bien qu'Amurat a juré ma ruine;[8]
> Je sais à son retour l'accueil qu'il me destine.
> Tu vois, pour m'arracher du cœur de ses soldats,
> Qu'il va chercher sans moi les sièges, les combats:
> Il commande l'armée; et moi, dans une ville,
> Il me laisse exercer un pouvoir inutile.
> Quel emploi, quel séjour, Osmin, pour un Visir!
> Mais j'ai plus dignement employé ce loisir:
> J'ai su lui préparer des craintes et des veilles,
> Et le bruit en ira bientôt à ses oreilles.

[8] Well do I know that Amurath has sworn
My ruin. I know what greeting his return
Will bring to me. That he may drive me now
Out of his soldiers' hearts, thou seest how
He seeks without me siege and battle. He
Himself commands the army; as for me,
He leaves me in a city, where I wield
A futile power. What task is this, what field,
Osmin, for me, me, a vizier! But I
Have used my leisure not unworthily.
Vigils have I prepared for him, and fears,
And soon the news thereof will reach his ears.

Seeing that Roxana is the key to the situation, he contrives to arouse first interest and then love in her for the helpless prince, and offers himself as their instrument for success, with the hand of Atalide to be his reward—purely with an eye to self-preservation in the future, as he scornfully tells his friend Osmin, who asks him if he loves her:

> Voudrais-tu qu'à mon âge[9]
> Je fisse de l'amour le vil apprentissage?
> Qu'un cœur qu'ont endurci la fatigue et les ans
> Suivît d'un vain plaisir les conseils imprudents?
> C'est par d'autres attraits qu'elle plaît à ma vue:
> J'aime en elle le sang dont elle est descendue.
> Par elle Bajazet, en m'approchant de lui,
> Me va contre lui-même assurer un appui.
> Un visir aux Sultans fait toujours quelque ombrage:
> A peine ils l'ont choisi, qu'ils craignent leur ouvrage.
> Sa dépouille est un bien qu'ils veulent recueillir,
> Et jamais leurs chagrins ne vous laissent vieillir.
> Bajazet aujourd'hui m'honore et me caresse;
> Ses périls tous les jours réveillent sa tendresse.

> [9] Wouldst thou that at my age
> I should submit to love's vile tutelage,
> Or that a heart long years of toil made hard
> Should blindly seek vain joys as its reward?
> She charms my gaze because of other things;
> I love in her the stock from which she springs.
> Bajazet binds me to himself through her
> And thus assures me of a succorer
> Against him. Ever doth a vizier irk
> The souls of Sultans. They mistrust their work
> As soon as they have chosen him. They deem
> His fall a thing desirable for them,
> And their displeasure never lets us see
> A ripe age. Bajazet now honors me
> And courts me. Every day the risks he runs

Ce même Bajazet, sur le trône affermi,
Méconnaîtra peut-être un inutile ami.
Et moi, si mon devoir, si ma foi ne l'arrête,
S'il ose quelque jour me demander ma tête . . .
Je ne m'explique point, Osmin. Mais je prétends
Que du moins il faudra la demander longtemps.
Je sais rendre aux Sultans de fidèles services;
Mais je laisse au vulgaire adorer leurs caprices,
Et ne me pique point du scrupule insensé
De benir mon trépas quand ils l'ont prononcé.

He himself attends to everything, overlooks nothing that
might be of advantage:

> . . . . j'ai su déjà par mes brigues secrètes[10]
> Gagner de notre loi ses sacrés interprètes:
> Je sais combien crédule en sa dévotion
> Le peuple suit le frein de la religion.

Rekindle his affection. But when once
Firm on the throne, then may this Bajazet
Think me a friend whom he would fain forget.
For my part, if my aid and loyalty
Restrain him not,—if he dares ask of me
My head some day . . . Osmin, I leave the rest
Unsaid. But I intend that he at least
Will have to ask it a long time. I know
How to serve Sultans faithfully, but to
The common herd I leave the worshipping
Of their caprices, and I will not bring
Myself to such a senseless fealty
As to give thanks when doomed by them to die.

[10] I have already contrived secretly,
By intrigue, to bring over to our side
The expounders of our sacred law. To guide
The credulous throng, I know religion's power.

All is so well devised—only he does not foresee in others
the possibility of those insurgent feelings of which he himself
is devoid. At least, when these wreck the whole edifice of his
carefully-laid plans, he does not lose his head or waste any
time in futile anger. He knows he has gone too far to be
able to turn back now, stakes all on one desperate but coolly
calculated effort to retrieve the situation, and when it fails
by the narrowest of margins, has a ship ready for his escape
from the death which overtakes the others.[11]

Love—the rank sort of love to be expected in the inmate
of a harem—together with ambition rules Roxana, and she
is determined to gratify both at once. Her infatuation makes
her easily believe her love is returned, but Bajazet must
give her the one thing that Amurath has withheld, the name
of wife, or she will let him perish. When she unexpectedly
meets with a refusal little softened by the practical considerations which he urges, the conflict within her bosom between
her first fury and her heart's passion for the Prince finds
eloquent utterance in a tempestuous scene of great dramatic
power :

> Ne m'importune plus de tes raisons forcées.[12]
> Je vois combien tes vœux sont loin de mes pensées.
> Je ne te presse plus, ingrat, d'y consentir.
> Rentre dans le néant dont je t'ai fait sortir.

---

[11] He saves with him those who have compromised themselves
by their loyalty to him (his pride makes them his chief concern;
for his own life he cares little, amid the ruin of his fortunes)
and would save Atalide, too, if she would let him. His consideration for her, even now, is noteworthy.

[12] Vex me no more with logic drawn so fine.
I see how distant are thy hopes from mine.
No longer will I urge thee, thankless man,
To grant my wish. Back to the night again
From which I drew thee forth!

.   .   .   .

Ah! je vois tes desseins. Tu crois, quoi que je
    fasse,
Que mes propres périls t'assurent de ta grâce,
Qu'engagée avec toi par de si forts liens,
Je ne puis séparer tes intérêts des miens.
Mais je m'assure encore aux bontés de ton frère :
Il m'aime, tu le sais ; et, malgré sa colère,
Dans ton perfide sang je puis tout expier,
Et ta mort suffira pour me justifier.
N'en doute point, j'y cours, et dès ce moment même.
    Bajazet, écoutez : je sens que je vous aime.
Vous vous perdez. Gardez de me laisser sortir.
Le chemin est encore ouvert au repentir.
Ne désespérez point une amante en furie.
S'il m'échappait un mot, c'est fait de votre vie.

BAJAZET.

Vous pouvez me l'ôter : elle est entre vos mains.

.   .   .   .

        Oh, I perceive thy thought!
Thou deemest mine own peril, no matter what
I do, assures thy pardon,—that I am tied
To thee with bonds too strong to dare divide
Thy interests from mine. But I am still
Certain thy brother holds me in good will.
Thou knowest he loves me; and, despite his wrath,
Thy false blood can atone for all, thy death
Suffice to exculpate me. Do not doubt
This very moment 'twill be brought about!
    Bajazet, hear me! I find that all too well
I love thee. Thou art destroying thyself. Still, still
The way lies open to repent. Take care
Thou lettest me not go hence, nor to despair
Drivest a woman mad with love. If one
Word leaves my lips, thy life is o'er and done.

BAJAZET.

Thou canst deprive me of it. 'Tis in thy hands.

Peut-être que ma mort, utile à vos desseins,
De l'heureux Amurat obtenant votre grâce,
Vous rendra dans son cœur votre première place.

ROXANE.

Dans son cœur? Ah! crois-tu, quand il le voudrait
    bien,
Que si je perds l'espoir de régner dans le tien,
D'une si douce erreur si longtemps possédée,
Je puisse désormais souffrir une autre idée,
Ni que je vive enfin, si je ne vis pour toi?

And when she finally learns the whole deception that has
been practiced on her, her savage, almost incoherent frenzy
of rage is truly awesome:

Avec quelle insolence et quelle cruauté [13]
Ils se jouaient tous deux de ma crédulité!
Quel penchant, quel plaisir je sentais à les croire!
Tu ne remportais pas une grande victoire,
Perfide, en abusant ce cœur préoccupé,

Perhaps my death will further best thy plans,—
Will from triumphant Amurath win grace
And give thee in his heart thy former place.

ROXANA.

In *his* heart? Dost thou dream though he should fain
Have me, that if I lose the hope to reign
In thine, when I so long have cherished that dear
Delusion, I a different thought could bear
Henceforth, or live unless I lived for thee?

[13] How cruelly and how insultingly
They both made sport of my credulity!
I was so glad, so ready, to believe!
No mighty deed, false wretch, didst thou achieve
In cozening this heart already yielded,

Qui lui-même craignait de se voir détrompé.
Moi, qui, de ce haut rang qui me rendait si fière,
Dans le sein du malheur t'ai cherché la première,
Pour attacher des jours tranquilles, fortunés,
Aux périls dont tes jours étaient environnés;
Après tant de bonté, de soin, d'ardeurs extrêmes,
Tu ne saurais jamais prononcer que tu m'aimes!

. . . .

Tu pleures, malheureuse? Ah! tu devais pleurer
Lorsque, d'un vain désir à ta perte poussée,
Tu conçus de le voir la première pensée.
Tu pleures? et l'ingrat, tout prêt à te trahir,
Prépare les discours dont il veut t'éblouir.
Pour plaire à ta rivale, il prend soin de sa vie.
Ah! traître, tu mourras.

. . . .

Toi, Zatime, retiens ma rivale en ces lieux.
Qu'il n'ait en expirant que ses cris pour adieux.

Which feared to lose the dream that it had builded.
I first, from that high place which made me proud,
Myself have sought thee, 'neath misfortune bowed—
To link my days, quiet and with blessings crowned,
To perils wherewith thine were girt around—
And after favors, care, and love so free,
Thy tongue can never say thou lovest me!

. . . .

Thou weepest, unhappy woman? Ah, that day
Shouldst thou have wept when foolish impulses
First bred thy fatal wish to see his face!
Thou weepest? and he, resolved on perfidy,
Prepares the words with which to hoodwink thee.
He fain would live, such being thy rival's will!
Oh, thou shalt die, thou traitor!

. . . .

Do thou, Zatima, keep my rival here.
No last farewell shall reach his dying ear

Qu'elle soit cependant fidèlement servie.
Prends soin d'elle: ma haine a besoin de sa vie.
Ah! si, pour son amant facile à s'attendrir,
La peur de son trépas la fit presque mourir,
Quel surcroît de vengeance et de douceur nouvelle
De le montrer bientôt pâle et mort devant elle,
De voir sur cet objet ses regards arrêtés
Me payer les plaisirs que je leur ai prêtés!

Even yet, however, she will spare Bajazet if she can possess him; and in confident reliance on the power of her physical charms if these are habitually encountered, she makes him a last proposal:

Ma rivale est ici: suis-moi sans différer;[14]
Dans les mains des muets viens la voir expirer,
Et, libre d'un amour à ta gloire funeste,
Viens m'engager ta foi: le temps fera le reste.

—upon his rejection of which, she utters the terrible *"Sortez!"* ("Begone!") that sends him to his death.

Except her screams. But take care of her. Give
The best of tendance to her. She must live.
My hate requires it. Ah, if she can be
Moved for her lover's sake so easily
That fear of his death almost caused her own,
What added vengeance and new sweetness soon
To show him to her lying pale and dead,
See her eyes fixed upon him, and be paid
Thus for the raptures which they had through me!

[14] My rival is here. Follow me instantly
And see her die by the mutes' hands. Set free,
Then, from a love fatal to glory's quest,
Plight me thy troth. Time will do all the rest.

But the man who created her gave his leading actress the part, not of this fierce and passionate creature, this magnificent human animal, but of the miserable Atalide. *She,* evidently, was in his opinion the more important, the more interesting, the more effective role!

CHAPTER XII

RACINE'S *MITHRIDATE*

A FTER *Bajazet,* Racine's position as the leading tragic dramatist in France was assured. He had decidedly bested Corneille in the duel of "the two *Bérénices.*" He had triumphed with *Bajazet* while Corneille was failing with *Pulchérie.* He was soon to be received into the French Academy. But he was not yet entirely satisfied. In the eyes of the public, especially of older people who had worshipped Corneille in his prime and who clung to him with dogged devotion in his later, less happy days, Racine was still only the writer of tragedies of love, who was incapable of treating historical subjects concerned with war and politics, the special province of their aging favorite. The success of *Britannicus* had been slow in coming, and was therefore of questionable impressiveness. Its author wanted to prove, beyond dispute, that he too could write a historical drama; he wanted to write one which would be generally recognized as equal or superior to any of Corneille's.

In some degree he would write it in his own fashion, as he did *Britannicus.* Let Corneille try to capture the spirit and circumstances of a given moment of history and show it, above all, in its political aspects, taking the greatest liberties with important historical figures as best suited his purpose. It was precisely those noted figures in whom Racine found his chief interest, and whom he was at pains to portray—to the extent that he could under the dramatic conventions to which he was subject—as he conceived them really to have been. Accordingly, he did not select, as Corneille usually did, personages who were not well known and who could therefore be distorted without a shock to his audience. In *Britannicus* he had painted portraits of Nero and Agrippina; and now in his new play, to compete with Corneille at his very best in historical drama—that is, with *Nicomède*—he chose no unfamiliar Prusias or Nicomedes for his central character in a play dealing with the resistance of the Near East to Roman aggression, but the great and terrible Mithridates.

Of the death of this famous king of Pontus, history tells that when attempting to renew his war with Rome after being routed and becoming a fugitive, he met with treachery at the hands of his own son, Pharnaces, in consequence of which he killed himself. Here were proper elements of drama ready to hand. But the unfilial conduct of Pharnaces had to be motivated, and it was not enough that he should merely be in sympathy with that conquering nation which was the object of his father's lifelong hate. Moreover, in addition to the external conflict resulting from their opposite attitudes towards Rome, there had to be provided, to secure the most potent dramatic effects, some struggle within the breast of Mithridates himself.

"To explain and excuse the odious treason of Pharnaces as being caused by a rivalry in love," says N. M. Bernardin, "must have been the first idea that occurred to Racine." [1] Certainly. It could not have failed to be the first idea to occur to him, for it was the absolutely stereotyped sort of motivation that all romanesque dramatists were employing. And that would have been the best of reasons for rejecting it. But Racine sought no further; he adopted it. He was still largely taking "the easiest way." After all, the invariable formula of French-classical tragedy called for a love-element, in which nearly always the protagonist himself was involved. Corneille had more than once depicted an elderly man in love, not intending him to be a grotesque, ridiculous figure as such a one traditionally is in comedy, but dignified and

---

[1] Translated from *Mithridate,* ed. by L. R. Lewis, New York, 1921, p. xlvii, which reprints Bernardin's study of this play.

"sympathetic"—thus Martian in *Pulchérie* only the year before, to say nothing of Sertorius earlier. In contrast, Racine would show how fearsome a thing the love of an aging man can be when the man is Mithridates—its sensitiveness, its suspiciousness, its ferocious jealousy.

The object of that stark passion could not love Pharnaces and remain, herself, a "sympathetic" character; his perfidy is too infamous. So Racine had to supply Mithridates with another son, Xiphares, for his heroine, Monime, to love; and in order that their mutual affection might be subject to no possible blame, she and Xiphares are depicted as each having secretly loved the other before Mithridates ever saw her.

Thus did the dramatist's material take shape—in a decidedly conventional mould (mingling love and affairs of State, and having all the prominent male characters, regardless of their age, in love with the same woman) yet with great opportunities for powerful scenes and for the arousing of strong sympathies in any audience. Unfortunately, with the work of his rival so much in his mind—work which it was his first aim to parallel and to surpass—there was bound to be a larger element of artificiality in what he produced than when he was wholly intent on the "convincing" dramatization of his subject. We have seen in earlier chapters that a greater-than-usual remove from the lifelike invariably results when the author of a play imitates another play rather than life—as witness Du Ryer's imitation of Corneille in *Scévole* and Corneille's imitation of his own *Cinna* in *Pompée*—and we shall see it later in the degeneration of French "classical" tragedy, throughout the eighteenth century. We have observed, with Racine himself, the increase of conventionality in *Bérénice,* where he was primarily competing with Corneille. In *Mithridate* he again and again sacrifices truth-to-life for convenience in plot-development or to secure a momentary stage effect or to have opportunities for "dramatic" speeches—as a brief review of this tragedy will disclose.

At the opening of the play the half-brothers Pharnaces and Xiphares, on the report of their father's defeat and death, have come to Nymphaeum in Tauris (the Crimaea), where Mithridates had sent Monime, his affianced bride, for her safety during the war whose outbreak prevented their nuptials. Declaring that Pharnaces is the most odious of men to her and that she would kill herself sooner than marry him, she begs Xiphares to protect her against him; he assures her that he will do so, and then undertakes to make known to her his own love. In view of her helplessness, her fears, and her dependence upon him, the situation is a delicate one, requiring great tact in his avowal, as he is well aware. But this is how he begins:

XIPHARÈS.[2]

Madame, assurez-vous de mon obéissance;
Vous avez dans ces lieux une entière puissance.
Pharnace ira, s'il veut, se faire craindre ailleurs
Mais vous ne savez pas encor tous vos malheurs.

MONIME

Hé! quel nouveau malheur peut affliger Monime,
Seigneur?

---

[2] XIPHARES.
Madam, of my obedience have no doubt.
Here thy authority is absolute.
To make himself feared, Pharnaces may go
Elsewhere. But thou still knowest not all thy woe.
MONIME.
Alas, what new woe can afflict Monime,
Sir?

Xipharès.

Si vous aimer c'est faire un si grand crime,
Pharnace n'en est pas seul coupable aujourd'hui;
Et je suis mille fois plus criminel que lui.

Monime.

Vous!

Xipharès.

Mettez ce malheur au rang des plus funestes;
Attestez, s'il le faut, les puissances célestes
Contre un sang malheureux, né pour vous tour-
    menter,
Père, enfants animés à vous persécuter.

He could hardly have found an approach more certain to
alarm and dismay her, even if he had tried; and no one, except in a play, could have failed to realize this. But his ineptness causes tension and suspense, and therefore Racine
represents him as being thus unbelievably inept.

The stupidity which this alert, capable, and usually far-
from-stupid young man is made to display on this occasion
is as nothing, however, beside that which the dramatist ascribes to him later. Though Monime, on his confession of his

---

Xiphares.

If to love thee is so great a crime,
Not Pharnaces alone is guilty now.
I am far guiltier than *he* is.

Monime.
Thou?

Xiphares.

Of thy misfortunes, reckon this the worst.
Invoke the gods against a race accurst,
Destined to bring unhappiness to thee,
Ever inspired—the father formerly,
And now the sons—to do thee some ill turn.

love, does not tell him that she returns it, she does tell him that he may continue to see her—a significant concession for a heroine of French-classical tragedy to make under such circumstances. She reiterates to Pharnaces, in Xiphares' presence, her inflexible determination to wed no friend of Rome; and Pharnaces makes obvious insinuations as to her real reason for refusing him. Then the supposedly dead Mithridates appears. He thinks that it is only Pharnaces, not Xiphares, who loves Monime; he concludes from her coldness to himself that she loves this recreant son of his, and complains to Xiphares that she does. And Xiphares more than half believes him! Xiphares, who has seen and heard so much with his own eyes and ears, and who knows how fatal it would be for Monime to reveal to the despot her true feelings, promptly entertains the idea—on Mithridates' mere assertion that it is a fact—that she loves Pharnaces, after all! And when she protests to him, in horror, that she does not, he still fails to suspect—in spite of all that he has seen and heard—that it is he himself whom she loves; and when she confesses that it is, he can hardly credit his ears. Had ever man so little sense, outside of a play? A "dramatic" scene, however, is thus obtained.

At length the King discovers, by trickery, who is the real object of Monime's affections; and Xiphares is warned by his friend Arbates that his father knows all and that he must fly. He hastens to Monime to inform her of this and take a hurried last farewell. Some hidden foe, he tells her, has betrayed their secret—who, he cannot imagine. Whereupon:

MONIME.[3]
Hé quoi? cet ennemi, vous l'ignorez encore?

[3] MONIME.
    Dost thou not know,
Then, even yet, who is thy secret foe?

XIPHARÈS.

Pour surcroît de douleur, Madame, je l'ignore.
Heureux si je pouvais, avant que m'immoler,
Percer le traître cœur qui m'a pu déceler!

MONIME.

Hé bien! Seigneur, il faut vous le faire connaître.
Ne cherchez point ailleurs cet ennemi, ce traître;
Frappez; aucun respect ne vous doit retenir.
J'ai tout fait; et c'est moi que vous devez punir.

Great surprise of Xiphares! Effective climax, well worked up. Yet in real life he would be bound to guess who has revealed his secret. For he knows that only two—or at most three—people besides himself knew it: Arbates and Monime, and Monime's confidante, Phaedima. Pharnaces divined it and accused him before Mithridates; but evidently someone has now confirmed the charges of Pharnaces against him and Monime, which the King hitherto had refused to credit. This could only have been one of those two or three people; and Arbates has warned him of his danger, and he well knows Monime's guilelessness and his father's infernal cunning. But it is theatrically effective for him to be amazed, and for Monime to offer her breast to his vengeance and say "Strike!" though she must have realized that Xiphares

---

XIPHARES.

To crown my grief, madam, I know him not.
How gladly would I pierce, before I got
My death, that false and treacherous heart of his!

MONIME.

Well then, sir, I must tell thee who it is.
Seek not elsewhere the foe that did such harm
To thee. Strike. No respect should stay thine arm.
I am the traitor. Thou shouldst punish me.

would not want to strike *her* in any case—even if her betrayal of him had not been wholly innocent, as it was.

Her own ingenuousness, however, and her incapacity for dissimulating are represented as too extreme; such over-simplification of a character belongs rather to melodrama than to tragedy. Common report could not have left her ignorant of Mithridates' possessive, suspicious, vengeful nature, unrestrained in its savagery by any human ties. She knows it would mean ruin for Xiphares as well as for herself if she should arouse the jealousy of this passionate tyrant and he should guess whom she loves. Yet when he seeks hungrily for some evidence of concern for him in her breast, she makes no effort to represent herself as anything but the unresisting victim of his will. She might at least have said then, quite truthfully, what she does say later when defending herself against his recriminations in the fourth act: that she was glad to be able to give happiness to so great a man. But she will not say even this when it would be helpful. Again, when Mithridates perpetrates his cruel fraud to discover her heart's secret (pretending he now wishes her to wed Xiphares instead of himself but believes that she loves the infamous Pharnaces, with whom he will therefore join her in marriage) and she is finally convinced of his sincerity, it is altogether too much that she forthwith confesses all her feelings,—that she stakes everything on not being deceived, without any reticence as a protection against the possibility that she is,—instead of merely assuring him that she detests Pharnaces and would much prefer Xiphares if she must marry one of the two. Here once more we have a conventional ineptness which serves the ends of drama—or rather of melodrama—but which would be almost unbelievable in real life.

It is also a convention of French-classical tragedies to magnify the prowess of their heroes; and in doing so, this play falls, near its end, into sheer absurdity: we are told that when Mithridates, brought to bay by overwhelming numbers and determined to die fighting, showed himself at the gates of the palace, the Romans all recoiled a short distance on beholding their redoubtable foe, and some of them in panic even fled back to their ships. Racine probably had in mind the great passage in the *Iliad*, when the Trojans recoiled at the mere sight of Achilles across the trench, unarmed though he was; but in *Mithridate* it is not Trojans but the veteran legionaries of all-conquering Rome who we are asked to believe were thus dismayed when confronted by a man whom they had beaten again and again!

Yet this drama, though conventionally plotted and though marred by false touches, has excellences which go far towards redeeming it. Its "story" is a good one—sure to appeal, as we have already observed, to an audience, and especially to people who are not too critical. In witness of this fact is the testimony of a teacher in an American college, that *Mithridate* "is by far the best play with which to begin the study of Racine," he having found, over a period of twenty-five years, that it "enlists, in higher degree than *Andromaque, Britannicus, Iphigénie, Phèdre*, or *Athalie*," the interest of his classes.[4] Its Xiphares, despite his occasional, out-of-character lapses of intelligence, is a rather attractive, if conventional, figure—as none of Racine's other young-men-in-love is. And the play has two very notable pieces of characterization in Mithridates himself and—aside from the one flaw in her portrayal discussed above—Monime.

Mithridates, with his sanguinary greatness and violent passions, more nearly accords with the conception of a "tragic hero" held by Shakespeare and his fellow Elizabethans than does any other protagonist of Racine. He answers

---

4 L. R. Lewis, *op. cit.*, p. v.

well, in many respects, to our conception of the Mithridates of history—however much more concerned with love, to satisfy the requirements of French-classical tragedy. Menace lurks in his smoothest words, as in the first that we hear him utter, on his arrival, to his sons:

> Princes, quelques raisons que vous me puissiez dire,[5]
> Votre devoir ici n'a point dû vous conduire,
> Ni vous faire quitter en de si grands besoins,
> Vous le Pont, vous Colchos, confiés à vos soins.
> Mais vous avez pour juge un père qui vous aime.
> Vous avez cru des bruits que j'ai semés moi-même;
> Je vous crois innocents, puisque vous le voulez;

and the wild-beast fangs of the savage Oriental ruler are bared in his admonition regarding Monime:

> En un mot, c'est assez éprouver ma faiblesse: [6]
> Qu'elle ne pousse point cette même tendresse,
> Que sais-je? à des fureurs dont mon cœur outragé
> Ne se repentirait qu'après s'être vengé.

His indefatigable, undismayed resilience in defeat, his grandiose plans and overweening hopes of success against

---

[5] Princes, whatever reasons ye profess,
    Duty could ne'er have brought you to this place
    Nor made you quit, when issues bulked so large,
    Thou Pontus, Colchis thou, left in your charge.
    But 'tis a loving sire who judges you.
    Ye thought the rumors which I spread were true.
    I deem you guiltless, since ye will have it thus.

[6] My love's indulgence hath enough been tried.
    Let her not drive that very love, defied,
    To how know I what frenzy, which my soul
    Would not repent of till avenged in full.

mighty Rome are revealed with a virile eloquence in one of
the most famous monologues (and the longest one) that
Racine ever wrote—a supreme effort to surpass Corneille in
the elder dramatist's own field:

Ne vous figurez point que de cette contrée[7]
Par d'éternels remparts Rome soit séparée.
Je sais tous les chemins par où je dois passer;
Et si la mort bientôt ne me vient traverser,
Sans reculer plus loin l'effet de ma parole,
Je vous rends dans trois mois au pied du Capitole.
Doutez-vous que l'Euxin ne me porte en deux jours
Aux lieux où le Danube y vient finir son cours?
Que du Scythe avec moi l'alliance jurée
De l'Europe en ces lieux ne me livre l'entrée?
Recueilli dans leurs ports, accru de leurs soldats,
Nous verrons notre camp grossir à chaque pas.
Daces, Pannoniens, la fière Germanie,
Tous n'attendent qu'un chef contre la tyrannie.
Vous avez vu l'Espagne, et surtout les Gaulois,

[7]   Deem not that we are separated here
From Rome by an eternal barrier.
I know the roads to follow, every one;
And if death does not come to thwart me soon,
Within three months—I need no longer time—
We shall be camped beneath the Capitoline.
Cannot the Euxine bear me to the place
At which the Danube empties, in two days?
Will not the pact the Scythians swore with me
Thence into Europe give me entrance free?
Admitted to their ports, joined by their host,
We shall at each step greater numbers boast.
Dacians, Pannonians, Germans—all await
Only a leader 'gainst Rome's tyrant State.
Ye have seen Spain, yes, and still more the Gauls

Contre ces mêmes murs qu'ils ont pris autrefois
Exciter ma vengeance, et jusque dans la Grèce,
Par des ambassadeurs accuser ma paresse.
Ils savent que sur eux prêt à se déborder,
Ce torrent, s'il m'entraîne, ira tout inonder;
Et vous les verrez tous, prévenant son ravage,
Guider dans l'Italie et suivre mon passage.
   C'est là qu'en arrivant, plus qu'en tout le chemin,
Vous trouverez partout l'horreur du nom romain,
Et la triste Italie encor toute fumante
Des feux qu'a rallumés sa liberté mourante.
Non, Princes, ce n'est point au bout de l'univers
Que Rome fait sentir tout le poids de ses fers;
Et, de près inspirant les haines les plus fortes,
Tes plus grands ennemis, Rome, sont à tes portes.
Ah! s'ils ont pu choisir pour leur libérateur
Spartacus, un esclave, un vil gladiateur,
S'ils suivent au combat des brigands qui les vengent,

Urge me to vengeance against those same walls
Which formerly they stormed, and even in Greece
Ambassadors blame me for my slothfulness.
They know this torrent, about to burst on them,
Will, if it sweeps me down, all else o'erwhelm,
And to prevent this they will every one
Guide me to Italy and then follow on.
   There shall ye, more than on the route we came,
Find everywhere the horror of Rome's name
And hapless Italy all smoking yet
With fires her dying liberty hath lit.
No, princes, 'tis not earth's remotest folk
That Rome makes feel the full weight of her yoke,
As she inspires near-by the bitterest hate,
Her greatest foes are at her very gate.
Ah, if they once chose for their liberator
Spartacus, a vile slave, a gladiator,
Or followed brigands to avenge their wrongs,

De quelle noble ardeur pensez-vous qu'ils se rangent
Sous les drapeaux d'un roi longtemps victorieux,
Qui voit jusqu'à Cyrus remonter ses aïeux?

. . . .

Marchons; et dans son sein rejetons cette guerre
Que sa fureur envoie aux deux bouts de la terre.
Attaquons dans leurs murs ces conquérants si fiers;
Qu'ils tremblent, à leur tour, pour leurs propres foyers.

. . . .

Brûlons ce Capitole où j'étais attendu.
Détruisons ses honneurs, et faisons disparaître
La honte de cent Rois, et la mienne peut-être;
Et, la flamme à la main, effaçons tous ces noms
Que Rome y consacrait à d'éternels affronts.

Yet except for this one speech, Mithridates is so pre-occupied with his fierce love and jealousy throughout the play that the most frequent criticism made of it is that we are not prepared for his sparing the young lovers in the end and consigning them to each other. This criticism, however, does not seem to me warranted. The motivating reasons for either vengeance or mercy on his part have been clearly

---

How nobly will they flock in ardent throngs
To the standard of a long-victorious king
Who knoweth his line doth e'en from Cyrus spring!

. . . .

Then onward! Let us bear into her breast
The havoc that she spreads from east to west.
Attack these conquerors proud behind their walls;
Make them in their turn fear for hearth and halls.

. . . .

Burn down this Capitol, where I was to be
A captive; wreck its trophies and efface
A hundred kings' disgrace and my disgrace—
Yea, torch in hand obliterate each name
That Rome hath blazoned with eternal shame!

shown, and no one could say certainly to which of two such possible alternatives the mind of a dying man would incline. His decision in favor of either was not inevitable, but can be accepted—whichever it is—for that very reason without incredulity; and that is enough.

Monime is generally considered the most attractive of all Racine's heroines. Gentle and innocent though she is, she displays a self-respecting pride, a quiet courage, strength of will, and devotion to duty which make her "Corneillian"— in Racine's own, very different way. The sweet, modest dignity with which she commences her account of herself wins every heart.

> Je crois que je vous suis connue.[8]
> Ephèse est mon pays; mais je suis descendue
> D'aïeux, ou Rois, Seigneur, ou héros, qu'autrefois
> Leur vertu, chez les Grecs, mit au-dessus des Rois.
> Mithridate me vit. Ephèse, et l'Ionie,
> A son heureux empire était alors unie.
> Il daigna m'envoyer ce gage de sa foi.
> Ce fut pour ma famille une suprême loi:
> Il fallut obéir. Esclave couronnée,
> Je partis pour l'hymen où j'étais destinée.

And her becomingly restrained but fearless defiance of the

---

[8] I think thou knowest my story. My own home
Is Ephesus, but in mine ancestry
Are kings—or else, sir, heroes whom their high
Deeds, in the eyes of Greece, made greater men
Than kings are. Mithridates saw me. Then
The prosperous empire that he ruled contained
Ephesus and Ionia still. He deigned
To send this token of his troth to me.
It was a mandate to my family
Which had to be obeyed. A crownèd slave,
I went to make the marriage that Fate would have.

tyrant when she is finally pushed to the wall cannot but thrill every heart.

> Je n'ai point oublié quelle reconnaissance,[9]
> Seigneur, m'a dû ranger sous votre obéissance.
> Quelque rang où jadis soient montés mes aïeux,
> Leur gloire de si loin n'éblouit point mes yeux.
> Je songe avec respect de combien je suis née
> Au-dessous des grandeurs d'un si noble hyménée;
> Et, malgré mon penchant et mes premiers desseins,
> Pour un fils, après vous le plus grand des humains,
> Du jour que sur mon front on mit ce diadème,
> Je renonçai, Seigneur, à ce prince, à moi-même.
>
> .   .   .   .
>
> Et même de mon sort je ne pouvais me plaindre,
> Puisque enfin, aux dépens de mes vœux les plus doux,
> Je faisais le bonheur d'un héros tel que vous.
> Vous seul, Seigneur, vous seul, vous m'avez arrachée
> A cette obéissance où j'étais attachée;
>
> .   .   .   .

[9] I have not forgotten, sir, thy favors. They
Should truly have made me subject to thy sway.
However great my lineage formerly,
Its distant glory hath not dazzled me.
Respectfully do I recall how far
Above my birth thy nuptial grandeurs are;
And though my feelings formerly inclined
Unto thy son, the foremost of mankind
Save thee, when once I wore this diadem
I gave him up, gave up all thoughts of him.

.   .   .   .

Nor could I even lament my destiny,
Since, having renounced my dearest hopes, I now
Brought happiness to a hero such as thou.
None, sir, but thee—yes, none but thee—hath torn
My heart from that obedience it had sworn;

.   .   .   .

Et le tombeau, Seigneur, est moins triste pour moi
Que le lit d'un époux qui m'a fait cet outrage.

. . . .

Non, Seigneur, vainement vous croyez m'étonner.
Je vous connais; je sais tout ce que je m'apprête,
Et je vois quels malheurs j'assemble sur ma tête;
Mais le dessein est pris: rien ne peut m'ébranler.
Jugez-en, puisque ainsi je vous ose parler,
Et m'emporte au delà de cette modestie
Dont jusqu'à ce moment je n'étais point sortie.
Vous vous êtes servi de ma funeste main
Pour mettre à votre fils un poignard dans le sein.
De ses feux innocents j'ai trahi le mystère;
Et, quand il n'en perdrait que l'amour de son père,
Il en mourra, Seigneur. Ma foi ni mon amour
Ne seront point le prix d'un si cruel détour.
Après cela, jugez. Perdez une rebelle;
Armez-vous du pouvoir qu'on vous donna sur elle;
J'attendrai mon arrêt.

And the grave, sir, would be easier to endure
Than that man's couch who thus hath treated me.

. . . .

Nay, sir, in vain thou thinkest to make me quail.
I know thee—know the doom that I invite—
And see what woes upon my head shall smite.
But my resolve is fixed. 'Twill not grow weak.
Judge of it, seeing how I dare to speak
To thee and how put off that modesty
Which I till now have worn continually.
Thou hast employed my hapless arm to run
A dagger through the bosom of thy son.
I have revealed the innocent secret of
His heart, and if it cost his father's love
Alone, 'twould kill him, sir. My fealty
Or love shall ne'er reward a treachery
So cruel. Decide, then. Slay one who defies thee.
Assume the power o'er me that none denies thee.
I shall await my death.

One thing she always longs for in her soul, with almost the keenness of a physical craving, and she repeatedly gives wistful expression to that desire: to be free. Free she has never been—to wed as she chooses, to love as she chooses, not even to die as she chooses—and she eagerly receives the poison cup sent her by Mithridates, happy to be thus free at last.

He relents before she can drink of it, and unites her with Xiphares.[10] It is not unnatural, perhaps, that this ever-loyal son should weep for him as he lay dying; for Xiphares, though well aware of his father's ruthlessness, cruelty, and guile, had sincerely loved and admired him. But I cannot believe that Monime, too, would weep then, beseeching Mithridates to live, as Racine represents her doing. Thankful she might indeed be, that she was spared and was granted her heart's dream of happiness; but his sins against her and against the man whom she adored had been too great and too recent for her to feel any affection for him; he had made her suffer too much.[11] One does not love a tiger that has been mangling him—not though the beast, for some reason, should capriciously refrain at last from tearing out his throat. But no other conduct on the part of her and Xiphares would have been acceptable to audiences in the France of Louis XIV; to them, monarchs were sacred, privileged beings, who must not only be pardoned for all their past wickedness but loved, too, as soon as they do one good deed. With such indulgence for the faults of kings, people in Racine's time doubtless found Mithridates a more "sym-

[10] This denouement, like that of *Bajazet,* is melodramatic in that it depends on the mere luck of time-sequence. Monime would have died if the intervention of Arbates had been two seconds later than it was.

[11] The only kind of tears she might really have shed at that time were tears of relief—in a natural reaction from the strain of her ordeal just ended.

pathetic" figure, in his greatness and his sufferings through jealousy in the hour of his defeat, than he is for us now. Audiences of the twentieth century will realize that, however great and however tortured he is, stroke after stroke of the dramatist's brush has painted him as a villainous monster—the slayer formerly of other women he loved and of other sons—and will wish only to see him removed from the path of those whose lives he threatens and whose happiness he prevents. Obviously, the play is more effective, more powerful, if he can be sympathized with; and this goes to show *Mithridate* to be a play of greater value for the age in which it was written than "for all time."

In that age it enjoyed a success marred by no important adverse criticism. Racine had achieved his purpose; his long duel with Corneille was finished at last, and he was completely victorious. Now he could finally return to his own preferred field of endeavor, the world of Greek tragedy he so much loved, from which that duel had kept him so long. He never thereafter wrote any play—nor is said to have considered writing any—except in that field, redepicting that world, until, late in life, he sought instead to apply the methods of Greek drama, fundamentally a religious drama, to themes connected with the religion of his own land.

CHAPTER XIII
RACINE'S *IPHIGENIE*

THE appraisal of *Iphigénie* has varied strangely. Though it did not create a sensation like *Andromaque* when first presented, of all the tragedies of Racine it was the most universally admired in his lifetime. In the eighteenth century, Voltaire regarded it and *Athalie* as the supreme achievements of French drama;[1] in the nineteenth, Sainte-Beuve quoted approvingly the opinion of "a talented man," considered by him well qualified to judge, that it ranks second only to *Athalie* and higher than *Andromaque*, *Phèdre*, and *Britannicus* among its author's "five masterpieces"; and he believed the man thought that as a finished and effective work, best exhibiting the beauties characteristic of Racinian tragedy, it has a right to stand first.[2] Yet for the last two generations, at least, it has not generally been classed with *Andromaque*, *Britannicus*, *Phèdre*, and *Athalie*, but as one of Racine's plays of the second grade. Such is the position assigned to it by N. M. Bernardin (with *Bajazet* and *Mithridate*),[3] by Mary Duclaux (with *Mithridate*, above

[1] *A un académicien, Œuvres complètes de Voltaire*, Paris, 1879, vol. xxv, p. 225.

[2] *Portraits Littéraires*, Paris, n.d., vol. i, p. 114. This statement occurs in a study dated Jan. 15, 1844. Earlier, Sainte-Beuve had judged differently—and better. In December, 1829, he wrote (*op. cit.*, p. 85): *"Britannicus, Phèdre, Athalie, . . . ce sont là les trois grands titres dramatiques de Racine et sous lesquels viennent se ranger ses autres chefs-d'œuvre* (. . . these are the three great dramas of Racine, below which his other master-works take their places)"—a dictum with which I entirely agree.

[3] In Petit de Julleville's *Histoire de la Langue et de la Littérature française*, vol. v, pp. 95-96.

Bajazet—but all three below *Bérénice!*),[4] and by Emile
Faguet (immediately below "the four miracles").[5] Jules
Lemaître goes so far as to say that if we had to lose two
of the secular tragedies of Racine (disregarding, of course,
the immature productions before *Andromaque*) he would
least unwillingly sacrifice *Mithridate* and *Iphigénie*, for they,
beyond all the rest, smack of the pseudo-classical age in
which they were written; and he appears to value *Iphigénie*
even less than *Mithridate*.[6]

In reality, aside from its style, which is somewhat "stately," *Iphigénie* is not more romanesque than most of Racine's
other dramas, but less so. Returning in this play, for the first
time since *Andromaque*, to a subject treated by one of the
great Attic masters, its author seems, as was the case in his
maiden effort of *la Thébaïde*, to be trying to reproduce a
classical tragedy on the French stage with the least modification that would make it acceptable to his public. And it is
to be doubted whether he came so near to doing this even in
Phèdre as he did here except in the part where Eriphyle is
concerned. Scene after scene is derived from Euripides'
Iphigenia in Aulis.[7] Many speeches have the true classic note.

[4] *The Life of Racine*, p. 110.
[5] *Propos de Théâtre*, vol. iii, p. 79.
[6] *Jean Racine*, pp. 222-225.
[7] Both plays open with a dialogue between Agamemnon and a
faithful attendant, whom he informs of the plan to sacrifice Iphigenia and dispatches with a letter countermanding his summons of
her. (The imitation in this scene is close.) After an interval, there
is in both a colloquy between the King and someone who is determined that the sacrifice shall be carried out (Menelaus in one play,
Ulysses in the other); and in both, this talk is interrupted by the
arrival of Clytemnestra and Iphigenia, destroying Agamemnon's
last hope of averting the girl's death. Both present the meeting of
father and daughter in a number of brief speeches, largely questions and answers, on the part of each—he in agony which he attempts to dissemble, she happy in seeing him again but puzzled by

STUDIES IN FRENCH-CLASSICAL TRAGEDY

Clytemnestra's indignant appeal to her husband does not
suffer when compared with the one in Euripides; though
somewhat more rhetorical than its Greek analogue, it is
perhaps even more moving,—and it works up to a more impressive climax:

> Vous ne démentez point une race funeste.[8]
> Oui, vous êtes le sang d'Atrée et de Thyeste.
> Bourreau de votre fille, il ne vous reste enfin
> Que d'en faire à sa mère un horrible festin.
> Barbare! c'est donc là cet heureux sacrifice
> Que vos soins préparaient avec tant d'artifice?
> Quoi? l'horreur de souscrire à cet ordre inhumain
> N'a pas, en le traçant, arrêté votre main?
> Pourquoi feindre à nos yeux une fausse tristesse?

his mood. In both plays, Agamemnon bids Clytemnestra not to go
with Iphigenia to the altar, and they have a dispute over this. In
both alike the revelation of his real purpose is made to Clytemnestra,
Iphigenia, and Achilles by the domestic who was given the never-
delivered letter and who now seizes the chance to disclose all, and
the Queen kneels to Achilles and begs his aid. Lastly, in both plays
Agamemnon comes to fetch Iphigenia when she has not gone to
him, and Clytemnestra calls her and shows him that they know the
truth; then both mother and daughter try unsuccessfully, each with
a single long speech, to persuade him to relent.

A few passages in *Iphigénie* are based on the *Iliad*. For the most
part they are in connection with Achilles.

[8] Thou showest thyself not false to a fell brood.
Yes, thou'rt of Atreus' and Thyestes' blood.
Butcher of thine own daughter, for the rest
Thou only needest to set a dread repast
Before her mother. Barbarous monster, this,
Then, is thy fine, fair-seeming sacrifice!
   Did not the horror of that dire command,
When thou didst sign and seal it, stay thy hand?
Why put feigned sadness on before our eyes?

Pensez-vous par des pleurs prouver votre
    tendresse?
Où sont-ils, ces combats que vous avez rendus?
Quels flots de sang pour elle avez-vous répandus?
Quel débris parle ici de votre résistance?
Quel champ couvert de morts me condamne au
    silence?
Voilà par quels témoins il fallait me prouver,
Cruel, que votre amour a voulu la sauver.
Un oracle fatal ordonne qu'elle expire.
Un oracle dit-il tout ce qu'il semble dire?
Le ciel, le juste ciel, par le meurtre honoré,
Du sang de l'innocence est-il donc altéré?
Si du crime d'Hélène on punit sa famille,
Faites chercher à Sparte Hermione, sa fille:
Laissez à Ménélas racheter d'un tel prix
Sa coupable moitié, dont il est trop épris.
Mais vous, quelles fureurs vous rendent sa victime?
Pourquoi vous imposer la peine de son crime?

Thinkest thou to prove thy love by tears and sighs?
Where are the struggles thou didst undertake?
What streams of blood hast thou shed for her sake?
What carnage doth of thy resistance tell?
What field bestrewn with dead bids me be still?
    Those are such proofs as I must have, cruel man,
That thy love sought to save her. She must be slain—
So a grim oracle decreeth? Nay,
Do oracles say all they seem to say?
Is heaven, just heaven, with a murder pleased?
By innocent blood is it to be appeased?
If Helen's kin for Helen's sin ye slaughter,
In Sparta seek Hermione, her daughter.
Let Menelaus at such a price redeem
His guilty wife, who is too dear to him.
But thou—what madness makes thee sacrifice

Pourquoi moi-même enfin me déchirant le flanc,
Payer sa folle amour du plus pur de mon sang?
Que dis-je? Cet objet de tant de jalousie,
Cette Hélène, qui trouble et l'Europe et l'Asie,
Vous semble-t-elle un prix digne de vos exploits?
Combien nos fronts pour elle ont-ils rougi de fois!
Avant qu'un nœud fatal l'unît à votre frère,
Thésée avait osé l'enlever à son père.
Vous savez, et Calchas mille fois vous l'a dit,
Qu'un hymen clandestin mit ce prince en son lit,
Et qu'il en eut pour gage une jeune princesse,
Que sa mère a cachée au reste de la Grèce.
Mais non: l'amour d'un frère et son honneur blessé
Sont les moindres des soins dont vous êtes pressé.
Cette soif de régner, que rien ne peut éteindre,
L'orgueil de voir vingt rois vous servir et vous
        craindre,
Tous les droits de l'empire en vos mains confiés,

Aught thine? Why must thou expiate her vice?
And why must I thus cause my heart to bleed,
And pay for her mad loves with my pure seed?
    What say I? She who giveth strife such cause,—
Who troubleth Europe's peace and Asia's,—
This Helen,—is she worth high deeds of fame?
How often hath she dyed our cheeks with shame!
Ere thy poor brother wedded her, withal,
Theseus had taken her from her father's hall;
Unpublished nuptials placed her in his bed,
Thou knowest—so Calchas many times hath said—
And that a princess was the fruit of these,
Whom she hath hidden from the eyes of Greece.
    Oh, no, a brother's love, his honor stained,
Are the least things by which thou art constrained.
Thy thirst for sovereignty, which naught can slake,
Thy pride, that twenty kings serve thee and quake,
The rule entrusted thee, who all devisest—

Cruel, c'est à ces dieux que vous sacrifiez;
Et loin de repousser le coup qu'on vous prépare,
Vous voulez vous en faire un mérite barbare.
Trop jaloux d'un pouvoir qu'on peut vous envier,
De votre propre sang vous courez le payer,
Et voulez par ce prix épouvanter l'audace
De quiconque vous peut disputer votre place.
Est-ce donc être père? Ah! toute ma raison
Cède à la cruauté de cette trahison.
Un prêtre, environné d'une foule cruelle,
Portera sur ma fille une main criminelle,
Déchirera son sein et d'un œil curieux
Dans son cœur palpitant consultera les Dieux!
Et moi, qui l'amenai triomphante, adorée,
Je m'en retournerai seule et désespérée!
Je verrai les chemins encor tout parfumés
Des fleurs dont sous ses pas on les avait semés!
Non, je ne l'aurai point amenée au supplice,

These are the gods to whom thou sacrificest,
Hard heart! Thou dost not spurn the task now set
For thee; thou makest a virtue out of it!
Fearful that some should envy thee thy powers,
Thou fliest to pay for them with blood of ours,
And fain by such a price wouldst terrify
Whoe'er might challenge thine authority.
　Are fathers, then, like that? Ah, all my reason
Totters, confronting this inhuman treason!
A priest, amid relentless warrior bands,
Will lay upon my child his wicked hands,
Will pierce her breast and seek, with curious eye,
From her yet-throbbing heart some augury. . . .
And I, who brought her here, so loved, elate—
I shall go back alone and desperate;
And I shall see the roads still perfumed sweet
With flowers that were strewn before her feet!
Nay, 'twas not for her death I brought her here,

Ou vous ferez aux Grecs un double sacrifice.
Ni crainte ni respect ne m'en peut détacher.
De mes bras tout sanglants il faudra l'arracher.
Aussi barbare époux qu'impitoyable père,
Venez, si vous l'osez, la ravir à sa mère.

The Iphigenia of Racine, however, is a quite different
person from the shrinking and afterwards heroic child of
the *Iphigenia in Aulis*. She is a grown woman, a gracious,
self-possessed princess, who is prepared, throughout, to let
herself be sacrificed if it is indeed her father's will, and
whose acquiescence springs from filial devotion and not
from any fervor of patriotism. Her nature is beautifully
revealed when—as in Euripides, but how differently!—she
makes her plea to Agamemnon:

> Mon père,[9]
> Cessez de vous troubler, vous n'êtes point trahi:
> Quand vous commanderez, vous serez obéi.
> Ma vie est votre bien. Vous voulez le reprendre:
> Vos ordres sans détour pouvaient se faire entendre.
> D'un œil aussi content, d'un cœur aussi soumis
> Que j'acceptais l'époux que vous m'aviez promis,

Or Greece shall have *two* victims! Neither fear
Nor duteous respect can force me hence.
She must be torn out of mine arms' defense,
Bleeding. Thou savage husband, sire accurst,
Come take her from her mother if thou durst!

[9] Father,
Do not be troubled. Thou art not betrayed.
When thou commandest, thou shalt be obeyed.
My life is *thy* gift. Thou wouldst have it back.
Thou needest but only speak thy will, and take.
With no more shrinking glance nor heart more loath
Than if I wedded him thou didst betroth

Je saurai, s'il le faut, victime obéissante,
Tendre au fer de Calchas une tête innocente,
Et respectant le coup par vous-même ordonné,
Vous rendre tout le sang que vous m'avez donné.
Si pourtant ce respect, si cette obéissance
Paraît digne à vos yeux d'une autre récompense,
Si d'une mère en pleurs vous plaignez les ennuis,
J'ose vous dire ici qu'en l'état où je suis
Peut-être assez d'honneurs environnaient ma vie
Pour ne pas souhaiter qu'elle me fût ravie,
Ni qu'en me l'arrachant un sévère destin
Si près de ma naissance en eût marqué la fin.
Fille d'Agamemnon, c'est moi qui la première,
Seigneur, vous appelai de ce doux nom de père;
C'est moi qui si longtemps le plaisir de vos yeux,
Vous ai fait de ce nom remercier les Dieux,
Et pour qui tant de fois prodiguant vos caresses,
Vous n'avez point du sang dédaigné les faiblesses.

To me, I would bow down a guiltless head,
A willing sacrifice to Calchas' blade,
And reverencing the blow decreed by thee,
Give thee again that life thou gavest me.
    Yet if my filial obedience
Deserves, thou thinkest, a different recompense,
And if thou pitiest a mother's grief,
I shall say frankly that just now my life
Seems amid such fair honors to be set
That I would fain not lose it, but would regret
That, snatching it, a cruel destiny
So soon after my birth should make me die.
    A daughter of Agamemnon, she I am
Who was the first to call thee by the name
Of "Father," who brought joy unto thine eye
So long and made thee thank the gods on high
For that dear name, and whom thou wouldst caress,
Nowise ashamed to exhibit tenderness

Hélas! avec plaisir je me faisais conter
Tous les noms des pays que vous allez dompter;
Et déjà, d'Ilion présageant la conquête,
D'un triomphe si beau je préparais la fête.
Je ne m'attendais pas que pour le commencer,
Mon sang fût le premier que vous dussiez verser.
Non que la peur du coup dont je suis menacée
Me fasse rappeler votre bonté passée:
Ne craignez rien: mon cœur, de votre honneur
　　jaloux,
Ne fera point rougir un père tel que vous;
Et si je n'avais eu que ma vie à défendre,
J'aurais su renfermer un souvenir si tendre.
Mais à mon triste sort, vous le savez, Seigneur,
Une mère, un amant attachaient leur bonheur.
Un roi digne de vous a cru voir la journée
Qui devait éclairer notre illustre hyménée.
Déjà sûr de mon cœur à sa flamme promis,

For thine own child.
　　　　　　　　　Alas, I numbered through,
With joy, the lands thou goest to subdue,
And even now, foreseeing Ilium's fall,
Was planning a triumphant festival!
I little dreamed that to begin thy task
My blood would be the first which Fate would ask.
　'Tis not from dread of what is threatened me
That I recall thy past love unto thee.
Fear naught; I, who am jealous for thy fame,
Will ne'er make such a father blush with shame,
And if I had only my life to shield,
Deep in my breast these memories would be sealed.
But on my lot, thou knowest, sir, my mother's
Happiness doth depend,—also my lover's.
A prince well worthy of us thought the day
Had come which was to join our hands for ay.
Sure of my plighted heart already, he

Il s'estimait heureux: vous me l'aviez permis.
Il sait votre dessein; jugez de ses alarmes.
Ma mère est devant vous, et vous voyez ses larmes.
Pardonnez aux efforts que je viens de tenter
Pour prévenir les pleurs que je leur vais coûter.

Though such a characterization of Iphigenia loses the effect produced by her sudden change in the Greek play, which is one of the most heart-stirring things in literature, it is a quite legitimate and well-executed variant.[10]

The love between her and Achilles is not the sheer romanesque invention that uninformed traditional criticism has pronounced it. Anyone who reads Euripides intelligently ought to see that before the end of his tragedy Iphigenia is consciously or unconsciously half in love with the splendid young hero who has offered himself as her champion, and that Achilles is wholly in love with Iphigenia.[11] Racine neither invented their love nor derived it necessarily from Rotrou's *Iphigénie,* where it also appears, just as he did not invent or derive from Rotrou that of Antigone and Haemon

---

Deemed himself blest; thy pledge for this had we.
He has learned thy purpose, now; judge of his fears.
Here stands my mother, and thou seest her tears.
Forgive me for thus having tried to keep
Unshed those which my death must make her weep!

[10] A similar conception of her character is found in an earlier play on the same subject by Rotrou. Racine owes little if any other debt to that drama.

[11] "The gods would make me happy," he tells her, "if I might win thee for my bride. . . . A yearning for thy love lays hold on me the more that I have seen thy nature, how noble is thy heart. Look now; I fain would save thee—fain would bear thee to my home." (*Iphigenia in Aulis,* ll. 1404-1405, 1410-1413.) And not the least of the reasons that persuade Euripides' heroine to accept her doom is the fear that Achilles will come to harm in defending her.

in *la Thébaïde;* in each case he merely expanded and emphasized a "heart-interest" that was in his original—as almost any author of today, no less than one in Racine's day, would be sure to do in treating a Greek subject. Actually, by representing Iphigenia as already betrothed to, loved by, and loving Achilles before the action of the play begins, he is not as romantic as Euripides, who with greater dramatic effectiveness makes their love be born of the girl's peril and felt only in the moment when it is hopeless. What Racine's changes do accomplish is to give their love a more prominent place in his play than it had formerly held.

His Achilles himself is also based on the classical sources. If he is not the Achilles of Homer, he at least comes as near the popular conception of him, derived from the *Iliad,* as would have been possible in the Age of Louis XIV. As in Homer, he is brave, impetuous, hot-tempered, eager to win glory; also he is something of an egotist, as in Homer— and in the extant text of the *Iphigenia in Aulis.* In that play, Achilles first consents to defend Iphigenia not so much out of pity as because of his anger at the unauthorized use of his name to decoy her to her death; he cares nothing for the fate of any mere girl. This touch, if not an interpolation as F. Melian Stawell has persuasively argued,[12] is a characteristic example of Euripides' disillusioning treatment of the heroes of legend. Racine has softened it, but has not wholly omitted it. Though his own Achilles, too, is preoccupied with the fact that his name has been thus vilely used, the excuse can be made for him that he is so sure of his ability to save Iphigenia that he takes it for granted and therefore gives free scope to his resentment of the outrage done him. Yet even at best it is an unlovely trait in him that he thinks, at such a time, of his own wrongs in-

[12] *The Iphigenia in Aulis of Euripides,* New York, 1929, p. 112.

stead of Iphigenia's, and that he looks at almost everything primarily in relation to himself.[13]

The fact is that Racine's Achilles is no insipidly stereotyped figure of a young "hero" and lover, no "Timocrate" or "Astrate"—not even a Xiphares or a Bajazet. He employs, of course, the language of gallantry in speaking of love (as everyone does in the tragedies of the period), but he is well and consistently individualized. True, when Iphigenia refuses to let him shield her in defiance of her father's orders, he exclaims that she is inspired more by hatred of himself than by filial respect; this, however, is not merely an instance of the habitual tendency of the characters in romanesque plays to impute the worst possible motive to anything that displeases them in the conduct of those whom they are represented as "loving." Racine here has at the same time followed convention and rationalized and transcended it. He has made the hackneyed thing the natural and characteristic thing. Such an outburst is natural and characteristic in Achilles; it does not give utterance to his real

---

[13] This defect in him is to some extent a defect in the play; for Racine, unlike Euripides, can have had no reason to cheapen the character of Achilles. Far, then, from departing unduly from his sources, he has here followed them "not wisely but too well."

Nor is this the only instance in which he has done so. When his Clytemnestra, like the Clytemnestra of Euripides, kneels before Achilles and begs him to protect her daughter, her action and her words too (though she does remind him that he and Iphigenia are betrothed) seem more appropriate to the situation in the Greek drama, where he is a stranger, than here where the presumption is that he will be concerned, without urging, over the fate of his plighted bride.

Again, the whole project of the marriage between Iphigenia and Achilles at the end of the war, clashes with the common knowledge that he is fated to die in the expedition. Racine should have suppressed that detail of the story. But this inconsistency would probably not be noticed in presentation.

belief, but is simply an explosion of his baffled anger at Iphigenia's obstinacy. Not for a moment does he lapse from his determination to save her, and it should be realized that it is he who, in the event, does save her : with a small band of soldiers he breaks through the mass of men about the altar and, holding off the entire army, effects a delay which gives Calchas time to learn and declare the true will of the gods. Such an Achilles need not be judged unworthy of his name.

The Agamemnon, the Clytemnestra, and the Ulysses of *Iphigénie* are in the same way essentially transcripts from the Greek. The most prominent trait in Agamemnon is pride of authority; but Racine has made his character somewhat more "sympathetic" by the invention of his renewed efforts to save his daughter when the time for her sacrifice arrives. Clytemnestra is depicted as less intractable than in Euripides : she finally bows to Agamemnon's command that she shall not witness the wedding of Iphigenia; and indeed it would have been shocking to a French audience in the days of the *grand monarque* if she had defied the will of her husband and king as she does in the Greek play. Racine's Ulysses, like the traditional Odysseus, sets public interest above all else, yet he is not wantonly cruel; when the sacrifice of Iphigenia is no longer required, it is he who hastens to bring the good news to her mother.

The romanesque element in this play is in fact mostly confined to that portion of it which deals with Eriphyle, whom, alone of the important dramatis personae, Racine created practically out of whole cloth and introduced into the action because he felt that his public would find the slaughter of so blameless a heroine as Iphigenia unendurable and yet could not accept the alternative version of the Greek legend, according to which she was saved miraculously. Thus thrown on his own resources without the guidance of the classics, Racine promptly reverted to the literary fashions of his time. That Eriphyle, as well as Iphigenia,

is in love with Achilles, and that her unrequited passion
breeds in her a deadly jealousy, is a complication thoroughly characteristic of pseudo-classical drama. The only genuine confidant in *Iphigénie* (for Arcas appears but briefly in
this function, and so does Argina) is Doris, to whom
Eriphyle unbosoms herself—somewhat against likelihood
when she tells of her secret love though she thinks it shameful and though it is for the man who killed Doris' father.

Not only is the role of Eriphyle in the play conventionally
romanesque; it begets romanesquely conventional conduct in
others. How insane is Agamemnon's choice of a story to prevent Iphigenia from coming to Aulis: that Achilles had
changed his mind about marrying her, and that Eriphyle was
said to be the cause of his loss of ardor! It had every prospect of resulting in serious complications with Achilles, and
there was no necessity for it. Many other pretexts were possible—for instance, that the young hero had been summoned
to the aid of his father, Peleus, which was indeed the case;
even some distorted report of the intended sacrifice itself
would have been safer. But a French dramatist in the seventeenth century was sure to select a reason involving a second woman and furnishing an occasion for jealousy. The
violent outburst of this passion to which Iphigenia presently gives vent seems somewhat out of character, as also does
her immediate acceptance, with apparently no surprise, of
the idea that Eriphyle loves Achilles and has captured his
heart—out of character, that is, except according to the conventional romanesque notion that everyone in love is prone
and prompt to be violently jealous on every possible occasion.[14] That a misunderstanding as to the object of

[14] Sarcey maintained that the reproaches heaped upon Eriphyle
by Iphigenia are spoken not in anger but in tearful distress, for
only thus would they be natural to her. In proof that they should
be so interpreted, he offers line 711, "Vous triomphez, cruelle, et
bravez ma douleur." ("Thou triumphest, cruel girl, and mock'st my

Achilles' affections should arise out of the situation in which he and the two women are placed, is an inevitable detail of romanesque tragedy.

But Eriphyle no more than Achilles is a featureless puppet of conventional design. If she does not belong to the heroic world of the distant past, she looks towards the future. She is the feminine counterpart of the Orestes of Racine's *Andromaque,* anticipating like him (as Lemaître pointed out in regard to them both) the morbid heroes of nineteenth-century romanticism, who are imbued with the idea that they are the especial victims of relentless fate, who derive a melancholy pleasure from this distinction, and who think it justifies them in any conduct.[15] Eriphyle recalls in lingering detail—her relish of it is a daring touch for the decorous Racine—that she was carried off insensible by Achilles and recovered consciousness to find herself held fast in his bloody arms. Her jealousy is sharpened by the envy which she, a girl of unknown parentage and doubtful estate, who has been reared under another's roof and on another's

---

woe"—not "rage," but "woe," "*douleur.*" Sarcey is quoted—from *Chronique théâtrale* of the *Temps,* November 8, 1880—in N. M. Bernardin's *Théâtre complet de Jean Racine,* vol. iii, *Iphigénie,* p. 76, note 1.) But he overlooks the fact that immediately afterwards (ll. 715-718) she threatens her "rival" with Agamemnon's vengeance:

> Toutefois vos transports sont trop précipités.
> Ce même Agamemnon à qui vous insultez,
> Il commande à la Grèce, il est mon père, il m'aime,
> Il ressent mes douleurs beaucoup plus que moi-même.

> (Thou art too quick, however, to exult.
> This Agamemnon, whom thou dost insult,
> Commands all Greece; he is my father; he
> Loves me. My sorrows wound him more than me.)

[15] *Op. cit.,* p. 246.

bounty, feels towards the favored child of fortune to whose
happy home she is consigned when a captive's lot has just
been added to her already full store of ills. "If she hates
Iphigenia"—I translate from Félix Hémon's well-stated
analysis of her character—"it is not only because Iphigenia
is the betrothed of Achilles, but because she is the daughter
of Agamemnon, is a princess respected by all, loved, worshipped, for whom the present is bright and the future more
glorious still." [16] As a self-pitying egoist, Eriphyle craves
the affection that she has never received, and whose imagined sweetness, which she has missed, she continually
dwells upon. She says to Doris:

> Hé quoi? te semble-t-il que la triste Eriphile [17]
> Doive être de leur joie un témoin si tranquille?
> Crois-tu que mes chagrins doivent s'évanouir
> A l'aspect d'un bonheur dont je ne puis jouir?
> Je vois Iphigénie entre les bras d'un père;
> Elle fait tout l'orgueil d'une superbe mère;
> Et moi, toujours en butte à de nouveaux dangers,
> Remise dès l'enfance en des bras étrangers,
> Je reçus et je vois le jour que je respire,
> Sans que mère ni père ait daigné me sourire;

and afterwards to Iphigenia:

[16] *Cours de Littérature: Iphigénie,* Paris, n.d., p. 30.

[17] Nay, could sad Eriphyle, dost thou deem,
    Look on their happiness with tranquil mien?
    Thinkest thou my misery will vanish, where
    Good fortune is which I can never share?
    A daughter in her father's clasp, I see;
    Her regal mother's only pride is she—
    And I, whom always some new evil harms,
    Consigned from infancy to strangers' arms,
    Was given life's gift, and live, yet know not still
    Either a father's or a mother's smile.

Hélas! à quels soupirs suis-je donc condamnée,[18]
Moi, qui de mes parents toujours abandonnée,
Etrangère partout, n'ai pas même en naissant
Peut-être reçu d'eux un regard caressant!
Du moins, si vos respects sont rejetés d'un père,
Vous en pouvez gémir dans le sein d'une mère.

The monstrous ingratitude and treachery with which she repays all the great kindness shown her are the measure of the deep wells of bitterness in her soul.

Eriphyle, if considered only as a character and apart from her introduction of a marring element into the play, is not a blemish there, but one of the chief excellences.

Next to the romanesque features of *Iphigénie,* its theme itself has most often been the target for adverse criticism. That the Olympian gods demand a human sacrifice is an initial assumption too barbarous to be made by civilized Christian audiences, we are told. But the fact is that the idea of human sacrifice was no less revolting to intelligent Athenians of the fifth century B.C. than to the contemporaries of Racine or even to us, and Euripides' tragedy on the same subject was eminently successful when it first appeared and has not diminished in fame since that time. No inconceivable moral problem is posed in either the Greek play or the French; the sacrifice of Iphigenia is not represented as being actually desired by the gods, but as being made the price for the taking of Troy, and thus an obstacle to the destruction of that city, which they, traditionally, loved. Agamemnon is at liberty, his army is at liberty, to

[18] Alas, then, to what sighs am I condemned—
I, whom my parents left and never claimed,
A stranger everywhere, who even perchance
At birth has never had a loving glance!
If now thy father is unkind, at least
Thou still canst weep upon a mother's breast.

give up the war instead.[19] Unless such a course is indeed an alternative which they are free to choose, and not merely an impious refusal to obey the will of heaven, there can be no real indecision for Agamemnon, and his indecision is the very core of both dramas.

Moreover, the idea of human sacrifice is not so strange to us that we cannot project ourselves imaginatively into a situation dealing with it. The parallel between us and the Greeks of Euripides' time is peculiarly close in this respect. Just as human sacrifice, an atrocity which they would not dream of perpetrating, was familiar to them as a rare but well-known detail in their ancient, semi-sacred legends, whereas other sacrifices held a prominent place in their religion,—so, too, is human sacrifice familiar to our minds because of the Old Testament stories of Jephthah's daughter and Abraham-and-Isaac, and the idea of propitiatory sacrifice is basic in Christianity.[20] And we have the legends of Greece besides as part of our own mental background— tales that we have known from childhood. It is true that the Greeks of Euripides' day themselves believed in the Olympian gods concerned in the story of Iphigenia, and we do not; but our disbelief in them does not hinder our ap-

[19] This is not so evident in Racine as in Euripides, for the characters in *Iphigénie* often express the contrary view as a result of misgivings or wishes. But we are not obliged to agree with them, and their interpretation of the quoted words of the oracle, though possible, is not the natural one. The signs with which the gods receive the sacrifice indicate nothing more than their acknowledgment of its consummation and their readiness to keep their side of the bargain.

[20] Such a sacrifice must have seemed less unnatural still to the Age of Racine, a period of greater religious faith—and superstition— than ours. In this connection, Lemaître has noted the alleged belief of Madame de Montespan that the blood of an infant child, shed by a recreant priest, would preserve for herself the love of Louis XIV and rid her of Madame de Fontanges (*op. cit.*, p. 243).

preciation of the tragedies of the Attic dramatists, and there is no reason why it should hinder our appreciation of *Iphigénie.*

Emile Faguet has argued that Racine was grievously at fault in not making the prophet Calchas one of the dramatis personae and indeed the central figure of his play.[21] But Calchas does not appear in Euripides' play, either. The same critic also deplores the assignment to so unimportant a character as Arcas of the important function of disclosing the intentions of Agamemnon to Clytemnestra, Iphigenia, and Achilles; Arcas, he says, is too *"vulgaire"* a personage to be worthy of this revelation and the fine *coup de théâtre* that it makes. Yet the same function is discharged in Euripides by the corresponding character, who is not given there even a name. The most terrific revelation and the most tremendous *coup de théâtre,* perhaps, in the whole range of drama is the disclosure of the parentage of Oedipus in Sophocles, and it is effected by a nameless herdsman, who speaks, in all, twenty-five complete lines and four incomplete lines. I cannot help suspecting that this last criticism of Faguet's was inspired by some survival, conscious or unconscious, in him of the old notions of decorum and degree, those fetishes of pseudo-classical *littérateurs,* in deference to which Corneille changed the opening of the *Cid*—"because Elvira was not of sufficient dignity to be seen in conversation with the Count de Gormas."

Why, then, does *Iphigénie* enjoy no higher esteem today than it does? Why is it now produced only at rare intervals, *"de loin en loin"* as Bernardin says? Mainly, I think, for two valid reasons—reasons which no one has mentioned, yet by which I believe people have been unconsciously influenced in their attitude towards this drama.

In the first place, Racine has never elsewhere followed

[21] *Op. cit.,* pp. 82 ff.

so closely another play that was the source of his own, yet in no important respect has he surpassed or indeed equaled his Attic model. We are instinctively dissatisfied, even if we do not realize why, with an imitation that contributes practically nothing of superior value to previous treatment of the same theme. The *Iphigenia in Aulis* of Euripides, judged by any plausible reconstruction (such as F. Melian Stawell's) of its corrupt text, is a very great play; it is not one of the half dozen Greek tragedies which constitute together with Shakespeare's four tragic masterpieces the supreme achievements in the dramatic literature of the world, but it stands in a group immediately below these. Its failure to rival them is in large measure due to a certain lack of unity, a shift in interest and emphasis, that would seem almost unavoidable with its subject matter. A similar fault is to be found in another tragedy of approximately the same degree of greatness and by the same author, the *Hippolytus,* from which Racine derived his next play. But whereas in *Phèdre,* as I point out in my study of that drama, he corrected the chief imperfection of his Greek original, in *Iphigénie* he worsened it.

Unity of a sort is of course not wanting in either his or Euripides' version of the affair at Aulis; in both plays the issue is whether or not Iphigenia will be sacrificed. But this would appear, in the first three-quarters of the *Iphigenia in Aulis,* to depend on Agamemnon; he is on that account the central figure, and the all-important question is, What will he decide to do? Then, after line 1275, when he has declared his unalterable purpose and gone finally away, it is Iphigenia who becomes the central figure, and the question is thenceforth, What will she herself do? Now in Racine's *Iphigénie* also, the problem of Agamemnon's choice remains long dominant—though not so completely as in Euripides, for Iphigenia's misunderstanding about Achilles and her consequent jealousy divert attention from her dan-

ger, on which it ought to be fixed. But Agamemnon's decision is reached at the end of Act IV; he determines to save
his daughter if he can. Thereupon the question becomes
merely one of whether or not she can succeed in escaping
from the camp; and then, when this proves impossible, of
whether Achilles can persuade her to accept his protection;
and then of whether he will save her in spite of herself;—
and then at the last, to crown all, she fortuitously owes her
life to the recoil of Eriphyle's wickedness upon her own
head, a surprise-ending! There is plenty of action, excitement, suspense, and strong emotion in the fifth act of *Iphigénie*, but not the substance of great drama.[22]

A second reason for the relative disregard of this play
in modern times is the fact that it contains none of Racine's
finest characters. Among its dramatis personae there is no
one comparable to Achmet or Roxana in *Bajazet*, or to
Mithridates or Monime in *Mithridate*. Such figures challenge the skill of great actors and actresses, and invite
critical study. The fascination they exert makes one return
again and again to a play in which any of them appears,
and perhaps grow to love it in spite of its blemishes; the
praise of them reflects glory upon it.

But *Iphigénie* is nevertheless, we should not fail to realize,
superior to both *Mithridate* and *Bajazet*. Though it has in
it no remarkable piece of characterization, it is peopled
with a larger number of well-conceived, thoroughly individualized men and women than any other tragedy of

[22] Not only is the material in this act melodramatic in itself, but
its manipulation is that of melodrama. Clytemnestra was hardly
the sort of woman to faint; her reported swoon is but a transparent
device to cause and explain her absence when Achilles finds Iphigenia. She appears as soon as he is gone; had she been present
earlier, during the contention between the lovers, there is no saying
what would have been the result. It is pure chance and a matter
of a few minutes that she was not present.

Racine. There are six of them: Agamemnon, Achilles, and Ulysses; Clytemnestra, Iphigenia, and Eriphyle.[23] These characters, as Faguet observed, clash continually—Achilles with Agamemnon, Clytemnestra with Agamemnon, Ulysses with Agamemnon, Iphigenia with Eriphyle, Iphigenia with Achilles. The tension, therefore, is almost as incessant as in *Andromaque*. *Iphigénie* certainly cannot compare in structural excellence with that miracle of plot-design, nor can it boast of such exquisite poetry; and Hermione is one of the greatest creations of Racine. But on the other hand, *Iphigénie* exhibits much less of pseudo-classicism in language and sentiments and method of treatment than *Andromaque*, and much more that is truly classical and thus harmonious with its subject; and it is marred by no character like Andromache herself, for whom sympathy is required yet whose code and conduct, rightly judged, are both wrong and absurd. On the whole, one may, perhaps, fairly conclude that though *Iphigénie* is far inferior to *Britannicus*, not to speak of *Phèdre* and *Athalie*, it deserves a place with *Andromaque* just outside the circle of dramas that can properly be called "great."

[23] *Athalie* and *Britannicus* have only five each (if the little-developed Joash and the unsatisfactory prince Britannicus are excluded from the reckoning, as they should be), the rest in no instance more than four.

CHAPTER XIV

RACINE'S *PHEDRE*

PHEDRE is perhaps Racine's masterpiece; it is certainly the highest achievement of French-classical tragedy. *Athalie* is thought by many to be a greater work; but *Athalie* stands apart, representing, together with *Esther,* a unique experiment not conformable to the type established by Pierre Corneille. Of that type, *Phèdre* is the supreme example. Though less ingeniously plotted for sustained tension than *Andromaque,* and though centering its interest upon a single character, it is yet pre-eminent by virtue of the more compelling sweep and power of its passions, its finer poetry, and its loftier tone in general. It is superior also to *Britannicus,* for the same reasons.

The Greek legend of Phaedra and Hippolytus was the subject of the *Hippolytus* of Euripides, of the *Phaedra* of Seneca, and of several French dramas prior to *Phèdre.* Racine was indebted to these last for only a few minor touches. Euripides was his chief source, from which he derived the general outlines of his play and of the characters of Phaedra, Theseus, and the Nurse, and some phases of the character of Hippolytus. He followed Seneca, however, in making Phaedra herself declare her love to Hippolytus and in making the nurse originate the slander against him, which is lent color of truth by his loss of his sword (whereas in Euripides it is the Nurse who, unknown to Phaedra, informs Hippolytus of the Queen's passion for him, and it is Phaedra who, when the shame of this exposure and of his abusive words drives her to suicide, leaves in death a letter accusing him of having dishonored her); as in Seneca, the absence of Theseus at the beginning of the play is identified with that hero's fabled expedition to Hades, and Phaedra

believes him dead; again as in Seneca, she survives Hippolytus and in a dying confession clears him of all blame.
But Racine's borrowings from his classical models are not
limited to characterization and turns of plot; he at times
imitates their scenes, as to both development and language.[1]

His imitation of Euripides is closest in the dialogue between Phaedra and the Nurse at the end of the first act.
Here, as in the *Hippolytus,* the Queen enters exhausted and
distraught, longing to carry her woes and her shameful
secret with her to the grave; she chafes at the oppressiveness of her attire and vexes the Nurse with the swift changes
of her whims; she wishes dreamily that she were amid forest shades and where chariots are racing (for that is where
she would be likely to find Hippolytus), and then starts
from her reverie in terror lest she has betrayed herself, and
tries to avert suspicion from her blushes and tears. For three
days she has refused all food, says the Nurse, who now
begins to plead with her to reveal what is troubling her and
to desist from her resolve to die; because her death will

---

[1] Passages deriving from Seneca are a portion of the scene in
the second act between Phaedra and Hippolytus (his attempt to reassure her that Theseus is alive and her denial of the possibility of
any return from the realms of the dead, then his misunderstanding
of the cause of her perturbation, and her speech comparing him to
Theseus at the time he slew the Minotaur: 618-652), Phaedra's
prayer to Venus to make Hippolytus love (813-824; in Seneca the
Nurse prays to Diana to bend him to the yoke of Venus), the dialogue between Phaedra and Oenone in which the latter protests
the impossibility of winning Hippolytus and the Queen over-rides
all objections (787-790), the plan of the Nurse to defame Hippolytus (886-889), Theseus' claim of his boon from Neptune which
he had refrained from asking for hitherto even when a captive
(1069-1073), the description of the sea-monster as fire-breathing
and shaped like a bull in front and like a scaled dragon further
back (1517-1519, 1533-1534), and the final confession of Phaedra
(1618-1619, 1623-1624).

leave her motherless children at the mercy of the Amazon's son, Hippolytus—and at the mention of his fatal name, Phaedra cries out in protest. The Nurse, misunderstanding her reaction, is encouraged and presses the point, but without success. "It is surely not that your hands are stained with blood?"—"They are pure; would that my soul were as stainless!"—"Then what terrible thing is the matter?" Phaedra will not tell her. The old woman becomes frantic; her own death will be upon her mistress' head if her suppliant prayers are not heeded.—"But to know the truth would only make you wretched, too."—"What greater wretchedness could be mine than to lose you?"—"I shall die in any case, but more honorably if I die silent." Still beset, Phaedra at length consents to speak. But she finds much difficulty in beginning; she apostrophizes her mother, who loved so fearsomely, and her sister Ariadne, who loved and was betrayed. Again the Nurse misunderstands, thinking that she is censuring her unhappy kindred, but the Queen declares herself to be the third of her house to fall a victim to love.— "You love? Whom?"—Phaedra cannot name his name; ". . . the son of the Amazon," she manages to articulate.— "Hippolytus!"—"It was you that said it, not I!" she wails; and the Nurse is overwhelmed with horror, but later accepts the fact and counsels hope. These minute and striking correspondences between the text of *Phèdre* and that of the *Hippolytus* occur in a scene that has no analogue in Seneca's tragedy, and the same is true of the other extended passage where the French dramatist follows Euripides in detail.

This is the scene in which Hippolytus is banished. In both plays Theseus reflects, on seeing him, that nature ought to provide signs by which one could distinguish a true man from a knave, and Hippolytus begins by asking his father to confide in him. Then Theseus launches his terrible accusation and decrees exile to his son, with threats that if the youth ever again sets foot within the lands he rules, he himself will slay him as he slew so many miscreants in the past; Hippolytus in his defense urges his blameless repute, and declares that he is entirely chaste. He vainly proffers his oath; he asks the conditions of his exile, and is told to begone to the ends of the earth; he asks who will receive him when charged with such a crime, and is told to consort with those who delight in honoring the basest of men. Finally, when Theseus threatens immediate physical violence if he delays longer, he submits to necessity and goes. A notable difference in handling this scene lies in the fact that in Euripides it is before the entrance of Hippolytus that Theseus invokes the aid of the sea-god; in *Phèdre* his fatal prayer comes, more effectively, at the climax of his rage.

When one great dramatist so obviously builds upon the work of another great dramatist and so deliberately vies with him, comparisons are inevitable. It must be clearly understood at the outset that one difference between the *Hippolytus* and *Phèdre* is not, as some French critics assert, that the subject of the former is a contest between two goddesses, between Aphrodite and Artemis, in which the human characters are but irresponsible puppets, instead of free agents as in the play of Racine. Such an idea can spring only from the error of taking one's notion of classical deities from Ovid and other late writers of mythological fairy tales, and thus quite failing to understand the real Greek concept of the gods as somehow at once quasi-human personalities and unhuman physical forces. Racine's Phaedra herself says that she perishes "by will of Venus," and that Venus has "fastened on her prey." She builds a shrine to placate the goddess; she cries to her for mercy and for aid. Yet all this, as everyone knows, does not mean that she is the helpless victim of a supernatural being; nor has the Phaedra of Euripides one whit less of choice and free will than she. The shadowy figure of the Cyprian Aphrodite appears in the prologue of the *Hippolytus,* the voice of Artemis speaks from a cloud in the final scene, but all the action throughout the body of the play moves on a purely human plane and admits of rationalistic motivation. The conception of Aphrodite as "a Force of Nature or a Spirit working in the world" (against which, as an unarguable fact, it is entirely possible to speak of Hippolytus as "sinning," and which for purposes of drama is made into a person and represented in human form) is brought out by the words of the Nurse:

> She ranges with the stars of eve and morn,
> She wanders in the heaving of the sea,
> And all life lives from her.

And in the *Trojan Women* of Euripides a similar interpretation is given of the story that this goddess caused Helen to love Paris:

> . . . thine own heart, that saw and conned
> His face, became a spirit enchanting thee.
> For all wild things that in mortality
> Have being, are Aphrodite; and the name
> She bears in heaven is born and writ of them.[2]

Let us make no mistake about it: the *Hippolytus* of Euripides and the *Phèdre* of Racine are both human dramas.

Nor can any very important difference be established between the heroines of the two plays, though admirers of each have extolled its Phaedra at the expense of the other. There are, indeed, some points in which the characters are not identical. In destroying Hippolytus, both are actuated by desire to protect their good repute and thereby their children. The Phaedra of Euripides combines this motive with resentment at the young man's excessive abuse of her and

---

[2] These two verse quotations, and also the next one a few pages later, are from Gilbert Murray's translations.

at his failure to comprehend the agonized struggle which she
has made to preserve her purity; the Phaedra of Racine,
when in a revulsion of feeling she is ready to save Hippolytus at any cost, is checked by her discovery that he loves
Aricia, which fills her with jealous madness and then, in consequence, with utter horror at herself and with such confusion of soul that she is paralyzed, as it were, and incapable
of action until too late. The Greek Phaedra has a sense of
the essential rightness of her inmost heart in spite of all;
she is less the morbid and frenetic prey of her passions—is
not driven helplessly by them to do things she did not intend
to do, like her French sister, and would probably not have
been murderously jealous under similar circumstances,
whereas the self-loathing of Racine's Phaedra is so great
that she might have borne the insults of Euripides' Hippolytus meekly. The French dramatist has sought to extenuate
the guilt of his heroine; to this end he has employed the false
report of Theseus' death and increased the persuasiveness
and forcefulness of the Nurse; yet withal he has not drawn
a more appealing, more piteous, or more human character
than his model. He has, however, elaborated and exploited
the figure of Phaedra to a greater degree than did Euripides,
and has more clearly, though not more subtly, motivated her
conduct.

The point in which Racine's play departs furthest from
the Greek original, is the role of Hippolytus, and this is also
the point on which adverse criticism of *Phèdre* has been
focused. Such criticism, from Boileau and Dryden down
to the present day, has very imperfectly recognized what is at
fault. Racine's mistake was not, as generally is declared, that
he made Hippolytus in love; to do so was to create a quite
legitimate variant of the story, and served the valuable purpose of giving grounds for an access of jealousy in Phaedra
and in this way accounting for her failure to save Hippolytus
from the fate which threatened him. The intention of the

dramatist was evidently to depict a bold young huntsman, unversed in courtly ways and always hitherto absorbed in such manly interests as horses and the chase, until the beauty and wistful charm, and perhaps also the very misfortunes, of the dispossessed princess Aricia aroused in him those feelings for which he had till then had a boy's disdainful aversion. Again and again, in references to him by various characters, his fierce pride, his unpolished manners, and his wild, free mode of life are stressed. The figure of Hippolytus, as thus conceived, is artistically valid; but his own language is completely at variance with it. Racine clearly did not dare to put into his mouth, when he wooes Aricia or at other times, the simple if not faltering speech that would alone be natural to such a character. The fashionable world in seventeenth-century France would never have tolerated uncourtliness in a "sympathetic" hero; he must express himself like a young gentleman, with all the customary phrases of gallantry; and with these the author accordingly supplied him. Between what is said of Hippolytus in the play and all that he himself says, there is a hopeless incongruity; and it is therefore, and not because he is represented as being in love, that he chiefly offends us.

But he offends us also by the priggishness and fantastic absurdity of his conduct, of which we are expected to approve. "Priggishness" is only too kind a word for it when he proposes at once, on the report of Theseus' demise, to procure the throne of Athens for Aricia. He properly might have declined to accept it himself, if he thought it rightly hers, or might even have refused to defend it for his little half-brother against her; but to set himself up as a judge of his father's legitimacy and to undertake to use the power and prestige which he had gained as Theseus' supposedly faithful son to frustrate his father's will and despoil his father's heir in favor of a hereditary enemy as soon as the great hero-king and not unloving sire lay (he believed) helpless in death, is an ugly combination of complacent self-righteousness and disloyalty, which appears but the uglier the longer it is scrutinized. From his unfilial design he passes presently to an exaggerated squeamishness of filial scruples, and back again. The snaring promise of secrecy which prevents the Hippolytus of Euripides from refuting the charge brought against him is needed to motivate his failure to clear himself by exposing Phaedra in the French play. The only reason he has there for silence is that it would be unbecoming of him to offend his father's ear with the shameful truth; and this consideration seals his lips though at the risk of his life and though his beloved Aricia, as well as he, would gain by his speaking out. But when he goes into exile, he plans to enlist friends at Argos and Sparta and make war on his country to regain his rights and Aricia's! That is indeed to strain at the gnat and swallow the camel. The code of Racine's Hippolytus is not of one piece with the moral code of mankind in general; it is at times the sort of far-fetched, arbitrary, and purely personal code which, as Jules Lemaître observed, is commonly had by the characters in French romanesque dramas.[3]

But despite the blemish of the unsatisfactory figure of the prince, Racine's tragedy, taken as a whole, stands on an approximate parity with that of Euripides. It is strange indeed that two plays dealing with the same subject should be so nearly equal in greatness that the superiority of either may be plausibly argued but not convincingly established. Poetically, the *Hippolytus* doubtless bears off the palm; for though the poetry of each is almost its author's best, Euripides is a poet of loftier, lovelier strain and far more varied music than Racine. The *Hippolytus,* moreover, is full of a fresh, simple charm and a picturesque beauty which are foreign to French-classical drama. And there are subtleties

[3] Cf. p. 319.

in the work of the great Athenian that have no parallel in
Phèdre. One minor and one major example of them may be
cited, both typical of the genius of their author.

The first of these is where Theseus, bending over the
dead body of his wife, espies a tablet fastened to her hand.
It contains, in reality, the slanderous charge against Hippolytus, but her husband supposes it to be a message about
some last wish, some dying request, and observing the
familiar seal upon it, says:

> Ah, see
> How her gold signet here looks up at me,
> Trustfully.

Nothing could be truer or more pathetic than this chance
flash of tender, whimsical fancy crossing the mind of a grief-
stricken man; it is a characteristic touch of "Euripides, the
human,"—one of "his touches of things common till they
rose to touch the spheres." French-classical tragedy was too
rhetorical and hence dealt too generally with things in the
large and with obvious things to bring thus to light the in-
timate trivial phenomena of the heart.

Another and more impressive instance of the subtlety of
the Attic dramatist is a master-stroke to which Gilbert Norwood has called attention in his volume, *Greek Tragedy*.[4]
The Phaedra of Euripides, he points out, is a noble and
spirited woman. She has, it is true, a hereditary predisposition to unchastity: lawlessness is in her veins; her mother
and sister both have sinned;—but though she cannot help
her instincts, she can and will dispute their power over her
life. Her heart is finally broken when, to the argument that
the gods themselves are against her, is added the proof that
man is utterly unable to realize her devotion to what is pure

[4] Boston, 1920, pp. 210-214.

and of good repute or the hard fight that she has made.[5] "If thy life had not been in such danger," says the Nurse, "and thou *hadst happened to be a chaste woman,* I would not thus lead thee on," and again: *"Thy duty, to be sure, forbids sin; but as things are,* be advised by me." This hideous purring is perhaps Phaedra's bitterest shame. No one can understand. Then comes the betrayal of her secret, and the intolerable endless speech of condemnation by the man whom she loves and who is hence the cause of all her suffering. No one can understand. In an agony of terrified protest she destroys him and herself—and thereby wins that appreciation for lack of which she died. For there *was* one who could understand, after all—the one who seemed the least able to understand, and whose understanding she would most have craved: the Prince himself. Her suicide, her very slander which must bring about his death, opens his eyes to her real nature; it is he, the moral idealist, who can apprehend her tenacious and (as he now divines) not alien ideals; and in the shadow of his own doom he exclaims:

> Unchaste of passion, chaste of soul was she;
> But I am shamed by my cold purity.[6]

Here we have that supreme manifestation of genius, "the utterly unexpected, which we instantly accept," as in Shakespeare and a few other writers. There is nothing like this touch anywhere in Racine; it is quite outside his imaginative range.

[5] It must be confessed that she in large measure confuses in her mind actual *character* and mere *reputation,* as early civilizations like the Greek were prone to do—and as not a few people do still.

[6] The translation of the first line is Norwood's, as is much of the wording of the first part of the paragraph before it. The renderings both of Murray and of Way fail to bring out the significance of the passage.

On the other hand, *Phèdre* possesses a unity lacked by its rival. Though the *Hippolytus*, by intention of its author, is the "tragedy" of a young man whose persistent disregard of everything relating to sex results in his being unable to handle with intelligence and sympathetic tact a difficult, delicate situation with which he is confronted, Phaedra is the real center of interest until her death in the middle of the play; and after that the intensity of Theseus' passions makes him as prominent as the titular hero. Racine's tragedy subordinates everything to Phaedra herself; and such is the skill with which the plot is constructed to exhibit her with a maximum of sympathy and in situations requiring her to run the gamut of unrestrained and tragic emotions, and such eloquence is found for the expression of those emotions, that this drama is one of the most effective acting plays ever written and its heroine has become the great traditional role of the French stage as Hamlet is of the English. Every French actress aspires to play Phaedra, as every English actor aspires to play Hamlet, yet Sarah Bernhardt said that she never undertook the part without a feeling of terror at its illimitable possibilities and her inadequacy to do justice to them.

The greatest of Racine's secular tragedies, *Phèdre* was also the last. That he at this time forsook his career as a dramatist, when he was only thirty-seven years old and in the fullness of his powers, is generally ascribed to his disgust at the tactics of his enemies, which imperiled the fortunes of the play when it was first performed, and to the Jansenist influences which had colored his upbringing and which now regained control over him and convinced him of the sinfulness of his life and work. There should be no doubt of the importance of both these factors in shaping his decision, and they were probably paramount. Yet it is reasonable to think that discouragement, too, influenced him—discouragement at his initial scant success here again, as in the case of *Britan-nicus,* when he departed furthest from pseudo-classical con-ventions. We know from the *Mémoires* of his son, Louis Racine,[7] that he wanted to depart even further from these conventions after writing *Phèdre;*—that he planned to go back to the pattern of ancient classical tragedy and show that the love-element could be dispensed with in French drama as well as in Greek. He thought of attempting the subject of Oedipus and treating it in its essential simplicity as Sophocles had done, without introducing any factitious love-episode like Corneille before him or Voltaire after him.[8] He did begin and almost finish a play on the story of Alces-tis, which contains only conjugal love. But he may well have felt that the disappointing reception of *Phèdre* was not to be wholly attributed to malicious intrigue, and that, on the contrary, the failure to be adequately appreciated at first, which was common to this play and to *Britannicus* and was experienced by none of his other tragedies, indicated plainly that his public would not relish such approximations to a true classicism as alone would satisfy his own taste. At any rate, whatever his reasons, he destroyed his nearly completed *Alceste* and wrote no plays for some twelve years. Then came a brief resumption of his old activities, in the religious dramas of *Esther* and *Athalie*—all too brief, indeed, but sufficient to prove that his genius was undiminished and to suggest poignantly how much mankind was deprived of by his retirement.

This study of *Phèdre,* as I state in the Introduction, was written for my volume of translations, *The Best Plays of Racine,* which was published in 1936. In 1940 Henry Car-

[7] *Œuvres de J. Racine,* ed. by P. Mesnard, Paris, 1885, vol. i, pp. 268-269.

[8] Fénelon, *Lettre à M. Dacier sur les occupations de l'Académie* (1774).

rington Lancaster published Part IV of his great *History of French Dramatic Literature in the Seventeenth Century,* which is the part dealing with "the Age of Racine." Here he maintains (1) that *Phèdre* did not encounter unfriendly audiences even at first, (2) that its author's "conversion" did not occur till many years later, near the end of his life, and (3) that the sole reason he stopped writing plays was his appointment by Louis XIV as Royal Historiographer at this time. Lancaster disproves the colorful story of the wholesale purchase of theater seats by the enemies of Racine; but I cannot accept any of the three conclusions at which he arrives, and therefore I have not much altered my original version of the last paragraph above, which I believe is an essentially correct statement of the facts.

Though the earliest extant assertion that *Phèdre* was badly received when it first appeared is the testimony of Valincourt half a century later, this is at least the testimony of an eye-witness who states that he himself "saw Racine in despair." That "may well be . . . an old man's exaggeration," argues Lancaster. It may be; on the other hand, it may not be; in any case it is not likely to be an outright invention. Certainly Boileau's *Epître VII,* immediately contemporaneous, shows that Racine was greatly disturbed then by hostile criticism. Whether the machinations of his enemies were effective or not, he must have beheld with anxiety the ever-increasing lengths to which they went. It would have been very natural for him to feel a revulsion against writing under such conditions.

As for Racine's religious conversion, no doubt it was only in the very last years of his life that he came to regard playwrights as *"empoisonneurs publics";* he continued, for a long time after *Phèdre,* to take some interest in the stage, and he twice brought out revised editions of his dramas. But it is one thing to do in retirement such revising and editing, and quite a different thing to write and produce new plays with the contacts thus involved with the theatrical world and all its passions and allurements, where first la Du Parc and then la Champmeslé had been Racine's mistress. His appointment by Louis XIV to the position of royal historiographer would perhaps be sufficient to account entirely for his abandonment of dramatic composition; but it does not account for his complete departure from his old way of living and for his marriage, in that very year, with a simple, pious woman who never read even one of his plays. His new duties could as well have been assigned him because the King, learning that he had resolved to sever all connection with the theater, wanted to help him in this crisis in his life by providing him with highly honorable, official employment and a consequent pension. Indeed, I submit that this is much more likely to have been what occurred than that a royal mandate took Racine, regardless of his own wishes, from the writing of plays; for however great importance Louis attached to the chronicling of his military achievements, he was bound to realize, as an intelligent man, that this author had no unique qualifications for that task but was quite irreplaceable as a dramatist—and Racine was in fact the favorite dramatist of *le grand monarque,* who was a devoted patron of drama. (The choice of Boileau for the same work was a more natural one.)

The gossip, some six months later, of Madame de Sévigné and of the *Mercure galant,* cited by Lancaster, is no real evidence that Racine's appointment as historiographer was the cause of his break with the stage; they of course knew of the appointment and of this break, but they may well have been ignorant of what took place within his own mind. It is noteworthy that A. F. B. Clark, whose *Jean Racine*[9] appeared less than a year before Lancaster's discussion of this subject, and who was equally familiar with the data concern-

[9] Cambridge (Mass.), 1939.

ing it, saw no reason for rejecting the traditional explanations of Racine's "retirement." [10] Clark's treatment of the whole matter seems to me admirably judicious, and I would modify his conclusions only by my suggestion made above, that Racine was probably also influenced to some extent by his apparent difficulties in making a truer classicism, which his own taste craved, acceptable to his audiences.[11]

[10] The most recent work dealing with this subject, however, Raymond Picard's *la Carrière de Jean Racine,* Paris, 1956, presents views similar to Lancaster's.

[11] There remains to account for the prose outline, which survives in Racine's own handwriting, of the first act of an *Iphigénie en Tauride.* We know that his method of literary composition was to make such an outline, in great detail, for an entire play before composing any of the verse at all, and, indeed, that he felt his real labor was done when the outline was completed. This fragment is the only such chip from his workshop that we possess, and consequently is very interesting and valuable. To the student of his career, however, the striking thing about it is that it prefigures a drama decidedly more romanesque than *Phèdre* or even than *Iphigénie.* What is the most reasonable explanation of this fact? How does it fall in with our conjectures about the motive forces influencing his successive plays?

The answer depends on another fact which we do not—cannot—know: the time at which Racine made this outline. His son J.-B. Racine believed it to be the sole remaining vestige of the "several tragedies" that he considered writing after *Phèdre,* before he entered the service of the King. La Grange-Chancel said that Racine told him that he hesitated for some time as to whether to write his *Iphigénie* about the subject of the *Iphigenia in Aulis* or the *Iphigenia in Tauris* of Euripides, and decided in favor of the former "only after realizing that the other play did not have material for a fifth act"—whereof Lancaster comments (*op. cit.,* p. 119), "This shows that Racine had the work in mind about 1673, not that he then wrote out the plan of Act I. The evidence is certainly not sufficient to make us reject J.-B. Racine's statement." I agree with the last sentence quoted, but not with the first one; for it is improbable that Racine went back, after *Phèdre,* to a subject which he had found definitely unsuited for treatment. Either J.-B. Racine or La Grange-Chancel was mistaken, and we do not know which.

If the outline in question was written after the completion of *Mithridate* and prior to *Iphigénie*, it is without any particular significance. At that time he was slowly working away from romanesque drama, and the projected play about Iphigenia in Tauris would, it seems, have been little if any advance beyond *Bajazet* and *Mithridate* in this respect, but probably no retrogression from them. Somehow he grew bolder when he came to grips with the story of Iphigenia in Aulis. But if his fragment of an outline for a *Tauride* was made after *Phèdre*, it must have been with the same intention of surrendering to the preferences of his public as had caused him to follow the coldly received *Britannicus* with *Bérénice*. Does this unfinished outline show that after *Phèdre* he considered repeating his former policy of recurrence to what was sure to be acceptable—and then found that he was not willing to do it again?

A THALIE is not universally admitted to be Racine's greatest play, but beyond all question it justifies a higher estimate of his genius than does any other. For it is by all means his most original work. *Phèdre,* his own favorite, may be as great or greater; but there he was indebted to Euripides both for general outline and for many effective details, and also in some measure to Seneca. *Athalie* is entirely his; no one else had ever treated the theme which he took from Second Kings and Second Chronicles.[1] And in structure, too, it is peculiarly his own. His secular tragedies substantially adhere to the dramatic form current in his day, though they are distinguished by less intricacy of plot and by subtler and more human characterization. But in *Athalie* Racine, following the lead of his own *Esther,* achieved a fusion of French "classical" tragedy with that of ancient Greece, re-introducing the Chorus but, instead of keeping it continually present, bringing it on to the stage on only four occasions to punctuate with lyric interludes the otherwise uninterrupted progress of the action—for though these choral songs nominally divide the play into the customary five acts, there is really no more act-division than in a Greek tragedy. And just as in a Greek tragedy, in this masterpiece every possible sort of artistic appeal—drama, poetry, spec-

---

[1] No one, that is, in a published drama. An *Athalia* in Latin was played in the Jesuit college of Clermont in 1658; its program, which outlines its plot (romanesque and reminiscent of *Héraclius* and other plays of Corneille), is preserved. Racine may have read the program; it is hardly possible that he read the play itself, which must have had few resemblances to *Athalie.* See R. Lebègue in the *Revue bleue,* vol. xxxiv (1936), pp. 357-359.

tacle, music, and dancing—is combined in one harmonious whole.

The subject of *Athalie,* taken as it is from Holy Scripture, was a happy one for Racine. His own piety, his earnest religious convictions, here found ampler scope for expression than was afforded in classical or oriental plays. Moreover, he was now able, since he worked along new lines, to shake off most of the trammels of prevailing literary fashion. With the complete elimination of all love-interest—an element which he doubtless considered inappropriate in a sacred theme, but an unescapable requisite in all other dramas of the period—vanishes the conventional language of gallantry that jars in his treatment of Greek legend and Roman history. Gone, too, is the stereotyped, insipid confidant. Previously, this figure had taken on life only by transcending its role and becoming almost or quite a major character; that is what Narcissus and Burrus do in *Britannicus* and Oenone does in *Phèdre.* But Nabal in *Athalie* has a very minor part and discharges exactly the functions of a confidant. And yet he is a real man; in the few lines that he utters, the personality of this cool, predatory, callous ruffian is somehow created and vividly revealed.

There is another respect in which *Athalie* is superior to the secular dramas of its author. One of the chief flaws of French-classical tragedy in general, and one of the chief obstacles to our enjoyment of it today, is its lack of what we call "local color." Though its characters bear familiar names of olden times or far-distant lands, in speech and behavior they seem to us French courtiers of the Age of Louis XIV. Yet it is probably a mistake to suppose that the dramatists of that age were guilty of such incongruities through intent or indifference. We know that literary criticism then had a great deal to say about ascribing to historical figures the sentiments that would have been natural to them, and dealt severely with whatever was considered a failure to do so. We know that Corneille was especially interested in the re-creation of history in his plays; his admirers declared that his Romans expressed themselves better than real Romans, his Greeks better than real Greeks; and there has been a book on "Corneille the Historian." But Corneille made Sertorius gallant and Attila in love! He really offends worse than Racine. The truth appears to be that the seventeenth-century plays falsified their dramatis personae because seventeenth-century playwrights could supplement the bare facts of history with but scant data concerning the lives and minds of Greeks or Romans or Asiatics, and that their most outrageous anachronisms did not annoy their critics and audiences because the critics and audiences knew no more about these things than did the authors themselves—whereas the progress of historical research and the development of the historical imagination have now made us better informed as to such matters, and hence we demand a truer picture of the past. But the Bible and Josephus, which are still our main authorities for the Old Testament period, were as familiar to Racine as they are to ourselves; the conception of ancient Hebrew civilization which is traditional with us is not greatly different from what it was then; we see that where the dramatist had some acquaintance with the distinctive features of a remote environment, he was careful to preserve them; and as there is here no violent clash between what he depicts and what we imagine, our appreciation of his masterpiece is unimpaired.

A masterpiece it truly is. No beginning could possibly be finer than its opening scenes with their slow, majestic, ascensional movement—the meeting of high priest and solitary first-come worshipper within the neglected Temple in the dusk of dawn, the story of accumulated wrongs which cry out for vengeance and of the reassuring wonders of God's might, the first rays of the sun gilding the pinnacle of the sanctuary, the dialogue between Jehoiada and Jehosheba culminating in the great prayer of each. And the so-called "second act" (what lies between the first chorus and the second) is finer still; containing, as it does, the Queen's dream, her interview with the child in which with diabolical cunning she besets him with all her wiles yet is baffled at every turn by his simple innocence, her sudden outburst of fury at Jehosheba when she feels herself balked, and her marvelous revelation of her inmost heart, it is the finest act that Racine ever wrote. In its central situation, the dialogue between Athaliah and little Joash, he for the first and only time in his career improved upon a Greek model which he was directly imitating. He had fallen short of his original in *Iphigénie* and perhaps equaled it in *Phèdre;* but in this breathless scene, suggested by the meeting of Creusa and her son in the *Ion* of Euripides, he immeasurably surpassed the work which had inspired his own.

Had the rest of *Athalie* maintained the standard of excellence achieved in the first two "acts," this drama would scarcely yield in greatness to any tragedy of Aeschylus or Sophocles. But the fact is that after the second chorus there is a slight falling off. The poetry is as magnificent as ever—Racine's most beautiful poetry is in this play—but the tension is somewhat relaxed, and therewith comes a certain coldness. For Athaliah herself does not appear again until the very end, and in the physical absence of this, the figure of greatest imaginative value and one of the two principals of the action, the necessary grip and intensity could be preserved only by sheer force of religious exaltation. And this Racine simply did not possess in a sufficient degree to imbue his lines with it. A sincere Christian, he was nevertheless at heart a worldling, despite his Jansenist rearing and his ill-advised attempts to renounce the world. Sainte-Beuve's famous and too-laudatory statement that *Athalie* is "as beautiful as *Oedipus the King* with the true God added" is misleading. *Athalie* and *Oedipus* are both triumphs of dramatic construction, and *Oedipus* indeed has a hardness of texture which seems to bear a kind of analogy to the coldness of *Athalie*. But the hardness of *Oedipus*, as it were a mathematical proposition of horrible fatality, is artistically desirable; but the coldness of *Athalie* is certainly not desirable. Set its most eloquent and moving passages, such as Jehoiada's address to the assembled Levites and Azariah's answer (ll. 1326-1380), beside an excerpt from the *Choëphoroe* of Aeschylus, and it will be plain what fervor of spirit Racine lacked and his religious tragedy was in want of.[2]

ORESTES.

O Zeus, Zeus, gaze thou on this sight!
Behold a brood bereft of its father, thine eagle,
    killed in the twisted coils of a dreadful viper.
The nestlings, orphaned, are perishing with hunger,
    for they are not grown to bear the prey their
    father brought to the eyrie.
Even so, I and she who is with me here,—
    I name Electra,—
    stand in thy sight two children fatherless,
    both suffering like banishment from home.

ELECTRA.

And if thou leave to death the brood of him
Whose altar blazed for thee, whose reverence
Was thine, all thine,—whence, in the after years,
Shall any hand like his adorn thy shrine
With sacrifice of flesh? The eaglets slain,
Thou wouldst not have a messenger to bear

---

[2] That this fervor may be shown to reveal itself in any medium of translation, one speech is here quoted in a poetic prose rendering by Canon Orville E. Watson, and another, its antiphonal response, in the blank verse of Morshead, of which I have altered the last two lines.

Thine omens, once so clear, to mortal men;
So, if this kingly stock be withered all,
None on high festivals will fend thy shrine.
Preserve us, and raise up a mighty house
From this low state in which thou seest us now!

But the struggle that is joined in *Athalie* is at least nobly conceived and aligns against each other two champions of no petty stature. These tower up from among the other characters of the play—the gentle, anxious Jehosheba, the worthy but commonplace Abner, and Mattan the arch-villain, themselves delineated with sure and delicate strokes. Athaliah is not so wonderful a creation as Phaedra or perhaps Hermione, but of all Racine's heroines she is the grandest figure. Some French critics have sought to establish a similarity between her and Agrippina in *Britannicus,* and have compared them to the advantage of Agrippina. Such criticism is demonstrably wrong. It really compares the mother of Nero with Athaliah solely as the latter appears in the play, when she is, as Mattan says, no longer what she has been up to that time.

> Ce n'est plus cette Reine éclairée, intrépide,[3]
> Elevée au-dessus de son sexe timide,
> Qui d'abord accablait ses ennemis surpris,
> Et d'un instant perdu connaissait tout le prix.

Mattan was certainly in a position to understand her thoroughly, and in the next breath he speaks of her as "this great soul." No one could have called Agrippina that. She

---

[3] No more
Is this the bold, clear-sighted queen of yore,
Her timid sex transcending—she that flew
To overwhelm astonished foes and knew
The value of an instant lost.

was a clever, resourceful intriguer, with endless patience and carefulness in details and with no scruples whatever in the pursuit of her ends; but we have no evidence of her administrative ability in affairs of magnitude, for though she says she formerly guided Nero in his policies, she was not his only adviser and nothing of importance resulted from her domination. Athaliah, on the other hand, could boast of a brilliantly successful reign (ll. 471-484). And though her guilt is emphasized throughout the play, and though that of Agrippina is intentionally obscured in *Britannicus*, it may reasonably be maintained that Athaliah was not only the abler but also the less wicked of the two, for she felt herself involved in an implacable vendetta with Jehovah and the house of David, in which her parents and all her brothers had been slain, and she fought to avenge them—especially her mother, whom she unquestionably loved, whereas Agrippina loved not even Nero in comparison with her ambition. Indeed, in her great speech avowing her feud with Jehovah, Athaliah is for the moment a distinctly appealing figure. After all, victory was once within her grasp and she could have preserved her life and crown, had she chosen to carry off Joash at the end of their conversation in the Temple; for Mattan was at hand with her Tyrian mercenaries and against such force the resistance of Jehoiada and the handful of Levites whom he had hastily assembled would have been vain. It is a violation of dramatic logic and fitness, and the most serious positive defect in the play, that her doom is thus, because of her failure to strike then at the child, made to depend upon the single good impulse recorded of her, instead of being wholly the fruit of her sins.

One may feel that this terrible queen would have been a match for her human foes, and may find one's sympathies, contrary to the author's intention and the proper effect of the play, inclining towards her as a splendid even though criminal combatant who is unfairly compelled to fight against

God as well as against men. One might prefer to see her
worsted by Jehoiada in a more equal contest of intelligence
and craft, without having her mental fiber hopelessly impaired by Heaven to render certain the triumph of the high
priest. But that is a purely modern viewpoint. To Racine the
real protagonist of the drama is God himself, who after suffering this blood-stained, impious woman to live long in her
iniquity, at last majestically avenges the moral law upon
her. A rationalist need not interpret her fall thus, and can
easily, if he chooses, explain her irresolution and impru-
dence, which brought it about, as the natural consequences
of old age and of a vicious circle of shaken nerves and dis-
quieting dreams; but she herself declares that it is God alone
who has accomplished her destruction.

It is not merely just retribution nor the protection of helpless innocence nor the restoration of the rightful heir to the
throne nor even the return of the Jews to the faith of their
fathers which are at stake. The little Joash is the last surviving descendant of David in unbroken male succession, and it
is from David's line of kings that the promised Messiah,
the Redeemer of Israel and of the world, is to be born. Again
and again in the course of the play, this fact of cosmic significance is brought to mind, more or less unmistakably, until
it receives its final confirmation and culminating emphasis in
Jehoiada's rapt vision of futurity—the New Jerusalem and
the Savior Christ. On the fate of Joash hangs the fate of
all mankind, the vindication of God's word, the fulfilment
of the Divine purpose.

Jehoiada is no mean agent of the Lord of Hosts. "His
unswerving faith, even under the most trying circumstances,
and under conditions that would discourage and appal the
bravest spirits; his inflexible determination to proceed at all
hazards with the task he has undertaken; his profound belief
in the religion of which he is the high priest, and his assured demeanor in the presence of the gravest danger; his

foresight, his magnetic influence over his followers, the boldness of his plans, his consummate knowledge of human nature, mark him at once as a born leader of men and a foe of
the most redoubtable sort." [4] He divides with the vizier
Achmet in *Bajazet* the distinction of being the most notable
study of a man that Racine, pre-eminently the portrayer of
women, has painted. He is not a simple figure. To Voltaire,
himself engaged in relentless war with ecclesiasticism, he appeared a bloodthirsty bigot who conspires against his sovereign and murders her. Racine surely must have intended
him to be regarded with entire sympathy as the stern but
upright man of God, cherishing the good and ruthlessly ex-
tirpating that which is compact of evil. If so, the hand of the
artist wrought more subtly than his conscious mind conceived; for Jehoiada is indeed what his creator meant him
to be, but he is also what Voltaire thought him. All the qualities of the Hebrew priest of Old Testament times, if not
of the typical priest of primitive civilizations in general, are to
be found in him—all the steadfast faith and the fierce intolerance, the devotion to the God he worships, the desire for
theocratic domination, the protective care for his people, the
patience, the shrewdness, the superstition, the capacity to
go into trances, the common sense, the keen knowledge of
men and affairs, the skill at intrigue, the sanguinary fanati-
cism, the guile, the vindictiveness, the heroism. To one of us
one aspect of him will show more prominently, to another
of us another; and we shall each feel differently about him,
as we shall each feel differently about Athaliah and as each
of us views with different opinions and different sympathies
the people and the problems that we encounter in real life.
Athalie is one of those rare plays, like the *Philoctetes* of
Sophocles and the *Misanthrope* of Molière, in which it is
possible to side with any of the characters or with none of

---

[4] *Athalie,* ed. by F. C. de Sumichrast, New York, 1902, p. xxxvii.

them; and that is to say that in such plays can be found the very stuff of life itself.

It must have been with high hopes that Racine undertook the composition of *Athalie*. He had been asked by Madame de Maintenon to devise some scenes on a religious subject to serve as a vehicle for training the school-girls at Saint-Cyr in dramatic recital, and his *Esther* had been the result. As a play, it is but a slight thing, of merit chiefly by virtue of its lyrical passages; yet its presentation was greeted with tremendous acclaim. To the poet who, because of his chagrin and his tormenting scruples, had ceased to write for the stage years before, an immense new field, a new career, seemed to be opening. It was surely no sin but rather a work of piety to compose dramas on Biblical themes, which would be performed not by corrupt actors and actresses but by carefully reared young girls. Writing no longer for the professional stage, he was now freed from the yoke of its conventions and could write as he pleased, in close imitation of his Greek masters; and the success of *Esther* gave assurance that, writing thus, he would find favor.

A cruel disappointment awaited him. In the interval since the appearance of his first sacred drama, voices had been raised in protest against the elaborate theatrical activities of the pupils of Saint-Cyr. *Esther* had succeeded only too well. It was alleged that their triumphs had turned the heads of some of the young misses and that the devout atmosphere of the school was becoming contaminated. Therefore, instead of being produced with pomp and circumstance as its predecessor had been, *Athalie,* which far more than any other work of Racine demands the support of music and sumptuous setting to secure the intended effect, was very inadequately presented and, as a result, had a cold reception. Not until 1702, eleven years afterwards, was it played with the accessories which had been designed for it; from that time its fame slowly mounted, and at length Voltaire hailed it as *"le chef-d'œuvre de l'esprit humain."* But Racine, who was too much discouraged to make any further effort in the field of drama, had died in 1699.

CHAPTER XVI

AFTER RACINE: CAMPISTRON

THE minor French dramatists who wrote tragedies
during the last years of Racine's life were less original,
less interesting, and of smaller stature than those most
prominent in the group about Corneille a half-century earlier.
There is no one quite comparable to Rotrou, Du Ryer, or
Tristan l'Hermite among these later men. They exhibit the
flagging inspiration, the reworking of old themes, the stereotyped conventionality or the attempt to avoid it by the choice
of strange and sensational subject-matter, that are commonly
associated with the decline of a great dramatic movement.

The last thin strain of Corneillian tradition is exemplified
in the *Régulus* of Pradon. It is universally regarded as the
"best" of his plays; but when the best is so bad, one is not
encouraged to acquaint oneself with the others. The figure of
the captured Roman general, whom the Carthaginians
paroled that he might induce his countrymen to make peace
with them but who counseled instead a continuation of the
war and then, true to his promise, returned to his disappointed
captors though fully aware that their vengeance awaited him,
is well suited for tragedy; and Pradon cleverly preserves the
"Unities" by representing the mission of his hero to be not
to Rome but to the camp of the invading Roman army, before Carthage. His Regulus has not suffered defeat and the
loss of that army, as in history—for the *gloire* of the tragic
hero must not be impaired—but has been made prisoner
while reconnoitering a weak point in the defenses of the
city. The "love-interest" invariably found in French-classical
tragedies is secured by making him a widower to whom the
daughter of Metellus, the Roman general associated with
him, is betrothed; this girl, Fulvia by name, is present in

the camp, having come there to nurse her father when he was
wounded, and so is Regulus' son, Attilius, a child ten years of
age. Regulus now is anxious to send both of them away to
a safer place, and takes up the matter with Metellus:

> Tous les jours votre fille augmente nos alarmes: [1]
> A nos moindres périls elle donne des larmes.
> Que serait-ce, grands Dieux! si de pressants mal-
> heurs
> Méritaient quelque jour de plus justes douleurs?
> Mon fils (vous le savez) veut me suivre sans cesse:
> L'un et l'autre à son tour m'arrête, m'intéresse;
>
> .   .   .   .
>
> Et Rome, Métellus, n'en est pas mieux servie.

The two men believe that Regulus can be more successful
in reconciling Fulvia to their decision than her father could,
and that Metellus can best break the news of it to Attilius;
but Regulus proves quite unable to persuade Fulvia, and
Metellus reports similar ill success with the boy:

> Votre fils veut partir encor moins que Fulvie.[2]
> J'ai parlé, mais en vain j'ai voulu préparer
> Son cœur à ce départ qui l'a fait soupirer;

[1] Thy daughter every day augments our fears;
    At our least dangers she gives way to tears.
    How would it be, great gods, if serious evils
    Some day afforded better grounds for grief!
    My son, thou knowest, would follow me every moment;
    They both by turns hinder me, occupy me;

    .   .   .   .

    And Rome is not thus better served, Metellus.

[2] Thy son wishes to go still less than Fulvia.
    I spoke to him, but vainly sought to school
    His heart for this departure, which distressed him.

Protestant que plutôt il cessera de vivre,
Loin de partir, seigneur, il s'apprête à vous suivre.

Such deference to the wishes of a child when he is trouble-
some in a camp of war is surely absurd, not only in ancient
Romans but also in seventeenth-century Frenchmen unless
in the case of a young king or prince. But Regulus is touched
by his son's eagerness and permits him to remain—and
Metellus likewise yields to Fulvia's supplication, exclaiming
as soon as she gives voice to a single spirited sentiment (Je
dois près de vous vivre, ou près de vous mourir[3]), though it
is belied by all her previous conduct:

Puisque vous faites voir un si noble courage,[4]
Demeurez: vous verrez l'attaque de Carthage.

In the later acts of the play his mistake is abundantly demonstrated, for she "makes a scene" on every possible occasion. For instance, when frightened about Regulus (the
news that he is a prisoner has been kept from her, but she
suspects that something is wrong) and told that he is safe
but that matters of vital importance require an immediate,
secret consultation, she cries:

Si vous me dites vrai, s'il faut que je vous croie,[5]
Dès ce même moment souffrez que je le voie.

Protesting he would rather die, instead
Of going, sir, he prepares to follow thee.

[3] I ought to live near thee, or die near thee.

[4] Since thou exhibitest such noble courage,
Stay; thou shalt witness the assault on Carthage.

[5] If truth thou tellest me, if I must believe thee,
This very instant suffer me to see him.

She has, however, considerable provocation. Metellus tries to conceal from her the capture of Regulus (brought about, as we might expect, by the treachery of his rival in love!) and afterwards the fate that hangs over him, but in each case says enough to fill her with the greatest anxiety, and then refuses to say more and leaves forthwith, forbidding her to investigate further.[6]

There is genuine vigor in Fulvia's rebuke of the perfidious rival lover, Mannius, when he presumes to make advances to her. There is vigor also in the lines of Regulus when, on his return to the camp, he urges war instead of a peace costly to Rome. Pradon shows marked skill in building the action up to a climax in which the hero encounters first his betrothed and then his little son, yet is not shaken in his high resolve. But when in spite of them he departs, and Fulvia falls half-fainting into her confidante's arms, we have the following grotesque dialogue between the boy (ten years old,[7] let us remember) and his tutor, Lepidus:

ATTILIUS.[8]

Ah! sans verser de larmes,
Le fils de Régulus doit recourir aux armes.

---

[6] Yet he takes so little real care to prevent her from discovering the truth that, each time, someone else enlightens her the very next moment. And he is meant by the author to be an intelligent man!

[7] So those who discuss the play state, without a dissenting voice. The play itself says "A peine a-t-il encor deux lustres accomplis" ("Scarcely has he completed yet two lustrums"). A lustrum is usually a period of five years, but this seems not to have been invariably true. Yet if Attilius were much older, he would hardly have been carried in the soldiers' arms in the assault.

[8] ATTILIUS.
Ah! without shedding tears
The son of Regulus should rush to arms.

Pourquoi m'arrêtez-vous? un Romain, quoiqu'
    enfant,
Ne doit-il pas apprendre à combattre en naissant?

LÉPIDE.

Ah, seigneur!

ATTILIUS.

            Est-ce ainsi que vous devez m'in-
    struire?
Vous devez au combat vous-même me conduire.
Je suivrai Métellus: (à FULVIE) marchant à son
    côté,
Je combattrai, Madame, en pleine sûreté.
Mais hélas! vous pleurez. Ah! généreux Lépide,
Hé quoi? n'est-il pas temps que la vertu me guide?
Et que mon père enfin puisse voir aujourd'hui,
Qu'il laisse à sa patrie un fils digne de lui?

Why dost thou stay me? Though I am a child,
Should not a Roman learn, when born, to fight?
LEPIDUS.
Ah, sir!
ATTILIUS.
        Is it thus thou oughtest to instruct me?
Thou oughtest thyself to lead me to the combat.
Metellus will I follow!
            (to FULVIA) I shall fight
In perfect safety, madam, at his side.
Alas, thou weepest!
            What, noble Lepidus!
Is it not time that valor guided me,
And that my father now should see that he
Leaves to his country a son worthy of him?

LÉPIDE.

Hé bien? seigneur, allons; il faut vous satisfaire.

One would like to know why it was necessary to satisfy this preposterous child rather than to bring him to his senses. But he is the son of a hero of French-classical tragedy; and the war-hardened legionaries of Rome recoiled at the mere sight of Racine's Mithridates. Everyone takes Attilius seriously. Fulvia's attendant comforts her with the assurance,

> Du bras de Métellus vous devez tout attendre.[9]
> Priscus et les Romains, le jeune Attilius,
> Tous veulent s'immoler pour sauver Régulus.

and eventually we are told that

> Le jeune Attilius amené par Lépide,[10]
> Porté par des soldats, montre un air intrépide;
> Et pour sauver son père affrontant les hasards,
> Sait nous servir de chef, d'aigles, et d'étendards.

Some critics have praised Pradon for his rarely precedented introduction of a child into his play, but one cannot rightly call praiseworthy that which begets absurdities.

LEPIDUS.
Well then, come, sir. I needs must satisfy thee.

[9] Thou shouldst expect all from Metellus' arm.
Priscus, the Romans, young Attilius,
All would fain perish to save Regulus.

[10] The young Attilius, brought by Lepidus,
Carried by soldiers, shows a fearless mien;
And, for his father's rescue, scorning danger,
Serves us for leader, for eagles, and for banners.

It should be added that the style of *Régulus* is often of an extraordinary lameness; the language is jejune and inexact; the author continually uses the second-best or fifth-best word or phrase in his effort to write verse. Thus when Metellus advises Regulus:

> Allez trouver Fulvie en ce péril extrême; [11]
> A ce départ, seigneur, disposez-la vous-même,

there is nothing that could possibly justify calling the situation resulting from Fulvia's presence in the camp a *péril extrême,* except the mere need for a rhyme. And only for rhyme's sake would the capture of Regulus have been called a *sacrifice* in the lines,

> Xantippus est vainqueur, et par son artifice[12]
> Il a fait à Carthage un si grand sacrifice;

—the turn thus given to the thought is a decidedly unnatural one. And again, in

> laissez-moi dégager ma parole,[13]
> Priscus; soutenons mieux l'honneur du Capitole,

how unnatural to say *Capitole* instead of *Rome!* There are countless examples of this ineptitude in the play.[14]

[11] Go and find Fulvia in this peril intense;
Win her consent thyself, sir, to go hence,

[12] Xanthippus triumphs, and by his artifice
Has made to Carthage this great sacrifice.

[13] Make me not, Priscus, violate my parole;
Preserve the honor of the Capitol.

[14] H. C. Lancaster in his *History of French Dramatic Literature in the Seventeenth Century,* Part IV, p. 227, quotes several lines

The most prominent tragic dramatist in the last years of
the seventeenth century was Campistron, who was regarded
as in some measure the chosen disciple of Racine and the

---

from *Régulus* which he says Corneille might have written. It is true
that such lines are not infrequent in this tragedy, and no one can
doubt that it attempts deliberately to capture something of the general manner and spirit of Corneille. But that it has a specific source
in him is not so easily granted. As a rule, Lancaster tends to be
skeptical about the alleged influence of one French-classical play on
another—and rightly so; for their range of themes and conduct and
emotions was comparatively limited, and resemblances of detail or
phrasing, which often occur in them, are less significant than such
resemblances would be elsewhere. Actual indebtedness, though undoubtedly frequent in these plays, is not easily distinguishable from
the mere chance similarities which must also have been plentiful
when different men were constantly at work upon much the same
sort of thing. It is somewhat surprising, therefore, to find that Lancaster categorically asserts (pp. 225-227) that Pradon in *Régulus*
imitated *Horace*. I do not think he proves his case, which he attempts
to do by arguing that the characters in the one play parallel those
in the other. But the resemblance of Regulus and Metellus to the
Horatian son and father is not strikingly close; Priscus, unlike
Curiatius, actually would make public interest yield to private interest; any supposed analogy between poor, frantic Camilla and the
unscrupulous villain Mannius, on the ground that both "lack patriotism" and are "moved primarily by love," seems to me far-fetched
indeed. Lancaster says that Fulvia, like Sabina, "encourages the man
she loves to risk his life." That is not my interpretation of the text.
The first passage at issue occurs when Regulus tells her that she
must leave the camp, where her fears embarrass his conduct of the
war. She then says:

> Si je n'ai pas gardé d'empire sur mes sens,
> Pardonnez-moi, Seigneur. Courez à la victoire,
> J'ai de quelques moments retardé votre gloire :
> C'est un crime, il est vrai, que mon cœur a commis ;
> Il était le plus grand de tous vos ennemis :
> Pour l'en punir, partez, oubliez sa tendresse,
> Et que la gloire soit votre unique maîtresse.

continuer of his work. Estimates of Campistron vary greatly. Lanson considered him not worth reading, and pronounced his inventions commonplace, his characters feature-

---

(If I have not kept mastery o'er my feelings,
Forgive me, sir. Hasten to victory.
I have delayed thy glory a few moments.
'Tis a crime, truly, that my heart hath done;
It was the greatest of thine enemies.
To punish it, go forth; forget its love;
And let thy glory be thy soul's one mistress.)

It is a speech which seems to me almost certainly ironical; if she
is really condemning herself here, it is out of keeping with everything else that she says or does, before or later, until the other moot
passage is reached. This is when Regulus persists in his determination to return to Carthage according to his promise. She approaches
him with these words:

Ne croyez pas, Seigneur, que pour vous attendrir,
Je pousse devant vous quelque indigne soupir.
Je connais votre cœur, votre vertu farouche:
Je sais que les soupirs, les pleurs, rien ne vous touche.
Je viens vous applaudir de votre grand dessein.
Vout êtes, il est vrai, véritable Romain:
Je serai comme vous véritable Romaine.
Partez, Seigneur; allez où la gloire vous mène.
Vous aurez à mes yeux un cœur, prêt à percer;
Et j'aurai comme vous du sang prêt à verser.

(Think not, sir, that to melt thy bosom I
Shall heave before thee some unworthy sigh.
I know thy heart, thy virtue fierce. I know
That neither sighs nor tears nor aught will move thee.
I come to applaud thee for thy lofty purpose.
Thou art, in very truth, a genuine Roman.
I, too, will be, like thee, a genuine Roman.
Depart, sir. Go where honor leads thee. Thou
Wilt have a heart that waiteth to be pierced
Before my very eyes; and I shall have

less, and his style invertebrate, languid, and a perpetual echo of Racine.[15] But Lancaster admits only his stylistic weakness, and asserts that his *Andronic* and *Tiridate* "are, among the tragedies of the century, surpassed only by those of Corneille and Racine." [16]

Like thee some blood that waiteth to be shed.)

This surely is not said to encourage him in his resolve; it is, on the contrary, the final card which she plays to turn him therefrom. Clearly, he recognizes it as such, for he replies:

Dieux! que me dites-vous? je frémis: ah! Madame,
Quel chemin prenez-vous pour ébranler mon âme!

(What dost thou tell me? Gods! I shudder, madam.
Ah, what course takest thou to shake my soul!)

When she sees that she cannot sway him by her threat, she cries:

Fidèle aux Africains, à Fulvie infidèle,
Vous osez la quitter, et vous brûlez pour elle?
Vous m'abandonnez donc, et gardez votre foi
A nos fiers ennemis, Seigneur, plutôt qu'à moi?

(Faithful towards Africans, to Fulvia faithless,
Thou darest to leave her, and thou lovest her?
Thou then abandonest me, and keepest faith
With our cruel foes, sir, rather than with me?)

and forthwith she begins to weep again; we have no further talk from her about sharing his fate. If Fulvia resembles anyone in *Horace,* it is Camilla, not Sabina; if the Camilla of *Horace* resembles anyone in *Régulus,* it is Fulvia, not Mannius.

[15] See Lanson's *Esquisse d'une Histoire de la Tragédie française,* pp. 104-105.

[16] *Op. cit.,* Part IV, p. 277. Elsewhere (Part V, p. 101) in the same work he records his opinion that the best plays by the minor tragic dramatists between 1670 and 1700 are Campistron's *Andronic* and *Tiridate,* La Fosse's *Manlius Capitolinus,* Péchantré's *Géta,* and Thomas Corneille's *Ariane* and *le Comte d'Essex.* These, together with the last named author's *Stilicon* and, in the period before 1650, Tristan l'Hermite's *Mariane, la Mort de Sénèque,* and *la Mort*

A study of *Andronic,* by common consent the better of
the two,[17] will reveal—at least to those who do not share the
usual French obsession that style is all-important—substan-
tial grounds for so high an estimate of it. As compared
with the best plays of Du Ryer, Rotrou, and Tristan, it is
somewhat lacking in vigor and in grasp of realistic detail;
it is more artificial and conventional; it has the blurred outlines, the grey tints, and the thin, plaintive note of a tragedy
essentially elegiac in type. Yet it is competently fashioned,
is not blemished by any glaring absurdity such as may be
found at least once or twice in almost all of the lesser "classical" French tragedies,[18] and is notable for a consistency,
complexity, and subtlety of characterization which will sus-
tain a searching analysis as will the dramatis personae in
perhaps none of the others.

Andronic takes its plot from the well-known story of Philip

---

du Grand Osman, Rotrou's *Saint Genest, Venceslas,* and *Cosroès,*
and Du Ryer's *Saül* and *Scévole* appear to constitute his list of the
most notable French tragedies, outside of Pierre Corneille and
Racine, from the inception of the "classical" type with Mairet's
Sophonisbe to the end of the seventeenth century. To conform it to
my own judgment, the changes that I would make in it with the
least uncertainty would be the omission of *Saint Genest* and the
substitution of Thomas Corneille's *Laodice* for his *Stilicon. Géta*
has been praised by no other critic, so far as I can recall, and is
little known; but it perhaps deserves inclusion. I think *Sophonisbe*
itself more surely does.

[17] Victor Fournel, however, in his article "Contemporains et
successeurs de Racine" in *Revue d'Histoire littéraire de la France,*
vol. i (1894), declared, to the contrary, that *Tiridate* "passe gen-
éralement pour son [Campistron's] chef-d'œuvre" (p. 255), and
himself pronounced it not only "le chef-d'œuvre de Campistron" but
"certainement l'un des chefs-d'œuvre du théâtre de second ordre" in
the seventeenth century (p. 257).

[18] The hero's ecstasies over the "unexampled kindness" of the
heroine in merely showing solicitude for his life when he is held
a prisoner are absurd, but they are too brief and unimportant to
mar the play seriously.

II of Spain, Elizabeth, and Don Carlos; Campistron has transferred this, with changed names, to the Byzantine Empire in the days of the Palaeologi. The exposition of essential facts is accomplished naturally enough by a conversation between two ministers of State, Leo and Marcenus, who have hitherto been mortal foes but are now brought together by their common dread of Prince Andronicus, the heir to the throne. The Emperor has recently wedded Irene, the daughter of the ruler of Trebizond; she was formerly betrothed to the Prince, and these ministers fear that his vengeance will fall on them, to whose counsels he ascribes the marriage. Moreover, they know that Andronicus is trying to secure justice for the oppressed Bulgarians, who have been goaded to sedition by the cruelties of the imperial governors; and if the realm is tranquil, the Emperor will find his ministers less necessary to him.

The plea of the Bulgarian envoy is harshly rebuffed, and the Prince begs permission of his father to go and pacify the insurgents himself; when the Emperor declines to allow this, he resolves to go secretly. Any further stay in Byzantium has become intolerable to him. His sensitive, restless, passionate nature is well portrayed. Like Racine's Orestes, he is a prototype of the ill-fated, self-pitying hero of romantic drama; but he better preserves a sense of moral values.

> Irène est trop charmante, et je sens mon amour,[19]
> Sans espoir, sans désirs, s'accroître chaque jour.
> Je la vis, je l'aimai dès sa plus tendre enfance;
> Cet amour s'est nourri de cinq ans d'espérance;
> Ses yeux sont plus puissants qu'ils ne l'étaient alors,

[19] Too strong is Irene's spell. I feel my love,
Hopeless and purposeless, grow more each day.
I saw her, loved her, from her earliest childhood;
This love hath by five years of hope been nourished,
Her glance can move me more than earlier,

Et je ferais contre eux d'inutiles efforts.
Mais ce feu malheureux que je ne puis éteindre
Peut-être plus longtemps ne pourrait se contraindre.
Je ne puis voir mon père, avec tranquillité,
Possesseur d'un trésor que j'avais mérité.
Il m'a fait trop de maux en m'enlevant Irène.
Il s'élève en mon cœur des sentiments de haine
Que toute ma vertu ne saurait étouffer;
Ce n'est qu'en m'éloignant que j'en puis triompher.
Je sais tous les égards que je dois à mon père,
Et le ciel m'est témoin combien je le révère.
Je voudrais faire plus; mais il m'a tout ôté.
Son choix . . . N'en parlons plus, je suis trop agité:
Je ne me connais plus, et je me crains moi-même.

His unhappiness did not begin with his loss of Irene.

L'empereur, soupçonneux, esclave de son rang,[20]
Ne m'a jamais fait voir les tendresses du sang.

And I would strive quite uselessly against it.
But this unhappy flame that I can quench not
Perhaps no longer could control itself.
I cannot with a calm mien see my father
Possess a treasure which I had deserved.
He did me too much wrong in taking Irene
From me; within my heart he kindled hate
Which all my rectitude cannot suppress.
Only by absence can I triumph o'er it.
I know how much respect I owe my father,
And heaven witnesseth my reverence for him.
I fain would do still more; but he has robbed me
Of all. His choice . . . but let us speak no further
Of this. I am too deeply moved. I know
Myself no longer, and I fear myself.

[20] The Emperor, suspicious and the slave
Of his own rank, has never shown to me

Les plus saints mouvements que la nature imprime
Dans son austère cœur passeraient pour un crime :
Et pour être né prince, il ne m'est pas permis
D'éprouver tout l'amour d'un père pour son fils.

Most of all, he chafes at the inaction that is imposed on
him. From childhood he has been thrilled by the great deeds
of his ancestors; now he is determined to follow their example at whatever hazard. But he wishes to speak with Irene
once more before he goes.

She, no less unhappy than he, shrinks from the thought
of seeing him :

Je ne puis m'exposer à ce triste entretien; [21]
C'est trop de mon tourment sans y joindre le sien :
C'est trop pour triompher de toute ma constance,
Hélas! d'avoir quitté les lieux de ma naissance,
Ces lieux où tout semblait prévenir mes desirs,
Où mon cœur n'a jamais connu que les plaisirs.
O bienheureux séjour! aimable Trébisonde!
O murs où je vivais dans une paix profonde!

A parent's tenderness. The holiest feelings
Instilled by nature would to his heart austere
Seem criminal, and 'tis not permitted me,
Being born a prince, to know a father's love.

[21] To this sad interview I cannot expose
Myself. My torture is too great without
His own being added to it. Alas, it shakes
My constancy too much to have left my birthplace,
The place where all things seemed to anticipate
My wishes, where my heart knew never aught
But happiness! O fortunate abode!
Dear Trebizond! O walls wherein I lived

Que n'ai-je, en vous perdant, de mes funestes jours
Par une prompte mort vu terminer le cours!
Je m'éloignai de vous en ces lieux entraînée
Par le trompeur espoir d'un heureux hyménée.
Je croyais qu'Andronic, à mon destin lié,
Pour jamais avec moi serait associé.
Nos pères l'ordonnaient; Trébisonde et Bysance
Sur cet illustre hymen fondaient leur espérance.
Je venais avec joie en célébrer les nœuds:
Le prince était aimable, il était amoureux.
Vains projets, vain transports, espérance inutile!
J'arrive enfin: à peine entré-je en cette ville
Que je me vois livrée à des maux infinis:
Il me faut épouser le père au lieu du fils;
Nos destins sont changés: un ordre de mon père
Détruit dans un instant le bonheur que j'espère.

In peace profound! Why did I not, when I
Lost you, by speedy death cut short the course
Of my sad days? I left you, carried hither
By the false prospect of a happy marriage.
I dreamed that Andronicus, linked with me
In fortune, would be always my companion.
So said our fathers; Trebizond and Byzantium
On this illustrious marriage based their hopes.
I came with joy to celebrate the nuptials.
The Prince was lovable; he was in love.
   Vain plans, vain transports, futile expectations!
At length I arrive; but scarcely have I entered
This city, when I find myself consigned
To infinite ills. I needs must wed the sire
Instead of the son. Our destinies are changed.
An order from my father in one instant
Destroyed the happiness for which I hoped.
A victim of State policy, and bound

En victime d'état contrainte d'obéir,
Pour conserver ma gloire il fallut me trahir.

Yet, she continues,

Qui jamais a caché ses chagrins mieux que moi . . .[22]
Observée avec soin par une cour austère
Où les yeux les plus chers me semblent ennemis,
Où je n'ai rien des biens que je m'étais promis,
Où, sans cesse livrée à ma douleur extrême,
Mon cœur tyrannisé combat contre lui-même;
Que vous dirai-je enfin? où ce cœur malheureux
Est souvent malgré moi moins fort que je ne veux!

Andronicus enters before she can withdraw as she intended. In the scene that follows, the elegiac vein which is dominant in this play finds its fullest and most pathetic expression:

IRÈNE.[23]

. . . Quel est votre dessein de venir en ces lieux
Me faire malgré moi recevoir vos adieux?

To obey, I had to be for duty's sake
Mine own betrayer.

[22] Who hath e'er better hid her grief than I . . .
Scrutinized closely by an austere Court
In which the dearest eyes seem foes to me;
In which I have naught good that I was promised;
In which, committed without cease to anguish,
My sore oppressed heart fights against itself—
What shall I say? in which this heart so wretched
Is oft less strong, despite me, than I wish!

[23] IRENE.
. . . What is thy purpose when thou comest hither
To make me hear adieus against my will?

Puisque vous êtes prêt à sortir de Byzance,
N'en pouviez-vous partir avec votre innocence?
Avez-vous oublié qu'un serment solennel
Nous impose à tous deux un silence éternel;
Qu'il n'est plus entre nous d'entretien légitime;
Qu'un seul mot, qu'un regard, qu'un soupir est un
    crime;
Que, sans cesse attentive à remplir mon devoir,
Je mets tout mon honneur à ne vous plus revoir;
Et quels que soient les maux que vous avez à
    craindre,
Qu'il ne m'est pas permis seulement de vous
    plaindre?

ANDRONIC.

Qu'entends-je! Juste ciel! de quoi m'accusez-vous?
Madame, qu'ai-je fait digne de ce courroux?
Viens-je vous demander que d'un œil pitoyable
Vous donniez quelques pleurs au malheur qui
    m'accable?

Since thou art ready now to leave Byzantium,
Couldst thou not go still innocent of wrong?
Hast thou forgotten that a solemn vow
Imposes on us, both, eternal silence;
That no more talk between us is legitimate;
That one word, one glance, one sigh is a crime;
That, ever careful to perform my duty,
I staked my honor nevermore to see thee;
And be whate'er they may the ills thou facest,
That I can do nothing but pity thee?

ANDRONICUS.

What do I hear? Just heaven! of what dost thou
Accuse me, madam? What have I done deserving
This anger? Do I come to thee to ask
That thou shouldst give some tears from sorrowing eyes
To the woes that crush me? Do I come to thee

Viens-je vous demander que vous me permettiez,
Puisqu'il me faut mourir, d'expirer à vous pieds?
Ah! de votre repos plus jaloux que vous-même,
J'ai soin de m'exiler, parceque je vous aime.
Pardonnez-moi ce mot pour la dernière fois;
Et songez que je pars sans attendre vos lois;
Qu'en vain à me bannir vous étiez résolue,
Puisque déjà mon cœur vous avait prévenue.
Depuis le jour fatal qu'arrachée à ma foi,
Madame, vous viviez pour un autre que moi,
Quoique toujours brûlé jusques au fond de l'âme,
Vous savez si mes yeux ont parlé de ma flamme;
Si le moindre transport, un indiscret soupir,
Vous ont fait soupconner quelque injuste désir.
Tout a gardé, madame, un rigoureux silence:
Mais un cœur n'est point fait pour tant de violence.
Je sais tous les combats qu'il me faudrait livrer,

To ask thee to allow me, since I needs
Must die, to perish at thy feet? More jealous
For thy peace than art thou, I have taken pains
To exile mine own self, because I love thee.
Forgive my saying those words, for the last time.
Note well that I awaited not thy bidding
To go,—that thou hast needlessly resolved
To banish me, because I have already
Anticipated thy decision. Since
That fatal day when thou, torn from me, madam,
Gavest thy life to someone else, although
Love's flame hath ever burned deep in my heart,
Thou knowest if mine eyes have spoken of it;
If the least sign, if an imprudent sigh,
Hath caused thee to suspect some wrong desire.
I have in all respects kept strictly silent.
   But human hearts are not made to be done
Such violence. I well know all the struggles
Of which I needs must be the prey if under

Si sous un même ciel nous osions respirer.
Je sais enfin, je sais tout ce que pourraient dire
Vos ennemis, les miens, peut-être tout l'empire:
Ils ont su mon amour, et doivent présumer
Que qui vous aime un jour doit toujours vous
    aimer;
Peut-être oseraient-ils soupçonner l'un et l'autre:
Sauvons de leurs soupçons et ma gloire et la vôtre.
Je cherche à m'éloigner; vous, pressez l'empereur
D'accorder à mes vœux cette unique faveur.
Heureux si par vos soins mon attente est remplie!
J'irai des révoltés apaiser la furie;
Ils me veulent pour chef, et je ne doute pas
Que je ne sois bientôt maître dans leurs états;
Qu'au gré de mes désirs leur valeur toujours prête,
Ils n'entreprennent tout, si je marche à leur tête.
Je viens donc vous offrir leurs armes, mon pouvoir.
Le ciel qui me condamne à ne jamais vous voir,

The same sky we should dare to breathe. I know,
I know only too well, all that thy foes,
And mine, and the whole realm, mayhap, might say.
They have known I loved thee, and should know that he
Who loves thee for one day must love thee always.
They would perchance dare to suspect us both.
Let us save from suspicion my fair fame
And thine. I seek to go away. Urge thou
The Emperor to grant me this one favor.
Ah, joy, if by thy help mine aim succeeds!
  I go to appease the rage of some insurgents.
They want me as their chieftain, and I doubt not
That I shall soon be master in their lands,
That, with their valor ever prompt to serve
My wishes, there is nothing which they will
Not undertake, if I march at their head.
I come to offer thee their swords, my power.
Heaven, which condemns me ne'er again to see thee,

Qui me fait étouffer une flamme si belle,
Ne saurait pour le moins s'offenser de mon zèle.
S'il défend à mon cœur des sentiments trop doux,
Il permet à mon bras de combattre pour vous;
Et si jamais ce bras vous était nécessaire,
Ou pour aller servir l'empereur votre père,
Ou pour faire périr, ou chasser de ces lieux
Ceux de qui la présence y peut blesser vos yeux,
Appelez-moi, madame, et je pourrai tout faire.
Je ne veux que la gloire ou la mort pour salaire:
A vous donner mon sang je borne mon bonheur,
Puisqu'il m'est défendu de vous donner mon cœur.

IRÈNE.

En vain vous me flattez de ces fameux services:
Mes vœux n'aspirent point à ces grands sacrifices.
Quand vous aurez quitté ce funeste séjour,
Qu'aurai-je à craindre encor, prince, dans cette
    cour?

Which bids me to suppress a love so fair,
At least can in such zeal find no offense.
If it forbids my heart thoughts all too sweet,
It lets mine arm do battle for thy sake!
And if that arm should e'er be needed by thee,
Either to go to serve the Emperor
Thy father, or to slay or to drive hence
Any whose presence here offends thine eyes,
Summon me, madam; and I can do all this.
I wish but honor or death for my reward.
I seek no blessing save to give my blood
To thee, since 'tis forbidden me to give thee
My heart.

IRENE.

Thou vainly flatterest me with these
Distinguished services. My wishes do not
Aspire to such great sacrifices. When thou
Hast left this baneful place, what shall I have

Hélas! j'y verrai tout avec indifférence.
M'exercer aux vertus dignes de ma naissance;
Accoutumer mon cœur, trop souvent mutiné,
A chérir un époux que le ciel m'a donné;
Obéir à ses lois; ne songer qu'à lui plaire;
Me sacrifier toute à mon devoir sévère;
Soulager les sujets qui vivent sous ma loi:
Voilà jusqu'à la mort quel sera mon emploi.
J'avouerai cependant, et je le puis sans crime,
Que vous aurez toujours ma plus parfaite estime;
Que pour vous applaudir, pour louer vos exploits,
Je joindrai mon suffrage à la commune voix;
Que pour tous mes plaisirs, le seul que j'imagine,
C'est de voir les hauts faits où le ciel vous destine,
Et de votre grand nom cent monarques jaloux,
Justifier le choix que j'avais fait de vous.
Après cela, partez. A votre exil fidèle,
Ne revenez jamais que je ne vous rappelle.

Further to fear, Prince, in this Court? Alas!
I shall see all here with indifference.
To practice virtues worthy of my birth,
Accustom my too oft rebellious heart
To cherish a husband given me by heaven,
Obey his hest, seek only how to please him,
Wholly devote myself to my stern duty,
Lighten those subjects' lot whose lives I rule—
That will be mine employment till I die.
Yet I confess (and without sin I can)
That thou wilt always have my highest esteem,—
That to commend thee and to praise thine exploits,
Unto the general voice I shall add mine,—
That all my joy, the only one I picture,
Will be to see the great deeds for which heaven
Destines thee, and a hundred monarchs' envy
Prove right the choice which I had made of thee.
  After this, go. Stay faithfully in exile,
Nor e'er come back unless I should recall thee.

Faites-vous un bonheur sous de nouveaux climats,
Qu'aux lieux où je serais vous ne trouveriez pas.

ANDRONIC.

Est-il temps ? Ce bonheur dont vous flattez mon
    âme,
Hélas! en vous perdant je l'ai perdu, madame!
Et je n'en connais plus où je puisse aspirer:
Cette perte est un coup qu'on ne peut réparer.
Si quelque soin encore occupe mon courage,
C'est de faire rougir le destin qui m'outrage;
D'apprendre à l'univers, par quelque illustre effort,
Qu'un cœur comme le mien mérite un autre sort:
Et, payant de mon sang ma première victoire,
D'élever de mes maux un trophée à ma gloire.
Vous, cependant, madame, oubliez mes malheurs;
Et tandis que, nourris de soupirs et de pleurs,
Mes déplorables jours vont courir à leur terme,
Régnez, et . . .

Achieve a happiness in other climes
Which thou wouldst never find where I would be.

ANDRONICUS.

E'en yet? This happiness thou paintest to me—
Alas! in losing thee I have lost it, madam!
And I no longer know where I can seek it;
My loss is one which I cannot repair.
If any purpose still is in my soul,
It is to put injurious Fate to shame;
To show the world by some illustrious act
That hearts like mine deserve a different lot,
And, buying my first victory with my blood,
Make from my wrongs a monument to mine honor.
Do thou forget, however, my misfortunes,
Madam, and while my lamentable days,
Nourished with sighs and tears, speed towards their end,
Reign, and . . .

IRÈNE.

Croyez-vous ma constance si ferme?
Ce reproche cruel, plus que tous vos regrets,
Etonne mon courage et confond mes projets.
Ah, prince! pensez-vous qu'insensible, inhumaine,
Mes yeux sans s'émouvoir regardent votre peine?
Que pendant les horreurs d'un exil rigoureux,
Vous soyez seul à plaindre et le seul malheureux?
Mais que dis-je! où m'entraîne une force inconnue!
Ah! pourquoi venez-vous chercher encor ma vue!
Partez, prince, c'est trop prolonger vos adieux.

Their parting has lasted too long, indeed; at this moment
the Emperor enters, and he observes their perturbation.
Irene explains that Andronicus was asking her to second
his petition to be sent to deal with the Bulgarians—whereupon the Emperor turns to him sternly:

Je vous ai dit tantôt, moins en maître qu'en
    père,[24]
Que je n'approuvais point ce départ téméraire.

IRENE.

Dost think my fortitude so great?
This cruel slur, more than all of thy repinings,
Dismays my courage and confounds my purpose.
Ah, Prince! supposest thou that inhuman, heartless,
I look unmoved upon thy pain,—that midst
The horrors of thine exile, thou alone
Art to be pitied and art alone unhappy?
But what say I? Where doth some power sweep me?
Oh, why didst come again, trying to see me?
Go, Prince. Too long have lasted our farewells.

[24] I told thee, more as father than as ruler,
    That I approved not of this rash forth-faring.

C'en était trop, je crois, pour vous persuader
Que vous m'offenseriez à la redemander.
Mais puisque malgré moi, puisque, sans com-
plaisance,
Vous me parlez encor d'un projet qui m'offense,
Ne vous étonnez pas de mon juste refus.

ANDRONIC.

Ah, seigneur! voulez-vous . . . ?

L'EMPEREUR.

Ne me répiquez plus.
Songez à m'obéir d'une âme plus soumise.
Dans un profond oubli laissons cette entreprise,
Et ne fomentez point des soupçons dangereux
Dont nous pourrions un jour nous repentir tous
deux.

ANDRONIC.

Eh bien, seigneur, je sors: mais c'est trop me
contraindre;

'Twas overmuch, I think, to have convinced thee
That thou'dst displease me by its further mention;
But since despite me, since unduteously,
Thou askest me again for what offends me,
Do not, then, wonder at my just refusal.

ANDRONICUS.

Ah, sire! wouldst thou . . .

THE EMPEROR.

Reply to me no further.
Learn to obey me with a more submissive
Spirit. Let us forget this enterprise
And give no food to dangerous suspicions
Of which we both hereafter might repent.

ANDRONICUS.

Very well, sire; I take leave of thy presence.

Dans l'état où je suis je ne saurais plus feindre;
Et d'un si dur refus les perfides auteurs
Me pourraient bien un jour payer tous mes
    malheurs.

[Exit ANDRONIC.

L'EMPEREUR.

Quelle témérité! quel discours! quelle audace!
A mes yeux . . . !

LÉON.

Vous voyez, seigneur, qu'il nous menace.

Leo and Marcenus tell the Emperor that Andronicus' intention is to march in arms against him at the head of the rebels; and he himself begins to suspect the relations between his son and Irene. He gives orders that the Prince shall be carefully watched.

Andronicus is more determined than ever to escape. Bitterly he sums up his plight:

On me prive à jamais de tout ce que j'adore;[25]

But thou imposest too much constraint on me.
I can no longer feign in such a plight,
And the instigators of thy harsh refusal
May yet for all my sorrows pay me dearly.

[Exit ANDRONICUS.

THE EMPEROR.

What words! What boldness! What audacity!
Before my face . . .

LEO.

Thou seest, sir, how he threatens us.

[25] I lose forever all that I adore.

Je vois dans la splendeur deux hommes que
    j'abhorre,
Dont l'injuste pouvoir, à me nuire obstiné,
Me rend presque odieux le sang dont je suis né.
Malgré tant de raisons, malgré tant de contrainte,
Laissé-je un seul moment échapper quelque plainte?
J'étouffe mes soupirs, j'étouffe mes regrets:
Je ne punis que moi des maux que l'on m'a faits;
Et, nourrissant mon cœur de ma mélancholie,
D'un malheur éternel j'empoisonne ma vie.
Enfin, lassé de voir des objets si cruels,
Pour m'épargner des coups ou des vœux criminels,
Moins soigneux de mes jours que de mon innocence,
Je demande par grâce à partir de Byzance,
Et d'aller exercer mon courage et mon bras
A soumettre, à calmer de rebelles états:
On me refuse encor l'emploi que je demande;
On soupçonne ma foi, je vois qu'on m'appréhende;

I see raised high two men whom I detest,
*Both bent on injuring me; their wicked power
Makes me loathe, almost, mine own parentage.
Despite so many grounds, so much coercion,
Have I once let some plaint escape from me?
My sighs I stifle, my regrets I stifle;
I punish but myself for evils done me;
And as my heart feeds on its melancholy,
My life is poisoned by my eternal sorrow.
At last, now, tired of seeing things so cruel,
To fly from deeds or wishes that are wrong,
Of life less careful than of my innocence,
I ask to leave Byzantium, as a favor,
And to go try my courage and my arm
To subjugate and pacify some lands
That have rebelled. The employment which I ask for
Is still refused me; my own loyalty
Is doubted, and I see that I am feared.

On m'impute à forfait le soin de m'éloigner;
On me croit dévoré de l'ardeur de régner,
Et tout prêt de tenter, par un orgueil extrême,
Ce que je n'ai point fait en perdant ce que j'aime.
Sur ces fausses raisons on me retient ici:
Je vois contre mes pleurs qu'un père est endurci;
Je vois mes ennemis triompher de ma peine;
On me lie à mes maux d'une plus forte chaîne.

He bids farewell to the home in which he grew to manhood,
invoking its protection of Irene:

O vous dont si longtemps j'ai chéri la présence,[26]
Lieux à mes vœux si doux, sacrés murs de Byzance,
Palais de mes aïeux où je reçus le jour,
Je me prive à jamais de votre heureux séjour,
Je fuis: mais en partant mon amour vous confie
Un trésor à mes yeux bien plus cher que ma vie;
Heureux dans votre sein de pouvoir l'enfermer!

My wish to go away is laid to criminal
Intentions. I am thought consumed with longings
To reign, and ready to attempt, through pride's
Excess, that which I did not even do
When robbed of her I loved. For these false reasons
I am kept here. I see my father harden
His heart against my tears. I see my foes
Triumphing o'er me in my anguish. They
Have bound me to my woes with stronger chains.

[26] O places where so long I loved to dwell,
   Dear to my heart, Byzantium's hallowed walls,
   The palace of my fathers, where I first
   Beheld the light of day, I rob myself
   Forever of your blest abode. I flee.
   But when I go, my love entrusts to you
   A treasure dearer far to me than life.
   Yea, blest are ye to hold her in your close!

Je l'aime, je l'adore, et ne l'ose nommer.
Pour lui plaire, à l'envi redoublez tous vos charmes;
Voyez couler ses jours sans trouble, sans alarmes;
Et, le ciel sur moi seul épuisant ses rigueurs,
Puissiez-vous n'être plus les témoins de ses pleurs!

But in the moment of departure he is apprehended; his
sword, when he tries to kill himself, is torn from him; and
he is led away, under guard. Irene's attempt to dissuade
the Emperor from extreme measures only serves to strength-
en the suspicions of that mistrustful monarch:

IRÈNE.[27]

A cet excès pousser votre colère,
Quelle horreur!...
Peut-être j'en dis trop; mais mon zèle, seigneur,
Ne tend qu'à prévenir un repentir vengeur,
Qu'à vous sauver enfin d'une indigne mémoire.

L'EMPEREUR.

Madame, c'est assez, j'aurai soin de ma gloire.
Je vois ce que prétend ce zèle officieux

I love, I worship, and I dare not name her. . . .
To give her pleasure, double all your charms.
See her days pass untroubled, unafraid.
May heaven expend on me alone its harshness,
And may ye nevermore behold her tears.

[27] IRENE.
To push thy wrath to this excess—
How horrible!...
I may have said too much, sir; but my zeal
Seeks only to prevent thy keen remorse
And save from all unworthiness thy memory.

THE EMPEROR.
Madam, that is enough. I can take care
Of mine own honor. I see what is the meaning

Qui vient en ce moment d'éclater à mes yeux;
Je connais votre cœur, je sais tout ce qu'il pense.
Allons . . .

The Prince considers his execution a virtual certainty,
but a letter from Irene begging him to make every possible
effort to save his life persuades him to do what in his pride
he had sworn that he would not do: appeal to his father for
clemency. The interview between sire and son is perhaps
the most specifically dramatic scene in this too elegiac play.
Andronicus, as always, has not the tact and shrewdness
needed to gain his ends. "Do not crush me; I am desperately
unhappy, and I am your son; you owe compassion to your
son"—such is the substance of his pleas: in short, even when
he is most abject, a claim that he has a right to benignity
from his father; there is not the slightest protestation of
affection, nor, on the other hand, is there any reasoned
argument that he is innocent, instead of a mere denial of
guilt. The Emperor, on his side, desires above all things
that his son, ever intractable, shall be completely humbled
before him. "Will he fall down at my feet?" he says to
himself when he first enters the room; and when he finally
does see him kneel, he cannot at once declare him pardoned
but must preserve an inexorable harshness to savor the
situation for a moment longer—a moment too long, as it
proves.

L'EMPEREUR.[28]
Prince, n'avez-vous rien à me dire de plus?

Of this officious zeal which has been just
Displayed before mine eyes. I know thy heart;
I know its every thought. Come . . .

[28] THE EMPEROR.
Prince, hast thou nothing more to say to me?

ANDRONIC.

Non; d'en avoir tant dit je suis même confus.
Ah! ce n'est point l'horreur du coup qui me menace
Qui m'a fait mendier une honteuse grâce;
Et mon cœur en effet n'attendait pas de vous
Après tant de rigueurs un traitement plus doux.
Je sais trop que pour moi vous êtes insensible,
Et la mort à mes yeux n'offre rien de terrible:
Si l'on ne m'eût contraint à cet indigne effort . . .

L'EMPEREUR.

C'est assez, je t'entends.

ANDRONIC.

      Ordonnez de mon sort.
Hâtez le coup fatal d'une lente justice;
La vie est désormais mon plus cruel supplice;
Et je mourrais bientôt de honte et de regret

ANDRONICUS.

No. To have said so much makes me ashamed.
Ah! 'twas no horror of what threatens me
Which has abased me thus to beg for mercy,
And I did not indeed expect from thee,
After such sternness, any kindlier treatment.
I know well that thy heart is hard towards me,
And death has nothing terrible to show me.
If someone had not made me make this effort . . .

THE EMPEROR.

Enough! I understand thee.

ANDRONICUS.

      Sentence me.
Hasten the fatal blow of tardy justice.
Life is henceforth my cruelest punishment,
And I would soon die of regret and shame

De m'être à vos genoux abaissé sans effet.

[*Exit* ANDRONIC.

Andronicus' reference to the letter which prevailed on him to ask for mercy removes the Emperor's last doubt that Irene loves his son, and thus seals the doom of both. With this assured at the end of Act IV and what small tension the play has hitherto possessed now relaxed, the final act decidedly drags. It is devoted to the last reflections of the Prince, which add little to what he has said already, an account of his death—given the choice of its manner, he has his veins opened in a bath, in the old Roman fashion—and Irene's sorrows and fate. She drinks poison, and, as she nears her end, summons her husband and makes him hear the truth:

Ni votre fils, ni moi, jusqu'au dernier soupir,[29]
N'avons jamais formé de criminel désir.
Il partait pour me fuir; à mon devoir fidèle,
Mon cœur lui prescrivait une absence éternelle.
C'est dans ce même temps qu'un sacrifice affreux
A vos tristes soupçons nous immole tous deux.

.   .   .   .

Je ne vous dis plus rien. J'ai consommé mon sort;

That I have humbly kneeled to thee in vain.

[*Exit* ANDRONICUS.

[29] Neither thy son nor I, till our last breath,
Has ever had a criminal desire.
His going was to flee me. With a duteous
Heart, I imposed on him eternal absence.
'Twas then that both of us were sacrificed
Horribly to thy miserable suspicions.

.   .   .   .

I say no more. I have fulfilled my lot.

Je passe sans regret dans les bras de la mort,
Puisqu'elle rompt les nœuds de l'hymen qui nous
    lie.

This is a strong note near the close. The Emperor's sudden qualm, which follows it and concludes the play, is an unfortunate, but fortunately brief, epilogue.[30]

"*Tiridate* had a prodigious and to us inexplicable success," says Arthur Tilley[31]—merely translating Bernardin's statement that it "*remporta un succès prodigieux et qui nous paraît aujourd'hui inexplicable,*" to which is added the dictum that it is perhaps the most insipid (*fade*) of Campistron's tragedies.[32] Encountering such opinions, one cannot but wonder whether these critics really ever read *Tiridate*. For though its verse is no doubt of somewhat greater insipidity than that of *Andronic,* and though its excellence is less well sustained and its characterization less subtle, its best scenes are more dramatic, more vigorous, and more interesting, and its fifth act, instead of being the weakest as in the case of *Andronic,* is one of its best as a whole—perhaps its only act that contains no serious flaw. Lancaster was thoroughly justified in praising both plays in the same breath, while he agrees with the general verdict that, of the two, *Tiridate* is the inferior.

The subject of this tragedy is the incestuous love of a young prince for his sister. Campistron asserts in his Preface

---

I pass without regret into death's arms,
Because it breaks the marriage-bonds that join us.

[30] Bernardin (in Petit de Julleville's *Histoire de la Langue et de la Littérature française,* vol. v, p. 147) says that the fifth act of *Andronic* is "*d'une gaucherie ridicule.*" But though it is indeed weaker and less interesting than the earlier acts, I can see no maladroitness in it flagrant enough to be called "ridiculous."

[31] *The Decline of the Age of Louis XIV,* Cambridge, 1929, p. 75.

[32] *Op. cit.,* vol. v, p. 146.

that "the most extraordinary emotions are the most effective
on the stage, provided their portrayal is veracious and properly tempered." [33] Such doctrine is of course characteristic
of a period of dramatic decadence, and *Tiridate* naturally
brings to mind the famous treatment of incest between a
brother and sister in decadent Elizabethan drama, Ford's
'Tis Pity She's a Whore. There are certain similarities but
also great differences between these two plays.

Both tragedies contain good work and bad, side by side;
in both, the main theme is entangled with subordinate issues,
and it is in the scenes dealing with these that the chief defects occur, whereas the part devoted to the hero's perverse
infatuation is in general distinctly better than the rest of
the play. In Campistron's drama Tiridates, who is the eldest
son of Arsaces, King of Parthia, is engaged to Thalestris,
the Queen of Cilicia, who loves him and is waiting at the
Parthian court to be married to him; he has repeatedly put
off the wedding, and his gloom and anguish of mind are a
mystery visible to all. His sister, Erinice, is being wooed
by a distant relative, Abradatas; and Tiridates violently
opposes their union, professedly because this suitor is not
a king. Now, not only are Abradatas and Erinice the conventional lovers, so commonly found in the tragedies of the
period, who will die if their wishes are disappointed; actually, when Abradatas is informed that Arsaces has decided, in view of his son's condition, to postpone their marriage for a few days, *though with this news comes also the
King's assurance that Erinice shall certainly be his,* he forthwith exclaims:

Je n'espère plus rien. . . .[34]

[33] *Les sentiments les plus extraordinaires sont ceux qui réus-
sissent le plus sur la scène, pourvu qu'ils soient justes et adoucis.*

[34] I have no more hope. . . .

Trahi de tous côtés, il ne me reste plus
Qu'à terminer des jours désormais superflus;
On me hait, on m'accable, et je me hais moi-même.

These silly "transports" are followed not long afterwards
by a piece of conventional bad psychology in the portrayal
of Tiridates himself: he thinks of his old friendship with
Abradatas and resolves to compel himself to be kind to
him, but at the sight of the man his aversion immediately
flares up anew. Of course his natural reaction, when he
first sees his former comrade thus alone, dissociated from
Erinice, would be favorable to him, instead of the reverse—
but an abrupt change of his mood on the appearance of "his
rival" was theatrically effective clap-trap.

On the other hand, the incestuous passion of the Prince
is treated with no little subtlety and forcefulness—and,
it scarce need be added, with the delicacy which rarely fails
a French author even when writing about the most difficult
of subjects. Tiridates does not justify or indulge his criminal love like Ford's Giovanni; he fights against it always,
with all his strength; his moral perceptions are never destroyed; and when at last he betrays his heart's heinous
secret, he promptly kills himself. Hence he is more like
another Elizabethan hero in supposedly similar plight, Beaumont's Arbaces in *A King and No King*. These lines to his
friend, Mithranes, who begs to be told the cause of his
misery, are quite in Arbaces' vein:

Ah! que plutôt des Dieux le pouvoir redoutable,[35]

Nothing is left me, on all sides betrayed,
Except to end my life, henceforth quite useless.
They hate me, crush me, and I hate myself.

[35] Ah, rather may the gods' dread power, to hide

Pour dérober à tous ce secret effroyable,
Obscurcisse à jamais ce soleil qui nous luit,
Et couvre l'univers d'une éternelle nuit!
Je ne sais quel forfait irrite leur justice;
Je crains, en te parlant, de t'en rendre complice:
Mais de tout leur pouvoir leur courroux soutenu,
Punit sans doute en moi quelque crime inconnu,
En laissant concevoir à mon âme parjure
Mille injustes projets dont frémit la nature;
Mille indignes transports, mille horribles désirs,
Qui font en même temps mes maux et mes plaisirs,
Que ma vertu combat, et jamais ne surmonte,
Et dont ma mort ne peut assez cacher la honte.

So are the lines which preface his terrible disclosure:

Je vais, par cet aveu, perdre ton amitié;[36]
Tu me refuseras jusques à ta pitié:
Indigné, tu fuiras ma vue abominable;

and so are his repinings:

From all men's eyes this fearful secret, darken
For evermore the sun which gives us light
And shroud the world in an eternal night!
I know not what ill deed hath vexed their justice—
I fear in speaking to thee to involve thee
Herein—but all their power serves their wrath
To punish me for some unknown-of sin
By letting in my recreant soul be born
Thousands of vile thoughts whereat Nature trembles,
Wicked emotions, horrible desires,
Which are at once my woe and my delight,
'Gainst which my virtue struggles, but ne'er triumphs,
Nor can my death enough conceal their shame.

[36] I shall by this confession lose thy friendship;
Thou wilt not even let me have thy pity;
Shocked, thou wilt flee from mine abhorrèd sight.

Il m'est donc défendu de couronner ma sœur? [37]
Et je puis élever une esclave à l'empire,
Sans qu'une loi barbare ose me contredire!

and:

Hélas! pourquoi le sort impitoyable[38]
Forma-t-il entre nous ce lien qui m'accable?
Pourquoi d'un même sang, et dans les mêmes lieux,
Nous fit-il recevoir la lumière des cieux?
Et pourquoi dans le sein d'une terre étrangère,
Inconnue à l'Asie, inconnue à mon père,
Où vos divins appas auraient pu se cacher,
Ne me permit-il pas de vous aller chercher?

No account of the origin of his aberration is given—this is decidedly a fault in the play—but according to Thalestris its effects were first apparent some six months earlier, which would seem to have been about the time when he returned victorious from the wars; and we may conjecture that these had lasted for several years, and that during his absence Erinice had grown up and become possessed of her remarkable beauty, which was evidently, as many passages indicate, the chief cause of his undoing. Really excellent is

[37] Is it, then, forbidden me to crown my sister?
And I can raise a slave-girl to the throne,
With no cruel law daring to say me nay!

[38] Alas! wherefore hath pitiless Fate
Formed between us this tie which breaks my heart?
Wherefore of one blood and in one same place
Were we first made to see the light of day?
And wherefore in the heart of a strange land—
Unknown to Asia, unknown to my father—
In which thy loveliness divine could hide,
Was it not granted me to come to seek thee?

the scene in which Tiridates reveals the horrible truth about
himself to his friend; excellent, too, the first scene between
the brother and sister, in which he almost reveals it to her,
especially in the last line when, half-fainting, he repulses
her efforts to assist him from the room, ". . . Si vous
m'aimez, ne me secourez pas!" [39] showing his dread of
physical contact with her; and also their second scene together, in which he can keep his secret from her no longer—
a moral collapse well motivated by the strain of his interview with her lover just before, which added a final straw
to the burden that obviously he was bearing with more and
more difficulty. A really fine touch, for it is quite unexpected but very natural, appears in his cry to her,

> Vous voyez d'où partaient mes caprices? [40]
> Ainsi, justifiez toutes mes injustices,

where even in the first horror of having betrayed himself
he finds a desperate relief in being able to explain at last
why he has behaved as he has.

Erinice's shame and self-loathing, after she discovers
what feelings she has inspired, are another detail worthy
of high praise. The figure of Arsaces is effective throughout: a monarch with real dignity, yet a solicitous, kindly
father, he recalls Rotrou's Wenceslaus; he can be stirred to
righteous wrath when he learns of his son's abominable
passion, but is quick to forgive when he realizes how well
it was resisted and with what agonies atoned for. And when,
before he knows the whole truth about it, he offers to avenge
the humiliated Thalestris on Tiridates, the Cilician queen
has her one great moment:

[39] ". . . If thou lovest me, nay, do not help me!"

[40] Thou seest whence my caprices sprang?
Acquit me, thus, of all my past injustice,

ARSACE.[41]

Je ne suis plus son père.

TALESTIS.

Et moi, désespérée
De ses malheurs, des miens, des vôtres pénétrée,
Je suis toujours pour lui ce que je fus jadis,
Quand mes vœux se bornaient à l'hymen de ce fils.

. . . .

Souffrez que je le voie; et, s'il faut qu'il périsse,
Qu'il connaisse du moins que je lui rends justice;
Que, sans lui reprocher les pleurs que je répands,
Contre un père irrité seule je le défends . . .

There is nothing in *Tiridate*, however, that can compare
with the best scenes in Ford's *'Tis Pity*. Those have a power
and a beauty and a poignancy which are altogether beyond
any minor French dramatist, and which would, if sustained
throughout their author's work, have lifted him quite out
of the class of minor dramatists. On the other hand, there
is nothing in *Tiridate* that is as bad as the poorest parts of
'Tis Pity. But neither in his strength nor his weakness is
Ford any proper analogue for Campistron, despite the parallel which is obvious between these two plays. The real Eng-

---

[41] ARSACES.
I am no more his father.

THALESTRIS.
And I, hope gone,
With heart pierced by his woes and mine and thine—
I am always towards him what I was before,
When marriage with that son was my sole wish.

. . . .

Now let me see him, and if he must die
Let him at least know that I judge him justly,
And, not reproaching him for tears I shed,
Alone defend him 'gainst his angry sire . . .

lish analogue to Campistron is Shirley, "the last of the Elizabethans" as Campistron was the last prominent tragic dramatist of seventeenth-century France—if we do not count
La Fosse with his one notable play. True, even Shirley's
facile verse is poetically superior to Campistron's; almost
all the Elizabethans were poets to a degree to which the
minor French seventeenth-century dramatists, except Rotrou
and possibly Tristan l'Hermite, were not.[42] But both Shirley
and Campistron dexterously manipulated the dramatic material supplied them by their predecessors; they had a certain
amount of technical competence, but their work is obviously
imitative, is of the theater rather than of life, and has something essentially feminine about it. Shirley wrote nearly
forty dramatic productions, Campistron fifteen; but the
number of tragedies by each is almost the same (seven and
ten, respectively), and though Shirley's are only a small
part of his total corpus, some of his best plays are in that
field, two of which, *The Traitor* and *The Cardinal,* stand
out far above the rest, precisely as two of Campistron's do.
The French dramatist has no comparable achievement in
comedy, and his other tragedies deserve all the disparage-
ment that has been lavished upon them,[43] but *Andronic* and

[42] Poetically, a better analogue of Shirley would be Quinault.

[43] Lancaster speaks of *Arminius,* generally recognized as the
best—we should rather say "the least bad"—of them, as "a play of
love and patriotism, in which," he strangely states, "the latter element receives the greater emphasis" (*op. cit.,* Part IV, p. 248).
This is of course how it should be; for the hero of the play is that
famous German chieftain who destroyed the legions of Varus in
the Teutoburger forest. Of the second act, which contains a debate
in the manner of Corneille as to whether submission or resistance
to Rome is the better policy, Campistron was very proud; and it is
a fact that throughout his plays there are passages which show a
grasp of situation and human nature that might have carried him
far if he had lived in more propitious times. But the Arminius
whom he depicts is engaged to Ismenia, the daughter of another

even *Tiridate* are very much better than anything from the pen of Shirley.

German chief or "king," Segestus, who has gone over to the Roman side and now is determined to marry her to Varus instead. Into the camp of Segestus and Varus comes this Arminius, the most important figure in his people's opposition to Rome, and he will not heed Ismenia's warning that he should leave at once while flight is still possible; "he thinks of nothing but the love which guides him" ("Il s'abandonne entier à l'amour qui le guide"), for he and Ismenia are another pair who must needs die if they cannot wed. Seized by order of Segestus, but secretly released by Segestus' son, Sigismund, he is prepared to escape to his army near by, who await only his leadership to launch an attack; but Ismenia does not want them to launch it, because her father might be killed, and asks her lover if he would compel her to hate him. He vainly tries to reassure her:

> S'il se trouve au combat je veillerai sur lui,
> Moins jaloux mille fois d'emporter la victoire,
> Que de sauver ses jours aux dépens de ma gloire.

> (If he is in the fight, I will watch o'er him,
> Less anxious far to win the victory
> Than save his life, though at my glory's cost.)

"I forbid . . . ," she begins, as though her desires, in comparison with the effective prosecution of the war for her country's liberty, are of sovereign importance; and so they indeed appear to be, for Arminius begs her, "Revoke so cruel a command, or fear the evils which Rome prepares for us."—"I cannot consent. Let us talk no more of it."—"And I, I no more wish to go. I shall return to my imprisonment." That is how patriotism fares against love in this play.

However, Ismenia does change her mind, for purely personal reasons, and the Romans are defeated. Segestus is about to butcher his son, his daughter, and Arminius' sister (affianced to Sigismund, of course), when Arminius stops him—but bears no malice towards him.

> Je ne veux d'autres prix, je ne veux d'autre gloire,
> Que le charmant espoir d'être de vos amis,

Et le parfait bonheur de me voir votre fils.

(I wish no other prize, no other glory,
  Except the precious hope to be thy friend
  And the perfect bliss of seeing myself thy son.)

Virginie, about Appius Claudius and Virginia, is still poorer; it was Campistron's first play and shows this fact by its continual sacrifice of consistency, rationality, and everything else to secure momentary effects, and by its constant inanely bad choice of words. Lancaster calls it "a psychological tragedy" (*op. cit.,* Part IV, p. 246); but its many vicissitudes so fill it that there is little room for a study of Appius and little emphasis is placed on him. *Alcibiade,* though better than *Virginie,* is saturated with cloying gallantry. The rest of Campistron's plays are not even worthy of comment.

CHAPTER XVII

MANLIUS CAPITOLINUS

ANTOINE DE LA FOSSE was the author of four dramas, but whatever fame has been his derives solely from one of these, his *Manlius Capitolinus,* which is worthy of note for several reasons. It has considerable merit; La Harpe thought it and Rotrou's *Venceslas* the two best tragedies written by minor dramatists in seventeenth-century France. Appearing in 1698, it was the last French tragedy of any importance in that century. And it was the first French play known to have been based on an English play.

Its source was Otway's *Venice Preserved,* which somehow acquired and has largely maintained to this day the reputation of being vastly superior to all other Restoration tragedies—except, perhaps, Dryden's *All for Love*—though really there is little to choose between it and the rest of them.[1] The only rational explanation for the praise accorded *Venice Preserved* in modern times is that most of its admirers first encounter it after drearily perusing some of the other tragedies of the period, dealing with far-fetched, very exceptional situations, and are pleased at finding in it a theme which is, in essence, an excellent one, with broad human appeal and great emotional potentialities. But the finest subject matter in the world can be brought to naught by wretchedly bad workmanship.

Stated in barest outline, so as to show the opportunities it offered, this is the plot of *Venice Preserved.*[2] Jaffier, a young

---

[1] William Archer utterly demolishes its pretensions (*The Old Drama and the New,* New York, 1929, pp. 160-164), yet even his recital of its defects is far from complete.

[2] I use in part the succinct phraseology of Archer's synopsis of it.

Venetian gentleman, rescued Belvidera, the daughter of a senator named Priuli, from drowning; they fell in love, and she eventually eloped with him. Determined to support her "in the style to which she was accustomed," he has exhausted his modest means at the opening of the play, and his house and domestic goods are now seized by his creditors. He vainly appeals for assistance to his wife's unrelenting father. In his distress and desperation, he listens eagerly to the suggestion of his friend Pierre, a soldier with a grievance, that he shall join in a conspiracy that has been formed for the massacre of the Senate and the subversion of society. At a meeting of the conspirators, he encounters distrust, because of his marital connections, whereupon he gives them his wife as a hostage for his loyalty. But when she discovers the nature of their plot she persuades him to save the State and her father's life by turning informer on promise of pardon for himself and his associates. Except in regard to Jaffier, however, the Senate does not keep its word; and with two blows of his dagger he saves his friend from the shame and pain of death by torture, and shares his fate, while Belvidera first goes mad and then kills herself.

In its actual elaboration this promising material is completely spoiled. The earlier scenes of the play create no sympathy for Jaffier and his friend; Jaffier especially is presented as an abject, contemptible person. His delicate task of committing his wife to the keeping of the other conspirators could not have been discharged in a way that would shock and terrify her more; and his manner of revealing to her the object of the conspiracy is, of all possible ones, that which is most certain to dismay her.[3] Not less

---

[3] She says that he must tell her what is intended, or she will tell the Senate what she knows and suspects. He begins:

I've bound myself by all the strictest sacraments . . .
To kill thy father—

incredible is the behavior of her custodian, who instead of guarding her carefully, first attempts her honor with violence and then allows her to escape and rejoin her husband. When the conspirators next meet, Jaffier's deportment towards her would-be ravisher is grotesquely unnatural, as also is that of Pierre, who has been told of the outrage. From the plans outlined for the uprising, its purpose would seem to be not, as announced, the overthrow of the ruling classes but a general slaughter of the citizens and the destruction of the entire city.[4] The psychology of Jaffier in betraying his comrades is unconvincing: he does not temporarily believe this the right course and then sooner or later have a revulsion of feelings; he goes to the Senate protesting all the while that he is acting wrongly, but goes none the less—spell-bound, as it were, by Belvidera—and is in despair the very instant after he has given his information. But the climax of wanton and perverse ineptitude is to be found in Otway's handling of the betrayal itself. Jaffier is arrested while still on his way to the Senate-house, and hence still able to change his mind, so that his appearance before the civic authorities is not voluntary, as the dramatic situation demands that it be. He has a list of the conspirators written down, on his person; no one need bargain with him for their names; the paper can be seized.

"My father!" she cries, in horror; and Jaffier continues:

> Nay, the throats of the whole Senate
> Shall bleed . . . whilst thou, far off in safety,
> Smiling, shalt see the wonders of our daring,
> And when night comes, with praise and love receive me.

This is a fair sample of the imbecility which characterizes Otway's conduct of the scenes of his drama.

[4] The same criticism can be made of Ben Jonson's *Cataline*. Was Otway influenced by this earlier play about an attempted revolution?

The Senate has already learned, somehow, about the conspiracy and is in session regarding it when Jaffier enters, and he has hardly revealed who are the people concerned in it when they are brought in—arrested already, as a result of nothing that he has done! Further discussion of such a play would be useless; but mention, at least, should be made of what are perhaps the most flagrant of all its many faults: the constant unlifelike development of the details of the action and the inappositeness, rant, exaggeration, and inappropriate imagery of the dialogue, in which "not nature but robustious un-nature" was the goal of the dramatist. Also, there are scenes interpolated for "comic relief," depicting the senile lust of a fatuous old Senator, which are simply nauseating.

La Fosse fuses the story of *Venice Preserved* with Livy's account of the plotting and death of Manlius, the savior of the Capitoline Hill from the Gauls. In the resulting play the background is Roman, the personal relation of the characters to each other chiefly Otway's. In a number of brief passages, some of which are cited by Lancaster,[5] the French dramatist follows the text of his English source quite closely.

Almost at every turn he has improved on his model. True, in his play, the character who corresponds to Pierre becomes the titular hero; but Servilius, his analogue to Jaffier, still has the most prominent role, albeit the difference in the importance of the two friends in this play is less than in *Venice Preserved*. *Manlius Capitolinus* is in fact a tragedy of them both—of Manlius because, though shrewd and masterful, he was blinded by friendship; of Servilius because he was by nature weak and unstable, even if nothing like so much so as Jaffier.

[5] In his *History of French Dramatic Literature in the Seventeenth Century*, Part IV, pp. 389-390.

It is moreover true that the "tragic guilt" of Servilius is less overt than that of his prototype, and hence the moral issues are less clearly drawn in his case than in *Venice Preserved*. He did not betray, he never intended to betray, anyone or anything. His wife, Valeria, divined that there was a conspiracy against the State, taxed him with this, begged him to abandon it, and when she could not persuade him, herself struck a bargain with the Senate by which they were informed of the plot against them and in exchange agreed to pardon all the participants. Servilius' error lay only in his failure to deal effectively with the situation in which Valeria placed him. Confronted by her accusations, he weakly admitted everything, considering all denials useless in the face of her certitude; he neither took any steps himself to ensure her silence nor revealed to his fellows that she had become aware of their designs, for he feared for her life if the others should learn this fact and she promised that she would keep his secret. He was unwise, it proved, in trusting her word, especially as her father was one of those to be killed; but the young man's problem was an extremely difficult one, and La Fosse has posed it skilfully. The blurring of Servilius' guilt is more than compensated for by the increased respect and sympathy which he commands in this version of the story.

Indeed, the characters in *Manlius Capitolinus* are all of far greater dignity than those in *Venice Preserved*, and the details of the action are far more impressive. Servilius has rescued Valeria, not from drowning in a mere boat-accident, but from the Gauls during the sack of Rome. His offense against his wife's father was far greater than Jaffier's: he did not merely elope with her but carried her off from before the altar itself, where she was about to wed someone else by parental command; and her father, Valerius, had refused her to him for the excellent reason that she was already plighted to another, and had offered him as a bride her sister instead. A fugitive from Rome as a result of his high-handed course, at the opening of the play Servilius has returned there, with whatever risk to himself, upon learning that his friend Manlius is in serious trouble with the authorities; and he becomes a conspirator only after his property has been confiscated by the Senate in compliance with the wishes of his implacable father-in-law and he has thus, by no improvidence of his, been reduced to beggary.

As for Manlius, because of his past exploits he is an imposing figure—the hero of the Gauls' assault—and his affection for Servilius makes him an appealing figure also, whereas the attempt of Valerius, in the very first act, to persuade successively each of the two friends to renounce the other, tends to alienate one's sympathy from their adversaries and prepares one for the eventual perfidy of the government which Valerius represents. In that very perfidy, however, there is a difference from *Venice Preserved;* the revocation of the Senate's promise of amnesty is not wanton and general, but applies only to Manlius and Rutilus, the leaders of the conspiracy, who are considered too dangerous to be spared by men to whom no pledge is sacred when the safety of the State is involved. For Manlius has another side; his self-seeking ambition, his pride, his vengefulness, and his unscrupulous pretense of devotion to the cause of the people in their struggle against the ruling aristocracy are portrayed in his initial scene with his confidant, Albinus:

Justes dieux! quand viendra le temps d'exécuter? [6]
Quand pourrai-je à la fois punir tant d'injustices

[6] Just gods! when will the time of action come?
When can I punish all the wrongs at once

Dont ces tyrans de Rome ont payé mes services?
Oui, je rends grâce, Albin, à leur inimitié,
Qui, me débarrassant d'une vaine pitié,
Fait que de ma grandeur, sur leur perte fondée,
Sans scrupule aujourd'hui j'envisage l'idée.
Car enfin, dans mes vœux tant de fois démenti,
Quand du peuple contre eux j'embrassai le parti,
Je voulais seulement, leur montrant ma puissance,
A me mieux ménager contraindre leur prudence.
Mais, après les affronts dont ils m'ont fait rougir,
Ma fureur ne saurait trop tôt ni trop agir:
Je veux leur faire voir, par un éclat terrible,
A quel point Manlius au mépris est sensible;
Combien il importait de ne rien épargner,
Ou pour me perdre, Albin, ou bien pour me gagner.

Albinus warns him that the rabble are not to be depended
on; they had gathered to espouse his cause when he was
arrested, and then had not dared to do anything. Manlius
replies:

With which Rome's tyrants have repaid my service?
I thank their enmity, Albinus, which,
Divesting me of useless pity, makes me
Able to envisage without qualms today
The thought of building upon their destruction
My greatness. For indeed, when I, so often
Cheated of my desires, espoused the cause
Of the populace against them, I wished only,
By showing them my power, to contrive
To teach them to behave more prudently
Towards me. But after the affronts wherewith
They have made my face burn scarlet, my rage cannot
Act either too soon or too much. I wish
To make them see, by one dread lightning bolt,
How ill does Manlius bear contumely,—
How vital 'twas, Albinus, to spare naught
To win me or, if not that, to destroy me,

Ils ont forcé du moins le sénat à me rendre.[7]
Leur repentir accroît leur zèle et mon espoir ;
Mes fers par eux brisés leur montrent leur pouvoir,
Et que, pour abolir une injuste puissance,
Tout le succès dépend de leur persévérance.
Car enfin, des efforts qu'ils ont faits jusqu'ici,
Souvent même sans chef, combien ont réussi !
Ils ont fait des tribuns, dont l'appui salutaire
A l'orgueil des consuls est un frein nécessaire ;
Aux plus nobles emplois on les voit appelés ;
Les plus fiers des Romains par eux sont exilés ;
Ils ont forcé les grands, en leur donnant leurs filles,
A souffrir avec eux l'union des familles ;
Ils se font partager les terres des vaincus ;
Et que faut-il, Albin, pour les faire oser plus,
Que leur montrer un chef dont les soins, le courage,
Soutiennent les efforts où l'ardeur les engage ?

[7] At least they forced the Senate to release me.
  Their zeal and my hope grow from their repentance.
  Breaking my chains revealed their power to them
  And this fact, that to end an unjust yoke
  Their whole success depends on perseverance.
  How many of the efforts they have made,
  Oft even without a leader, have succeeded !
  They have won tribunes, whose good aid supplied
  A needed curb unto the consuls' pride.
  They have been seen to engage in nobler tasks :
  The haughtiest Romans have been exiled by them ;
  They have compelled those of the highest station,
  In wedding with their daughters, to permit
  The union of their families thus with them.
  They have acquired a share in conquered land ;
  And what, Albinus, do they need to make them
  Dare more, except to show to them a leader
  Whose skill and courage will aid the undertakings
  In which their ardor may engage them ?

Here we behold a wealth of detail and allusion, giving a lifelike sense of background, which is usual indeed in Corneille and Racine, but can hardly be matched among the minor tragic dramatists of seventeenth-century France after Rotrou's *Cosroès*. The author's imbuement with his subject is most notable in the earlier acts of the play, but persists in a quite large measure throughout. It appears in the eloquent marshaling of arguments with which Valeria urges her husband to betray the conspiracy:

VALÉRIE.[8]

. . . Voulez-vous aujourd'hui qu'une heureuse industrie
Sauve tous vos amis, en sauvant la patrie?
Nous le pouvons, seigneur, sans danger, sans effort.
Votre amitié pourra s'en alarmer d'abord:
Mais l'honneur, le devoir, la pitié l'autorise.

SERVILIUS.

Comment?

VALÉRIE.

Il faut oser révéler l'entreprise,
Mais ne la révéler qu'après être assurés

---

[8] VALERIA.

. . . Wouldst thou today that a successful shift
To save thy country should save all thy friends?
It can, sir, without danger, and with ease.
Friendship may make thee shrink from it at first;
But honor, duty, pity authorize it.

SERVILIUS.

The means?

VALERIA.

We must disclose what is intended,
But not till we have been assured the Senate

Que le sénat pardonne à tous les conjurés.
Garanti par nos soins d'un affreux précipice,
Peut-il d'un moindre prix payer un tel service?

SERVILIUS.

Qu'entends-je, Valérie? et qui me croyez-vous?

VALÉRIE.

Tel qu'il faut être ici pour le salut de tous.
Je sais à vos amis quel serment vous engage,
Et vois tout l'embarras que votre âme envisage,
Quels noms dans leur colère ils pourront vous
    donner:
Mais un si vain égard doit-il vous étonner?
Est-ce un crime de rompre un serment téméraire,
Qu'a dicté la fureur, que le crime a fait faire?
Un juste repentir n'est-il donc plus permis?
Quoi! pour ne pas rougir devant quelques amis,
Que séduit et qu'entraîne une aveugle furie,

Will pardon all of the conspirators.
Saved by our efforts from a fearsome fate,
Can it with less reward repay such service?

SERVILIUS.

What do I hear? What thinkest thou me, Valeria?

VALERIA.

The man thou must be for the safety of all.
I know what pledges bind thee to thy friends.
I perceive all the plight which thou perceivest,
What names they in their rage may give to thee;
But should so trifling a consideration
Daunt thee? Is it wrong to break rash oaths
Which wrath has prompted, and which 'twas wrong to
    swear?
Is true repentance, then, no more permitted?
What! to avoid blushing before some friends
Seduced and carried away by their blind rage,

Vous aimez mieux rougir devant votre patrie!
Devant tout l'univers! Pouvez-vous justement
Entre ces deux partis balancer un moment?
De l'un et l'autre ici comprenez mieux la suite:
Si nous ne parlons pas, Rome est par eux détruite;
Si nous osons parler, quel malheur craignons-nous?
Rome entière est sauvée, et leur pardonne à tous;
Et quand, de ce bienfait consacrant la mémoire,
Elle retentira du bruit de votre gloire,
Parmi tous les honneurs qui vous seront rendus,
Leurs reproches alors seront-ils entendus?
Enfin, retracez-vous l'épouvantable image
De tant de cruautés où votre bras s'engage;
Figurez-vous, seigneur, qu'en ces affreux débris
Des enfants sous le fer vous entendez les cris;
Que, les cheveux épars et de larmes trempée,
Une mère sanglante aux bourreaux échappée,
Vient, vous montrant son fils qu'elle emporte en
    ses bras,

Thou wouldst prefer to blush before thy country!
Before the whole world! Canst thou reasonably
Waver one instant between these two courses?
See better now what must result from each.
If we do not speak, Rome will be destroyed.
If we dare speak, what evil can we fear?
All Rome is saved, and pardoneth all of them;
And when, remembering thy holy deed,
She makes resound the glorious story of it,
Midst all the honors which will unto thee
Be paid, will *their* reproaches then be heard?
Trace for thyself the terrifying picture
Of all the cruelties to which thou art sworn.
Conceive, sir, that amid the dreadful wreckage
Thou hearest the cries of children 'neath the sword-edge;
That with disheveled hair and tear-stained cheeks
A bleeding mother comes, fleeing her slayers,
To show to thee her son, whom in her arms

Se jeter à genoux au-devant de vos pas :
Votre fureur alors est-elle suspendue?
Un soldat inhumain l'immole à votre vue;
Et du fils aussitôt, dont il perce le flanc,
Fait rejaillir sur vous le lait avec le sang.
Soutiendrez-vous l'horreur que ce spectacle inspire?

A no less striking imaginative grasp of the situation is shown when Servilius, with characteristic fluctuable impulsiveness, admits to Manlius that he has revealed all— making no effort to extenuate his infamy, though he could truthfully have said that it was really his wife who was the informer, and that the conspirators' plan to slay even women and children in the senatorial families, so as to avoid all chance of subsequent reprisals, was a heinous barbarity which he had never anticipated when he became a party to the plot. Manlius is thunderstruck by his avowal:

MANLIUS.[9]

. . . Qui? toi? tu me trahis? L'ai-je bien entendu?

SERVILIUS.

Il est vrai, Manlius. Peut-être je l'ai dû.
Peut-être, plus tranquille, aurais-tu lieu de croire

She bears, and fall upon her knees before thee :
Is thy rage stayed then? an inhuman soldier
Kills her before thine eyes, and at the same time
Makes the blood of her son, whose side he pierces,
Spurt over thee together with her milk.
Wouldst thou endure the horror of this sight?

[9] MANLIUS.
. . . Who? thou? thou hast betrayed me? Heard I rightly?
SERVILIUS.
It is true, Manlius. 'Twas perhaps my duty.
Perhaps, when tranquil, thou'dst have grounds for thinking

Que sans moi tes desseins auraient flétri ta gloire.
Mais enfin les raisons qui frappent mon esprit
Ne sont pas des raisons à calmer ton dépit;
Et je compte pour rien que Rome favorable
Me déclare innocent quand tu me crois coupable.
Je viens donc, par ta main, expier mon forfait:
Frappe. De mon destin je meurs trop satisfait,
Puisque ma trahison, qui sauve ma patrie,
Te sauve en même temps et l'honneur et la vie.

MANLIUS.

Toi, me sauver la vie!

SERVILIUS.

Et même à tes amis.
A signer leur pardon le sénat s'est soumis:
Leurs jours sont assurés.

MANLIUS.

Et quel aveu, quel titre,

That without me thou wouldst have stained thine honor.
But still the reasons that have impressed my mind
Would not avail to allay thy bitterness,
And naught care I that Rome, approving, doth
Declare me innocent when thou deemest me guilty.
I come, then, at thy hands to expiate
My crime. Strike. I shall die content with my
Fate, since my treason, which hath saved my country,
Saves for thee at the same time life and honor.

MANLIUS.

Thou, save my life!

SERVILIUS.

And even thy friends' lives.
The Senate hath been forced to sign their pardon.
They all are safe.

MANLIUS.

And what consent, what warrant

De leur sort et du mien te rend ici l'arbitre?
Qui t'a dit que pour moi la vie eût tant d'attraits?
Qui veux-tu que je puisse en faire désormais?
Pour m'y voir des Romains le mépris et la fable?
Pour la perdre peut-être en un sort misérable,
Ou dans une querelle, en signalant ma foi,
Pour quelque ami nouveau, perfide comme toi?
Dieux! quand de toutes parts ma vive défiance
Jusqu'aux moindres périls portait ma prévoyance,
Par toi notre dessein devait être détruit,
Et par l'indigne objet dont l'amour t'a séduit!
Car, je n'en doute point, ton crime est son ouvrage,
Lâche, indigne Romain, qui né pour l'esclavage,
Sauves de fiers tyrans soigneux de t'outrager,
Et trahis des amis qui voulaient te venger!
Quel sera contre moi l'éclat de leur colère!
Je leur ai garanti ta foi ferme et sincère;
J'ai ri de leurs soupçons j'ai retenu leurs bras

Made thee the arbiter of their fate or mine?
Who told thee that life had such charms for me?
What wouldst thou I might henceforth do with it?
See myself here the Romans' scorn and byword?
Lose it perhaps in a most wretched lot
Or in a quarrel while showing confidence
In some new friend, perfidious like thee?
Gods! when at every point my wariness
Made me foresee the very smallest dangers,
By thee our purpose had to be defeated
And by the unworthy one whose love seduced thee!
For thy crime is her work, I have no doubt,
Thou base, unworthy Roman, born for slavery,
Who savest proud tyrants bent on wronging thee
And dost betray the friends that would avenge thee!
How fierce will burn their rage against me! I
Have guaranteed thy staunch fidelity,
Have laughed at their distrust, have stayed their hands

Qui t'allaient prévenir par ton juste trépas.
A leur sage conseil que n'ai-je pu me rendre!
Ton sang valait alors qu'on daignât le répandre;
Il aurait assuré l'effet de mon dessein:
Mais sans fruit maintenant il souillerait ma main;
Et trop vil à mes yeux pour laver ton offense,
Je laisse à tes remords le soin de ma vengeance.

The alien influence, perhaps not of *Venice Preserved* so much as of English drama in general to whatever extent La Fosse was acquainted with it, may be seen in two ways in *Manlius*—one good, one bad. Here for the first time, perhaps, we encounter in French tragedy a depiction of connubial love's growth and ripening with continued association. Valeria says to Servilius, when she learns that her father will not forgive them:

Quelques malheurs sur nous que le destin assemble,[10]
Nous souffrons, mais unis; nous fuyons, mais
    ensemble:
Tous lieux sont pleins d'attraits aux cœurs qui
    s'aiment bien.
Eh! peut-on être heureux, sans qu'il en coûte rien?

Which by thy deserved death would have forestalled thee.
Why could I not accept their wisdom's counsel?
Thy blood was worth the trouble, then, to shed it.
'Twould have assured my plans' accomplishment;
But now it fruitlessly would soil my hand,
And since it is too vile to wash out thine
Offense, I leave to thy remorse my vengeance.

[10] Whate'er misfortunes Fate assembles for us,
    United we shall suffer them; together
    We flee. All places have unnumbered charms
    For hearts that love each other truly. Ah,
    Can one be happy without any cost?

. . . .

Venez; que de ma foi la vôtre convaincue
Apprenne qu'avec vous mon cœur trouve en tous
    lieux
Sa gloire, son bonheur, sa patrie et ses dieux.

And he replies, with less conventionalism of thought than
of language:

Quel exil avec vous peut m'affliger encore? [11]
Quel bien me peut manquer? Je conserve pour vous
Tous les feux d'un amant dans le cœur d'un époux.
Que dis-je! vos beautés, vos vertus, dans mon âme
Allument de plus près une plus vive flamme;
Et mon cœur, chaque jour, surpris de tant d'attraits,
Voit toujours au-delà de ses derniers souhaits.

Genuinely moving is the scene in which he takes final
leave of her, to go and die with his friend. In his shock
of realization that she has brought this friend to such a
fate, he has even had a fleeting impulse to avenge him on
her, but now he speaks with all passion spent.

. . . .

Come; let thy love, convinced by mine, learn this:
With thee my heart finds everywhere its honor,
Its happiness, its country, and its gods.

[11] With thee what exile can afflict me further?
What blessing can I lack? I have for thee
A lover's fervor in a husband's breast.
What do I say? thy beauty and thy goodness,
Seen intimately, make my love flame higher;
And every day, enthralled by countless charms,
I always see more than mine utmost dreams.

SERVILIUS.[12]

    Ressouviens-toi de ce malheureux jour
Où la haine des dieux alluma notre amour.

VALÉRIE.

Malheureux! juste ciel!

SERVILIUS.

            Quoi! déjà ton courage . . .

VALÉRIE.

Et puis-je avec constance écouter ce langage?
Ainsi ce jour, témoin de ma félicité,
Est un jour malheureux, et par vous détesté!
Que votre amour, seigneur, dans ses transports sin-
    cères,
S'en souvenait, hélas! sous des noms bien con-
    traires!

SERVILIUS.

Cet amour insensé ne regardait que soi:

---

[12] SERVILIUS.
    Dost thou recollect that ill-starred day
On which the gods' hate kindled first our love?
          VALERIA.
Ill-starred? Just heaven!
          SERVILIUS.
    What! e'en now thy courage . . .
          VALERIA.
And can I hear without dismay such words?
So *that* day, which beheld my happiness,
Is now a day ill-starred and hateful to thee?
Alas, with names how different, sir, thy love
Recalled it in thy unfeigned ecstasies!
          SERVILIUS.
That mad love had no thought but of itself.

Il ne prévoyait pas les malheurs que sur toi
Déploieraient les destins depuis ce jour sinistre,
Et qu'il devait lui-même en être le ministre;
Qu'il te ferait quitter un sort tranquille, heureux,
Pour attacher tes jours à mon sort rigoureux;
Que par lui, que pour lui, tu te verrais réduite
Aux affronts de l'exil, aux travaux de la fuite;
Et qu'enfin aujourd-hui des transports inhumains
Contre ton propre sang exciteraient mes mains.

We are far from the conventions of gallantry here.

On the other hand, we find at times in *Manlius Capitolinus* a too-hurried development, an inadequacy of preparation or motivation, which is unfortunately common in Elizabethan and Restoration drama, but which is hardly paralleled hitherto in French tragedies between 1640 and 1700. The conduct of their dramatis personae is often fantastic if judged according to the ideas of people in other periods, but it is in keeping with their own ideas—with their concepts of *gloire* and romanesque love. They do not undertake anything, they do not change their minds or their purposes, without sufficient pressure of arguments or feelings or circumstances to make it appear natural, in view of the notions current in their world, for them to do so. Whatever the shortcomings of French-classical tragedy, until now it has con-

---

It ne'er foresaw the miseries that the Fates
Would bring on thee after that baleful day,
Nor that it was itself to be their agent;
That it would make thee leave thy tranquil, happy
Lot, to attach thy life to my grim fortunes;
That through it—for its sake—thou'dst undergo
The wrongs of exile, the hard toil of flight;
And that at last today my savage passions
Would against thine own blood incite my hands.

tained nothing analogous to the easy seduction of Heywood's Mrs. Frankford in *A Woman Killed with Kindness* or to Charalois' unregretful, almost casual "untwisting" of his "long web of friendship" with Romont in *The Fatal Dowry* of Massinger and Field. But we do find something of the sort in *Manlius*. Too precipitant, for instance, are the disclosure of the conspiracy to Servilius, the proposal that he shall join it, and his eager assent; they do not quite achieve verisimilitude.

The main blemish in this play, however, is the behavior of the conspirators in making a hostage of Valeria. It is, of course, nothing like so absurd as Otway's treatment of the corresponding part of his tragedy; a truly clever touch by La Fosse is the consignment of his heroine to the care of Manlius, who felt the whole ado about her to be entirely unnecessary and who hence might be expected to guard her very little, so that it does not appear unnatural that she had no difficulty whatever in seeing her husband or in negotiating with the Senate. But there was never any real need for Servilius to absent himself from her without an explanation or even a leave-taking; this was just the way to excite her suspicions; and though he himself, as portrayed, might have lacked the good sense to realize that fact, Manlius and Rutilus would assuredly have realized it and would have refused to agree to so foolish a course. The disaster that overtook them was altogether a result of the incredibly bad judgment which the author makes them exhibit at this point.

As the outcome hangs upon it, we have here, beyond question, a serious defect. *Manlius Capitolinus,* but for that, might have deserved the primacy ascribed to it by La Harpe; and even as it stands, it is a decidedly good play. Nowhere in its five acts does the interest flag; its characters are well drawn; its forceful, competently fashioned verse is probably superior to that of any other minor French dramatist between Quinault and Crébillon—if not, indeed, between

Rotrou and Voltaire. Its slight yet palpable, marring yet not ruinous, remove from reality is no greater in degree than that which we observe in the best romantic dramas of Beaumont and Fletcher, of which *A King and No King* is the most notable example; and though by no means equal in excellence to that finest of Elizabethan tragi-comedies, which far surpasses it in variety, picturesqueness, poetic beauty, and emotional power, *Manlius Capitolinus* is much worthier of comparison with it than with so botched an enormity as *Venice Preserved*.

CHAPTER XVIII

NEO-CLASSICAL TRAGEDY
IN THE EIGHTEENTH CENTURY

SOMEWHAT as D'Avenant is the link between Elizabethan and Restoration drama, La Grange-Chancel is the link between French-classical tragedy of the seventeenth century and of the eighteenth. Of his nine surviving plays,[1] the earliest was produced in 1694 and three others appeared before 1700; but his best ones, *Amasis* and *Ino et Mélicerte* were first acted in 1701 and 1713, respectively. Like Campistron he enjoyed some intimacy with Racine and considered himself a disciple—the last disciple—of the great dramatist and a continuer of his dramatic tradition. But he little resembled his professed model and master: as a poet he was inferior even to Campistron, filling his verses with clichés and frequently using lame or inexact phraseology for the sake of rhyme; and in several respects his tragedies anticipated the work of later playwrights.

He certainly was no disciple of Racine as regards simplicity of subject matter. He displayed a good deal of skill in the invention and handling of intricate plots. His *Amasis* is based on the old story of Merope, which was treated by Euripides, in a lost play, before him and by Voltaire and Alfieri after him, as well as by many others. He relocated it in ancient Egypt, renamed the characters, and introduced —not ineffectively—several complications. With him, a love affair of the rightful inheritor of the throne receives almost as much stress as the ordeal of the sorely tried mother. When he has exhausted all the possibilities for striking situ-

---

[1] His total seems to have been fourteen, of which the rest, including his only comedy, were never published.

ations, he brings his tragedy quickly to a close which is little dependent on the previous vicissitudes of the action. Yet he made a really much better play out of the Merope theme than did either of his more noted successors, and offended far less against rationality and human nature—though this, in truth, is no great praise, as we shall presently see.

Ino et Mélicerte, considered his next-best drama and the most typical of all, has a still more complicated plot. Indeed, in this respect it rivals Thomas Corneille's *Timocrate;* like *Timocrate* it makes scarcely any effort to distinguish the time or place of its setting—in this instance the world of Greek mythology, which was the usual source on which its author drew—and the credibility of its assumed circumstances will hardly better bear inspection. It is thus patently a specimen of romanesque tragedy yet is one of the best of that meretricious type. The involved situation which obtains at its outset is explained with remarkable succinctness, though the explanation is very poorly motivated; and thenceforth the action proceeds unflaggingly to its very end.

Aside from the banality of the verse, there is more vigor in these plays of La Grange-Chancel than in *Andronic* or *Tiridate;* but the characters that appear in them are not thoroughly conceived persons and do not arouse an interest in themselves like Campistron's Andronicus and the Emperor, Irene and Tiridates. The interest both in *Ino et Mélicerte* and in *Amasis* arises purely from the developments of the plot. Hence they are not properly tragedies at all, but melodramas, romanesque melodramas; one might almost call them romantic melodramas, for it has been remarked that La Grange-Chancel had the soul of a romantic dramatist, born more than a hundred years too soon.[2] The

[2] H. C. Lancaster, *A History of French Dramatic Literature in the Seventeenth Century,* Part V, p. 100.

people he depicts are as a rule entirely good or entirely bad.[3] And he frequently employs the stock melodramatic device of the *voix du sang,* that impulse of affection or attraction which one is alleged to feel towards one's unknown kindred; Pierre Corneille had made merry with it long before in *Héraclius* and *Don Sanche d'Aragon,* but it runs riot in eighteenth-century drama.

The chief names in French "classical" tragedy after 1700 are Crébillon and Voltaire. Both men enjoyed a contemporary and even a subsequent renown as dramatists which was out of all proportion to their actual achievement. As Renan said of John Stuart Mill, their apparent eminence "is largely due to the flatness of the surrounding country."

Crébillon attempted to excite horror in his audience, rather than terror as prescribed by Aristotle. He sought the "extraordinary" and the "atrocious," with such subjects as the revolting story of Atreus and Thyestes. He wrote, in all, ten tragedies, but he is remembered for only one of them, *Rhadamiste et Zénobie.* The story is told that when Racine's friend, the great critic Boileau, lay on his death-bed, someone read its first two scenes to him—whereupon: "Do you want to hasten my last hour?" he protested. "This is an author beside whom the Boyers and the Pradons are veritable luminaries." But La Harpe admired *Rhadamiste et Zénobie*

---

[3] An exception is Athamas in *Ino et Mélicerte.* His behavior, as represented, is that of a character of some complexity: a man who has been so possessed by ambition for the crown that he put away his beloved wife to marry a woman in alliance with whom he could obtain it, intending to pass it on to his son after him; and who then saw that dear first wife and that cherished son of theirs die (so he thought) as a result of his actions, while he found his second wife to be an evil, scheming woman, and who consequently was half mad with remorse. But the author did not write the lines which would reconcile Athamas' past misdeeds with his nature as exhibited in the play; hence he is a quite unconvincing figure.

greatly, declaring that only its opening act and the inferior poetic powers of Crébillon prevented it from standing among the best French tragedies; and it is still generally accorded some measure of respect, though with reservations.

In reality, its last act is quite as bad, in a different way, as its first; and its involved, far-fetched plot is sheer melodrama, without human values or any universal significance whatever, as a brief outline of the plot will show.

A clumsily introduced and not very clear exposition establishes the following facts. Pharasmanes, king of Iberia, and Mithridates, king of Armenia, were brothers. The former's son, Rhadamistus, was reared by the latter, who promised his daughter, Zenobia, to him. But the wicked Pharasmanes suddenly attacked Armenia in concert with Tiridates, the king of Parthia; and Mithridates, in desperate straits, tried to disrupt the alliance against him by offering Zenobia in marriage to Tiridates. Rhadamistus, enraged at the prospect of losing his betrothed, entered the war; he captured Mithridates and killed him, and then proceeded to wed Zenobia, who thought that her father was still living and would be saved by her marriage. But the truth about Mithridates' fate became known to the Armenian people; they rose in fury at such impious nuptials; Rhadamistus fled, bearing off his bride, and finally, overtaken in his flight and maddened by the prospect of Tiridates possessing her, stabbed her with his own hand and threw her into the Araxes river. She was supposed to have perished—and he, too, was universally believed to have been slain—but in reality she was rescued, and wandered incognita through Media, under the name of Ismenia, until she was brought, ten years later, as a prisoner of war to the capital of Iberia by Arsames, the younger son of Pharasmanes. The Prince loved her, and she secretly loved him; but Pharasmanes also became enamored of her. At this point the play begins—and all the antecedent action is tediously explained by Zenobia to her fellow captive and bosom friend, Phenice, who had never dreamed who she really was!

In Act II a Roman embassy to Pharasmanes arrives, and the ambassador—his identity concealed—is none other than Rhadamistus, who also had been rescued from death, had served unrecognized under the Roman general Corbulo, and finally had made himself known to the Romans and had been assigned to his present office because Rome expected to profit by his hatred of his father, who had caused all his woes. There is a certain amount of power in the author's depiction of Rhadamistus' feverish misery and remorse for the past; and the scene in which he finally encounters Zenobia —whom Arsames, of course not suspecting who they are, has persuaded him to take under his protection and carry away with him surreptitiously to save her from the King— is very famous, and not undeservedly so. But a less celebrated passage in the act which follows (Act IV) is better still and indeed the most admirable thing in this far from admirable play: it occurs when Rhadamistus finds Zenobia saying farewell to Arsames and learns that she has revealed to the young prince his identity and hers—at which his jealous nature takes umbrage, despite his brother's protest. Zenobia, who has forgiven Rhadamistus and offered to follow him, first addresses Arsames:

> Laissez agir, seigneur,[4]
> Des soupçons en effet si dignes de son cœur.
> Vous ne connaissez pas l'époux de Zénobie,
> Ni les divers transports dont son âme est saisie.
> Pour oser cependant outrager ma vertu,

[4] Leave a free course, my lord,
To doubts indeed so worthy of his heart.
Thou dost not know the husband of Zenobia
Nor all the paroxysms that seize his soul.
  To dare, though, to insult my rectitude,

Réponds-moi, Rhadamiste: et de quoi te plains-tu?
De l'amour de ton frère? Ah, barbare! quand même
Mon cœur eût pu se rendre à son amour extrême,
Le bruit de ton trépas, confirmé tant de fois,
Ne me laissait-il pas maîtresse de mon choix?
Que pouvaient te servir les droits d'un hyménée
Que vit rompre et former une même journée?
Ose te prévaloir de ce funeste jour
Où tout mon sang coula pour prix de mon amour;
Rappelle-toi le sort de ma famille entière;
Songe au sang qu'a versé ta fureur meurtrière;
Et considère après sur quoi tu peux fonder
Et l'amour et la foi que je t'ai dû garder.
Il est vrai que, sensible aux malheurs de ton frère,
De ton sort et du mien j'ai trahi le mystère.
J'ignore si c'est là le trahir en effet;
Mais sache que ta gloire en fut le seul objet:
Je voulais de ses feux éteindre l'espérance,

Rhadamistus, answer me: of what complainest thou?
Thy brother's love? Ah, cruel man, if indeed
My heart had yielded to the greatness of it,
Would not thy death's report, confirmed so often,
Have left me mistress of my choice? What rights
Over me does a marriage give to thee
Which one same day saw broken as well as made?
Dare, dare to boast of that grim day on which
My blood was poured out to requite my love!
Recall the fate of my whole family.
Think of the gore thy murderous frenzy shed,
And then consider on what to base thy claim
That I should harbor love or faith for thee.
'Tis true that, pitying thy brother's woes,
I have revealed the secret of thy lot
And mine. I am ignorant if this indeed
Is to betray it; but understand, thine honor
Was my sole aim therein. I sought to extinguish

Et chasser de son cœur un amour qui m'offense.
Mais, puisqu'à tes soupçons tu veux t'abandonner,
Connais donc tout ce cœur que tu peux soupçonner ;
Je vais par un seul trait te le faire connaître,
Et de mon sort après je te laisse le maître.
Ton frère me fut cher, je ne le puis nier ;
Je ne cherche pas même à m'en justifier ;
Mais, malgré son amour, ce prince, qui l'ignore,
Sans tes lâches soupçons l'ignorerait encore.
    (*à* ARSAME.)
Prince, après cet aveu je ne vous dis plus rien.
Vous connaissez assez un cœur comme le mien,
Pour croire que sur lui l'amour ait quelque empire.

This speech would not have been unworthy of Pierre
Corneille, or of Racine. But it is altogether inconsistent with
Zenobia's attitude earlier in the act, when she was blind to
these very considerations which she would afterwards present so well, and absurdly condemned herself; to Phenice's
inquiry as to whether she grieves for Arsames, she has replied:

His passion's hope, and to expel a love
Which wronged me from his breast. But since thou wishest
To give thyself up thus to thy suspicions,
Know, then, this heart entirely which thou doubtest.
I mean to make thee know it with one utterance,
And then I leave thee master of my fate.
I loved thy brother; I cannot deny it.
I do not even seek to justify it.
But this prince, who, despite his love, ne'er knew it,
Would still not know it, but for thy base doubts.
(*To* ARSAMES) Prince, after this avowal, I say no more
To thee. Thou knowest too well a heart like mine
To think that love has any mastery o'er it.

Loin de te confier mes coupables douleurs,[5]
Que n'en puis-je effacer la honte par mes pleurs!

and when reflecting on how hard it is for her to forgive her husband's savagery, she has said to herself:

Le cœur plein de feux illégitimes,[6]
Ai-je assez de vertu pour lui trouver des crimes?
Et me paraîtrait-il si coupable en ce jour,
Si je ne brûlais pas d'un criminel amour?

In the fifth act Arsames is brought before his father, who has learned of his secret meeting with the Roman ambassador, believes its purpose treasonous, and threatens him with death. The youth, who has been spoken of throughout the play as "the virtuous Arsames" *ad nauseam,* is a typical romanesque lover, but at this crisis he stands up to Pharasmanes with a stirring manliness quite unusual in that type:

ARSAME.[7]

Ces reproches honteux, dont en vain l'on m'accable,
Ne rendront pas, seigneur, votre fils plus coupable.
Que sert de m'outrager avec indignité?

[5] Far from telling thee of my guilty grief,
Would I might with my tears efface its shame!

[6] With a heart in which
Unlawful fires are kindled, have I virtue
Enough to point out crimes in him? Would he
Appear to me so culpable today
If I did not burn with a sinful love?

[7] ARSAMES.
Shameful reproaches, which are vainly heaped
Upon me, make thy son no guiltier, sir.
What serves it thee to abuse me thus with insults?

Donnez-moi le trépas, si je l'ai mérité:
Mais ne vous flattez point que, tremblant pour ma
    vie,
Jusqu'à la demander la crainte m'humilie.
Qui ne cherche en effet qu'à me faire périr
En faveur d'un rival pourrait-il s'attendrir?
Je sais que près de vous, injuste ou légitime,
Le plus léger soupçon tint toujours lieu de crime;
Que c'est être proscrit que d'être soupçonné;
Que votre cœur enfin n'a jamais pardonné.
De vos transports jaloux qui pourrait me défendre,
Vous qui m'avez toujours condamné sans m'en-
    tendre?

PHARASMANE.

Pour te justifier, eh! que me diras-tu?

ARSAME.

Tout ce qu'a dû pour moi vous dire ma vertu;
Que ce fils si suspect, pour trahir sa patrie,

Give death to me if death is my desert,
But flatter not thyself that I shall fear it
So much that, trembling, I shall beg for life.
Could he grow tenderer who really seeks
To make me die only because a rival?
I know that in thy mind the least suspicion,
Legitimate or unjust, convicts of crime,
That to be doubted is to be proscribed,
And that thy heart, moreover, never pardons.
Who could defend me from thy jealous frenzies,
O thou who e'er condemnest me unheard?

PHARASMANES.

In thy defense, well, what canst thou say to me?

ARSAMES.

All that my character should say to thee:
That this suspected son ne'er came to seek thee

Ne vous fût pas venu chercher dans l'Ibérie.

Now the news arrives that the Roman ambassador is carrying off "Ismenia"; and the King rushes out, followed by his guards, and presently returns with sword red with the blood of Rhadamistus, who soon afterwards is carried in, dying. Seized with a sudden qualm of conscience when assailed by his father, he has not defended himself—which is of course out of keeping with his character as previously portrayed. To make matters worse, Crébillon at this point introduces the time-worn nonsense of the *voix du sang;* he represents Pharasmanes as being obscurely perturbed and filled with ever-increasing horror and confusion from the moment when he dealt Rhadamistus his mortal wound. Not only is there no such mysterious instinct; even if there were, it would not have unsettled Pharasmanes, who had long supposed that he had effected the death of that very son of his, and just now was about to put to death his other son. This violation of the consistency of his character is continued when he learns who his victim is and bitterly grieves over him. But it no doubt soothed the harrowed feelings of audiences for whom stage conventions had taken the place of life's realities in the theater; and as it permitted a denouement in which a repentant father resigns the lovely, much-tried Zenobia to the virtuous Arsames and sends them to reign over Armenia, those audiences of eighteenth-century France thus had the further pleasure of seeing happiness crown their favorites in the end—a fitting climax to some two hours of titillation with strange vicissitudes and passionate speeches. One can easily understand the renown which this play acquired; but a candid appraisal of it today, unbiased by the prestige which that renown has conferred on it, must rate it, in comparison for instance with the

---

Here in Iberia to betray his country.

tragedies of Thomas Corneille, some of which are somewhat analogous to it, decidedly below the best of them and
no higher than the average of the "Corneillian" plays of that
author. All traditional estimates to the contrary notwithstanding, Campistron's *Andronic* is far superior to *Rha-*
damiste et Zénobie.

The fact is that in France, as in England, there is a fundamental difference—indeed, much the same difference—between the tragedies of the great national dramatic period
and those of the period that followed it. Despite their mannerisms and artificialities—or, we may say, through the
distorting prism of those mannerisms and artificialities—the
French dramatists of the seventeenth century were trying to
depict human life, as they conceived that it was or had been
or might be. But the writers of tragedy in eighteenth-century
France, like those in Restoration and post-Restoration England, endeavored to put on the stage not a representation of
life, however idealized or conventionalized, but some con-
coction of stereotyped theatricalities. In England, even when
so great a man as Dryden is at his best in *All for Love,* his
characters are lay figures in a stage-world; they declaim
somewhat inappositely instead of coming to grips with the
situation confronting them; hardly any developments are
brought about with an illusion of reality comparable to that
which we find in any of the better Elizabethan plays. And
just as even Dryden failed in England, even Voltaire could
not succeed in France.

In his own times his reputation as a dramatist was immense; he was regarded by many as the equal of Corneille
and Racine—if not their superior. To this day his fame
resulting from very different work, as the ironic champion
of humanity and enlightenment, makes him also remembered
as a dramatist; the reflected light which illumines his tragedies exhibits them in a false perspective.

It is, of course, a well-known fact of literary history that

Voltaire's residence for three years in England familiarized him with Shakespeare, some knowledge of whom he was the first to introduce into France. Greatly impressed, originally attracted and later repelled by an art so alien to the French tradition, he was influenced by it to some extent—notably in *Zaïre,* generally considered his best play, which derives in part from *Othello.* But his tragedies, like Crébillon's, are essentially melodramas, with incognitos, recognitions, and misapprehensions important factors in almost all of them.

The heroine of *Zaïre,* for whom it is named, is a slave of Orosmanes, the Sultan of Jerusalem in the days of the Crusades. A captive from infancy and knowing nothing of her parents, she had some reason to think that they were Christians; but she is content to remain a Mahometan as she was reared, for she has long adored Orosmanes and is loved by him and she does not want to have the religion of his enemies. He is about to wed her as his sole queen, contrary to the usual practice of Moslems, with whose attitude towards women this noble potentate has little sympathy.

About two years earlier a fellow prisoner of Zaïre's, a young Christian knight named Nerestan, between whom and her there was a strong mutual attachment, had been paroled that he might try to raise a ransom for some of the captives. At this juncture he returns to Jerusalem with the necessary funds; but Orosmanes, though regally generous as regards all others, declines to set free at any price the last Christian king of Jerusalem, the aged Lusignan, considering him a figure around whom the Crusaders would rally. Naturally he will not give up Zaïre, either; but when she herself intercedes for the release of Lusignan, he cannot refuse her prayers. She brings the old man to Nerestan, and it transpires that she and Nerestan are his children. Their joy at reunion is blighted by the fact that she is not a Christian. Swayed by her father's impassioned appeal, she promises to become one, and to keep their relationship a secret; and when in a second interview her brother learns of her intended nuptials with the Sultan, she placates his rage and horror by pledging herself not to marry until a Christian priest has instructed and baptized her. But the wedding is set for that very day; without explanation she begs Orosmanes to defer it, and being by nature easily jealous, he suspects her of loving Nerestan; he intercepts a letter from that young man to her, so worded that the worst interpretation is the natural one, but lets it reach her to see if she is indeed false to him or if Nerestan alone is culpable; and when she steals forth at night to keep the tryst to which it summoned her, he stabs her dead, and then, learning the truth too late, kills himself.

This synopsis of *Zaïre* indicates the basic and fatal defects which characterize it. Here are the stock devices of melodrama : recognitions and misapprehensions, and unfortunate promises of silence imposed with doubtful necessity, and mere ill chance.[8] Everything would have been cleared up if Orosmanes had confronted Zaïre with the intercepted letter and asked for an explanation, and he was going to do so; but his faithful officer, Corasmin, with the best of intentions, prevailed on him to test her instead—and thence only does the tragic denouement result.

But worse than all this, the very essence of the play is in contradiction to human nature. Zaïre had known always that she was probably of Christian origin, yet she had so loved Orosmanes that she would not embrace his foes' religion. She owed everything to his love, and radiantly awaited marriage to him within the hour. It is simply incredible, then, that she should in a twinkling, on the discovery that Lusig-

---

[8] In *Othello*, too, ill chance plays a part—as witness Desdemona's loss of the fatal handkerchief—but there it is disastrous because Iago seizes upon this accident and makes it serve his ends, and we feel that if no such thing had occurred, his infernal cunning would have found some other means to achieve the same result. But in *Zaïre*, ill chance is fatal of itself.

nan was her father, transfer her loyalty to that aged man, practically a stranger to her, and should cringe before him guiltily when he inquired what faith was hers, and say,

> Je ne puis vous tromper: sous les lois d'Orosmane . . .[9]
> Punissez votre fille . . . elle était musulmane.

It is simply incredible that she should now yield at once to her father's exhortation and be persuaded forthwith to accept Christianity; should deceive, disappoint, perplex, and torture the man who loved her, who granted all her desires and was raising her from slavery to be his queen; should wish that she had died before she loved him; should without even a protest hear her brother speak of him abusively and threateningly! It is only in a stage world, not in real life, that people are bowled over and hypnotically obsessed by the mere name of father, mother, or child, in the complete absence of any endearing habitual contact.

Now a good play might conceivably have been written about the problem presented in *Zaïre*—a play in which a daughter's sense of duty to her suddenly discovered, not previously suspected, race and to her ancestral religion inexorably opposes the dictates of her heart. Pierre Corneille might well have attempted such a theme, and with the sort

---

[9] I cannot lie to thee; 'neath Orosmanes . . .
Punish thy daughter . . . she was a Mahometan.

Observe that this is her immediate reaction to his question, before his great plea to her. Her words imply both his right to punish her and her willingness to acquiesce in being punished—though he had been set free only that morning by her intercession and Orosmanes' clemency, and was still in their power. She also urges Nerestan to kill her when he learns of her intended marriage. If she herself did not value her life, she might at least have considered the injustice to Orosmanes involved in her death, and the grief it would cause him.

of characters that he customarily drew—proud beings, ruled by ideas, in whom the intellect and the will are dominant over all softer passions—he perhaps would have made something of notable worth out of it, though there is equal likelihood that he would have bungled it. But the heroine whom Voltaire gives to an essentially Corneillian plot is a Racinian creature of emotion.

The reactions of Lusignan and Nerestan to the situation in which they find Zaïre are all natural enough; Orosmanes' magnanimity and their indebtedness to him would have softened no whit the bigotry to be expected in the men of the Crusades. And bigotry was no doubt still sufficiently general in Voltaire's audiences for him to be sure that the conversion of Zaïre would please most people in them, no matter what disloyalties it involved, and hence would not be examined too closely as regards credibility. A man of the theater to his finger-tips, he made her about-face as plausible as he could under its circumstances, lavishing all his powers on the fervent entreaty with which Lusignan wins his daughter's soul:

> Que la foudre en éclats ne tombe que sur moi! [10]
> Ah, mon fils! à ces mots, j'eusse expiré sans toi.
> Mon Dieu! j'ai combattu soixante ans pour ta gloire;
> J'ai vu tomber ton temple, et périr ta mémoire;
> Dans un cachot affreux abandonné vingt ans,
> Mes larmes t'imploraient pour mes tristes enfants;

[10] May thunder's bolts fall only upon me!
Ah, my son, without thee I should have died
At those words! For thy glory, God, have I
Fought sixty years. I have seen thy temple fall
And the memory of thee perish. Languishing
For twenty years within a fearful dungeon,
With tears I have implored thee to protect

Et lorsque ma famille est par toi réunie,
Quand je trouve une fille, elle est ton ennemie!
Je suis bien malheureux . . . C'est ton père, c'est
    moi,
C'est ma seule prison qui t'a ravi ta foi.
Ma fille, tendre objet de mes dernières peines,
Songe au moins, songe au sang qui coule dans tes
    veines;
C'est le sang de vingt rois, tous chrétiens comme
    moi;
C'est le sang des héros, défenseurs de ma loi;
C'est le sang des martyrs . . . O fille encor trop
    chère!
Connais-tu ton destin? sais-tu quelle est ta mère?
Sais-tu bien qu'à l'instant que son flanc mit au jour
Ce triste et dernier fruit d'un malheureux amour,
Je la vis massacrer par la main forcenée,
Par la main des brigands à qui tu t'es donnée!

My hapless children; and when through thy power
We are again united and I find
A daughter—lo, she is thine enemy!
I am indeed most wretched . . .
                           'Tis thy father.
'Tis I, 'tis my imprisonment, naught else,
Which reft thee of thy faith. Dear daughter mine,
Thou source of my last cares, think, think at least
What blood flows in thy veins. It is the blood
Of twenty kings, all Christians like myself;
It is the blood of heroes, the defenders
Of heaven's law; it is the blood of martyrs . . .
O daughter still so dear! knowest thou what portion
Was thine? Dost thou know who thy mother was?
Dost thou indeed know that within the moment
When she gave birth to this sad final fruit
Of our ill-fated love I saw her slaughtered
By a fell hand, the hand of the same brigands

Tes frères, ces martyrs égorgés à mes yeux,
T'ouvrent leurs bras sanglants, tendus du haut des
        cieux!
Ton Dieu que tu trahis, ton Dieu que tu blasphèmes,
Pour toi, pour l'univers, est mort en ces lieux
        mêmes;
En ces lieux où mon bras le servit tant de fois,
En ces lieux où son sang te parle par ma voix.
Vois ces murs, vois ce temple envahi par tes
        maîtres;
Tout annonce le Dieu qu'ont vengé tes ancêtres.
Tourne les yeux, sa tombe est près de ce palais;
C'est ici la montagne où, lavant nos forfaits,
Il voulut expirer sous les coups de l'impie;
C'est là que de sa tombe il rappela sa vie.
Tu ne saurais marcher dans cet auguste lieu,
Tu n'y peux faire un pas, sans y trouver ton Dieu;
Et tu n'y peux rester sans renier ton père,

With whom thou joinest thy destiny? Thy brothers,
Those martyrs slain before mine eyes, hold out
Their bleeding arms to thee from heaven's height.
Thy God, whom thou betrayest, whom thou blasphemest,
Died in this very place, for thee, for all men—
Here, where mine arm so often served his cause!
Here, where his blood calls to thee by my voice!
    Behold these walls; behold this sacred temple,
Seized by thy masters—all proclaims the God
Thine ancestors avenged. Look round about thee:
His tomb is near this palace; yonder stands
The mountain where, to wash our sins away,
He perished at the hands of impious men;
Yonder he rose, victorious, from his tomb.
Thou canst not walk within this holy place—
Thou canst not take one step—and not find there
Thy God; and neither canst thou here remain
Without denying thy father, and thy honor

Ton honneur qui te parle, et ton Dieu qui t'éclaire.

To unthinking audiences this harangue may the more likely seem adequate to bring about Zaïre's change of heart, in that they have known of the love between her and the Sultan only a little longer than they have known that Lusignan is her father; for at this point the second act of the play is not yet concluded. But to those whose view is less superficial and who can imaginatively enter into a dramatic situation, it must be evident that, having already chosen to reject Christianity in spite of its attractions for her and the probability that her parents were Christians, she could not be swayed now by the chance identification of her father and a few words from him, however eloquent, if her love for Orosmanes had any real depth or constancy whatever; and to those not ruled by religious prejudice—in other words, to a great majority of intelligent people in more modern times —she must needs appear no "sympathetic" character at all, but an abject creature without proper devotion, gratitude, or spirit. Any woman in her position who was not lacking in these essentials would have answered Nerestan's ferocious abuse of Orosmanes very much as Palmira, in the same author's *Mahomet,* answered abuse of the man whom she worshipped:

Vous me faites frémir, seigneur; et, des mes jours,[11]
Je n'avais entendu ces horribles discours.
Mon penchant, je l'avoue, et ma reconnaissance,
Vous donnaient sur mon cœur une juste puissance;

Which claims thee, and thy God who lights thy path.

[11] Thou makest me shudder, sir. In all my days
I ne'er have heard such hideous words as these.
My feelings, I confess, and thankfulness
Gave thee some power rightly o'er my heart.

Vos blasphèmes affreux contre mon protecteur
A ce penchant si doux font succéder l'horreur.

In a play like *Zaïre* it is absolutely vital that the heroine
should elicit our sympathy, or else the tragic effect is not
achieved; but the "heroine" of *Zaïre,* if we can waive our disbelief in the existence of such a person, ought rather to excite only irritation or disgust.

Mérope was the most carefully written of Voltaire's tragedies, and is usually regarded as the second-best of them. It
is unique in that none of its characters is infatuated with
anyone; its entire subject is a mother's love for her son. But
here this emotion is not the love that a mother normally
feels—a love indeed rooted in the protective instincts of
motherhood which are older than mankind, but developed
and augmented by the long-continued, affectionate associa-
tions of home and family and parental care. The mother-
love which the author of *Zaïre* now characteristically chooses
to depict is maintained solely by a mother's thoughts of her
son, long absent, whom she would not know even by sight;
when the play opens, Queen Merope has not seen Aegisthus
for sixteen years—not since her husband and her two older
children were murdered and this boy, still an infant, was
conveyed secretly out of the country, to save his life. She
has heard nothing of him for a long time, and is uncertain
whether he is alive. Yet she not only persists in trying to
keep the throne of Messenia vacant for him; that he is "her
son" and she is "his mother" makes him an obsession with
her—just as Zaïre's discovery that she could apply the
sacred name of "father" to a virtual stranger promptly made
her blind to everything else. Nor is Merope thereby an attractive figure, any more than Zaïre was. The wise providence,

---

Thy blasphemies against my kind protector
Make horror take the place of those sweet feelings.

the finer qualities and feelings of motherhood are not portrayed in her, but only sheer emotionalism, somewhat artificially induced by exercise of the fancy and untempered by practical realities—hence little rational or moral. She is "all mother"—and her "mother's love" only beclouds her wits when the unrecognized Aegisthus, who does not know that he is her son, is brought before her charged with her son's murder, so that she at once believes him guilty though the circumstances distinctly hint at the truth and would at least have prompted any clearer-headed person to further inquiry; her "mother's love" makes of her an unsexed Fury who insists on killing the supposed murderer with her own hands; and when a theatrical disclosure at the last moment has saved her from doing so, her "mother's love" robs her of the self-control needed to conceal his identity from the tyrant who seeks his life. In the end, his salvation and the denouement of the play are brought about by nothing that has gone before, but simply by his ability to spring quickly and strike effectively.

In spite of all their faults—the invariable melodrama, the stock stage devices, the conventionalized psychology—Voltaire's greatness appears now and then in his dramas. The influence of Shakespeare upon him is strikingly shown in the scene in which Orosmanes awaits the coming of Zaïre that he may kill her, where the deliberate creation of "atmosphere" and of suspense—the darkness and hush of the night, the imagined sounds which the Sultan thinks he hears, and his short, broken cries of passion—produces effects hitherto unknown in French tragedy. Occasionally Voltaire displays a breadth of historical vision, a firm grasp of the essence of a matter, and a sweep of imagination that cannot be matched even in Corneille or Racine. No less magnificent than Lusignan's celebrated appeal to his daughter, though less famous, is a scene in *Mahomet* between the Prophet (depicted in this play as a deliberately fraudulent self-seeker) and his mortal enemy, Zopir, the sheik of Mecca:

Mahomet.[12]

Approche, et puisque enfin le ciel veut nous unir,
Vois Mahomet sans crainte, et parle sans rougir.

Zopire.

Je rougis pour toi seul, pour toi dont l'artifice
A traîné ta patrie au bord du précipice;
Pour toi de qui la main sème ici les forfaits,
Et fait naître la guerre au milieu de la paix.
Ton nom seul parmi nous divise les familles,
Les époux, les parents, les mères, et les filles;
Et la trêve pour toi n'est qu'un moyen nouveau
Pour venir dans nos cœurs enfoncer le couteau.
La discorde civile est partout sur ta trace.
Assemblage inouï de mensonge et d'audace,
Tyran de ton pays, est-ce ainsi qu'en ce lieu
Tu viens donner la paix, et m'annoncer un dieu?

---

[12] Mahomet.

Approach. Since heaven would fain at last unite us,
Fear not to see Mahomet; blush not to speak.

Zopir.

I blush for thee alone; for thee whose trickery
Has dragged thy country to the brink of ruin;
For thee whose hand sows here felonious crimes
And brings to birth war in the midst of peace.
Thy name alone, among us, divides families,
Husbands and wives, sons, fathers, mothers, daughters;
This truce is but a new means to enable thee
To come and plunge a dagger in our hearts.
Intestine discord follows in thy wake.
O monstrous mixture of deceit and daring,
Thy people's tyrant, dost thou thus come hither
To give us peace and tell us of a god?

MAHOMET.

Si j'avais à répondre à d'autres qu'à Zopire,
Je ne ferais parler que le dieu qui m'inspire;
Le glaive et l'Alcoran, dans mes sanglantes mains,
Imposeraient silence au reste des humains;
Ma voix ferait sur eux les effets du tonnerre,
Et je verrais leurs fronts attachés à la terre:
Mais je te parle en homme, et sans rien déguiser;
Je me sens assez grand pour ne pas t'abuser.
Vois quel est Mahomet. Nous sommes seuls, écoute:
Je suis ambitieux; tout homme l'est, sans doute;
Mais jamais roi, pontife, ou chef, ou citoyen,
Ne conçut un projet aussi grand que le mien.
Chaque peuple à son tour a brillé sur la terre,
Par les lois, par les arts, et surtout par la guerre:
Le temps de l'Arabie est à la fin venu.

MAHOMET.

Had I to answer any other man
Than Zopir, I would make the god alone
Speak who inspires me. In my blood-stained hands
The sword and the Koran would then impose
Silence upon the rest of humankind.
My voice would sound like thunder in their ears,
And I would see their brows pressed to the earth.
But I would fain speak as a man to *thee,*
Without disguising aught; for I am conscious
That I am great enough not to deceive thee.
See now what manner of man Mahomet is.
We are alone. Listen: I am ambitious;
So all men are, no doubt; but never king,
Nor priest, nor chief, nor citizen hath conceived
A purpose as exalted as mine own.
Every nation in its turn hath blazed
In splendor o'er the world, through laws, through arts,
And most of all through war. Arabia's turn
Has come at last. Its people great of heart,

Ce peuple généreux, trop longtemps inconnu,
Laissait dans ses déserts ensevelir sa gloire;
Voici les jours nouveaux marqués pour la victoire.
Vois du nord au midi l'univers désolé,
La Perse encor sanglante, et son trône ébranlé,
L'Inde esclave et timide, et l'Egypte abaissée,
Des murs de Constantin la splendeur éclipsée;
Vois l'empire romain tombant de toutes parts,
Ce grand corps déchiré, dont les membres épars
Languissent dispersés sans honneur et sans vie:
Sur ces débris du monde élevons l'Arabie.
Il faut un nouveau culte, il faut de nouveaux fers;
Il faut un nouveau dieu pour l'aveugle univers.

En Egypte Osiris, Zoroastre en Asie,
Chez les Crétois Minos, Numa dans l'Italie,
A des peuples sans mœurs, et sans culte, et sans
   rois,
Donnèrent aisément d'insuffisantes lois.

Too long unknown, have let their just renown
Be buried in its deserts. The new days,
Destined for victory, are now at hand.
   Behold from north to south this earth laid waste:
Persia still bathed in blood, with tottering throne;
India enslaved and craven; Egypt humbled;
The glory gone from the walls of Constantine.
Behold the Roman Empire everywhere
Crumbling, its body rent, its broken members
Scattered afar, dishonored, without life.
Above this wreckage of the world now let us
Raise up Arabia. There needs to be
A new religion, a new discipline,
A new god found for this blind universe.
   Egypt's Osiris, Asia's Zoroaster,
Minos in Crete, Numa in Italy,
To brutish peoples without creeds or kings,
Dispensed their laws, which were not adequate.

Je viens après mille ans changer ces lois grossières:
J'apporte un joug plus noble aux nations entières;
J'abolis les faux dieux; et mon culte épuré
De ma grandeur naissante est le premier degré.
Ne me reproche point de tromper ma patrie;
Je détruis sa faiblesse et son idolâtrie:
Sous un roi, sous un dieu, je viens la réunir;
Et, pour la rendre illustre, il la faut asservir.

ZOPIRE.

Voilà donc tes desseins! c'est donc toi dont l'audace
De la terre à ton gré prétend changer la face!
Tu veux, en apportant le carnage et l'effroi,
Commander aux humains de penser comme toi:
Tu ravages le monde, et tu prétends l'instruire.
Ah! si par des erreurs il s'est laissé séduire,
Si la nuit du mensonge a pu nous égarer,
Par quels flambeaux affreux veux-tu nous éclairer?

After a thousand years I come in turn
To change those old, crude laws. A nobler yoke
I bring to entire nations. I abolish
Their false gods; and this purer faith of mine
Is the first step by which I grow to greatness.
Reproach me not with cozening my country;
I end its weakness and idolatry.
Under one king, one god, I would unite it;
And to make it glorious, I must master it.

ZOPIR.

These are thy schemes, then! thou dost, then, presume
To try to change the very face of the earth
To suit thy pleasure! Thou desirest to bring
Carnage and terror into it, to compel
Mankind to think like thee. Thou ravagest
The world, and thou pretendest to instruct it!
Ah, if it let itself be led astray
By error—if in darkness we have wandered—
With what dread torches wouldst thou light our way?

Quel droit as-tu reçu d'enseigner, de prédire,
De porter l'encensoir, et d'affecter l'empire?

MAHOMET.

Le droit qu'un esprit vaste, et ferme en ses desseins,
A sur l'esprit grossier des vulgaires humains.

ZOPIRE.

Eh quoi! tout factieux, qui pense avec courage,
Doit donner aux mortels un nouvel esclavage?
Il a droit de tromper, s'il trompe avec grandeur?

MAHOMET.

Oui; je connais ton peuple, il a besoin d'erreur;
Ou véritable ou faux, mon culte est nécessaire.
Que t'ont produit tes dieux? quel bien t'ont-ils pu
    faire?
Quels lauriers vois-tu croître au pied de leurs
    autels?

What right hast thou to teach, to prophesy,
To wear the mitre and assume the crown?

MAHOMET.

The right which a great soul, strong in its purpose,
Has over the gross souls of common men.

ZOPIR.

How now! Shall every factionist with bold
Imaginings give to mortals a new slavery?
Has he a right to practice fraud, if practiced
On a grand scale?

MAHOMET.

Yes. I well know thy people.
They need illusions. My religion, whether
'Tis true or false, is necessary to them.
What have thy gods availed thee? What good thing
Have they been able to confer on thee?
Thou seest what laurels grow beneath their altars?

Ta secte obscure et basse avilit les mortels,
Enerve le courage, et rend l'homme stupide;
La mienne élève l'âme et la rend intrépide.
Ma loi fait des héros.

ZOPIRE.

Dis plutôt des brigands.

Porte ailleurs tes leçons, l'école des tyrans;
Va vanter l'imposture à Médine où tu règnes,
Où tes maîtres séduits marchent sous tes enseignes,
Où tu vois tes égaux à tes pieds abattus.

MAHOMET.

Des égaux! dès longtemps Mahomet n'en a plus.
Je fais trembler la Mecque, et je règne à Médine;
Crois-moi, reçois la paix, si tu crains ta ruine.

ZOPIRE.

La paix est dans ta bouche, et ton cœur en est loin:

Thy lowly, groveling sect debases men,
Weakens their courage, makes them dull of wit.
Mine elevates the soul and makes it fearless.
My creed makes heroes.

ZOPIR.

Rather call them ruffians!

Carry elsewhere thy teachings, a fit school
For tyrants. Go, and boast of thine impostures
Unto Medina, where thou reignest now,
Where thy corrupted masters march beneath
Thy banners, where thou seest thine equals bowed
Low at thy feet.

MAHOMET.

Equals? Mahomet long
Has had none. I make Mecca tremble; I
Rule at Medina. Credit my words; accept
Peace from me if thou fearest destruction.

ZOPIR.

Peace

Penses-tu me tromper?

MAHOMET.

Je n'en ai pas besoin.
C'est le faible qui trompe, et le puissant commande.
Demain j'ordonnerai ce que je te demande;
Demain je puis te voir à mon joug asservi:
Aujourd'hui Mahomet veut être ton ami.

ZOPIRE.

Nous amis! nous? cruel! ah! quel nouveau prestige!
Connais-tu quelque dieu qui fasse un tel prodige?

MAHOMET.

J'en connais un puissant et toujours écouté,
Qui te parle avec moi.

ZOPIRE.

Qui?

Is on thy lips, not in thy heart. Dost think
To deceive *me?*

MAHOMET.
I have no need to do so.
The weak deceive; the powerful command.
Tomorrow I shall order what I now
Request of thee. Tomorrow I shall see thee
Subjected to my yoke. Today Mahomet
Wishes to be thy friend.

ZOPIR.
We friends! Cruel monster,
We? Ah, what marvel . . . Knowest thou any god
Who can work such a miracle?

MAHOMET.
I know
A powerful one, one always heard, who speaks
To thee with me.

ZOPIR.
What god?

MAHOMET.

La nécessité,

Ton intérêt.

ZOPIRE.

Avant qu'un tel nœud nous rassemble,
Les enfers et les cieux seront unis ensemble.
L'intérêt est ton dieu, le mien est l'équité;
Entre ces ennemis il n'est point de traité.
Quel serait le ciment, réponds-moi, si tu l'oses,
De l'horrible amitié qu'ici tu me proposes?
Réponds: est-ce ton fils que mon bras te ravit?
Est-ce le sang des miens que ta main répandit?

"Yes, it is your children that will unite us," Mahomet
answers. "They still live; they are in my power. I have
reared them and been like a father to them, but now their
life or death depends on whether you will help to spread
my religion or will oppose me."
Zopir replies:

Mahomet, je suis père . . .[13]

MAHOMET.

Necessity.

Thy interest.

ZOPIR.

Before such a tie unites us,
Heaven and hell shall first be joined together.
Thy interest is thy god; my god is justice.
Between these foes there is no truce at all.
What will there be—answer me if thou darest—
That can cement the horrible friendship which
Thou here proposest to me? Answer me:
Is it thy son, of whom mine arm has reft thee?
Is it my children's blood, which thou hast shed?

[13] Mahomet, I am a father . . .

Mais s'il faut à ton culte asservir ma patrie,
Ou de ma propre main les immoler tous deux,
Connais-moi, Mahomet, mon choix n'est pas douteux.

The rest of the play, as one might expect from this turn
of the plot, is merely the usual tissue of melodrama—un-
guessed identities and the *voix du sang* and recognitions,
here too late. Zopir does not know who his children are, and
they do not know that he is their father, and they kill him in
their blind devotion to Mahomet. Thus in Voltaire are
genius and charlatanry mixed.

There was yet to flourish, in the last quarter of the eighteenth century, one other important writer of the post-
renaissance version of classical tragedy; but he belongs not
to French but to Italian literature. Like Voltaire, Count
Vittorio Alfieri was a man of unusual mental powers who
became a dramatist because he resolved to do so. One could
hardly have been confronted, at the outset, by greater obstacles. He began, he says, "with an almost total ignorance
of the rules of dramatic composition," with nothing but
some recollection of French plays to guide him. A native of
Piedmont and speaking only the dialect of that region, he
actually wrote his first tragedies in French and then translated them into good Italian, which he taught himself "with
infinite labor." Nor did he ever acquire literary graces. His
style is vigorous and austere, marked by many inversions
and by frequent omissions of the definite article; "narrow
elevation" is Matthew Arnold's phrase for its quality.

The type of play which he made his own eliminates the
conventional gallantry that disfigured French-classical trag-

---

But if I must enslave to thy religion
My country, or with mine own hand slay them both,
Know this, Mahomet: my choice is not in doubt.

edy, but is of a similar rhetorical cast and preserves many other conventions of that school of drama. Moreover, it introduces new artificialities, equally conventional, characteristic of Romanticism, by this time well advanced: rhapsodies, for instance, on Friendship—or on Liberty, for which Alfieri felt the consuming passion of a Shelley or a Byron.[14] But except for the abuse of rhetoric which mars neo-classical and romantic tragedy alike, Alfieri practiced a literary economy so severe that one finds in passing from Corneille and Racine to him something of the difficulty which people accustomed to the amplitude of Elizabethan drama find in passing from it to Corneille and Racine. He reduces the action of his plays to absolute essentials, and also simplifies the characters of the dramatis personae and restricts their number to an absolute minimum. The confidants of French-classical tragedy had been thought to be needed in the absence of the Chorus of ancient tragedy, but Alfieri managed to dispense with both. His plays are even shorter than those of Corneille, Racine, or Voltaire; their dramatis personae are sometimes as few as four. Such economy often results in a failure to create any suggestion of background; his characters seem figures beheld in front of a blank screen. This is notably and oddly true in so fine a tragedy as *Philip*, Alfieri's version of the story of Philip II and Don Carlos, though all the life and stir of the populous Court of Spain must be going on just outside the room in which the action takes place. There is no lack of background, however, in *Saul*, his most famous play; and when he deals with Greek legends, associated in our minds with the simplicity of Attic drama, background does not greatly matter.

The inability of some historians of literature to compre-

[14] With the latter poet his life and character present striking analogies. Both men had violent emotions and scandalous love-affairs; but Alfieri, unlike Byron, eventually found a noble and abiding love, which had a good effect on his later years.

hend what constitutes a good play is exemplified by the statement of one of them that Alfieri's twenty-two tragedies are
all about equal in merit. The truth is that the work of neither
Corneille nor Shakespeare was more variable in degree of
excellence than his. Other critics have selected for especial
praise two of his worst productions, *Merope* and *Polynices*.
His *Merope* has all the faults of Voltaire's and some additional ones of its own. In *Polynices* he evidently intended to
write, from material furnished by the grim saga of Thebes,
a terrible tragedy in the grand, ancient manner. But its
Jocasta is a Voltairian mother, and Polynices himself eventually exhibits the same obsession about blood-ties; yet he
must have known when he resorted to arms that success
would probably involve his brother's death, and hence his
subsequent despair at having committed fratricide—and,
earlier, even at the prospect of committing it—is incredibly
inconsistent in him. Most of the time the characters "simply
spout at each other" (to borrow an apt phrase of William
Archer's) and each seems to stop his ears when the other
speaks, for they show no signs of taking in what is said to
them! The figure of Antigone is the only attractive feature of
this miserable play.

Its sequel, which bears her name, is, on the other hand, one
of Alfieri's very best dramas and illustrates his originality in
handling Greek subjects. In the *Antigone* of Sophocles,
Creon is a stiff-necked autocrat who forbids the burial of
Polynices' body on pain of death and then to his horror finds
that his own niece, his son Haemon's betrothed, defies his
mandate and leaves him no "face-saving" way to pardon
her. Alfieri's Creon is a scheming, hypocritical villain. His
intrigues have destroyed all the family of Oedipus except
Antigone, who alone of them has perceived his villainy. His
sole desire is the crown of Thebes for himself and for Haemon after him; he has acquired it, but it is rightly Antigone's. He denies burial to Polynices solely because he knows

she will disobey him and then he can put her to death. He
has not been aware of his son's love for her, and when the
young man avows it in pleading for her life, he says that if
she will consent to marry Haemon, she will be pardoned
forthwith. Haemon on his part is horrified at the idea of
constraining her to accept him, but despite his remonstrance
Creon makes her this offer. With her, however, as with
Sophocles' Antigone, family comes before everything else.
She feels that to wed the son of the arch-enemy and bane
of all her nearest and dearest would be disloyal to them; she
simply *cannot do it;* her feelings about such a union are like
those of a nineteenth-century heroine of fiction about the loss
of her chastity. Wrung with anguish and self-condemnation,
she confesses to Haemon that she loves him; but nothing
can persuade her to marry him, and yet she cannot bear the
thought of causing strife between him and his father, attach-
ing so much importance as she does to family ties. The
denouement of this drama is practically the same as in
Sophocles. Lovers of his *Antigone* may think such a radical
transformation of one of the great stories of the world
little short of sacrilege, but it cannot be denied that Alfieri
has succeeded in making of his variant a most excellent play.

Antigone and *Saul* and *Philip* are decidedly his finest
achievements. They rank at least with Corneille's *Horace*
and Racine's *Mithridate,* perhaps even with *Andromaque*
and *Iphigénie.* Judged by the most exacting standards, they
are on the border-line of greatness. Not a little inferior to
them, but still good plays, are Alfieri's *Agamemnon, Orestes,*
and *Myrrha*—somewhat of a class with *Cinna* in merit; and
his *Don Garcia, Octavia, The Conspiracy of the Pazzi, Agis,*
and more doubtfully *Virginia* and *Timoleon,* may be pronounced fairly or passably good. The first two acts of *The
First Brutus* are almost devoid of dramatic qualities; its last
three acts are really notable. *Rosamunda*—with its atrocities,

melodramatic force, and lack of truth-to-life—recalls *Rodogune.*

Although Alfieri's favorite subject is liberty—as witness *The Conspiracy of the Pazzi, Agis, Virginia, Timoleon, The First Brutus,* and *The Second Brutus*—it never inspired him to anything approaching his best work, but always to something stiff, frigid, and declamatory, except to some extent in the first-named one of these plays. His best-drawn character is the Clytemnestra of his *Agamemnon,* whom he depicts as torn between her wifely duty and her mad love for Aegisthus, who does not love her but uses her only to further his ambition. In *Orestes* her conflicting emotions are too stagey, and the manner in which they alternately possess her is unconvincing. This tragedy is more exciting, more filled with action and tension, than any of the others, but its hero is represented as so maniacally impulsive that Pylades could not have failed to realize his frenetic condition and would surely have refused to set out with him on his expedition of vengeance. The catastrophe in *Orestes* is "softened" in deference to modern sensibilities; the mother-murder is accidental and is momentarily unrealized, for Clytemnestra throws herself between Aegisthus and the sword which blind frenzy wields.

The illusion of life is never as well attained in Alfieri as it is in greater dramatists—or, indeed, in many less great than he. All his plays, good or bad, give a certain impression of being deliberately fashioned products of industry, not the output of a creative mind; nor is this to be wondered at, in view of the way in which he became an author by dint of sheer determination and perseverance. But in spite of his obvious shortcomings, it is he—not Crébillon or Voltaire, as each of them vaingloriously supposed himself and was supposed by his admirers—who stands with Corneille and Racine as one of the three major writers of neo-classical tragedy.

CHAPTER XIX

ELIZABETHAN AND FRENCH-
CLASSICAL DRAMA

DRAMA is the most enduring of literary forms. Not of recent origin like the novel, it has not lapsed like the epic and is almost as ancient. It has persisted in the Occident continuously, except during the Dark Ages, from about 500 B.C. to the present day. Yet in all that time almost every play that should indubitably be called "great" has been written in one or another of four relatively brief periods, during which drama flourished to an extraordinary degree.

Each of these four flourishings of drama is distinguished from the others by different themes, conventions, technique, and objectives; but they all have certain remarkable similarities. In each there is a great central figure—or perhaps more than one such figure—in whom the period culminates; in each, near its beginning, there is at least one pioneer of equal or not very much inferior genius, who in large measure created the dramatic type which characterizes that period; and in each there are many lesser dramatists who did as best they could the same kinds of things that the great men did superbly, and whose work is in consequence a valuable aid to a true comprehension of the great men themselves. None of these periods lasted more than a hundred years.[1]

---

[1] A fifth, somewhat similar flourishing of drama, initiated by Lope de Vega and culminating in Calderon, occurred in sixteenth and seventeenth century Spain. It was of much longer duration, and many more plays were written in it than in any of the others; but it produced nothing comparable in merit to the best work done in each of the four great periods.

509

The first of them is the Greek—or Attic, or Athenian—drama of the fifth century B.C., in which comedy and tragedy flourished at the same time but quite independent of each other. In tragedy, Aeschylus was the pioneer of genius, fully the equal of the culminating figures, Sophocles and Euripides. In comedy, it seems that Cratinus was the pioneer and that Eupolis as well as Aristophanes was of major importance, but all the plays of Cratinus and Eupolis are lost—as are all those of all the minor writers of either tragedy or comedy in fifth-century Athens, and all but a few of the plays of even Aeschylus, Sophocles, Euripides, and Aristophanes.

The most recent of the great periods is that international flourishing of drama which was heralded in Grillparzer and which, after the romantic drama of the early part of the nineteenth century and the well-made-plays of Scribe, was developed especially by Hebbel in Germany and Augier in France between 1840 and 1860, and culminated shortly afterwards in Ibsen. Its plays were, customarily, distinguished by having some social rather than merely individual aspect, some problem or thesis that relates the affairs of the dramatis personae to the larger life; they were, in the main, dramas of ideas. This period may be said to have ended with the beginning of the First World War.

The other two great periods were that of the neo-classical or pseudo-classical drama of seventeenth-century France and, just prior to this, what we speak of as Elizabethan drama (though it was evolved only in the latter part of the reign of Queen Elizabeth and extended through that of the first two Stuarts) in England. In French-classical drama, the pioneer of genius was, of course, Corneille; and Molière and Racine were the great central figures. In Elizabethan drama, Marlowe died so young and with so little accomplished that he does not stand out as a genuinely great dramatist, who prepared the way for Shakespeare, in the impressive manner in which the other pioneers of genius stand out in their respective periods, but such was indeed his role; and a judicious appraisal of his potentialities as they were indicated in his brief career will suffice to show him not unworthy of it.

Elizabethan drama had not quite reached its end when French-classical drama began; but we have no positive evidence that the former exerted any influence on the latter, or even that any French dramatist of the seventeenth century knew anything about the work of the Elizabethans. Yet between these two great flourishings of drama, which seem to have been totally unconnected but which took place in immediate succession and in two countries separated only by the narrow waters of the English Channel, there are at once striking similarities and striking contrasts.

Both were derived from the same two sources: the medieval popular drama (miracle, mystery, and morality plays) on the one hand and the Renaissance academic imitations of classical drama (chiefly of Seneca, Plautus, and Terence) on the other. But in England the influence of the medieval popular drama was the more important in shaping the type of play that resulted, whereas in France the academic, classical influence was preponderant. This difference was in keeping with the national character of the two peoples. The French type of play required a more civilized and sophisticated environment in which to flourish than the Elizabethan; and the creation of this environment, which would have taken time in any case, was delayed in France by the Huguenot wars of the latter part of the sixteenth century. Therefore, though the first tragedies and comedies in both countries were written at about the same time—the 1550s— French-classical drama was some half a century later than the Elizabethan in developing. It is possible, however, that the tardiness of the appearance of great drama in France was due merely or largely, instead, to the absence there, earlier, of any writers of the requisite genius.

At any rate, the final products of these two schools of drama were very unlike. Besides the usually mentioned ways in which French-classical drama differs from Elizabethan—self-conscious subjection to sophisticated literary criticism, observance of "the three unities," exclusion of acts of violence from the stage, concept of a play as a crisis, and ideal of concentration in contrast to the Elizabethan ideal of comprehensiveness—two others may be pointed out. In sixteenth-century France, tragedy had been conceived of, not as a catastrophe, but as a lament over a catastrophe; the tragic event, a great disaster to some great personage, occurred near the beginning of the play, the rest of which was devoted to expressing as eloquently as possible the anguish of that personage; and French-classical tragedy never ceased to be affected by this Renaissance conception, which imparted to it an essentially rhetorical cast—just as Elizabethan drama derived from the medieval "mysteries" from which it sprang its conception of a play as a story represented on the stage, wherefore its rambling, action-crammed complexity. The other difference was that the artificial pastoral note, which was made prominent in Elizabethan drama by Beaumont and Fletcher, was present in French-classical drama from the first. Thus the flavor of mannered artificiality which attaches to Elizabethan drama only in its decline was intrinsic in French-classical drama—comedy aside.

Elizabethan and French-classical drama of the great age ran their course in approximately the same length of time—sixty or seventy years.[2] Both ended with a similar degenera-

[2] The exact beginning and end of a dramatic period are not always easy to fix upon. Elizabethan drama did have a definite termination, the closing of the theaters in 1642 in the Puritan rebellion against Charles I. The period may be said to have begun with Lyly and

tion of tragedy (described in the chapter "Neo-classical Tragedy in the Eighteenth Century") and with especial and notable activity in the field of comedy, in which, however, a workmanlike competence did not altogether make amends for a loss of the verve that had characterized the comedies of the great age. In the Elizabethan period, the largest number of the best minor playwrights flourished during the middle and later parts of the career of Shakespeare, whereas in seventeenth-century France the chief group of them among the writers of tragedy flourished in the earlier part of the period.

As to the amount of merit to be found in each of the two periods, the number of good plays and of great plays produced in each and their degree of excellence, and the comparative stature of the dramatists in each, any estimate can represent only the judgment of the individual critic, and no two critics would exactly agree. The categoric appraisals which I shall venture to attempt are, of course, for the most part only my own, unless it is otherwise stated. They are but the opinions of one man, who can at least claim that he appreciates the good plays of every period of drama, without prejudice for or against any type. It is quite safe to say positively, however, that Brander Matthews' statement somewhere that the three supreme dramatists of

---

Kyd, with *Campaspe* and *The Spanish Tragedy*. The date of neither of these plays can be stated more precisely than 1580-1585. Roughly, then, we may reckon the duration of Elizabethan drama as sixty years. Neither the beginning nor the end of the great age in French drama is clearly defined; but the end of the career of Alexandre Hardy and the appearance of the first plays of Corneille, Rotrou, and Du Ryer (1628-1629) or of Mairet's *Sophonisbe* (1634) may be regarded as inaugurating it, and the *Manlius Capitolinus* (1698) of La Fosse as bringing it and the century alike to a close. If we should, instead, consider that it ends with *Athalie* (1691), its length is even more nearly identical with that of Elizabethan drama.

all time are Shakespeare, Sophocles, and Molière, was as fatuous as it was neat, and could have been made by no one with any real comprehension of the work of Aeschylus or Euripides; and that Lemaître's unbounded adulation of Racine, and Sainte-Beuve's preference for *Athalie* over *Oedipus the King,* could find little if any support outside of France. It is not only the English-speaking world but the world in general that regards Shakespeare as much superior to Racine. But if seventeenth-century France had no Shakespeare, it had in Racine and Molière, instead of a single great figure, two dramatists who were each fully the equal of Ibsen—and Corneille besides, whose greatness in his early prime was actual instead of merely potential like Marlowe's.

Potentially, Molière was perhaps greater than Racine; but his achievement was somewhat less, for the classical ideal of compression was not so well suited to comedy as the Elizabethan ideal of comprehensiveness. Only by comprehensiveness, by representing a whole cross-section of an age or a social group, could comedy make up for what it lacks of intensity, compared with tragedy. Had Molière been an Elizabethan, or had Ben Jonson possessed Molière's genius, we would probably have some much greater comedies than have ever been written.[3] But even working under the conditions that his environment forced upon him, Molière is the world's greatest comic dramatist. *Le Misanthrope* seems to me to stand quite markedly above all other comedies that we possess. Among those of Shakespeare, only *Twelfth Night* can rank with *Tartuffe, Don Juan,* and *les Femmes savantes;* the rest are much inferior to these and also to *l'Avare.*[4]

[3] Augier in *le Gendre de M. Poirier,* the greatest comedy of the nineteenth century, gives a suggestion of the kind of play I imagine, as nearly as an author of his caliber could give it.

[4] Traditional criticism groups together *le Misanthrope, Tartuffe, les Femmes savantes,* and *l'Avare* as Molière's masterpieces; *Don*

Though the artificial, "romanesque" element in French-classical tragedy has made Racine more alien than Molière to foreigners, in France he is considered fully Molière's equal. None of his plays approaches the four supreme tragedies of Shakespeare in greatness; but both *Phèdre* and *Athalie* are certainly not less great than Shakespeare's next-greatest plays, *Julius Caesar* and *Antony and Cleopatra*, and are perhaps somewhat greater than Ibsen's *Ghosts,* which the Norwegian dramatist himself and most other people, also, have considered his masterpiece. *Britannicus* is a rather greater play than any other drama of Shakespeare's or Ibsen's, even than *Coriolanus* or *Henry IV* or *The Wild Duck* or *The Pretenders*. The other French-classical tragedies which attain to greatness are the *Cid* and *Polyeucte*. *Iphigénie, Andromaque,* and *Horace* closely approach greatness, and *Mithridate, Bajazet,* and *Nicomède* somewhat less closely—yet all these, too, are excellent plays, much superior to the best tragedy or tragi-comedy by any of the minor dramatists of either period. Even *Cinna* and *Bérénice* have, along with their grave faults which we have noted, positive merits that stamp them as, at least, good plays—better, almost everyone would maintain, though with questionable correctness, than anything written by the contemporaries of Corneille and Racine.

These contemporaries of theirs have, to be sure, no such fame as the Elizabethans have enjoyed since the days of

---

Juan is too "irregular" for French critics, with their academic pseudo-classical bias. The great French actor, Coquelin, less affected by this bias, recognized the greatness of *Don Juan*. (Cf. his "Molière and Shakespeare," *The Century Magazine,* October, 1889.) Brander Matthews pronounced it one of Molière's four supreme plays, instead of *l'Avare,* an opinion which I have observed to be shared by other American scholars, who did not regard it as the least of the four in merit. *L'Avare,* I think, is only on the border-line of greatness.

Charles Lamb. The enthusiasm of no Swinburne has extolled any of them, and their study has been neglected as that of the Elizabethans long was. This persistent neglect has perhaps been largely due to the fact that, of them all, only Rotrou was a poet comparable to the best of the group about Shakespeare; Du Ryer and Thomas Corneille, two of the most capable as playwrights, were among the feeblest in poetic ability. No minor French-classical dramatist, let us recognize at once, was of a stature equal to that of the Elizabethans of the first rank, Jonson, Beaumont, and Webster—to say nothing of Marlowe. But except for these few men there was no great difference in the minor figures of the two periods as regards either ability or achievement. In making a detailed comparison, we shall limit ourselves to the field of tragedy (and more-or-less serious tragi-comedy) as we have done throughout this volume. Let us not fail to realize, however, that such a limitation of our survey is not to the advantage of the French-classical period. This could boast of more writers worthy of mention in the field of comedy than in that of tragedy: Desmaretz, Scarron, Chappuzeau, Poisson, Montfleury, Boursault, De Visé, Hauteroche, Champmeslé, Baron, Dancourt, Palaprat, Brueys, Regnard, and Dufresny—besides Rotrou, Thomas Corneille, and Quinault, all three of whom won distinction in both genres; and in seventeenth-century France a great many more comedies than "serious" plays were definitely or at least passably good.

Henry Carrington Lancaster, whose opinions on larger questions of critical appraisal are always worthy of thoughtful attention, says in speaking of Crébillon: "One may hesitate to agree with Dutrait that he should be ranked third among authors of [French] classical tragedy, but one may well grant him admission to a group of writers, each of whom has some claim to this distinction: Rotrou, Du Ryer,

Thomas Corneille, Campistron, and Voltaire." [5] I must confess, however, that I do not see by what logic Lancaster includes Crébillon in such a group, even with his estimate of *Rhadamiste et Zénobie,* which is far kindlier than mine. He himself says of this play merely that it seems to him "to deserve neither the enthusiasm nor the scorn that it has received"; [6] and if he can accord no higher praise than that to a play which (however poor) is recognized by all to be much the best that Crébillon wrote, how can he assign to that dramatist a position beside the others whom he names? Crébillon has more plays to his credit (or discredit) than La Fosse, but still not very many; to fame he is scarcely less a one-play author; and *Manlius Capitolinus* is in my judgment immensely superior to *Rhadamiste et Zénobie;* yet no one would consider putting La Fosse, because of it, on a level with men who did a much greater amount of work that is not of negligible quality.

The choice of all the other names listed by Lancaster is logical enough. Voltaire did not write even one play which is good as a whole; the time at which he flourished was out of joint for that, as we have seen. But his productivity as a dramatist, his innovations and varied work in the tragic field, the originality and force of intellect frequently exhibited in his plays, and the remarkable power of some of his scenes or passages give him the right to be reckoned among the foremost of the lesser men, if we are to include any from the eighteenth century—which we should not do, however, in comparing the great age of French-classical drama with the Elizabethan. The same right surely belongs to Rotrou, to Du Ryer, and to Thomas Corneille, as our chapters devoted to them sufficiently indicate. But about Campistron I would disagree. It is possibly true that his *Andronic*

[5] *Sunset,* Baltimore, 1945, p. 123.
[6] *Ibid.,* p. 119.

and *Tiridate* cannot be outweighed, as a pair, by any two tragedies that any of his rivals could set in the scales against them, though Rotrou produced *Cosroès* and *Vences-las,* Du Ryer *Saül* and *Scévole,* and Thomas Corneille *La-odice* and *le Comte d'Essex.* But Lancaster perceives merit in other dramas, too, of Campistron—*Arminius, Virginie, Alcibiade*—where I perceive little or none; and it is doubt-less for this reason that we estimate him differently. I should be much more inclined to accord a place—albeit the lowest—to Tristan l'Hermite in the first rank of minor French-classical dramatists; and in this preference for him over Campistron I believe almost all other students, past and present, of this period would agree with me.

If none of these four men—Rotrou, Du Ryer, Tristan, and Thomas Corneille—is comparable in magnitude to Beaumont or Webster, they are surely on a par with the Elizabethans of next-highest rank: with Fletcher, Middle-ton, Ford, and Massinger, in the last three of whom we have already observed similarities to the three last-named Frenchmen, respectively. Analogies have also been remarked between Campistron and Shirley. Of a class with Eliza-bethans of somewhat less importance are Mairet and La Calprenède (neither of whom, unfortunately, it has been found practicable to discuss in this book), Quinault, and La Fosse—and, around the turn of the century, La Grange-Chancel. Boyer and Pradon rate lower still, and there are many others of scant note.

In the number of plays which can be pronounced unques-tionably good that were written by the contemporaries of the great men, the two periods are again not uncomparable. I would say that there are not less than ten such plays among the French-classical tragedies of the seventeenth century: Mairet's *Sophonisbe,*[7] Tristan's *Mariane,* Du Ryer's

---

[7] Its earlier acts have something of the ineptitude that one might

Saül and *Scévole,* Rotrou's *Cosroès,* Thomas Corneille's *Laodice* and *le Comte d'Essex,* Campistron's *Andronic* and *Tiridate,* and the *Manlius Capitolinus* of La Fosse. Of these, *Cosroès, le Comte d'Essex,* and *Andronic* seem to me the best; *Laodice* and *Tiridate* the least good. Péchantré's *Géta* might raise the number to eleven. It is not likely, of course, that any two people would be altogether in agreement as to such a list; one would add this play or eliminate that one; most critics, probably, would include *Venceslas* and *Ariane;* but the number of plays and the choice of them would not be very different in the case of anyone.[8] In Elizabethan drama the genres are less sharply distinguished, and the prevailing tone of a "chronicle history play" might be either tragic or comic; but I would name as, in their entirety, good serious plays of that period *Edward II, A Woman Killed with Kindness, The Revenger's Tragedy, The White Devil* and *The Duchess of Malfi, The Maid's Tragedy* and *A King and No King, The Fatal Dowry, The Changeling,* and *The Witch of Edmonton*—also a total of ten.[9] Here again, the best in the Elizabethan period are somewhat superior to the best in seventeenth-century France. To such an Elizabethan list of good plays should be added two serious dramas of Shakespeare which also are good but are no better than they, *Richard II* and *Richard III;* and similarly to those on the French list can be added several of the less well known plays of Corneille—*Don Sanche, Othon, Attila,*

---

expect in the first French "classical" tragedy; its last part is hardly surpassed outside the work of the major dramatists.

[8] For Lancaster's selections, see p. 424, note 16.

[9] *Edward II* is included because Marlowe, though potentially more than a minor dramatist, did not develop enough to emerge from that category. *Doctor Faustus* would doubtless deserve inclusion if we possessed his own original version of it. Perhaps *A Fair Quarrel* or *Women Beware Women* should not have been omitted.

Pulchérie, Suréna, and perhaps *Héraclius*—besides, as aforesaid, *Cinna* and *Bérénice.*

Whether crudity and naïveté, such as we encounter in Elizabethan drama, are more objectionable than the artificiality which we find in French-classical tragedy, or less so, is a matter of individual taste. There is, however, an attractive amount of variety in Elizabethan drama which makes it much more colorful and interesting, even to those who are not prepossessed in its favor. The most fervent partisan of French-classical tragedy must admit that there is a dreadful sameness about it. It began with far better plays than the earliest Elizabethan tragedies—with *Sophonisbe* and *la Mariane*—and within three years of the former it produced a real masterpiece in the *Cid.* In that masterpiece were, side by side, the extremely dramatic figure of Chimene and the tiresome figure of the Infanta—and a "tragedy" of French-classical tragedy is that it never repeated its Chimene but put its Infanta, essentially, into play after play.[10] Not only do many details of plot or situation constantly recur in French-classical tragedy, but the same ideas are expressed over and over again: the supreme desirability of sovereign power, the fact that policy instead of love determines the marriages of those of royal blood, et cetera, et cetera, et cetera. But a certain circumscription of themes and ideas seems inevitable in classical drama of any era; the Greeks themselves were limited to their saga-world of myth and legend in their selection of subjects for tragedy, and if a large instead of only a pitifully small part of Attic drama had survived, we might discover that even in this greatest of dramatic periods there was far too much repetition.[11] But

[10] In the minor dramatists' seventeenth-century plays discussed briefly or at some length in this book—twenty-seven, I believe—something like her problem is present in at least six of them!

[11] As perhaps evidence of this, see Medea's famous speech before

whatever our preferences, we should recognize that there is little difference in actual achievement, as regards either the degree of excellence attained (except in Shakespeare's four supreme tragedies) or the amount of good work done, in Elizabethan and French-classical drama.

---

killing her children, in Euripides, and a surviving fragment from the apparently earlier, lost *Medea* of Neophron. English translations of both can be found in John Addington Symonds' *Studies of the Greek Poets* on pages 333-334 and 382, respectively, in the Third Edition of that book, London, 1920. The Greek text of Neophron's fragment is also printed on page 382.

INDEX

(Numbers italicized refer to the pages where the subject under which they are listed receives treatment.)